Cognitive Theory and Documentary Film

"The editors of *Cognitive Theory and Documentary Film* make ambitious claims about the usefulness of cognitive theory for understanding the documentary as well as the fiction film—and their volume more than delivers. Equipped with a fuller picture of the mind as embodied and socially networked, the authors here offer exciting approaches to a wide range of work including biographies, animations, nature films, docudramas and 'fake news' websites, while attending as well to the creative processes and aims of documentary filmmakers."
—Cynthia Freeland, *Professor of Philosophy, University of Houston, USA*

"Cognitive film research is about narrative fiction, or so it seems. This milestone volume presents the cognitive approach to documentary. Specialists in the field—some of them documentarists themselves—paint a vivid picture of the rich experiences that an exceptionally multifarious genre gives rise to. They document how people watching documentaries construct and engage with other people, their minds, emotions, realities, truths and actions. Moreover they highlight in convincing detail the amazing variety of aesthetics displayed by documentaries supporting viewers' experiences."
—Ed Tan, *Professor of Media Entertainment University of Amsterdam,*
The Netherlands

"Represents a welcome first foray into the relation of cognitive theory to documentary film studies. It not only expands our conceptions of documentary but asks us to consider not only how we see reality through films but how films shape our notions of reality. The ideas are complex but are made more accessible through the straightforward writing of many of its contributors."
—David MacDougall, *Professor of Visual Anthropology,*
Australian National University, Australia

"This unique collection is likely to become a landmark in documentary studies. It is ambitious, innovative, sometimes provocative but always rigorous. Its pioneering approach to the complex relationship between selfhood, emotion, subjectivity, cognition and the art of the record is utterly convincing and inherently valuable."
—Anita Biressi, *Professor of Media and Society,*
University of Roehampton, UK

"*Cognitive Theory and Documentary Film* is an exceptionally rewarding read. Featuring probing accounts of such timely topics as post-truth, stereotyping, trans-species empathy, and filmmakers' use of cognitive theory, the volume more than delivers on its ambitious promises. Featuring a formidable team of contributors and evidencing great clarity of purpose, *Cognitive Theory and Documentary Film* provides conceptual tools, arguments, and examples that deserve attention, within and beyond the academy."

—Mette Hjort, *Chair Professor of Humanities and Dean of Arts,*
Hong Kong Baptist University, Hong Kong

"This collection of essays, through the emphasis on thought processes, brings an original approach to documentary reception and representation. Even more important, this book will expand the reach and boundaries within the study of cognitive theory itself, which can only benefit from the further influence of documentary production on this field. Thus the reader has a view from both ends of the telescope, and in a truly interdisciplinary fashion, which surely has to be welcomed."

—Jane Chapman, *Professor of Communications,*
Lincoln University, UK

"Brylla and Kramer's impressive interdisciplinary and international selection of scholars lead a ground-breaking extension of cognitivist theory into documentary film studies."

—Trevor Ponech, *Associate Professor of English,*
McGill University, Canada

Catalin Brylla • Mette Kramer
Editors

Cognitive Theory and Documentary Film

palgrave
macmillan

Editors
Catalin Brylla
University of West London
London, UK

Mette Kramer
University of Copenhagen
Copenhagen, Denmark

ISBN 978-3-319-90331-6   ISBN 978-3-319-90332-3   (eBook)
https://doi.org/10.1007/978-3-319-90332-3

Library of Congress Control Number: 2018942708

Cover illustration: kgfoto
Cover Design by Tom Howey

Printed on acid-free paper

This Palgrave Macmillan imprint is published by the registered company Springer Nature Switzerland AG
The registered company address is: Gewerbestrasse 11, 6330 Cham, Switzerland

FOREWORD

The specter of madness plagues our love of methodology. Methods can narrow our field of vision, tie us to a predetermined dogma, limit our imagination, blind us to alternatives that call on us to forfeit fundamental assumptions, and yet, we embrace them. Film studies has embraced them with exceptional vigor from the early genre/auteur studies through structural, poststructural, psychoanalytic, Marxist, feminist, formalist and semiotic approaches and on to phenomenology and cognitive theory, among others. Clearly, there are benefits to such a wild embrace or this wagon train of methodologies would have pulled up into a defensive circle to watch others stream past with alternatives less beholden to a body of systematic thought.

One clear benefit, abundantly evident throughout this volume, is the opportunity to see things from the other end of the stick, as it were. That is exactly what Galileo did when he moved the earth to the periphery of the solar system and replaced it with the sun. Everything astronomical took on a new meaning and a fresh perspective. Much the same can be said for our pantheon of critical methodologies from an auteur theory that discovered the directorial "termites" within the seemingly monolithic studio system to semiotics that proposed we understand cinema as a language that lacked a grammar, and a psychoanalysis that regarded narrative as systematic, and highly gendered play in the field of desire.

Cognitive theory takes hold of the other end of the critical stick as well. It helps us see things anew by urging us to see them differently. As these essays demonstrate, this line of sight is not the same as what it was when cognitive theory first arrived as a formalistic, grammar-like catalogue of how mental processing takes place in relation to a film. Cognitive theory has grown in sophistication and complexity. It joins many of the issues that other methods tackle and, in Catalin Brylla and Mette Kramer's *Cognitive Theory and Documentary Film*, does so with particular reference to documentary. How is a documentary different from a fiction, if it is? What changes when we cognitively process a documentary versus a fiction or even a docudrama? How do we come to empathize with characters or social actors? Do animal characters in wildlife documentaries change the nature of our response? How do we experience emotions and embodied experiences through documentary? How do we assess truth value? What effect do preexisting cognitive schema and social stereotypes have on our understanding and engagement? What types of interviews prevail and how do their effects differ? Why do viewers differ in their response to specific works if our cognitive mechanisms are the same?

Such a rich array of questions was hardly in the forefront of my mind when I first encountered David Bordwell's *Narration in the Fiction Film* in 1987, but his introduction of neoformalist—cognitive theory into film study got me thinking. I saw things in a new light. I was not ready to sign up as a follower on a path that seemed profoundly misguided in certain ways, but I was ready to rethink assumptions I have taken for granted about the nature of documentary.[1] I asked myself I if could do something like what Bordwell had done, that is, Could I develop a more systematic, rigorous understanding of the documentary than had been proposed in previous work? Was documentary sufficiently accounted for by memoirs, interviews, and vaguely conceived histories? Were there not underlying principles of formal organization in need of exploration, such as the various modes of documentary that subsequently occurred to me? Could insights gained from the study of fiction film transfer to the nonfiction film? The answer became *Representing Reality* (1991), which, in turn, and to my surprise, became one of the starting points for what is now the richly cultivated field of documentary film studies. It strikes me that sometimes

[1] See my "Form Wars: The Political Unconscious of Formalist Theory," in Jane Gaines, ed., *Classical Hollywood Narrative: The Paradigm Wars* (Duke University Press, 1992): 49–77. Most of my critical view of Bordwell would now be understood as a rejection of the first wave of cognitive theory and its formal, structural, ahistorical, and decontextualized approach to narrative, cinema, and the viewer as a hypothetical entity more akin to a black box than a socially situated individual. As Catalin Brylla and Mette Kramer's introductory chapter, "Intersecting Documentary and Cognitive Theory," indicates, cognitive theory has moved significantly beyond that starting point.

the sidelong glance can provide a way forward and that is precisely what I think this volume provides for many of us who are not cognitive theorists in our own right.

In many ways, *Cognitive Theory and Documentary Film* is both a step forward and back. Forward in the evolution of cognitive theory toward a more complex view of human behavior from a neuroscientific perspective fused with strong elements of a variety of other more affect-oriented approaches such as phenomenology and social cognition, and back in a return to many of the preoccupations of classic rhetoric. Gone is the effort to formalize mental processing into abstract algorithms that apply to each and every one of us regardless of external factors. Present is a deep concern for the ways in which a text engages viewers and predisposes them to see the world, and even act in the world, in a certain way. This was always the great divide between rhetoric and fiction. Fiction is, in my view, an allegorical act aimed at creating a parallel universe in which we can identify qualities akin to the qualities we find in our everyday world. Rhetoric is a persuasive act aimed at offering us a distinct perspective on the world we already occupy. It is closer to a metaphor that's meant, a way of saying "Reality is *like this*, isn't it?" Rhetoric is the province of politicians, trial lawyers, essayists, reporters and many if not most documentary filmmakers. It is why I once described documentary as a "discourse of sobriety" in its more conventional forms.

Both fictional texts and rhetorical ones adopt aspects of narrative storytelling to achieve their ends. That has proven a source of confusion in many cases since it has been historically more tempting to align narrative technique with fiction than documentary. That was certainly the tactic of Dziga Vertov and John Grierson, among others, in the early days of documentary. But narrative can serve both masters. The line between fiction and documentary, as several essays here argue, is a finer, more fluid one than we sometimes suppose. There remains a tendency, in some of the essays here, and elsewhere, to continue to perform a mopping up operation to remind us of this: documentaries are not necessarily true—they tell stories; documentaries construct characters from social actors (real people), build suspense, and create empathy by means not unlike those of fiction films. They are, in fact, a fiction (un)like any other. These essays take us on a journey to discover some of the many ways in which documentaries are like and unlike fiction films.

Another way to say this is that documentaries take up the problem of *dissoi logoi* directly. This Greek term referred to cases where different points of view contend but no one point of view can claim, though claim it will, that it and only it represents the truth of the matter.[2] These are issues involving values and beliefs, understanding and interpretations, ideology, or what Catalin Brylla's chapter, "A Social Cognition Approach to Stereotyping in Documentary Practice," refers to as "folk-psychological narratives." God exists. God does not exist. Capitalism gives the greatest benefit to the greatest number. Capitalism immiserates vast numbers in its quest for profit. Central governments and diversely populated nation states deserve priority over local governments and more monolithic communities, or vice versa. Fossil fuels are a prime source of energy vital to our future. Fossil fuels are a prime cause of global warming; they endanger the future.

Values and beliefs, understanding and interpretations change with time and place but they take hold of the human imagination at a deep level. Documentaries explore what it means to hold one form of belief, to embody one set of values over another. They often set out to predispose us to see things one way rather than another. They do so rhetorically, and sometimes poetically. Cognitive theory, in these essays, contributes to our understanding of *how* they go about doing so. The essays explore the many "complex embodied cognitive activities," as Veerle Ros, Jennifer O'Connell, Miklós Kiss and Annelies van Noortwijk term it in their

---

[2] Richard Lanham develops the meaning and use of the term brilliantly in his *A Handlist of Rhetorical Terms* (University of California Press, 2012). The following explanation elaborates on Lanham's insights.

> In essence, *dissoi logoi* posits that one side (*logos*) of an argument defines the existence of the other, creating a rhetorical situation in which at least two *logoi* struggle for dominance. In contrast, Western culture's implicit assumption that argument is about truth or falsity urges one to assume that one side of the argument is true or more accurate and that other accounts are false or less accurate. Quite differently, Sophists acknowledge that one side of the argument might in a particular context represent the "stronger" *logos* and others the "weaker," but this does not preclude a weaker *logos* from becoming the stronger in a different or future context. Sophism assumes that the stronger *logos*, no matter how strong, will never completely overcome competing *logoi* and earn the title of absolute truth. Rather—and this is the heart of *dissoi logoi*— at least one other perspective is always available to serve as another to the stronger argument.

In Richard D. Johnson-Sheehan, "Sophistic Rhetoric," *Theorizing Composition: A Critical Sourcebook of Theory and Scholarship in Contemporary Composition Studies*, ed., Mary Lynch Kennedy (Greenwood, 1998).

chapter "Toward a Cognitive Definition of First Person Documentary," that go into this effort to predispose us to see the world as others want us to. Cognitive theory now goes beyond reason—as we routinely do as well. It tackles questions of the nature of emotions and emotional response, of empathy and its arousal or dissipation, of seduction and its sway, of stereotypes and their mobilization or subversion.

Documentaries are sometimes considered ways of conveying information. They inform us about the world. And yet, they are never simply that. Tables, charts, spreadsheets convey information but documentaries speak in the voice of a filmmaker and convey a perspective on the world. This is why the rhetorical tradition is such a crucial resource. It is far more than a way to make an argument effectively, although it is well known for its contribution to oration and court room debate. It is, more essentially, a way to win hearts and minds, to convince others in a compelling way that one way of seeing things is preferable to another. This is not a matter of factual detail alone, not when we enter the realm of *dissoi logoi*, although contradicting proven facts seldom makes for good rhetorical practice. It is more a matter of finding the ways and means of predisposing viewers to believe, internalize, and even act upon a particular view of how things "really" are in the world. It is a matter of credible, convincing, and compelling representations of the sort fruitfully explored by classic rhetoric.

Work to the margins of what we might consider the heart and soul of documentary—the stand-alone work by a specific individual who addresses a given topic in a distinct style and with a recognizable voice—makes this matter yet more clear. Reality TV shows like the *The Real Housewives* franchise, *American Ninja Warrior*, or *Duck Dynasty* strain credibility; they may not fully convince, and yet they may well be compelling. Truth is not in the air so much as absorption into a particular view of reality, quite often a view of reality as spectacle, that borrows heavily from a documentary tradition and the affective and cognitive activity it invites in order to predispose us to say "Yes, reality is *like this*—at least for the moment. Advertisements and political campaign ads carry out similar procedures but with even more blatant uses of rhetoric and style not only to predispose us to see things as they want us to but to act upon these predispositions in ways that have significant consequences.

In other words, placing documentary in general upon the shrine of sober discourse can be an error. It is not sobriety we seek so much as engagement, conviction, and belief. It is the use of rhetoric and narrative technique that so often provides it. In documentary films, information may serve more as bait or lure than as the heart of the matter. Knowledge may be a basic goal but it is heavily tempered by the voice and point of view of the maker and the specific form of predisposition desired from the viewer. In this light, cognitive theory can also help address questions regarding the particular conception and structure of documentaries from a film production perspective, as discussed in some of the essays. It is in the exploration of these matters that this collection invites us to see documentary from a different angle, to take up the other end of the stick.

What is at stake for us, ultimately, is the getting of wisdom, something non-transferable and inexplicable, something beyond words or the form and structure of any given work. Cognitive theory contributes to our understanding of the process by which we encounter, assess, internalize, and take guidance for our actions from the representations, documentary and otherwise, that we encounter. Wisdom contributes to the long-term survival of our society, if not our civilization. It relies on reasons, which reason may not know, but which we can understand and deploy. This volume invites us to take one more step on that journey toward wisdom that lies beyond the values and beliefs, myths and ideologies, categories and interpretations we may take for granted but not yet fully understand.

School of Cinema, San Francisco State University   Bill Nichols
San Francisco, CA, USA

CONTENTS

NOTES ON CONTRIBUTORS

Luis Rocha Antunes holds a PhD in Film Studies from the University of Kent and a PhD in Aesthetics from the Norwegian University of Science and Technology. He is the author of *The Multisensory Film Experience: A Cognitive Model of Experiential Film Aesthetics* (Intellect, 2016). His main research interests revolve around experientiality and the senses in film.

Ib Bondebjerg is Professor Emeritus in the Department of Media, Cognition and Communication at the University of Copenhagen. He was Chairman of The Danish Film Institute (1997–2000), founder and director of the Centre for Modern European Studies (2008–2011) and chairman of the Danish Research Council for the Humanities (1993–1997). He is co-editor of the book series Palgrave European Film and Media Studies and on the editorial board of the *Journal of Documentary Studies*. He was the co-director of three European research projects: Changing Media—Changing Europe (2000–2005), Media and Democracy in the Network Society (2002–2006) and Mediating Cultural Encounters Through European Screens (2013–2016). His most recent books in English are *Media, Democracy and European Culture* (co-edited) (Intellect, 2008); *Engaging with Reality: Documentary and Globalization* (Intellect, 2014), *European Cinema and Television: Cultural Policy and Everyday Life* (co-edited) (Palgrave Macmillan, 2015); and *Transnational European Television Drama: Production, Genres and Audiences* (co-authored) (Palgrave Macmillan, 2017).

Catalin Brylla is Senior Lecturer in Film at the University of West London. Focusing on documentary film studies, cognitive film theory, phenomenology and visual anthropology, his research aims for a pragmatic understanding of documentary spectatorship in relation to experience, empathy and narrative comprehension. He has co-edited, with Helen Hughes, *Documentary and Disability* (Palgrave Macmillan, 2017) and is currently writing a book on stereotypes and spectatorship in documentary film. As a practice-led researcher, he has made documentaries about blindness and women's football in Zanzibar. His films have been screened and broadcast internationally.

Juan Alberto Conde Aldana has a degree in Communication Studies, an MA in Philosophy and a PhD in Semiotics from the University of Limoges. He is Assistant Professor in Semiotics on the master's program in semiotics at the Jorge Tadeo Lozano University, Bogota. His research interests include visual semiotics, graphic narratives, interactive media and sound studies.

John Corner is Visiting Professor in Media and Communication at the University of Leeds and Professor Emeritus of the University of Liverpool. He has published widely since the 1970s in a range of international journals and in books. His monographs include *The Art of Record* (Manchester University Press, 1996) and, more recently, *Theorising Media* (Manchester University Press, 2011) and *Political Culture and Media Genre* (Palgrave Macmillan, 2012). His long-standing research interests include the history and development of documentary forms, theories of media power and the changing forms of political mediation.

Jens Eder is Professor of Audiovisual Media, Aesthetics and Storytelling at the Film University Babelsberg KONRAD WOLF. After studying philosophy and literature, he worked as a script editor for German television and taught film studies, media studies and communication studies at universities in Hamburg, Mainz and Mannheim. He has written several books and papers on audiovisual narrative, characters, digital media, transmediality, and representations of human nature, politics and emotions in the media. His publications in English include *Image Operations: Visual Media and Political Conflict*, edited with Charlotte Klonk (Manchester University Press, 2017); *Characters in Fictional Worlds*, edited with Fotis Jannidis and Ralf Schneider (De Gruyter, 2010); and three papers in the journal *Projections: The Journal for Movies and Mind*, including the most recent, "Films and Existential Feelings" (2016). He is currently writing a monograph about media and affects/emotions.

Dirk Eitzen is Professor of Film and Media Studies at Franklin & Marshall College, Lancaster, Pennsylvania, and an award-winning documentary producer. He has previously published in *The Velvet Light Trap*, *Post Script* and *Iris*, among other journals. His article, "When is a Documentary? Documentary as a Mode of Reception" has initiated debates amongst the cognitive film theory community, especially since it shifts the neoformalist focus from the film text to the actual reception process. He is therefore considered one of the few cognitive film scholars to have pioneered the analysis of documentary.

Michael Grabowski is Associate Professor of Communication at Manhattan College, New York. He is the editor of *Neuroscience and Media: New Understandings and Representations* (Routledge, 2014). His work on documentaries, feature films, commercials, music videos and news has played at the Guggenheim, the Smithsonian, film festivals, and on broadcast and cable networks. He serves as a Senior Research Consultant for Audience Theory, which advises television and cable networks, OTT providers and new media companies. Grabowski's work explores how different forms of mediated communication shape the way people think and act within their symbolic environment.

Torben Grodal is Professor Emeritus at the University of Copenhagen. In addition to several books and articles on literature, he has authored *Moving Pictures: A New Theory of Genre, Feelings, and Emotions* (Oxford University Press, 1997); *Embodied Visions: Evolution, Emotion, Culture and Film* (Oxford University Press, 2009); an introduction to film theory in Danish, *Filmoplevelse* (2003); and edited *Visual Authorship: Creativity and Intentionality in the Media* (Museum Tusculanum Press, 2005). He has also published articles on film, emotions, narrative theory, art films, video games and evolutionary film theory. His most recent articles include "How film genres are a product of biology, evolution and culture—an embodied approach" (Palgrave Communications, 2017) and "*Die Hard* as an Emotion Symphony" (*Projections*, 2017).

Miklós Kiss is Assistant Professor in Film and Media Studies at the University of Groningen. His research intersects the fields of narrative and cognitive film theories. Published in anthologies and academic journals (including *Projections, Scope, Senses of Cinema, Necsus, New Cinemas, New Review of Film and Television Studies*), he is an editorial board member of *[in]Transition*, the first peer-reviewed academic journal of videographic film studies. His recent books are *Film Studies in Motion: From Audiovisual Essay to Academic Research Video* (co-authored with Thomas van den Berg) (Scalar, 2016) and *Impossible Puzzle Films: A Cognitive Approach to Contemporary Complex Cinema* (co-authored with Steven Willemsen) (Edinburgh University Press, 2017).

Mette Kramer is a film lecturer at the University of Copenhagen. She has written on emotion and cognitive film theory in a number of Danish and international film journals and anthologies. She is currently finishing a book project on attachment, cognition and affect.

Jan Nåls is a scriptwriter, author and editor, film educator and communications scholar. He is currently Lecturer in Directing and Scriptwriting at Arcada University of Applied Sciences, Helsinki. He has been active in teaching and researching intercultural communication for the past decade, primarily in a documentary-film exchange program between South Africa, Ghana and Finland. His research interests include the functions and effects of empathy in visual narratives, a topic on which he has published extensively. His latest scriptwriting effort is an award-winning novella film, *Beware of Thin Ice* (2017). Author of several works on varied topics, such as sports betting and modern theatre, his most recent titles include a fictional biography of Finnish maverick and smuggler Algoth Niska (Borderline, 2015) and a work on set design in theatre (Skenographia, 2015).

Annelies van Noortwijk is a senior lecturer in the Department of Arts, Culture and Media Studies at the University of Groningen. Her current research concentrates on contemporary documentary practice, with a specific interest in questions of engagement, resistance and ethics, and the penetration of artistic discourse into non-traditional forms of art. Recent publications include "The Other, the Same: Towards a Metamodern Poetics with Heddy Honigmann" in *Female Authorship in Contemporary Documentary Media* (Edinburgh University Press, 2018) and "See Me, Feel Me, Touch Me, Heal Me, La question de la mémoire dans le documentaire à l'epoque métamoderne" in *Un Art documentaire: Enjeux esthétiques, politiques et ethiques* (Presses Universitaires de Rennes, 2017).

Jennifer M. J. O'Connell is a junior lecturer in the Department of Arts, Culture and Media at the University of Groningen. She graduated with honors with a thesis on first-person documentary. She is also the main film programmer of the International Film Festival Assen, a festival that centers on women and film. Her research focuses on documentary theory and film festival policy. Recent publications include two entries on the Netherlands in *Women Screenwriters: An International Guide* (Palgrave Macmillan, 2015) and an interview with Rada Šešić (co-authored with Annelies van Noortwijk) in *Documentary Film Festivals: History, Politics, Challenges* (Palgrave Macmillan, forthcoming).

Karen Pearlman is a senior lecturer at Macquarie University, Sydney, and the author of *Cutting Rhythms: Intuitive Film Editing* (Focal Press, 2016). Her creative-practice research film, *Woman with an Editing Bench* (2016), won the Australian Teachers of Media Award for Best Short Fiction and the Australian Screen Editors Guild (ASE) Award for Best Editing in a Short Film, along with six other film festival prizes. Other publications from her ongoing research into editing, cognition and feminist film histories include "Editing and Cognition Beyond Continuity" in *Projections: The Journal for Movies and Mind* (2017) and co-editing a special 2018 issue of *Apparatus: Film, Media and Digital Cultures of Central and Eastern European* on women and editing.

Carl Plantinga is Professor of Film and Media at Calvin College, Michigan. He is the author of three books, including *Rhetoric and Representation in Nonfiction Film* (Cambridge University Press, 1997), *Moving Viewers: American Film and the Spectator's Experience* (University of California Press, 2009), and *Screen Stories: Emotion and the Ethics of Engagement* (Oxford University Press, 2018). Plantinga is also co-editor of *Passionate Views: Film, Cognition, and Emotion* (Johns Hopkins University Press, 1999) and *The Routledge Companion to Philosophy and Film* (Routledge, 2008). He is currently working on a book about the relationship between realism and the imagination in narrative film and documentary with the working title, *Alternative Realities.*

Veerle Ros is a PhD student in Film and Media Studies at the University of Groningen. She is currently working on a dissertation that explores the cognitive and hermeneutic dynamics of authenticity attribution in documentary film viewing. Her recent publications include "Disrupted PECMA Flows: A Cognitive Approach to the Experience of Narrative Complexity in Film" (co-authored with Miklós Kiss) in *Projections: The Journal for Movies and Mind* (Spring 2018) and "The Living Landscape of Jakarta in Leonard Retel Helmrich's Documentary Triptych" (co-authored with

Annelies van Noortwijk) in *Filmurbia: Screening the Suburbs* (Palgrave Macmillan, 2017).

Aubrey Tang is a PhD candidate in the Department of Comparative Literature at the University of California, Irvine. Her research interests include the history and phenomenology of perception, sensations and cinema, Chinese and Sinophone film historiography, and Hong Kong cinema. Her essays on Chinese literature and cinema have appeared in the journal *Frontiers of Literary Studies in China* and the collected volume *Li Ang's Visionary Challenges to Gender, Sex, and Politics* (Lexington Books, 2013). She has contributed a chapter on Shanghai sensationalism, "The Sensations of Semicolonial Shanghai: A Phenomenological Study of the Short Stories by Liu Na'ou", to *Sensationalism and the Genealogy of Modernity: A Global Nineteenth Century Approach* (Palgrave Macmillan, 2017). A practicing Tibetan Buddhist, she has a great interest in the topic of compassion, and currently teaches college writing at Irvine Valley College.

Alexa Weik von Mossner is Associate Professor of American Studies at the University of Klagenfurt. Her research explores the theoretical intersections of cognitive science, affective narratology and environmental literature and film. She is the author of *Cosmopolitan Minds: Literature, Emotion, and the Transnational Imagination* (University of Texas Press, 2014) and *Affective Ecologies: Empathy, Emotion, and Environmental Narrative* (Ohio State University Press, 2017), the editor of *Moving Environments: Affect, Emotion, Ecology, and Film* (Wilfrid Laurier University Press, 2014), and the co-editor, with Sylvia Mayer, of *The Anticipation of Catastrophe: Environmental Risk in North American Literature and Culture* (Winter 2014).

LIST OF FIGURES

CHAPTER 1

Introduction: Intersecting Cognitive Theory and Documentary Film

Catalin Brylla and Mette Kramer

Preamble

This collection of essays is the first major study to explore the intersection between cognitive theory and documentary film studies. As such, it offers a vital interpretation not only of how we perceive reality *through* documentary, but also of how we perceive it *because* of documentary. Western audiences live in a mass-mediated culture that filters reality through the prism of factual media; hence, their emotional and cognitive comprehension of the world is, to a significant extent, informed and consolidated by documentary film. The essays in this volume seek to illuminate the production, exhibition and reception of documentaries, exploring intratextuality (in which filmmakers employ narrative and aesthetic strategies to achieve particular audience responses and effects) and extratextuality (whereby filmmaking practices and sociocultural traditions negotiate the indexical link between representations and their real-life counterparts). The interplay between these levels means that documentaries have a

C. Brylla (✉)
University of West London, London, UK

M. Kramer
University of Copenhagen, Copenhagen, Denmark
e-mail: mettekramer@mail.dk

© The Author(s) 2018
C. Brylla, M. Kramer (eds.), *Cognitive Theory and Documentary Film*, https://doi.org/10.1007/978-3-319-90332-3_1

greater potential than fiction films to impact our attitudes towards and interaction with the world, helping construct our social, cultural and individual identities. This collection aims to demonstrate that cognitive theory represents an invaluable tool for film scholars and practitioners, allowing them to comprehend the range of documentary's implications within a wider context than that of just filmmaking or film scholarship.

Although these essays are not concerned with the definition or historicity of the concepts (or disciplines) of "cognitive theory" and "documentary" (arguably, this could turn into a philosophical minefield, providing little insight into documentary spectatorship), it may be helpful to offer a brief explanation of the rationale behind the choice of title, particularly as it highlights the contributions' common denominators and provides a loose demarcation for the collection as a whole. Cognitive theory encompasses a variety of theoretical strands that span several disciplines, including film studies, neuroscience and social psychology. Broadly speaking, there have been three historical waves of cognitive (fiction) film analysis.[1] The first regarded film as a text to be deciphered using predominantly neoformalist and constructivist methods (e.g. Bordwell 1985; Branigan 1992). The second shifted the focus from film-as-text to film-as-reception, initially building on linguistic and computational models of cognition (e.g. Anderson 1998; Buckland 2000) but eventually moving towards multimodal approaches that transcend Cartesian mind–body dualism to consider embodied responses in addition to cognitive processes (e.g. Smith 1995; Tan 1996; Plantinga 2009a; Grodal 2009). The third and latest wave has theoretically and empirically explored cognition as grounded in the human body and its interaction with the environment (e.g. Hasson et al. 2008; Gallese and Guerra 2012; Smith 2013; Coëgnarts and Kravanja 2015a), and has tentatively begun to use contextual paradigms, such as spectators' individual differences and sociocultural settings (e.g. Barratt 2014; Tan and Bálint 2017; Bondebjerg 2017). This wide-reaching cumulative trajectory has solidified cognitivism into what Gregory Currie (2004, p. 106) calls a "programme" rather than a specific theory, encouraging the interdisciplinary deployment of various theories, adapted to the case study at hand. When applied to documentary, this

---

[1] Although cognitive theory has developed differently in separate disciplines, some common historical threads can be discerned—for instance, in media studies (see Nannicelli and Taberham 2014), psychology (see Pecher and Zwaan 2006), literature studies (see Goldman et al. 1999) and the philosophy of science (see Wang 2015).

paradigm enables the analysis of a multitude of spectatorship dimensions, such as sensory perception, narrative comprehension, character empathy and the evaluation of realism, as well as the examination of various dimensions of authorship, including creativity, ethics, reflexivity and activism.

Documentary is an equally multilayered term that has also undergone several modifications since its inception. These can be traced in a historical arc that reaches from John Grierson's (1966, pp. 147–148) early definition of documentary as the "creative treatment of actuality" to John Corner's (2000, p. 688) coinage of the term "post-documentary," which he describes as the "result of the widespread dispersal (and, in part, perhaps dissipation) of documentarist energies and appeals across a much larger area of audio-visual culture." Corner, however, is prudent to mention that the prefix "post" does not suggest the collapse of the concept of documentary into postmodern doubt; rather, the term refers to the fact that the concept has shifted from a rhetorical and didactic concern with generic requirements to a recognition of documentary's cultural and commercial popularity as mediated through a greatly expanded range of formats and new modes of realist-factual entertainment. Corner alludes to the heterogeneous array of popular and democratic audiovisual nonfiction genres *consumed* (but also to a large degree *produced*) by a mass society. This is the umbrella under which the documentary dimension of this book operates.

The collection, however, is not intended as a parochial counterpoint to the plethora of cognitive studies of fiction film; on the contrary, it aims to expand the very notion of film and highlight the permeable boundary between fiction and documentary. Indeed, the long-established divide between documentary and fiction is counterproductive when studying particular documentary forms. Nevertheless, on a methodological level, the book's focus on documentary (in its widest possible sense) and its exclusion of traditional fiction forms (which have been extensively covered elsewhere) is designed to expand scholarly research into uncharted territories. It addresses, on the one hand, the lacuna in cognitive film studies in relation to documentary analysis, and on the other, the omission of cognitive models in documentary studies. In terms of cognitive scholarship, our hope as editors of this volume is that the study of nonfiction film gains a momentum that propels it to the status that fiction film enjoys as an area of academic interest.

This focus on documentary is also intended to challenge archaic notions of the genre and encourage the reconfiguration and expansion of research frameworks to encompass a wide spectrum of nonfiction audiovisual media, including classical as well as contemporary documentary forms that deviate from the doctrine of factuality. In terms of its form and conception, documentary is far more prone than fiction to a bricolage approach, constantly intermixing different aesthetics, authorial interventions and modes of spectatorial address. Furthermore, the disciplinary or institutional contexts and extratextual functions that surround documentary production and reception often overlap, blurring the boundaries between, for example, reportage, ethnographic film, drama, educational film, promotional video and avant-garde film. Hence, documentary, as a malleable and rather elusive concept, provides the scholar with a flexibility that eschews the determinism and constraints found in other audiovisual genres. Essentially, our aim is to demonstrate that the synergy between cognitive and documentary studies yields rigorous yet pragmatic methodologies for mapping Corner's "post-documentaries," including such diverse formats as web videos, reality TV, essay films, performative documentaries, docudramas and animated documentaries.

THE INTERSECTION OF COGNITIVE THEORY AND DOCUMENTARY STUDIES

Far from wishing to categorize scholars as belonging to strictly demarcated disciplines or fields of inquiry, this collection in fact aims to bypass such perceived disciplinary boundaries. Yet, it may be helpful here to briefly map the possible reasons for the relatively ossified divisions that have historically inhibited a substantially evolving convergence between documentary and cognitive film studies, and to highlight the few scholarly works that have transcended these divisions.

Documentary scholars, on the one hand, generally deem cognitive models too limited: they lament these models' reliance on normative scientific paradigms that, firstly, only account for a universalized audience reception, neglecting sociocultural and historical framings (e.g. Smaill 2010, p. 8), and secondly, limit the scope of spectatorship to knowledge acquisition through rationalist inquiry (e.g. Renov 2004, p. 149). A glance at the existing body of work that uses cognitive models for film analysis appears to justify the first argument as, despite occasional theoretical acknowledgments of social, cultural, political and historical contexts (e.g. Peterson 1996; Plantinga 2009b; Bondebjerg 2017), applied studies have been scarce at best.[2] This is one of the gaps this collection attempts to address. In terms of the second assertion, cognitive film theory's evolution towards embracing non-rationalist approaches that account for affective and subjective viewer experience has had little exposure or acknowledgement outside the discipline itself. As a consequence, fossilized views about the stagnant nature of (classical) cognitive theory are still pervasive among non-cognitive film scholars.

On the other hand, cognitive film scholars have largely favored the analysis of fiction film over documentary—and nonfiction in general. This can be attributed to four factors. Firstly, cognitive film theory was established in the 1990s, arguably as an antithesis to the poststructuralist, Marxist, psychoanalytic and semiotic *Screen* tradition (Bordwell and Carroll 1996; Tan 1996; Plantinga and Smith 1999). Since the *Screen* scholars focused mainly on fiction, it was logical that the cognitivists would offer their alternative theories in the same territory. Secondly, the public popularity of mainstream fiction is believed to overshadow that of documentary, despite Corner's observation that documentary has increasingly moved towards the mainstream. As one of the cognitivists' declared aims is to understand our most common movie experience—our fascination with and the pleasure we derive from mainstream films—through analyzing prototypical narratives (Shimamura 2013, p. 4), it is perhaps not surprising that documentary is thought to offer little scope for the study of mainstream audiences. However, whereas it is true that cinema documentaries have a still-limited—albeit growing—popularity, documentary content on television (especially reality TV, infotainment and newscasts) and online (for example, compilation films, mashups and audiovisual memes) has become increasingly popular and ubiquitous.

The third factor also relates to the question of popularity. This is the classical notion of documentaries as rhetorical or didactic—in Bill Nichols' (1991, p. 3) words, "discourses of sobriety". They are considered incapable of eliciting the same emotions and character engagement as fiction narratives. But while this may hold true for certain documentary forms (wildlife films and current affairs, for example), this belief needs to be revised for forms such as character-driven observational documentaries and docudramas, which have a closer kinship with fiction. In contrast, the

---

[2] Notable exceptions include the cultural contextualization of spatiotemporal perception (e.g. Barratt 2014; Coëgnarts and Kravanja 2015b) and the cultural-historical contextualization of spectatorship (e.g. Hake 2012; William 2017).

fourth factor is the opposite perception that documentaries use the same aesthetics and produce the same cognitive responses as fiction films (e.g. Shimamura 2013, p. 21). This assumption is plausible if seen in terms of the viewers' sensory and low-level cognitive responses as these are identical for fiction and nonfiction film, leading to the conclusion that a multitude of cognitive models can be applied equally to both. However, this bottom-up approach excludes essential top-down considerations, such as reality-status checks to determine whether the viewed content is fiction or nonfiction (Barratt 2007) and consequentiality (the awareness of real-life implications) (Eitzen 2007). In any case, these two contradictory perspectives, one based on the opposition and one on the correspondence between documentary and fiction films, are symptomatic of the indeterminate nature of documentary due to the large spectrum of forms and functions involved in generating different modes of "documentary relationship" with viewers. Hence, these perspectives may be valid for particular case studies but are precarious as generalized positions, which is why the contributions to this volume avoid making a universal case for either.

Yet, despite all these hurdles, tentative intersections between documentary and cognitive theory do exist. Within documentary studies, for instance, explicit references to spectatorial cognition are occasionally made in relation to narrative and aesthetics (e.g. Richardson and Corner 1986; Austin 2007; Corner 2008) and the representation of space (e.g. Chanan 2010). Other than that, however, there are only faint traces of cognitive considerations, as when textual analyzes draw inferences about audience reception (e.g. Renov 1993; Nichols 1994; Winston 2008) and documentaries are categorized as certain "modes" (e.g. Nichols 2001; Ward 2005). While not applying cognitive models per se, documentary scholars, especially those adopting ethnographic (e.g. MacDougall 1998, 2006; Pink 2015) and psychoanalytic (e.g. Renov 2004; Cowie 2011; Piotrowska 2013) angles, have also addressed general questions about the emotions and embodied experiences at play in documentary production and reception. However, these texts are still too remote from the psychological frameworks based on empirical studies and theoretical discourses employed in the natural sciences.

Within the field of cognitive film studies, a handful of film scholars have engaged in the study of documentary, particularly with regard to its specificity when compared with fiction (e.g. Currie 1999; Ponech 1999; Carroll 2003; Plantinga 2005; Eitzen 2007), its different modes of narrative address (e.g. Odin 1989; Plantinga 1997; Smith 2007) and its spectatorial reception (e.g. Bondebjerg 1994; Eitzen 1995; Plantinga 2013). Although these texts are seminal landmarks that have provided key paradigms for this book, they remain largely embryonic and isolated. An overarching discussion that builds on, adapts, expands or revises their methodologies has yet to develop. Such a discussion needs to take into account that the vast divergence in documentary forms, institutions, exhibition platforms and audiences over the last few decades has rendered a categorical and generalized examination of documentary problematic. Carl Plantinga (2005) illustrates this point succinctly by extrapolating two recurrent documentary models found in scholarly work, "documentary as indexical record" and "documentary as authorial assertion," and arguing that their abstract generalization of the concept of documentary fails the applied test of real case studies. By contrast, almost all the contributions to this collection adopt a grounded methodology investigating a very particular body of films or a specific case study.

A Pragmatic Approach

Pragmatism, in combination with Merleau-Ponty's and Heidegger's phenomenological ideas, has been a major paradigm in the relatively recent strand of embodied cognition studies (Madzia and Jung 2016, pp. 3–5; Wang 2015), and several chapters in this book advance research questions related to the "4EA" (Embodied, Embedded, Enacted, Extended, Affective) attributes of cognition. Our understanding of pragmatic research follows in the same tradition, though on a more fundamental level: the premise that documentary spectatorship is shaped by the degree of filmic mediation relative to certain viewing contexts. Eitzen (1995, p. 92) provides the basis for this premise by proclaiming that documentary is a "mode of reception" and needs to be studied, not as a kind of "film text" but as a kind of "reading," an approach that is reminiscent of the shift mentioned earlier from the first to the second historical wave of film cognitivism. This reception-driven approach largely bypasses questions about the actual definition of documentary (p. 98). Eitzen also concludes that "[d]ocumentaries are *presumed* to be truthful, even though considerations about the veracity of particular [authorial] assertions may play little role in how viewers actually make sense of them" (p. 88). The study of documentary spectatorship, therefore, needs to analyze the spectator's cognitive and affective perception of the documentary's "mediated" reality, in which the degree of mediation is as variable as the spectator's awareness of it.

Similarly, Bondebjerg (1994, pp. 82–83) argues that the pragmatic approach requires the mapping of textual, social and cultural elements in relation to psychological frameworks as well as institutional practices. This mapping relates not only to audiences, but also to filmmakers themselves. Bondebjerg considers documentary reception as an intersubjective mediation of reality, involving a "communicative contract" between film/filmmaker and audience. This is shaped by filmmaking practices and the audience's schematic configurations of mental frameworks based on their perceptual and embodied capacities as well as their past experiences (pp. 66–67). Plantinga (2013, pp. 43–46), too, stresses the importance of a contextual, grounded and reception-focused line of inquiry, arguing that when confronted with truth claims (for example, in social-activist documentaries), audiences understand that documentaries are structured rhetorical discourses and evaluate the film's indexical veracity using textual cues, trust in the filmmaker or institution, critics' reviews and common-sense psychology.

Eitzen's, Bondebjerg's and Plantinga's pragmatic ideas integrate dimensions of documentary spectatorship based on intratextual, extratextual and intertextual considerations, thus enabling the researcher to survey of a wide spectrum of documentary forms and functions. A pragmatic-cognitive study of documentary production and reception requires the building of bridges between the natural sciences, the social sciences and the humanities, and between theory and practice. This is why this volume features contributions by filmmakers, film theorists and scientists. Bondebjerg (2015) argues that such an interdisciplinary collaboration is essential for an understanding of the way human cognition and emotion operate in culture and society; biology (particularly neurobiology) is necessarily embedded in that understanding. This perspective has played an important role in editing this volume, as it initially informed our selection of contributors, suggestions for revisions and, ultimately, the sectionalization of the book into four parts that represent four areas of scholarly interest we advocate for the cognitive study of documentary.[3]

1. The Mediation of Realities
2. Character Engagement
3. Emotions and Embodied Experience
4. Documentary Practice

[3] See Brylla and Kramer (forthcoming) for the development of a theoretical framework based on these research areas.

This first area of interest, "the mediation of realities," explores the complex relationship between represented and inferred reality as experienced and interpreted by the viewer, and addresses the perceived indexical relationship between audiovisual depictions and their real counterparts. This involves, for example, the evaluation of truth claims and ethical considerations, as well as the generation of emotions with implications in real life. The spectator's construction of reality is not only informed by the film text, but also by the way he or she frames the film according to their individual, social, cultural and historical dispositions, as well as by their previous knowledge (schemas and scripts) of the topics and characters represented—knowledge that may well be intertextual. These converging mediation processes can also be used to explore the viewer's evaluation of authorship: for example, in documentaries that reflexively reveal the production process or where the viewer has pre-knowledge or an intertextual awareness of the filmmaker's modus operandi.

The second area, "character engagement," covers emotion-generation through appraisal, automatic and controlled responses, moral evaluation and higher cognition in relation to screen characters and their situation. It focuses on the audience's engagement with screen characters, an area that has been of major interest to cognitive scholars such as Carl Plantinga and Murray Smith, albeit one that has predominantly centered on fiction films. This concern has usually been related to the narrative and aesthetic attributes of the film text, but it has also touched on the more fundamental question of whether the engagement with characters happens on a central (empathetic) or acentral (sympathetic) level (Smith 1994). For documentary, however, this question needs to be expanded to include the spectatorially inferred indexical relationship between screen characters and real characters, which may be informed by the audience's prior knowledge of the film (for example, through paratexts, the press or social media). This area also explores the audience's moral evaluation of screen characters and examines their engagement with characters of different demographics or even different species.

The third area, "emotions and embodied experience," addresses "online" or "moment-to-moment" processes in relation to somatic responses, and it stands in sharp contrast to the field's computational, Cartesian and neoformalist beginnings. Based on developments in the social sciences and philosophy, this area adopts 4EA concepts, such as "embodied cognition" (Shapiro 2011) or the "phenomenological mind" (Gallagher and Zahavi 2008). The meta-theoretical aim of this area is two-fold. Firstly, it calls for an expansion of the disciplinary term "cognitive" to include sensory responses and low-level emotions, as well as related high-level cognitive processes such as comprehension and interpretation. Secondly, this expansion inevitably requires a cross-disciplinary approach, highlighting the aforementioned intersection between the natural sciences and the humanities. In terms of character engagement, emotions and embodied experience may, to a certain degree, transcend the fiction–documentary division, relegating indexical links to real-life referents to the background of audience reception and rendering the film text as the primary referent for the characters. Such a bottom-up approach, however, also needs to consider, or at least acknowledge, top-down processes and the situational context of the reception process.

The fourth area of "documentary practice" is dedicated to revealing the actual construction process of documentary, highlighting the role of authorship. Despite the emergence of practice-based filmmaking research, there has been little attempt to embrace cognitive theory as a research paradigm for either fiction or documentary practice. Applied cognitive approaches have been limited to empirical studies that use neuro-cognitive research, for example, and quantitative and qualitative accounts of viewing practices. But, whereas such applications employ cognitive theory as a purely *analytical* tool, we advocate its use as a *synthesizing* tool for conceptualizing and producing documentary films.[4] The focus is on a quasi-reverse-engineering process, enabling the filmmaker to create a hypothetical spectatorship that can be used as a basis for production decisions about narrative structure, cinematography, editing and distribution, among other things. The focus can also be placed on the creative process itself— that is, on the decisions arising from the filmmaker's affective and cognitive interactions with the film's real characters and the filmmaking apparatus.

---

[4] Interestingly, the creative application of cognitive theory in practice has been popular in performance and theatre studies (e.g. May 2015) and creative writing (e.g. Skains 2016). There have also been some isolated attempts to implement cognitive models in documentary film practice (Keeney 2016; Brylla 2017) and film editing (Pearlman 2009). Also, although not an example of its direct application, the Danish Broadcasting Corporation (DR/ Danmarks Radio) has started using cognitive systems for gauging audience responses; the data is fed back to commissioning editors who may then ask for production practices to be tweaked accordingly (Gregersen et al. 2017, p. 3).

BOOK OVERVIEW

This edited volume contains sixteen chapters (divided into the four areas of interest described above), which touch on a few of the possibilities yielded by the intersection between documentary and cognitive theory. The majority of chapters embrace theoretical cognitive frameworks; however, in several, these frameworks underpin or are underpinned by empirical research in the form of either heuristic data collection or creative film practice. Given its subject matter, we believe that this collection will be of interest not only to theoretical and empirical scholars, but also to practice-led researchers who generate new scholarly knowledge through the making of documentaries, as well as filmmakers seeking critical methodologies to apply to their practice.

Starting with one of the most iconic dimensions of documentary, the first part of the book explores the "mediation of realities." Ib Bondebjerg opens this section by challenging classical notions of documentary, applying theories of the embodied mind and the role of narrative and imagination to the understanding of reality in the work of Danish documentary filmmaker Anders Østergaard. Next, Juan Alberto Conde Aldana proposes a cognitive linguistic analysis of animated documentary based on Conceptual Blending Theory (CBT). He argues that CBT allows us to comprehend the way the viewer is confronted with multimodality in the ambivalent blend of two seemingly incompatible genres: animation and nonfiction film. Dipping into the realm of avant-garde film, John Corner's chapter explores the topic of intentionality and "cognitive difficulty" in relation to diverging spectatorial responses to and polysemic readings of experimental documentaries, challenging the traditional notion of an abstract, universal audience. In direct contrast, Torben Grodal focuses on one of the most mainstream of documentary genres, the docudrama, which blurs the line between fiction and documentary. Grodal explores the dimensions of realism and veracity in the film *The Queen* (2006) as they are experienced and cognitively assessed by its audience. Closing this section, Dirk Eitzen offers an intricate explanation of the trend of narrativization in documentary filmmaking in a "post-truth" era, extrapolating its consequences and its functions for nonfiction media producers in general.

The second part tackles one of the classical cornerstones of cognitive film theory, "character engagement". Carl Plantinga first presents the case that documentary characters are inevitably constructed through narrative selection, omission, emphasis, emplotting and point of view, and he illuminates a range of formalist and cognitive aspects of characterization, including truth claims, character templates, ethical implications, social contexts and the generation of audience engagement. Jan Nåls then analyzes how inconsistencies in narrative characterization can undermine empathetic engagement. From a practitioner's perspective, Nåls highlights the discrepancy that exists between the claims of filmmakers and their actual achievement of empathetic spectatorial engagement by analyzing two South African documentaries, *Miners Shot Down* (2014) and *I, Afrikaner* (2013). Aubrey Tang's chapter, meanwhile, suggests that the documentary genre is unique in its ability to negotiate the viewer's moral boundaries through the effects of empathy and realism. As a case in point, she looks at audience responses to the figure of art forger Mark Landis in the documentary *Art and Craft* (2014), and analyzes how his empathetic portrayal transforms the viewers' notion of morality. The last chapter in this section looks at an often-neglected aspect of character engagement: namely, the engagement with nonhuman characters. Alexa Weik von Mossner draws on ecocriticism, affective neuroscience, cognitive film theory and cognitive ethology to outline mechanisms of trans-species empathy in relation to anthropomorphism in wildlife documentaries.

Hinging on the turn to embodied cognition, the third part of this volume covers "emotions and embodied experience". Jens Eder begins this section by looking at the mushrooming new area of political web videos. He presents a model of affective responses based on viewers' online comments and argues that these videos reflect existing power relations and trigger conflicting emotions according to the diverging views held by different social groups. While Eder highlights sociocultural contexts, Luis Rocha Antunes largely omits these in his bottom-up examination of the moment-to-moment experiences of Norwegian "slow TV" documentaries. Using a multisensory approach, Antunes links the perceptual and cognitive processes operating around vision, the vestibular sense and thermoception in the spectator. The second half of this section focuses on first-person documentaries. Taking a meta-theoretical perspective, Veerle Ros, Jennifer O'Connell, Miklós Kiss and Annelies van Noortwijk discuss the inadequacy of existing models when it comes to defining and categorizing first-person documentaries. Based on embodied subjectivity and cognitive framing, the authors suggest a new model that considers spectatorship on a textual, contextual and real-world level. Moving from meta-theory to the specifics of first-person films, Mette Kramer's contribution demonstrates that a framework consisting of attachment theory, as well as affective and developmental psychology, is a vital theoretical instrument that can be used to unlock the emotional and cognitive complexity of such documentaries from the viewer's perspective, linking it to the director's own performance and "relational knowledge."

The fourth and last part, "documentary practice," is the newcomer to the field; it expands theoretical pragmatism to encompass praxical application. Catalin Brylla explores the formation and maintenance of disability stereotypes. He maps these empirically in existing documentaries featuring blind protagonists and then uses this pre-production knowledge to conceptualize his own documentaries, which aim to reconfigure schematic social perceptions of blindness. Moving to the actual production process, Michael Grabowski discusses three interview contexts, EFP (Electronic Field Production), ENG (Electronic News Gathering) and direct address, investigating the how and why of related conventions using Grodal's PECMA Flow model, the perception of facial expressions and embodied simulation. The book closes with a look at the post-production stage of documentary filmmaking. Applying distributed cognition theory, Karen Pearlman accounts for authorial choices by studying the embodied interactions between the editor, the film rushes and the apparatus during the documentary editing processes. She develops a cognitive model consisting of five phases: watching, sorting, remembering, selecting and composing.

Acknowledgements We would like to thank John Corner and Carl Plantinga for their generous feedback during the writing of this chapter.

REFERENCES

Anderson, J. D. (1998) *The Reality of Illusion: Ecological Approach to Cognitive Film Theory.* Carbondale, IL: Southern Illinois University Press.

Austin, T. (2007) *Watching the World: Screen Documentary and Audiences.* Manchester: Manchester University Press.

Barratt, D. (2007) "Assessing the Reality-Status of Film: Fiction or Non-Fiction, Live Action or CGI?," in Anderson, J. D. and Anderson, B. F. (eds.) *Narration and Spectatorship in Moving Images.* Newcastle upon Tyne: Cambridge Scholars Publishing, pp. 62–79.

Barratt, D. (2014) "The Geography of Film Viewing: What Are the Implications of Cultural-Cognitive Differences for Cognitive Film Theory?," in Nannicelli, T. and Taberham, P. (eds.) *Cognitive Media Theory.* London: Routledge, pp. 62–82.

Bondebjerg, I. (1994) "Narratives of Reality: Documentary Film and Television in a Cognitive and Pragmatic Perspective *Nordicom Review*, 1, pp. 65–87.

Bondebjerg, I. (2015) "The Embodied Mind: When Biology Meets Culture and Society," *Palgrave Communications* [Online]. Available at: http://www.nature.com/articles/palcomms201515 (Accessed: November 25, 2017).

Bondebjerg, I. (2017) "The Creative Mind: Cognition, Society and Culture," *Palgrave Communications*, 3(19) [Online]. Available at: http://www.nature.com/articles/s41599-017-0024-1 (Accessed: November 25, 2017).

Bordwell, D. (1985) *Narration in the Fiction Film*. Madison: University of Wisconsin Press.

Bordwell, D. and Carroll, N. (eds.) (1996) *Post-Theory: Reconstructing Film Studies*. Madison, WI: University of Wisconsin Press.

Branigan, E. (1992) *Narrative Comprehension and Film*. New York: Routledge.

Brylla, C. (2017) "Mediating Subjectivity Through Materiality in Documentary Practice," in Markham, T. and Rodgers, S. (eds.) *Conditions of Mediation: Phenomenological Perspectives on Media*. New York: Peter Lang Publishing, pp. 223–236.

Brylla, C. and Kramer, M. (forthcoming) "A Pragmatic Framework for the Cognitive Study of Documentary". *Projections*, 12(2).

Buckland, W. (2000) *The Cognitive Semiotics of Film*. Cambridge: Cambridge University Press.

Carroll, N. (2003) *Engaging the Moving Image*. New Haven, CT: Yale University Press.

Chanan, M. (2010) "Going South: On Documentary as a Form of Cognitive Geography," *Cinema Journal*, 50(1), pp. 147–154.

Coëgnarts, M. and Kravanja, P. (eds.) (2015a) *Embodied Cognition and Cinema*. Leuven: Leuven University Press.

Coëgnarts, M. and Kravanja, P. (2015b) "With the Past in Front of the Character: Evidence for Spatial-Temporal Metaphors in Cinema," *Metaphor and Symbol*, 30(3), pp. 218–239.

Corner, J. (2000) "What Can We Say About 'Documentary'?," *Media, Culture & Society*, 22(5), pp. 681–688.

Corner, J. (2008) "Documentary Studies: Dimensions of Transition and Continuity," in Austin, T. and DeJong, W. (eds.) *Rethinking Documentary: New Perspectives, New Practices*. Maidenhead: Open University Press, pp. 13–28.

Cowie, E. (2011) *Recording Reality, Desiring the Real*. Minneapolis, MN: University of Minnesota Press.

Currie, G. (1999) "Visible Traces: Documentary and the Contents of Photographs," *The Journal of Aesthetics and Art Criticism*, 57(3), pp. 285–297.

Currie, G. (2004) "Cognitivism," in Miller, T. and Stam, R. (eds.) *A Companion to Film Theory*. Oxford: John Wiley & Sons, pp. 105–122.

Eitzen, D. (1995) "When Is a Documentary?: Documentary as a Mode of Reception," *Cinema Journal*, 35(1), pp. 81–102.

Eitzen, D. (2007) "Documentary's Peculiar Appeals," in Anderson, J. D. and Anderson, B. F. (eds.) *Moving Image Theory: Ecological Considerations*. Carbondale, IL: Southern Illinois University Press, pp. 183–199.

Gallagher, S. and Zahavi, D. (2008) *The Phenomenological Mind: An Introduction to Philosophy of Mind and Cognitive Science*. London: Routledge.

Gallese, V. and Guerra, M. (2012) "Embodying Movies: Embodied Simulation and Film Studies," *Cinema: Journal of Philosophy and the Moving Image*, 3, pp. 183–210.

Goldman, S. R., Graesser, A. C. and van den Broek, P. (eds.) (1999) *Narrative Comprehension, Causality, and Coherence: Essays in Honor of Tom Trabasso*. 1st edn. Mahwah, NJ: Routledge.

Gregersen, A., Langkjær, B., Heiselberg, L. and Wieland, J. L. (2017) "Following the Viewers: Investigating Television Drama Engagement Through Skin Conductance Measurements," *Poetics*, 64, pp. 1–13.

Grierson, J. (1966) *Grierson on Documentary*. Berkeley, CA: University of California Press.

Grodal, T. (2009) *Embodied Visions: Evolution, Emotion, Culture, and Film*. Oxford: Oxford University Press.

Hake, S. (2012) *Screen Nazis: Cinema, History, and Democracy*. Madison, WI: University of Wisconsin Press.

Hasson, U., Landesman, O., Knappmeyer, B., Vallines, I., Rubin, N. and Heeger, D. J. (2008) "Neurocinematics: The Neuroscience of Film", *Projections: The Journal for Movies and Mind*, 2(1), pp. 1–26.

Keeney, D. (2016) *The Issue of Emotion in Stories of Conflict: Documentary Filmmaking in a Post Conflict Northern Ireland*. PhD thesis. Queen's University, Belfast [Online]. Available at: http://ethos.bl.uk/OrderDetails. do?uin=uk.bl.ethos.706991 (Accessed: December 16, 2017).

MacDougall, D. (1998) *Transcultural Cinema*. Princeton, NJ: Princeton University Press.

MacDougall, D. (2006) *The Corporeal Image: Film, Ethnography, and the Senses*. Princeton, NJ: Princeton University Press.

Madzia, R. and Jung, M. (eds.) (2016) *Pragmatism and Embodied Cognitive Science, From Bodily Intersubjectivity to Symbolic Articulation*. Berlin; Boston: De Gruyter.

May, S. (2015) *Rethinking Practice as Research and the Cognitive Turn*. Basingstoke, Hampshire; New York, NY: Palgrave Pivot.

Nannicelli, T. and Taberham, P. (eds.) (2014) *Cognitive Media Theory*. London: Routledge.

Nichols, B. (1991) *Representing Reality: Issues and Concepts in Documentary*. Bloomington, IN: Indiana University Press.

Nichols, B. (1994) *Blurred Boundaries: Questions of Meaning in Contemporary Culture*. Bloomington, IN: Indiana University Press.

Nichols, B. (2001) *Introduction to Documentary*. Bloomington, IN: Indiana University Press.

Odin, R. (1989) "A Semiopragmatic Approach of the Documentary," in Greef, W. D. and Hesling, W. (eds.) *Image, Reality, Spectator: Essays on Documentary Film and Television*. Leuven, Belgium: Acco, pp. 90–100.

Pearlman, K. (2009) *Cutting Rhythms: Shaping the Film Edit*. Boston, MA: Routledge.

Pecher, D. and Zwaan, R. A. (eds.) (2006) *Grounding Cognition: The Role of Perception and Action in Memory, Language, and Thinking*. London; New York; Melbourne: Cambridge University Press.

Peterson, J. (1996) "Is a Cognitive Approach to the Avant-Garde Cinema Perverse?," in Bordwell, D. and Carroll, N. (eds.) *Post-Theory: Reconstructing Film Studies*. Madison, WI: University of Wisconsin Press, pp. 108–129.

Pink, S. (2015) *Doing Sensory Ethnography*. 2nd edn. London: Sage Publications.

Piotrowska, A. (2013) *Psychoanalysis and Ethics in Documentary Film*. Abingdon, Oxon; New York: Routledge.

Plantinga, C. (1997) *Rhetoric and Representation in Nonfiction Film*. Cambridge, MA: Cambridge University Press.

Plantinga, C. (2005) "What a Documentary Is, After All," *Journal of Aesthetics and Art Criticism*, 63 (2), pp. 105–117.

Plantinga, C. (2009a) *Moving Viewers: American Film and the Spectator's Experience*. Berkeley, NJ: University of California Press.

Plantinga, C. (2009b) "Spectatorship," in Livingston, P. and Plantinga, C. (eds.) *The Routledge Companion to Philosophy and Film*. New York: Routledge, pp. 249–259.

Plantinga, C. (2013) "'I'll Believe It When I Trust the Source': Documentary Images and Visual Evidence," in Winston, B. (ed.) *The Documentary Film Book*, Basingstoke: BFI—Palgrave Macmillan, pp. 40–47.

Plantinga, C. and Smith, G. M. (eds.) (1999). *Passionate Views: Film, Cognition, and Emotion*. Baltimore, MD: Johns Hopkins University Press.

Ponech, T. (1999) *What is Non-fiction Cinema?* Boulder, CO: Westview Press.

Renov, M. (1993) "Toward a Poetics of Documentary," in Renov, M. (ed.) *Theorizing Documentary*. New York: Routledge, pp. 12–36.

Renov, M. (2004) *The Subject of Documentary*. Minneapolis, MN: University of Minnesota Press.

Richardson, K. and Corner, J. (1986) "Reading Reception: Mediation and Transparency in Viewers' Accounts of a TV Programme," *Media, Culture & Society*, 8(4), pp. 485–508.

Shapiro, L. A. (2011) *Embodied Cognition*. New York: Routledge.

Shimamura, A. P. (ed.). (2013) *Psychocinematics: Exploring Cognition at the Movies*. New York: Oxford University Press.

Skains, L. (2016) "Creative Practice as Research: Cognitive Approach," *Creative Practice as Research: Discourse on Methodology* [Online]. Available at: http://scalar.usc.edu/works/creative-practice-research/cognitive-approach (Accessed: January 14, 2018).

Smaill, B. (2010) *The Documentary: Politics, Emotion, Culture*. New York: Palgrave Macmillan.

Smith, G. M. (2007) "The Segmenting Spectator: Documentary Structure and The Aristocrats," *Projections*, 1(2), pp. 83–100.

Smith, M. (1994) "Altered States: Character and Emotional Response in the Cinema," *Cinema Journal*, 33(4), pp. 34–56.

Smith, M. (1995) *Engaging Characters: Fiction, Emotion, and the Cinema*. Oxford: Oxford University Press.

Smith, T. J. (2013) "Watching You Watch Movies: Using Eye Tracking to Inform Film Theory," in Shimamura, A. P. (ed.) *Psychocinematics: Exploring Cognition at the Movies*. New York: Oxford University Press, pp. 165–191.

Tan, E. S. (1996) *Emotion and the Structure of Narrative Film: Film as an Emotion Machine*. Mahwah, NJ: Routledge.

Tan, E. S. and Bálint, K. (2017) "The Phenomenology of Characterisation: From Social Cognition of Real Persons to the Construction of Fictional Human-Like Figures in Narrative", *SCSMI* (June 12, 2017). Helsinki [Online]. Available at: http://research.ku.dk/search/?pure=en/publications/the-phenomenology-of-characterisation(35e94907-5613-45a5-b804-516146165890)/export.html (Accessed: December 4, 2017).

Wang, H. (2015) *Cognitive Science and the Pragmatist Tradition*. Phd thesis. École normale supérieure de Lyon [Online]. Available at: https://tel.archives-ouvertes.fr/tel-01223306/document (Accessed: November 25, 2017).

Ward, P. (2005) *Documentary: The Margins of Reality*. New York: Columbia University Press.

William, J. M. (2017) *Cognitive Approaches to German Historical Film: Seeing is Not Believing*. New York: Palgrave Macmillan.

Winston, B. (2008) *Claiming the Real: Documentary: Grierson and Beyond*. 2nd edn. London: British Film Institute.

PART I

The Mediation of Realities

A Documentary of the Mind: Self, Cognition and Imagination in Anders Østergaard's Films

Ib Bondebjerg

Traditional theories of documentary tend to stress that the genre belongs to Bill Nichols' (1991, p. 3) "discourses of sobriety," that it is somehow a more direct representation of the real than fiction, a rhetorical form of communication that presents a rational argument about the world. However, although rhetorical structures, argumentation and the more direct use of material drawn from a nonfictional space are important elements distinguishing the documentary form from fiction, most theoretical studies of documentary genres or modes, including Nichols' (2001), also acknowledge its complexity, variation and creative dimensions. Furthermore, general documentary studies have moved in new directions since Nichols' (1991) seminal book. Yet, despite these changes, cognitive theories of documentary are still relatively limited. In this chapter, I want to demonstrate how documentary films are strongly influenced by emotional and narrative structures, how they feed our images of reality, and how our embodied mind and self are at work in their production and reception.

I. Bondebjerg (✉)
University of Copenhagen, Copenhagen, Denmark
e-mail: bonde@hum.ku.dk

C. Brylla, M. Kramer (eds.), *Cognitive Theory and Documentary Film*, https://doi.org/10.1007/978-3-319-90332-3_2

Cognitive film theory has dealt far less with documentary than with fiction; however, Carl Plantinga's work, *Rhetoric and Representation in Nonfiction Film* (1997), is a pivotal starting point. He begins by expanding the concept of rhetoric to include what he calls "the richness, complexity, and expressiveness of nonfiction discourse." By defining documentary's different voices (formal, open and poetic) and citing John Grierson's famous definition of it as "the creative treatment of actuality," he opens the way for a view of documentary not as a unified discourse or specific mode of representing reality, but rather as a way of presenting the world that can take a variety of forms (p. 3). In essence, his argument attempts to distance the analysis of documentary from classical theories that claim that while stories and imagination lie at the heart of fiction, documentaries are simply rhetorical arguments about the real world (p. 84).

The basic problem with such classical theories, however, has deeper roots. As recent cognitive film theory and theories of emotion, narrative and metaphor have revealed, emotion and reason are profoundly interconnected in the ways in which we think about and experience the world. Consequently, narrative and imagination cannot be reduced to fictional elements; they are embodied in how we experience the self, others and the world in general (Bondebjerg 1994, 2014a, b, 2015, 2017). Emotions play a crucial role in our reasoning, and our suspicion towards them and tendency to downplay them compounds what neurologist Antonio Damasio (1994) has called "Descartes' error," a misconception prevalent in Western thought. Damasio (2010) contends that our sense of self and ability to interpret the world are based on emotional and narrative structures which build the "stages" of the self (a concept I discuss later in the chapter). Thus, narrative structures are not just connected to fictional forms of communication, they are part of the very fabric of our mind and imagination, an evolutionary construction of a sort of "inner Sherlock Holmes" (Gottschall 2012).

The belief in the dominance of rationality in our mental processes has been similarly undermined by the work of George Lakoff and Mark Johnson (Johnson 1987; Lakoff and Johnson 1980, 1999). Using cognitive linguistics, they demonstrate the role that metaphor plays in language and reasoning, arguing that the mind creates metaphorical structures that are fundamentally connected to both mind and body. According to Lakoff and Johnson (1980), metaphors are embodied categories and our thought processes are based on neural connections linking mind and body. Although their work is situated within the field of linguistics, the salient point of their theory is that our way of speaking and thinking is linked to image schemas—embodied ways of perceiving the world and of relating words to domains of meaning. As a result, embodied image schemas also influence science and philosophy, the basic ways in which we think and argue (Lakoff and Johnson 1999), refuting the myth of the opposition of objectivity and subjectivity.

Lakoff and Johnson's (1999, p. 73) theory of metaphors, therefore, is grounded in an embodied cognitive definition. They describe what they refer to as "primary metaphors" in three ways:

1. they are embodied through bodily experiences of the world which pair sensorimotor processes with subjective experience;
2. their source-domain logic arises from inferential structures of the sensorimotor experience;
3. they are instantiated neurally in the synaptic weights associated with neural connections.

These authors show how our whole system of primary and complex metaphors is part of our cognitive unconscious—for instance, thinking and speaking about "love" produces a rich cognitive, emotional and embodied experience, often taking place below conscious awareness. As they comment, "take away all those metaphorical ways of conceptualizing love, and there's not a whole lot left" (p. 72).

DOCUMENTARY AND THE SOCIOLOGY OF EMOTIONS

Recent writing on film in general, and on documentary in particular, has frequently alluded to the fact that "the role of emotions has been secondary or even buried" (García 2016, p. 3). For example, in Nichols' (1991, 2001) influential works, the term "emotion" is missing from the indices and there are only brief references to "emotional proof" (1991, p. 133), defined as an appeal to the viewer's emotional disposition, and "emotional realism" (2001, p. 93), referring to the way in which a documentary can seek to create a specific emotional state in its audience. Both terms are accepted as legitimate in documentary film theory, but emotions are not awarded any greater role in the understanding of how documentaries work and their relation to reality and the mind of the viewer.[1]

---

[1] Nichols (2001, p. 131) also occasionally uses the terms "affect" and "embodied subjectivity," which he attributes to the performative documentary mode. However, he does not provide a definition of these terms.

For researchers situated outside the cognitive field, the most obvious route to uncovering the role of emotions in documentary has been through psychoanalysis, phenomenology and the focus on personal and gendered issues and themes. This is the case for Michael Renov's *The Subject of Documentary* (2004), which deals with the history of the subjective documentary, and Belinda Smaill's *The Documentary: Politics, Emotions and Culture* (2010), which, apart from analyzing varied examples of more subjective and transgressive types of documentary, highlights the need to develop a theoretical understanding of the fundamental role emotions play in documentary. Smaill (2010, p. 4) argues against the dominance of rationality and "discourses of sobriety" in documentary theory and points to the importance of emotions in the formation of attitudes and social norms. However, both scholars remain vague about the concrete mechanisms of emotion-generation. Another significant contribution to documentary theory is Elisabeth Cowie's *Recording Reality, Desiring the Real* (2011), which describes the genre as "embodied storytelling" that "engages us with the actions and feelings of social actors, like characters in fiction." The concept of "the desire for the real" is based on the theories of Freud and Lacan, combined with the phenomenology of Foucault, Deleuze and Derrida; however, there is no reference to cognitive theory. The same holds true for Malin Wahlberg's *Documentary Time: Film and Phenomenology* (2008), in which he argues against the disregard of the aesthetic and affective dimensions in documentary analysis and seeks to expand phenomenological theories on time and image to encompass documentary film. Reference to embodiment and emotion, however, plays no part in this endeavor.

Cognitive film theory has taken up the challenge from a cognitive perspective (for example, Plantinga and Smith 1999; Tan 2011) but mostly in relation to fiction films. It seems that the error in Western thought highlighted by Damasio (1994), and the dualism between rationality and imagination/emotion that Lakoff and Johnson (1980) have identified in both philosophy and linguistics, still shape theoretical approaches to documentary. Indeed, as I have pointed out previously (Bondebjerg 2014a, p. 70), the distinction between fiction and nonfiction in film has until now been predominantly based on this dualism: fiction had been viewed as the genre of narrative, emotions and imagination, documentary as the genre of direct representations of reality, rhetoric and rational arguments.

However, even though this binary distinction between fiction and nonfiction, between a sort of "reality modus" and a "hypothetical modus," is pervasive in our culture and society and in our forms of communication, it does not change the fundamental way in which our mind and body interact, irrespective of genre.

SELF, OTHER AND IMAGINATION

Danish filmmaker Anders Østergaard's documentary strategy clearly illustrates just how meaningful it is to see emotions as "embodied carriers of knowledge, which result in self-knowledge, in knowledge of our bonds with the world" (Martínez and González 2016, p. 19). The way in which his films use emotions and the self to provide a broader representation of society, culture and history reflects the latest understanding of how the mind works. For instance, by telling the story of the late Swedish jazz musician, Jan Johansson, in *The Magus* (1999), through the emotional universe of music and lyrical images of the artist's life and times, Østergaard triggers embodied layers of the self, releasing our individual memories and experiences (and our perception of those of others) that constitute our past and present. The film also provides us with a rich store of information about jazz history, Scandinavian societies and Johansson's character and personal network; it gives us a visual and narrative feeling of *being there*, and this sense reinforces the factual knowledge. We see Johansson not only as a musician, but also as an individual inhabiting a specific time and place. Even though we may have no prior knowledge of Johansson or his world, Østergaard enables us to identify with him and to imagine the period and type of society he lived in.

As a creative documentary filmmaker, Østergaard is not directly inspired by modern theories of the mind and emotions. Nevertheless, his way of using the documentary genre illustrates Damasio's (2010, p. 8) perception of the self as a process rather than an entity and his contention that our mind-brain is inextricably connected to the body—what he terms the "body and brain bond" (p. 21). Damasio offers three different perspectives of the brain-mind: the "individual conscious mind," to which we have only subjective access; "watching the behavior of others," a perspective from which we rationalize and imagine what goes on in others' conscious minds; and, finally, the "neurological brain," which can be accessed under certain clinical conditions (p. 15). The first two states are clearly defining elements in Østergaard's documentary strategy: he is attempting to present a visual, narrative insight into another's creative mind, an area that is particularly difficult to access or document through film. His use of imagination, metaphor and emotional cues are crucial because they resonate to a large degree with common feelings and experiences.

Perhaps more important for the understanding of the way the self functions is Damasio's description of how mind and body work together in the formation of the self. Damasio (2010, p. 181) distinguishes between three levels of the self. The first, the "protoself," is the site for the most fundamental aspects of the representation of primordial and spontaneous sensations of the living body—we feel our body and know that we are alive. Secondly, the "core self" involves modifications of the protoself through the organism's interactions with objects outside the self, resulting in the rise of temporary but coherent patterns of feelings, images and narrative sequences in the mind. Finally, the "autobiographical self" is generated when objects in the protoself are activated, creating new, larger-scale and more coherent patterns of sequential narrative, including images and feelings. In sum, this process starts with spontaneous primordial feelings in the protoself, progresses through small-scale narratives with fleeting patterns of images and feelings in the core self, and ultimately reaches the stage of the formation of more coherent, permanent and large-scale narratives, emotions and feelings in the autobiographical self. Damasio's model indicates the significance of the body and related primordial and higher-level feelings in the construction and experience of the self. In this respect, the main "language" used by the brain and the self consists of images and narrative sequences. Thus, metaphorically speaking, our mind and our ways of thinking and experiencing are made of the stuff that films are made of.

As Damasio (2010, pp. 109–110) points out, it is also important to distinguish between emotions and feelings. Emotions are "complex, largely automated actions" that take place in our bodies, while feelings are "composite perceptions of what happens in our body" during emotional instances and bodily actions; they are images or perceptions executed by the brain on the basis of embodied emotions. Of course, narrative, emotions, feelings and imagination do not cover the full spectrum of mental processes; the human mind also operates in what Jerome Bruner (1986, p. 12) calls the "paradigmatic mode" of rational, logical thought and the processing of factual knowledge. Although we often refer colloquially to a rational debate being derailed by emotional responses, it is crucial to emphasize that embodied emotions and rationality (in Bruner's sense) are not separate but fundamentally linked. As his explicit use of poetics shows,

Østergaard's documentaries transcend the dualism of the rational versus the emotional. His films carefully take us from one layer of the self to the next by embedding factual insight in emotional and metaphorical structures.

ØSTERGAARD, MEMORY AND THE DOCUMENTARY OF THE MIND

Damasio as a neuroscientist is also highly concerned with philosophical and cultural issues; indeed, he has an almost poetic way of defining the role of memory and imagination, referring specifically to the power of art. He argues that art evolved from basic forms of communication that were gradually transformed into a privileged means of transmitting factual and emotional information between groups of people and between whole societies. Imagination, therefore, has become a means of exploring our own individual mind and the minds of others; hence, it influences both our deeper emotional layers and our ability to express and communicate our feelings. Damasio declares:

[The greatest human attribute is] the ability to navigate the future in the seas of our imagination, guiding the self craft into a safe and productive harbor. The greatest of all gifts depends once again, on the intersection of the self and memory. Memory, tempered by personal feeling, is what allows humans to imagine both individual well-being and the well-being of a whole society. (Damasio 2010, pp. 296–297)

Østergaard (cited in Hjort et al. 2014, p. 381) has defined his approach to documentary as "a documentary of the mind." By attempting to enter the subjective, psychological world of his main characters in an expressive and metaphorical style, and by letting the artistic universe of his protagonists flow into his films, he is situating his documentaries at the intersection of the body, mind, reason and emotion, and of the self and the external world. The way in which he takes reality and turns it into a narrative, an imaginative space, using mind and emotion as an entry point, reveals a great deal about the relationship of documentary forms to both factual-rational and poetic modes of filmmaking. Essentially, the process by which Østergaard builds his narrative around his characters is clearly illustrative of Damasio's three dimensions of the self, combined with a strong focus on memory and the different layers of the actual and historical dimensions of the self.

Openings are important in all forms of written and filmic communication as they frame the "contract" between the readers/audience and the text and introduce the perspective through which the writer/director wants us to view the work and the characters it depicts (Bondebjerg 1994). Østergaard has a characteristic way of opening his documentaries: they invite us into the narrative and imaginative world of a character in a specific time and place. In his portrait of Johansson, which is also a poetic story of Sweden from the 1930s to the 1960s, the opening sequences stimulate our emotions and memories, evoking the very feeling of the music. They begin with black-and-white archive footage of Johansson entering a studio and starting to play one of his characteristic compositions, mixing jazz with Swedish folk melodies. This cue, which speaks directly to our historical documentary mind, is combined with a contemporary color sequence of a scientific experiment focusing on the sorts of emotions his music arouses in individuals. A further aesthetic layer is added with animated abstract patterns reflecting the pulse and rhythm of Johansson's music.

The experiment's participants are a representative sample of the Swedish population. Although they are of different genders, ages and ethnic backgrounds, their reaction to the music is quite universal, as manifest by their facial expressions and body language. They also attempt to express their feelings, reflecting on the emotions they experience when listening to Johansson's music. But while their comments refer to such basic common emotions as joy, sadness or melancholy, the participants also exhibit the urge to reminisce, reliving individual memories, as well as remarking that the music displays a Nordic/Swedish character. These responses are followed by a shot of a professional musician, who analyzes the specific form and tonality of Johansson's music, his originality and the place he occupies in the jazz tradition. What this opening sequence illustrates is the different levels of the self. When the ordinary Swedes in the film (and the film's audience) are exposed to the music, an interaction appears to take place between the deep primordial feelings of the protoself and the more coherent interpretive dimensions of the core self: they experience the feelings evoked by the music and simultaneously try to define it, to connect it to a social and cultural context. This interaction is further enhanced when the expert, embodying the autobiographical self, explains Johansson's music and places it in a coherent historical context.

No one watching the first five minutes of this film would doubt that it is a documentary, but the viewer is guided into the story that subsequently unfolds along a certain emotional route, signaling that this is a specific type of documentary. In the rest of the film, Johansson's personal life story, his musical universe and a broader historical dimension are combined in what is both a linear narrative and a visual and musical montage. In an interview in 2014, Østergaard (cited in Hjort et al. 2014, p. 381) delineated his documentary method and his intentions, calling the film a kind of "mental documentarism" and explaining that "[v]isually and aesthetically speaking, the style and form of my portrait films ... tend to opt for a poetic approach to the artist as a human being, and to that person's artistic work... My intent is to capture the mental dimension: the psychological aspect, the person's consciousness" (p. 389).

The opening of *The Magus* illustrates Østergaard's modus operandi. The recurrent use of what Mark Johnson (1987) calls "metaphor as imaginative rationality" is also characteristic of the rest of the film, which speaks directly to our perception of Johansson as a musician and an historical figure, using visual and musical metaphors that support a more intellectual understanding. Like many documentaries, the film deploys testimonies from experts, friends and family members, and these situate Johansson as a person and as an artist. But it also uses a continuous stream of visual metaphors and varied sequences—some with music, some with inserted sounds, some silent and some constructed or reconstructed by adding sequences with a purely symbolic function or through montage and animation. Such sequences prompt imaginative and emotional responses to the narrative; they create networks of memory linking the viewer with the text. This also means that the film connects to all the layers of the self, from the most basic feelings and emotions to those where our own life story combines with a broader cultural context. This sort of film creates the complex metaphors Lakoff and Johnson (1999) speak of by connecting sensorimotor embodied experiences with subjective ones, using music, landscape and visual cues, for example. During our lifetimes, metaphors create networks of neural connections that influence our perceptions. These function as a kind of embodied understanding, a feeling of the reality of the story the film tells. In this sense, documentaries, like fiction films, are deeply dependent on narrative, imagination, emotion and memory, all of which (in addition to rational thought) enable our understanding of reality.

THE LIFE AND MIND OF HERGÉ

Østergaard's documentary *Tintin and I* (2004) is probably his most innovative and experimental film so far. At its core is a classical element found in most portrait documentaries that focus on one main character:

a long interview with Hergé (the pseudonym of George Remi) in October 1971, near the end of his life, conducted by a then-unknown French student, Numa Sadoul. This interview gives us an intimate view—both front and back stage—of the famous cartoonist's work, life and times, and this portrait of him is supported by the testimonies of experts and other commentators. However, the way Østergaard chooses to aesthetically organize Hergé's life story is quite unique, underlining the fact that the truth can be found not only in a factual first- or third-person account, but also in a mediated, emotional reality. The kind of narrative Østergaard (cited in Hjort et al. 2014, p. 390) constructs around Hergé and his universe goes beyond the story of a specific person and artist. As he says, "*Tintin and I* is a film that doesn't merely depict a concrete individual and specific artistic universe: the film is about what it's like to be human in the twentieth century, and it's also about the history of that century." What Østergaard is referring to here is that Hergé's life mirrors some of the key developments of his time in a very dramatic way and that this historical period is reflected in the world of his cartoons. Hergé's story is that of an (initially) very conservative Catholic boy, who feels the need to change, to free himself of his past. He does this slowly, over a period of time, after experiencing a series of traumatic events. Meanwhile, he stages his own existential dilemma, his relationship with the world, in the universe of his cartoons.

The opening scenes of the film, prior to the title sequence, are illustrative of its inner structure. The first images comprise frames from Hergé's cartoon, *Tintin in Tibet* (1959), depicting a plane crash in the snowy mountains of the Himalayas. The frames are animated by the camera, as it tracks and zooms into the scene, and by the wind on the soundtrack. After a few seconds, Hergé is heard in a voiceover admitting to Sadoul, "You are getting secrets from me that I have never told anyone before. I don't like talking about myself. I instantly build a wall around myself." At the end of this statement, the visuals change to a (reconstructed) shot of Hergé's studio, with figures from Tintin ranged along the windowsill. The camera pans the room to take in further objects, including the microphone and tape recorder. Then we return to the scene of the plane crash. While Hergé states, "It definitely carries a message. I can see now, the story was a way of expressing myself," his face appears, superimposed on the Tibetan landscape, but depicted graphically as a cartoon image. As the animated sequence continues, Hergé's face gradually fades from view.

Following this, Østergaard introduces a new type of sequence, in which Sadoul—now in real time—looks back at the interview. Visually, we shift between a recorder with its tapes rolling, archive stills of Hergé and the interviewer, and the gradual unfolding of metaphorical visual sequences, in which the world of Tintin comes alive as a huge montage of all the pages of Hergé's 23 volumes, representing (we are told) 47 years of work, translated into 58 languages and circulated in millions of copies. This vision of numberless pages is followed by a rapid montage of images from his various albums and a statement by Sadoul that Hergé has not only distilled 50 years of history, war, politics and everyday life in his work, but has also given us access to his inner life and personal experiences. This again is visualized by superimposing Hergé as a cartoon figure on a background consisting of all 23 albums, which exemplifies how the on-screen animation of the character's superimposed image functions as an embodied metaphor: Hergé is in some way his cartoons and his cartoons are an image of his life.

The opening sequences of *Tintin and I* carry the stamp of an imaginative, poetic and metaphorical filmmaker. The film does not simply document or explain the close link between mind, body, emotions and the way we are and how we live our lives, it embodies this through a visual strategy that allows us to both see and feel what we are being told. Explanation and experience, rationality and emotion are combined in a narrative that is as much the story of an historical and personal reality as it is a visualization of a particular creative mind and self. Based on a long interview, this film portrait is also a film about memory and about the three layers of the self. Confronted with his past and with interpretations of himself as an historical figure or as portrayed through his cartoons, Hergé is witnessed moving between primordial memories, the fleeting emotions of his core self, and reflections on and changes in his autobiographical self.

When the film shifts to historical footage of Belgian politics and social life or of Hergé's childhood, it uses archival images. By linking this iconic/mimetic archive footage to the more metaphorical images, Østergaard allows the viewer to experience the link between past and present, between collective and personal history. Despite these expressionistic techniques, the film still deploys the basic elements of traditional documentary, such as interviews and archives, in an expository manner. This adheres to what Nichols (2001, p. 105), in his typology of documentaries, calls the "expository documentary," based on a direct rhetorical, rational structure, or what Plantinga (1997, p. 110) terms the "formal documentary," which is defined by its epistemic authority and its stance towards the world and the viewer. As I have argued elsewhere (Bondebjerg 2014a), the basic proto-types of documentaries can be summarized using Nichols' and Plantinga's observations as a basis, as illustrated in Fig. 2.1.

Looking at the characteristics of the four basic documentary modes, it becomes apparent that Østergaard's films use elements from almost all of these and that he has an equally strong investment in the authoritative, the dramatized and the poetic-reflexive type of documentary. This directly relates to the way he works with more complex metaphorical structures and character subjectivities that are simultaneously linked to broader his-torical and social narratives. He often uses dramatization, both in the form of reconstructions and the visual and narrative play of different types of images, and regards narrative structure as a strong form of argumenta-tion, in keeping with the old adage, "show, don't tell." Although he has not signed up to cognitive theory, Østergaard appears to instinctively understand, as a documentary filmmaker, that our narrative experience of

Authoritative	Observational	Dramatized	Poetic-reflexive
Epistemic authority	Epistemic openness	Epistemic-hypothetical	Epistemic-aesthetic
Explanation-analysis	Observation-identification	Dramatization of factual reality	Reality seen through aesthetic form
Linearity, causality, rhetorical structure	Episodic, mosaic structure, everyday life	Reconstruction, narration, staging (drama-doc, doc-drama, mockumentary)	Symbolic montage, meta-levels, expressive, subjective form
Q & A, interview, witnesses, experts, Authoritative VO	Actor driven, human-institutional life world	Testing borders between reality and fiction	Form driven reality experience, the poetics of reality, framing reality
Information, critique, propaganda	Documentation of lived reality, social ethnology	Narrative drive, reality driven narrative. Media-reflexivity	Challenging reality concepts and traditional doc-forms

Fig. 2.1   The basic prototypes of documentary. Source: Ib Bondebjerg (2014a)

the world is at least as important as rationality and abstract thinking—in fact, these attributes are always directly linked in his films and not portrayed as discrete parts of a dual division of the mind. To experience through narrative, in this case, is to experience through identification and embodied understanding. Østergaard also uses the more poetic and metaphorical dimensions of his documentaries—his ability to play with images, forms and sound—as a further way of speaking to the embodied mind. In *The Magus*, for example, by letting us enter Johansson's universe through music, emotions and other characters' reactions to and experiences of this world, Østergaard activates qualitative dimensions of mind and body other than those normally identified with a traditional, authoritative documentary.

The same is true, but to an even greater degree, with *Tintin and I*, which imaginatively connects the fictional story world, Hergé's personal life and the historical epoch. This documentary clearly does not fall into the trap of dividing internal and external reality, the subjective and the objective, emotion and reason. We enter Hergé's universe and his work, his life and his place in society and history from a personal, visual and emotional viewpoint, in which his self and his creative work merge. He performs in an open, confessional mode, reflecting on all the dimensions of his self, and in doing so, comes to the realization that the whole of his creative work has been about himself and his relations with others and with the times he has lived in and been formed by.

In the film, the narrative and imaginative uses of the visual are directly related to the underlying basis of factual reality that lies at its core. This factual, often archive-based footage, however, has at least two sides: it presents Hergé's interviewer, Sadoul, and the two foreign experts on Hergé and Tintin expressing their views not only on camera but also as voiceovers to a montage of archive stills and footage of Hergé and his times, reconstructed visual sequences and photographs. Alongside the authentic and paradigmatic dimensions of the film, Østergaard works with an imaginative concept of reality, embedding factual knowledge in an emotional and narrative structure.

The first instance of documentary archive comes four minutes into the film, where Sadoul (in a voiceover) describes how he came to interview Hergé. While he speaks, we see black-and-white images of Brussels in (what we must assume is) 1971, with crowds of people arriving in or leaving the city by train and tram. This is rapidly followed by a cut to Sadoul in his flat in the present day recalling the interview, and then a cut to a running tape from which a live cartoon-like image of the filmed interview with Hergé emerges. Thus, Østergaard establishes a direct link between the factual and the imaginative parts of the film. This montage of generic historical archive material, archive footage of Sadoul's interview, voiceover narration and imaginative cartoon images of Hergé continues throughout the film; the entire documentary's narrative is constructed in this way and there is no sharp distinction between the disparate elements. In one instance, as Hergé and Sadoul discuss how much Tintin and his other cartoon characters (such as Captain Haddock) resemble Hergé himself, we see a sequence with the real Hergé acting on stage and Tintin imitating his gestures and body language. The same point is also illustrated with split-screen, cartoon-style images of Hergé alongside scenes from his cartoons; the stories may be fictional children's tales, but they also illustrate Hergé's life and the history of the twentieth century.

This central theme of intermingling personal and collective history also emerges through the portrayal of Hergé's life story—for example, his upbringing in an extreme, right-wing Catholic family and culture, and his links to a priest who had dubious connections to the fascist movement. This grim childhood is characterized by some of the experts interviewed as "grey," "mediocre" and "cruel," and, as becomes clear during the film, Hergé has struggled to overcome this past, taking refuge in his fictional cartoon world in an attempt to change his way of life and self-image. The emotional peak of his life story is reached when, later in life, he leaves his wife (who was "assigned" to him by the priest) and marries another woman. By combining historical archive footage, Hergé's memories and reflections, expert analyzes and a systematic use of Hergé's cartoon images, Østergaard merges Hergé's private story of personal liberation and the dramatic historical story of the twentieth century into a narrative whole.

As the film progresses, the cutting between and integration of the different narrative and aesthetic layers becomes increasingly elaborate. The montage of elements and the use of superimposition and marked dissolves or split screens intensify as Hergé's autobiographical self becomes increasingly reflexive and aware of the narrative layers and connections in his life and work. There is also a circularity in the film as it becomes evident that *Tintin in Tibet* (the film's opening images) represents a turning point in Hergé's career and personal life—it was at this time that he sought the help of a Swiss psychiatrist. This development, as in all Østergaard's films, is not just told but also shown: it is embodied on all visual narrative levels while we acquire this factual knowledge about Hergé himself.

IMAGINATION AND FACTUALITY: CONCLUSION

Østergaard's documentary films use the whole repertoire of narrative, imagination and visual metaphor; they combine the classic rhetorical strategies of journalism, and even scientific modes of communication, with storytelling and strong emotional and visual cues. The audience clearly perceives them as documentaries with a special relationship to a factual external reality, while at the same time the films appeal to the same areas of the embodied mind as do forms of fiction. Østergaard stages his presentation of reality in such a way as to give viewers a deeper emotional understanding of the historical persons and periods he is describing. In many of his films, he also uses a personal memory as an entry point: in *The Magus*, Østergaard's emotional memory of the 1960s pervades the film, and in *Tintin and I*, the closing sequence of the film depicts a boy visiting his local library, picking up some Tintin albums and cycling home through a typical Danish suburb, in which a Tibetan mountain landscape suddenly appears. The subjective and emotional memories are not diversions from a documentary reality, they are in fact venues for the audience's collective experience of and identification with lived history.

In his film *Gasolin'* (2006) (the most viewed documentary film in Denmark since the 1990s), Østergaard uses the story of a 1970s Danish rock band to engage with the country's postwar history. Again, by taking the emotional, narrative and metaphorical road, he is able to guide the viewer to a deeper understanding of the clash of cultural and social trends at the time. In one of the film's key scenes, he illustrates the twin roots of the band's music—a typical, popular, national folk tradition and an American-inspired rock style—as embodied by two contrasting characters in the band, Kim Larsen and Franz Beckerlee. Larsen's and Beckerlee's voice-over narration is combined with a vivid visual montage of images and music that illustrates both their personal stories and the story of wider national and global trends in the 1970s. Explaining his visual and narrative strategy, Østergaard claims that he deliberately chose a mythological framework for the film, which he rooted in well-established literary traditions and fairy tales. The core imaginative framework for the documentary is embodied in Hans Christian Andersen's figure of Clumsy Hans and the figures of Aladdin and Noureddin, the bright and dark princes, known from the tales of *One Thousand and One Nights*, as well as later forms of literature and popular culture (Østergaard, cited in Hjort et al. 2014, p. 393).

Østergaard's documentaries are powerful examples of the role played by narrative, imagination, emotion and the different layers of the self in documentary film. They show that we are wrong if we think that the configuration of feelings, emotions and narrative are not central to documentary; they are, on the contrary, the basis for all that we think and do. Damasio (1994, p. xv) argues that feelings "serve as internal guides, and they help us communicate to others signals that can also guide them ... [F]eelings are just as cognitive as other percepts ... They are the result of a most curious physiological arrangement that has turned the brain into the body's captive audience."

REFERENCES

Bondebjerg, I. (1994) "Narratives of Reality: Documentary Film and Television in a Cognitive and Pragmatic Perspective," *Nordicom Review*, 1, pp. 65–85.

Bondebjerg, I. (2014a) *Engaging with Reality: Documentary and Globalization*. Bristol: Intellect Books.

Bondebjerg, I. (2014b) "Documentary and Cognitive Theory: Narrative, Emotion and Memory," *Media and Communication*, 2(1), pp. 13–22.

Bondebjerg, I. (2015) "The Embodied Mind: When Biology Meets Culture and Society," *Palgrave Communications* [Online]. Available at: http://www.nature.com/articles/palcomms201515 (Accessed: March 12, 2017).

Bondebjerg, I. (2017) "The Creative Mind: Cognition, Society and Culture," *Palgrave Communications*. [Online] Available at: http://www.nature.com/articles/s41599-017-0024-1 (Accessed: March 13, 2017).

Bruner, J. (1986) *Actual Minds, Possible Worlds*. Cambridge: Harvard University Press.

Cowie, E. (2011) *Recording Reality, Desiring the Real*. Minneapolis: University of Minnesota Press.

Damasio, A. (1994) *Descartes' Error: Emotion, Reason and the Human Brain*. New York: Avon Books.

Damasio, A. (2010) *Self Comes to Mind. Constructing the Conscious Brain*. London: Vintage Books.

García, A. N. (2016) "Introduction," in García, A. N. (ed.) *Emotions in Contemporary TV Series*. Basingstoke: Palgrave Macmillan, pp. 1–13.

Gottschall, J. (2012) *The Storytelling Animal. How Stories Make Us Human*. New York: Mariner Books.

Hergé, (1959/1962) *Tintin in Tibet*. Translated by Leslie Lonsdale Cooper and Michael Turner. London: Methuen.

Hjort, M., Bondebjerg, I. and Redvall, E. N. (eds.) (2014) *The Danish Directors 3: Dialogues on the New Danish Documentary Cinema*. Bristol: Intellect Books.

Johnson, M. (1987) *The Body in the Mind: The Bodily Basis of Meaning, Imagination and Reason*. Chicago: Chicago University Press.

Lakoff, G. and Johnson, M. (1980) *Metaphors We Live By*. Chicago: Chicago University Press.

Lakoff, G. and Johnson, M. (1999) *Philosophy in the Flesh: The Embodied Mind and Its Challenge to Western Thought*. New York: Basic Books.

Martínez, A. G. and González, A. M. (2016) "Emotional Culture and TV Narratives," in García, A. N. (ed.) *Emotions in Contemporary TV Series*. Basingstoke: Palgrave Macmillan, pp. 12–25.

Nichols, B. (1991) *Representing Reality: Issues and Concepts in Documentary*. Bloomington: Indiana University Press.

Nichols, B. (2001) *Introduction to Documentary*. Bloomington: Indiana University Press.

Plantinga, C. (1997) *Rhetoric and Representation in Nonfiction Film*. Cambridge: Cambridge University Press.

Plantinga, C. and Smith, G. M. (1999) *Passionate Views. Film, Cognition and Emotion*. Baltimore: University of John Hopkins Press.

Renov, M. (2004) *The Subject of Documentary*. Minneapolis: University of Minnesota Press.

Smaill, B. (2010) *The Documentary: Politics, Emotion, Culture*. Basingstoke: Palgrave Macmillan.

Tan, E. (2011) *Emotion and the Structure of Narrative Film*. New York: Routledge.

Wahlberg, M. (2008) *Documentary Time: Film and Phenomenology*. Minneapolis: University of Minnesota Press.

CHAPTER 3

Little Voices and Big Spaces: Animated Documentary and Conceptual Blending Theory

Juan Alberto Conde Aldana

ANIMATED DOCUMENTARY AND THE VOICE

The encounter between documentary film and animation is not a new phenomenon, but in the last two decades it has become an increasingly frequent one: the inclusion of animated sequences in documentaries is now common practice, and animated films no longer focus solely on imaginary worlds but have also begun to depict the real world.[1] However, this encounter is not an easy one, as Anabelle Honess Roe points out:

> Animation and documentary make an odd couple. Theirs is a marriage of opposites, made complicated by different ways of seeing the world. The former conjures up thoughts of comedy, children's entertainment and folkloric fantasies; the latter carries with it the assumptions of seriousness, rhetoric and evidence. (Honess Roe 2013, p. 1)

---

[1] See, for example, the autobiographical docudrama *Approved for Adoption* (Laurent Boileau and Jung Henin 2012), and *Chicago 10* (Brett Morgen 2007).

J. A. Conde Aldana (✉)
Jorge Tadeo Lozano University, Bogotá, Colombia
e-mail: juan.conde@utadeo.edu.co

© The Author(s) 2018
C. Brylla, M. Kramer (eds.), *Cognitive Theory and Documentary Film*, https://doi.org/10.1007/978-3-319-90332-3_3

Nevertheless, Jeffrey Skoller celebrates the blurring of boundaries between the photographic realism of classical documentary and animation's expressive and imaginative characteristics:

> [T]he binaries between the truth claims of documentary cinema and the impressionisms of animated filmmaking seem increasingly irrelevant. … [T]he truth claims of non-fiction forms are no longer located in the "reality effects" of the photographic trace. Rather, they reside in a developing understanding that the realities that surround us and the events that structure our present are not always visualizable, that their meanings are unclear, and that documentary evidence is not always possible, revealing or clarifying. (Skoller 2011, p. 207)

In order to address these ambiguities, Honess Roe has created a typology based on three of the roles that animation can play in documentary film: mimetic substitution, non-mimetic substitution and evocation. In the first two, the function of animation is to replace filmic material. However, it is the third or evocative function that is of particular interest to this chapter. Its purpose is to represent "concepts, emotions, feelings and states of mind" in a way that will show "in an abstract or symbolic style… the world from someone else's perspective" (Honess Roe 2013, p. 25).

The three functions are not mutually exclusive. In this sense, animated documentaries and traditional documentaries share the complex relationship between film's aural and visual aspects. For example, when either type of documentary uses audio recordings of interviews, sound possesses its own realism or indexicality that is not fully dependent on the image. The voice, in particular, is generally understood as a vehicle for communicating—directly or indirectly—the viewpoint of the film. This is the idea behind Bill Nichols' (1991) concept of documentary modes, which describes the various functions of the voice, ranging from the didactic voice of god in the expository mode to the voice of the interviewer (disclosing their presence) in the participatory mode. Nichols (2001, pp. 42–60) argues that the voice should not only be understood in a literal sense; it is also associated with the film's perspective—that is, it conveys a sense of how the filmmaker has selected and arranged the sounds and images in such a way that they implicitly advance a specific argument. Carl Plantinga (1997, p. 106), meanwhile, proposes three types of documentary voice: the formal, the open and the poetic, "based on the degree of narrational authority assumed by the film (in the case of the formal and open voices), and on the absence of authority in favor of (broadly) aesthetic concerns in the case of the poetic voice." He also expands the notion of the voice to encompass that of the orator, allowing the analysis of documentary as a form of rhetoric rather than argumentation.

This approach is also applicable to animated documentaries. However, these films possess a distinguishing peculiarity—the actual bodies that produce the voices are substituted (in mimetic or non-mimetic ways) by drawings, puppets or other animated figures. For this reason, many scholars argue that the voice accompanying the animated image plays an indexical role, referencing a given reality (DelGaudio 1997; Strøm 2003; Ward 2005). Yet, although these disembodied indexical voices point to the testimonies and interviews of original sources in the real world, they are reenacted by the uncanny bodies that inhabit the world of animated objects. This chapter argues that a cognitive approach, using the "conceptual blending theory" (CBT), can provide a plausible account of how this peculiarity emerges from the animated film's conceptualization process, and how it is experienced by spectators.

In the first part of the chapter, I look at how scholars have inadvertently (and perhaps intuitively) described animated documentaries as "blends," and show how this description helps explain the way filmmakers create and spectators experience and interpret such films. In this context, blending— as a research paradigm—is a valuable tool with which to explore the link between the minds of the filmmaker and the viewer (Marston William 2017). In the chapter's second part, I use CBT to analyze the Colombian animated documentary, *Pequeñas Voces* (*Little Voices*) (Jairo Eduardo Carrillo, Oscar Andrade 2011), focusing on its conception, and in particular the way it blends the characters' (or witnesses') frames of reference with that of the producers. To deepen the analysis, I also introduce cognitive linguist Barbara Dancygier's (2008, 2012) concept of "narrative spaces," a theoretical approach that addresses aspects of traditional narrative theories from a CBT perspective.

CONCEPTUAL BLENDING THEORY: FROM LINGUISTICS TO ANIMATED FILM

CBT is a development of Gilles Fauconnier's mental space theory. Fauconnier (1997, p. 11) defines mental spaces as "partial structures that proliferate when we think and talk, allowing a fine-grained partitioning of our discourse and knowledge structures." Hence, they are "the domains that discourse builds up to provide a cognitive substrate for reasoning and for interfacing with the world" (p. 34). The construction of novel and imaginative meanings demands a cognitive operation that involves the fusion or integration of different mental spaces. This operation is called "conceptual blending." According to Fauconnier and Mark Turner (2002, p. vi), conceptual blending has played an essential role in human evolution: it is "responsible for the origins of language, art, religion, science, and other singular human feats, and... [it] is as indispensable for basic everyday thought as it is for artistic and scientific abilities."

Fauconnier and Turner provide a basic descriptive model of how conceptual blending works. This introduces four mental spaces: two inputs, a generic space and the blend. The inputs comprise long-term schematic knowledge presented in the form of packages of information about the world or stereotypical scenarios. The generic space captures "the structure that inputs seem to share," and its elements and relations are mapped onto the elements from the input spaces. The "blend" results from the projection of the structure in the two input mental spaces (Fauconnier and Turner 2002, p. 47). CBT is therefore a powerful theoretical tool whose use is not only limited to linguistics; it can be productively employed in other disciplines—for example, the theory has been applied to audiovisual media, and particularly to film (see, for example, Oakley and Tobin 2012; Dannenberg 2012; Rubba 2009; Boyle 2007; William 2017). Turner (2006), one of the originators of the theory, has even applied CBT to cartoons.[2] Nevertheless, documentary studies, in particular the study of animated documentaries, has yet to discover the benefits of CBT.

CBT's relevance to animated documentary is exemplified by the genre's description as a marriage of opposites (Honess Roe 2013) or hybridization (Skoller 2011); these attributes are embodied in the very expression "animated documentary," a term that captures the idea of blending two different filmic modalities. The implications of this new form of cinema can be addressed by cognitive metaphors or blends that help to schematize

---

[2] Some authors have also focused on general cinematic issues from a CBT perspective. For instance, Todd Oakley (2013) has reinterpreted cinematic apparatus theory by applying one of the developments of CBT, the so-called "Aarhus model"; and more recently, Christian Quendler's (2014, p. 56) entry on "Blending and Film Theory" in the *Routledge Encyclopedia of Film Theory* points to the role of "blending as a meta-theoretical framework for studying inferential structures in theorizing about cinema." Also, in contrast to David Bordwell (1985) for whom the viewer's cognitive activity is a purely rational process based on inferences, I have proposed CBT as an alternative way of addressing this activity, in which imagination plays a central role (Conde 2014).

and explain the intricate cognitive processes involved in its conception and reception. To achieve this, the domains that are blended together are constructed from "frames"—stereotypical scenarios or sets of elements and relationships drawn from previous experiences.[3] Based on Fauconnier and Turner's model, Fig. 3.1 illustrates conceptual blending using Honess Roe's (2013) idea of animated documentary as a marriage of opposites.

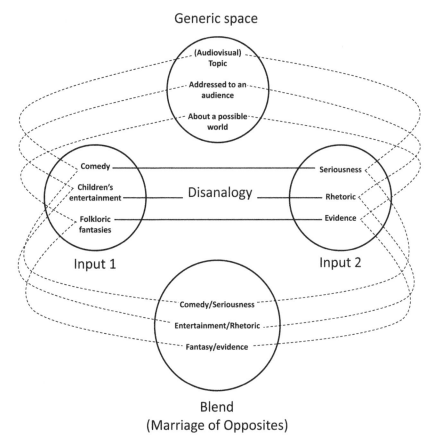

Fig. 3.1 A marriage-of-opposites blend. Source: Juan Alberto Conde Aldana (2016)

---

[3] In a similar way, Michael Sinding (2005, 2012) has used CBT to describe the phenomenon of "mixed genres" in literature.

In this diagram, the solid lines between the two inputs represent "vital relations," which are essentially connections between counterpart elements in the two mental spaces.[4] In this case, the marriage between elements from inputs 1 and 2 is based on the vital relation of "disanalogy," which in turn is based on analogy: for example, both documentary and animation are the values prescribed to their roles as "audiovisual genre/domain/modality." The blended structure is mainly generated in three ways (Fauconnier and Turner 2002, p. 48): through the *composition* of elements from the input spaces, revealing relationships between them that do not exist in the separate inputs; through *completion*, using the background knowledge and structures that we insert into the blend unconsciously; and through *elaboration*, by treating blends as simulations that we can experience imaginatively. In the case of animated documentary, there are disanalogies between the domains of animation and documentary, but by means of composition these are projected into the blend, and completion primes us to fill the frame "animation" with expectations of "expressiveness" or "artistry" and the frame "documentary" with ideas such as "rhetoric." Finally, through elaboration, animation becomes a "representational strategy in documentary" that offers "new or alternative ways of seeing the world"; it presents "the conventional subject matter of documentary (the "world out there" of observable events) in non-conventional ways" that help us visualize "the 'world in here' of subjective, conscious experience—subject matters traditionally beyond the documentary purview" (Honess Roe 2013, p. 2). Essentially, animated documentary is far more than the sum of its parts, a fact that is demonstrated later in the chapter in the case study of *Pequeñas Voces*.

Addressing the sound–image relationship, Michel Chion (1994, p. xxv) has coined the term "audio-vision" to express the way that "films, television, and other audiovisual media do not just address the eye. They place their spectators—their audiospectators—in a specific perceptual mode of reception." The perception of one influences the perception of the other—we do not perceive something in the same way if we not only see it but also hear it, and vice versa. This entails discarding notions of redundancy between these two major filmic elements (p. xxvi).

---

[4] CBT identifies fifteen vital relations: Change, Identity, Time, Space, Cause-Effect, Part-Whole, Representation, Role, Analogy, Disanalogy, Property, Similarity, Category, Intentionality and Uniqueness (Fauconnier and Turner 2002, pp. 93–102).

Fauconnier and Turner, however, assume that perception is already a form of conceptual integration, due to the vital relation between cause and effect:

> [T]he perception available to consciousness is the *effect* of complicated interactions between the brain and the environment. But we integrate that effect with its causes to create emergent meaning: the existence of a *cause*— namely, the cup—that directly presents its *effect*—namely, its unity, color, shape, weight, and so on. As a consequence, the effect is now in its cause: the color, shape, and weight are now intrinsically, primitively, and objectively in "the cup." (Fauconnier and Turner 2002, p. 78)

It is possible to extend this vital relation beyond the visual to all sensory information, including sound. In fact, the relationship between image and sound is usually explained as one of cause and effect. Indeed, the idea that all sound has a source, and the question of whether this source is on-screen or off-screen, has been a preoccupation of many of the theories on sound in film, including those concerned with vocalization. In this sense, Chion's audio-vision could be described as a blending process. But while Fauconnier and Turner assume that multimodal perception is the result of the general cause and effect of blending, Chion's term aims to express the idea that although the audiovisual relationship is based on our cognitive and perceptive abilities, it is an artifice, the result of filmic conventions and spectatorship practices.

Arguably, animated documentary is a good example of a specific form of audio-vision, and CBT can help us describe this phenomenon in all its complexity. The question of voice and of testimony is the most important, although other aural material also plays a role. As mentioned above, the interviews and testimonies in animated documentaries are assumed to be the components that guarantee that the viewer places the film in the realm of documentary, while the animated visuals are a kind of free, artistic or expressive interpretation of the subjects who "own" the voices by means of mimetic and non-mimetic substitution or through Honess Roe's concept of evocation. All three relations are examples of what Fauconnier and Turner call "double-scope blending networks":

> A double-scope network has inputs with different (and often clashing) organizing frames as well as an organizing frame for the blend that includes parts of each of those frames and has emergent structure of its own. ... [B]oth

> organizing frames make central contributions to the blend, and their sharp differences offer the possibility of rich clashes. Far from blocking the construction of the network, such clashes offer challenges to the imagination; indeed, the resulting blends can be highly creative. (Fauconnier and Turner 2002, p. 131)

According to this understanding, Honess Roe's conceptualization of animated documentary can be described as a double-scope network, particularly her idea of "vocalic bodies," as represented in Fig. 3.2

In this blend, the vocalic body emerges as a new structure, the result of the projection of the record of testimonies from input 1 onto the visual interpretation from input 2. The blending process is different if there is a mimetic or a non-mimetic substitution. In the case of mimetic substitution, according to Fauconnier's and Turner's description of perception in terms of blending, the vital relations that allow the mapping of elements from input 1 (subject's voice) onto elements from input 2 (Subject's iconic representation) are those of cause–effect and property: the animated "talking" character is the *cause* of its visual and aural *properties*, which act as *effects*. Representation is another vital relation that allows the mapping of the thing represented (the absent human body) in input 1 onto the element that represents it (the animated visual aspect of the character).

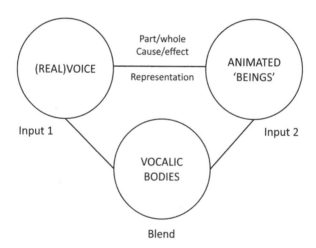

Fig. 3.2 Voice/image blend in animated documentary. Source: Juan Alberto Conde Aldana (2016)

Non-mimetic substitution works in a slightly different way: input 1 would be the same (subject's voice), but input 2 would be a rhetorical representation of the subject which may be distanced (to a greater or lesser extent) from his/her body (or physical appearance—the voice's source), including transformations based on analogies or disanalogies, or even on another vital relation such as category or role/value. The blended space would be a non-mimetic vocalic body.

The case of evocation is also different, as there is no visual representation of the subject's body; instead, there is a free interpretation of some of the different aspects of the subject's emotions or states of mind. In this case, the vital relations supporting the mapping of inputs 1 (subject's voice) and 2 (abstract or symbolic representations) can be multiple, depending on the visual interpretation of the animators. In fact, what is really represented is the subject's discourse in a blend that "evokes" inner states from a subjective perspective.

Honess Roe offers several examples that fit each of her types of animated documentary. Nevertheless, *Pequeñas Voces* challenges these categories—for example, there are elements of input 2 (visual representation) that are difficult to characterize according to her model.

REAL VOICES, CHILDREN'S PICTURES AND COMPLEX EVOCATIONS

Pequeñas Voces is composed of testimonies of child survivors of Colombia's armed conflict. It developed out of an earlier short film that the first director, Jairo Eduardo Carillo, made in 2003 with the same title and central premise—that is, to present a set of interviews with children who have been displaced by the violence from the countryside to the city, and to illustrate their testimonies with animated renderings of their drawings of their experiences. The short version was well received on its tour of international festivals and exhibitions, winning first prize in the documentary projects category at the Anabel Andujar Alfonso Festival in Caceres, Spain, in 2003. As a result, Carrillo decided to develop the project (with co-director Oscar Andrade) and turn it into a feature, with the inclusion of new interviews and testimonies. The long version was released in 2010, but with some important changes, the most dramatic being the film's conversion to a 3D format, enabling it to be screened in large film theaters—in fact, it was the first Colombian film to be released in 3D. It also uses more advanced animation techniques, mixing 3D backgrounds and objects with 2D animations. In the 2D component, the film combines animations made from the children's drawings with the work of professional animators. All this gives the film the appearance of a patchwork, a visual hybridity that could also be explained with the use of CBT, although this lies beyond scope of this chapter.

The film uses an animated talking-head schema for the introductory scenes presenting the main characters (and narrators); only then do the animated characters speak to the camera with what are (strictly speaking) lip-synced dialogues. In these scenes (one for each character), the children begin by talking about their day-to-day lives since arriving in the city of Bogotá with their families, fleeing the violence in their home regions. These scenes operate as a form of Honess Roe's non-mimetic substitution: the speaking subjects are represented as childlike cartoon characters, as is usually the case in animated documentaries.

After the prologue and the title, the subjects' testimonies are narrated in voiceovers while the stories themselves are brought to life by the animated characters. Thus, the testimonies are narrated in the first person (that is, from the narrator-character's perspective, known as "internal focalisation") but the images that appear on screen are what film narratologists call an "external (or zero) ocularisation" (Stam et al. 1992, p. 94)—the narrator-character is an agent who interacts with the other objects and beings of the represented world. Furthermore, the visual representation of these narrations is also a hybrid of the children's own drawings and the childlike illustrations of professional animators (Fig. 3.3). The differences between the two are emphasized by the fact that the children's drawings are executed in crayon and colored pencil and presented as 2D paper cut-outs (the soldiers), while the professional drawings are vivid, digital, 3D objects (the car and the grass in the background).

It is difficult to say if *Pequeñas Voces* continues in the mode of non-mimetic substitution or if it spills over into the mode of evocation, as it offers a symbolic representation of the children's interpretation of the events, particularly through their drawings. In relation to this, Carrillo's previous version of the subject uses an interesting visual-rhetorical device: the beginning of the short film includes a series of shots of the children in the act of drawing. Suddenly, as one of the children starts to tell his story, the camera zooms to a close-up of one of his eyes, and we see reflected there the drawing that opens the animated sequence; the film almost literally allows the viewer to enter the child's inner story. Although this device is not used in the long version, it is clear that the viewer witnesses directly the narrative worlds from the children's perspective.

Fig. 3.3 Children's and professional drawings. Source: Jairo Eduardo Carrillo, Oscar Andrade, *Pequeñas Voces* (2011)

There are also issues concerning the characterization of input 1 (the real voices). One of the main differences between the short and long versions of the film is that, in the second, Carrillo and Andrade have decided to intervene in a more evident way in the presentation of the stories. In Andrade's own words from the DVD extras:

> This is a movie, as it is said in Hollywood, "based on a true story," because children's stories are real, they suffer situations similar to those show[n] [i]n the film... There are some very tough situations there, so what we tried to do was to "recreate" the happy life in the countryside with scenes based on what the kids told us. The idea was to take the stories of several kids displaced by violence in Colombia in the internal war that we have in our country, and to offer a child perspective of this conflict from the victims' point of view... We want to show what the kids told us in the interviews but trying to connect the characters so the viewer does not see a pile of disconnected stories, but that he/she feels that there is a link between them... (Carillo and Andrade 2010)

The film accordingly blends a certain degree of fictionalization (the stories are merged to give the impression of a collective experience) with factual representation. Thus, the viewer can perceive the filmmaker's presence in both the visual and aural aspects of the film, even while sensing that the children are telling their own stories. This is a complex narrativization of real-life events that traditional CBT cannot fully explain unless the different stories are conceptualized as mental spaces or inputs that can be blended in different ways. Dancygier (2008, p. 54) calls these kinds of more elaborate mental space, triggered by a text (or film), "narrative spaces"; these require a more complex structure and extended mainte-nance to enable the mental construction of the story. She also proposes a theoretical model that addresses the question of viewpoint in narrative media from a CBT perspective, allowing a better understanding of the particular narrative strategy used by *Pequeñas Voces*. The prologue and the epilogue, both of which show the children's present-day situation in the city, comprise the framing story, while the central part of the film—five stories, each narrated by an individual child—are the narrative spaces. These spaces contain the stories of (1) the blonde sisters; (2) the boy and his dogs; (3) the child recruited by the guerrilla army; (4) the child trapped in the middle of a battle between the guerrillas and the national army; and (5) the child who has lost both an arm and a leg in a land-mine explosion.

Dancygier (2012, p. 63) further distinguishes between a story view-point (SV-Space), "the space where the 'narrator', or some features of narratorship, are located"; a main narrative space (MN-Space) that con-tains the narrative universe and its characters[5]; and ego viewpoint(s) (Ego-VP), where a character in the MN-Space is selected as the narrator. In the latter case, "the character's knowledge or intentionality provides the primary focus to the narrative mode" (p. 63). In *Pequeñas Voces*, the SV-Space is manifest not only in the film's general organization and the interlinking of the children's stories, but also in what David Bordwell (1985, p. 50) calls the film's style—that is, the particular way in which the filmmakers use animation, sound design, music and other expressive cin-ematic techniques.

As the visual aspects of the film have been covered, the chapter now turns to consider sound design.

Each narrative space is built from the narratives of the children them-selves. Nevertheless, as Andrade recounts in the DVD extras, besides the main stories of the children's experience of the conflict, they were also asked to share some everyday anecdotes in order to slightly soften the

---

[5] In some cases (as in the so-called "nested narratives"), the MN-Space may profile its own narrator(s); however, it usually relies "entirely on the SV-space structure" (Dancygier 2012, p. 63).

brutal impact of their testimonies. Using these anecdotes, the filmmakers show lighter scenes of the children laughing, playing or sharing in the daily routine of their family's work in the countryside. They also use these scenes to interlink the five stories, introducing random encounters between the children, and even a sort of "love story" between one of the blonde sisters and the boy with the dogs.

All these complementary scenes use the same strategy as the scenes of armed conflict narrated by the children: the protagonists are the only characters to have a recognizable voice, and this only when they are telling their stories in voiceover; the voices of the rest of the characters (and the children themselves when they are not the main narrator) are incomprehensible, reduced to a murmuring or mumbling, like the voices of adults in the Charlie Brown cartoons.[6] The sound design of these scenes is also constructed in a similar way to that of animated fiction films, using Foley effects of objects and body sounds; particular soundscapes to create the atmosphere of the countryside, the town, the war, and so on; and incidental (or non-diegetic) music to set the emotional tone of each scene (Cohen 2014).

The SV-Space is also configured by specific narrative strategies, the most important being the blending of the five independent stories into the same narrative scenario. In reality, all the child interviewees come from different villages and regions, but in the film they become characters who live in the same town and share the same public spaces, such as school, downtown, the village market or certain country roads. In this way, the town becomes a prototypical Colombian country town, one of the many plagued by violence. This blended narrative space results from the compression of several vital relations: role-value, category, time and space.

Each of these narrative spaces are individually configured by the Ego-VPs (individual viewpoints) of the children; by alternately allowing each of them to "hold the floor," the film achieves a polyphonic narration while simultaneously maintaining the singularity of each narrative space. This strategy achieves the goal expressed in the film's opening credits: to tell the story of the Colombian conflict from the perspective of the victims,

---

[6]According to Scott Curtis (1992), the traditional distinction between voices, sound effects and music does not work when describing the aural dimension of cartoon films. He particularly mentions the fact that in animated films music can produce sound effects or the character's voices become "noises". *Pequeñas voces* also blends these two sound-design strategies.

particularly the children, as a sort of collective narration. Nevertheless, the filmmakers' point of view is also manifest in the prologue's talking-heads device. The (animated) children talk to the filmmakers, who are hidden "behind the scenes," through a virtual camera. Figure 3.4 is an adaptation of Dancygier's representation of this kind of narrative structure.

This strategy allows the viewer to share in the film's blend between the filmmakers' perspective and the perspective of its characters—the children of the Colombian armed conflict.

Both versions of *Pequeñas Voces* start with similar textual statements on screen, citing statistics gathered by UNICEF:

> In Colombia, the number of people displaced by force between 1985 and 1999 represents approximately 1,900,000; 1,100,000 are less than 18 years old (57.9 %). (Carrillo 2003; my translation)

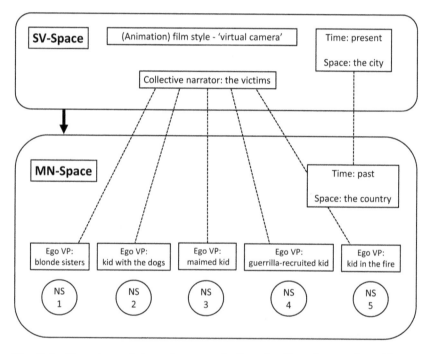

Fig. 3.4   Narrative and viewpoint spaces in *Pequeñas Voces*. Source: Juan Alberto Conde Aldana (2016)

In Colombia, there are about one million children displaced by violence. This film was told and drawn by some of them. UNICEF (Carrillo and Andrade 2011; my translation)

The first version is the more precise in terms of the information it provides, while the second adds that the film was co-created by the children themselves. Nevertheless, both statements convey that the films are related to actual situations by specifically locating the country, the period of time (in the first statement) and the group of people involved in this dramatic situation. The short version also gives the children's real names, although the feature film does not—in some of the children's stories certain names are mentioned but there is no indication of who these children are. The credit sequence of the feature film reveals the names of the children who "perform" the voices, but as if they were actors playing a role, and there is no precise information about the towns or regions of Colombia they come from; nor are these locations named.

Of course, the purpose of the feature film must be borne in mind—that is, to inform the wider public (both local and international audiences) about the situation of children caught up in the Colombian conflict. The blending of fictional narrative strategies and animation with the traditional techniques of documentary film is oriented on this goal.

In this sense, the conceptual blending proposed by animated documentary theories can be simplified to a more generic interpretation (Fig. 3.5), closer to the introductory statement of the first film.

CONCLUSION AND FURTHER DEVELOPMENTS: CONTEXT AND SPECTATORSHIP

The film's analysis will not necessarily resemble a non-professional spectator's interpretation. In order to gauge how closely this model is aligned with the way in which a general audience might perceive the film, it would be necessary to conduct experiments or interviews with specific groups of spectators, which lies beyond the scope of this study. Indeed, further developments of the approach the chapter outlines could consider some of the critiques of CBT, one of which is related to the theory's lack of a clear procedure of falsification, a requirement of modern scientific methodology (Glebkin 2015, p. 102). Nevertheless, by testing CBT's models with the qualitative methods used in social research it is possible to corroborate its descriptions of "the way people actually think"—or, at least, the thought

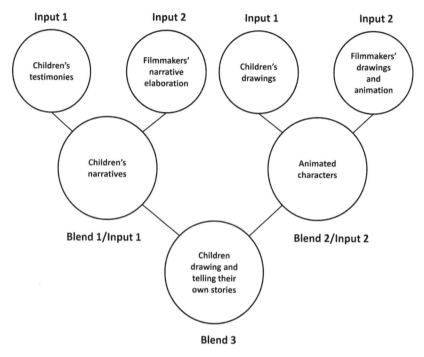

Input 1   Input 2   Input 1   Input 2

Children's   Filmmakers'   Children's   Filmmakers'
testimonies   narrative   drawings   drawings
                 elaboration   and
                                                   animation

Children's   Animated
narratives   characters

Blend 1/Input 1   Blend 2/Input 2

                 Children
                 drawing and
                 telling their
                 own stories

Blend 3

Fig. 3.5   The complete blending network of *Pequeñas Voces*. Source: Juan Alberto Conde Aldana (2016)

processes of specific groups of people, with specific tasks or goals, in specific settings. Arguably, Daniel Dennett's (1992, pp. 72–81) method of "heterophenomenology"—interpreted in this context as the qualitative analysis of spectators' views during or after the viewing of an animated documentary—could provide the data needed to describe their cognitive processes.

This question is related to another criticism of CBT, which points to its tendency to fail to take into account the situation in which the interpretative processes are embedded—that is, the context that helps determine the possible blends that take place in the viewer's mind (Brandt and Brandt 2005; Kövecses 2015). This is important as it addresses aspects of animated documentary that are related to the general problem of documentary spectatorship. As mentioned earlier, mental spaces and blends are constructed from frames, and frames are strongly context-related.

However, another solution to this problem might be found in conceptual metaphor theory. In the field of linguistic discourse, Zoltán Kövecses (2015, p. 176) has introduced a series of contextual factors that play a role in the production of metaphors. He groups these into four general types—situational, linguistic, conceptual–cognitive and bodily factors—arranged along a local-to-global gradient and a time gradient. The extrapolation of these factors to the study of audiovisual discourse in animated documentary could offer a powerful insight into the cognitive processes behind spectatorship. This is particularly the case with situational factors such as the viewer's knowledge of the main elements of the discourse; the surrounding discourse (for example, if the film is screened as part of an academic debate, in a classroom or at a festival); previous discourses on the same topic (p. 181); and the social and cultural situation of the viewer and the influence of history and memory on their interpretation (pp. 182–183). By taking these factors into consideration, it should be possible to discern differences in interpretation according to the provenance of the viewer—for example, the contrast between a Colombian viewer's construction of the meaning of *Pequeñas Voces* and a foreign viewer's, or between a viewer from one of the (primarily rural) more violent regions of the country and an urban viewer who has no personal experience of the conflict.

This chapter, therefore, has argued that CBT in general offers a productive new framework for an understanding of the cognitive processes that form the basis of the way in which any viewer makes sense of experimental forms of documentary storytelling, including animated documentary. Indeed, animated documentary, as an aesthetic phenomenon, demonstrates that the most direct way to grasp (and deal with) reality could be through freeing the imagination.

References

Bordwell, D. (1985) *Narration in the Fiction Film*. Madison: The University of Wisconsin Press.

Boyle, J. E. (2007) "When This Thing Grabs Hold of Us...: Spatial Myth, Rethoric, and Conceptual Blending in Brokeback Mountain," in Stacy, J. (ed.) *Reading Brokeback Mountain. Essays on the Story and the Film*. Jefferson: McFarland, pp. 88–104.

Brandt, L. and Brandt, P. (2005) "Making Sense of a Blend: A Cognitive Semiotic Approach to Metaphor," *Annual Review of Cognitive Linguistics*, 3, pp. 216–249.

Chion, M. (1994) *Audio-Vision. Sound on Screen*. New York: Columbia University Press.

Cohen, A. J. (2014) "Film Music from the Perspective of Cognitive Science," in Neumeyer, D. (ed.) *The Oxford Handbook of Film Music Studies*. New York: Oxford University Press, pp. 96–130.

Conde, J. A. (2014) "La integración conceptual y la experiencia fílmica. El escape psicológico en el cine," in Niño, D. (ed.) *Ensayos Semióticos II*. Bogota: Universidad Jorge Tadeo Lozano, pp. 221–252.

Curtis, S. (1992) "The Sound of the Early Warner Bros. Cartoons," in Altman, R. (ed.) *Sound Theory Sound Practice*. New York: Routledge, pp. 191–203.

Dancygier, B. (2008) "The Text and the Story. Levels of Blending in Fictional Narratives," in Oakley, T. and Hougaard, A. (eds.) *Mental Spaces in Discourse and Interaction*. Amsterdam: John Benjamins, pp. 51–77.

Dancygier, B. (2012) *The Language of Stories. A Cognitive Approach*. Cambridge: Cambridge University Press.

Dannenberg, H. (2012) "Fleshing Out the Blend: The Representation of Counterfactuals in Alternate History in Print, Film, and Television Narratives," in Hartner, M. and Schneider, R. (eds.) *Blending and the Study of Narrative: Approaches and Applications*. Berlin: De Gruyter, pp. 121–145.

DelGaudio, S. (1997) "If Truth Be Told, Can Toons Tell It? Documentary and Animation," *Film History*, 9(2), pp. 189–199.

Dennet, D. (1992) *Consciousness Explained*. New York: Back Bay Books.

Fauconnier, G. (1997) *Mapping in Thought and Language*. Cambridge: Cambridge University Press.

Fauconnier, G. and Turner, M. (2002) *The Way We Think. Conceptual Blending and the Mind's Hidden Complexities*. New York: Basic Books.

Glebkin, V. (2015) "Is Conceptual Blending the Key to the Mystery of Human Evolution and Cognition?" *Cognitive Linguistics*, 26(1), pp. 95–111.

Honess Roe, A. (2013) *Animated Documentary*. Basingstoke: Palgrave Macmillan.

Kövecses, Z. (2015) *Where Metaphors Come From—Reconsidering Context in Metaphor*. New York: Oxford University Press.

Nichols, B. (1991) *Representing Reality: Issues and Concepts in Documentary*. Bloomington: Indiana University Press.

Nichols, B. (2001) *Introduction to Documentary*. Bloomington: Indiana University Press.

Oakley, T. (2013) "Toward a General Theory of Film Spectatorship" [Online]. Available at: https://case.edu/artsci/engl/Library/Oakley-TheoryFilmSpectator.pdf (Accessed: August 28, 2017).

Oakley, T. and Tobin, V. (2012) "Attention, Blending, and Suspense in Classic and Experimental Film," in Hartner, M. and Schneider, R. (eds.) *Blending and the Study of Narrative: Approaches and Applications*. Berlin: De Gruyter, pp. 57–83.

Plantinga, C. (1997) *Rhetoric and Representation in Nonfiction Film*. Cambridge: Cambridge University Press.

Quendler, C. (2014) "Blending and Film Theory," in Branigan, E. and Buckland, W. (eds.) *The Routledge Encyclopedia of Film Theory*. New York: Routledge, pp. 56–62.

Rubba, J. (2009) "The Dream as Blend in David Lynch's Mulholland Drive," in Evans, V. and Pourcel, S. (eds.) *New Directions in Cognitive Linguistics*. Philadelphia: John Benjamins Publishing, pp. 227–261.

Sinding, M. (2005) "'Genera Mixta': Conceptual Blending and Mixed Genres in *Ulysses*," *New Literary History*, 36(4), pp. 589–619.

Sinding, M. (2012) "Blending in a Baciyelmo: Don Quixote's Genre Blending and the Invention of the Novel," in Schneider, R. and Hartner, M. (eds.) *Blending and the Study of Narrative*. Berlin: De Gruyter, pp. 147–171.

Skoller, J. (2011) "Making It (Un)real: Contemporary Theories and Practices in Documentary Animation," *Animation: An Interdisciplinary Journal*, 6(3), pp. 207–214.

Stam, R., Burgoyne, R. and Flitterman-Lewis, S. (1992) *New Vocabularies in Film Semiotics. Structuralism, Post-structuralism, and Beyond*. London: Routledge.

Strøm, G. (2003) "The Animated Documentary," *Animation Journal*, 11, pp. 46–63.

Turner, M. (2006) "Compression and Representation," *Language and Literature*, 15, pp. 17–29.

Ward, P. (2005) *Documentary: The Margins of Reality*. New York: Columbia University Press.

William, J. M. (2017) *Cognitive Approaches to German Historical Film*. Berlin: Springer.

CHAPTER 4

Documentary Spectatorship and the Navigation of "Difficulty"

John Corner

In this chapter I want to explore questions about the kinds of difficulty that can occur within the mental work documentary spectators perform in making cognitive and affective connections with the mediations presented to them. These hermeneutic, experiential difficulties often concern the referential status of material, its relationship to the real, and the structural and expressive relations of the parts within the whole. As a consequence, there is necessarily an aesthetic dimension involved too.

A key aspect of the mental difficulties I shall examine is that they are *intentionally* present, caused by a film's core features; they are points of friction, contradiction or breakdown purposefully "designed into" the film by the filmmaker through a strategic interaction between a variety of formal features, such as narrative structure, uses of speech, editing style and a range of other aesthetic elements. The origin of these difficulties lies in presenting spectators with a challenge that will encourage—if not force—serious reflection on the processes of mediation and understanding themselves, and the choices, tensions and even contradictions these involve. Such mental difficulty inevitably results in an increase in

J. Corner (✉)
University of Leeds, Leeds, UK
e-mail: J.R.Corner@leeds.ac.uk

© The Author(s) 2018
C. Brylla, M. Kramer (eds.), *Cognitive Theory and Documentary Film*, https://doi.org/10.1007/978-3-319-90332-3_4

spectatorial divergence (affectively and cognitively) and in polysemic readings. It presents a challenge not only to the viewer, but indeed to any classical spectatorship scholar who assumes a normative and universal audience response.

By offering such challenges, these types of documentary also position themselves within a broad and internally varied art-discursive space, which, since modernism, has associated intended difficulty in interpretation with serious creative and socio-critical ambition.[1] Their value for a cognitive approach to documentary study is enhanced by the fact that the films are not only concerned with the particular themes they represent, but also with the practices involved in the spectatorial cognition of these themes. The effect of this on the viewer is an intensified form of what Ib Bondebjerg (1994, p. 82) calls a "constant testing and re-evaluation of activated schemas", of stored mental representations of information, in order to, among other things, "assign reference" to what is seen and heard (p. 9).[2]

Documentaries that intentionally present difficulty in this way are often concerned not only with the specific problems of mediating the "reality" and "truth" surrounding their specific subjects, but also with the problems and contradictions, perhaps even impossibilities, involved in documentary-making at the levels both of representation and reception. This is rather different from the strategic use of difficulty and reflexivity in fiction films where, whatever the desire to problematize knowledge and modes of knowing, including through sub-generic conventions of storytelling and character (see, for instance, spectatorial divergence in puzzle films, ambiguous characters, and so on), subversion of "fiction" as a broad category of representation is a less achievable aim than subversion of the category "documentary." One reason for this is that fiction films, across their great variety, do not operate with the claims of epistemological privilege that, whether made explicit or simply presumed, have characterized the documentary mode and have also been a key focus for critical

---

[1] George Steiner (1978) provides a much-cited discussion of difficulty in the arts, including what he calls the "tactical" difficulty introduced by intention. However, his primary focus is on poetry, with consequent limitations on its application to other forms. For a broader appraisal of difficulty in the arts, see John Corner (2016).

[2] The difference between " difficulty" and " reflexivity" is important to note, especially given the widespread use of the latter term to indicate a recent progressive tendency in production approaches. A "reflexive" documentary primarily wishes to call attention to its status as a discursive construct; it does not need to confront the spectator with significant difficulties in following it in order to achieve this aim.

attention, especially from Bill Nichols (1981) onwards. Their "cognitive offer" is less generically prescribed—their referential schemes have a "license to be playful" and to work with teasing enigma as part of the delivery of narrative pleasure (see Buckland 2014).

This is in some contrast to the central representational precepts still underpinning much documentary production and guiding documentary spectatorship, precepts which inform what Bondebjerg (1994, p. 66) calls the "communicative contract" of documentary. Such a contract shapes, if it does not entirely define, the ontological relationship with the pro-filmic generated in viewing. This is a relationship in which aspects of the "actual world as portrayed" rather than "imaginary worlds" (Plantinga 2002, p. 26), figure directly and prominently, and where the drive to knowledge frequently takes precedence over the drive to pleasure in regulating schema deployment.

THE APPROACH

My approach will be to select two films for examination, *Surname Viet Given Name Nam* (Trin T. Min-ha 1989) and *Dial H-I-S-T-O-R-Y* (Johan Grimonprez 1997). The intent is not to explore the films' own distinctive profiles but to take them as examples of a much broader and formally varied range of documentaries in which "difficulty" is intrinsic to textual design. I discuss this broader range further in my conclusions.

A key idea is the familiar one of navigation: the attention to multiple and changing points of reference in narrative, expositional development and visual design, requiring regular (and, here, often frequent) reappraisals of schemas to reduce the risk of becoming "lost" and to "find a way back" when this happens.

In this project, close attention to the formal structures through which a sense of the film is generated is necessary. I take my principal bearings here from writings such as those of Carl Plantinga (2002, 2009) and Ib Bondebjerg (1994, 2014). Bondebjerg's (1994) "semio-pragmatic" perspective in particular provides an excellent model of accounting, one in which (as the name suggests) the transactional interplay between the signs of textual design and the incremental, constructive work of viewing practice, using diverse cognitive tools, is closely charted. At some points, I have inserted into my analyses a few anonymized citations from spectators' comments posted on particular websites, quite aware that no representativeness attaches to these comments in the way that might be sought in dedicated audience research studies. My concern is with *process*, not *difference*, in interpreted meanings, and I am interested in the way the anecdotal postings explicitly articulate encountered difficulty, positioning this either negatively or positively in relation to the full experience of the film.

Surname Viet Given Name Nam

Trin T. Min-ha's *Surname Viet Given Name Nam* (1989) has attracted a lot of attention due to the cognitive challenges it presents and the purposes behind those challenges. Grounded in a series of interviews with Vietnamese women within a rich context of archive footage and music, its project is to reflect on the recent history and contemporary circumstances of Vietnam, and specifically, on the position of women within Vietnamese society.

Surname Viet starts in a way that presents the viewer with several different cues for their entry into viewing and for their application of schemas. For nearly a minute, there is a slow-motion sequence of a group of women, in colorful traditional dress and straw hats, performing a graceful dance to music. Spectator engagement with the dancers' bodily elegance and co-ordination across the marked duration of the sequence sets up a strong aesthetic frame. After the titles, however, drumbeats are heard over a series of monochrome archive shots, moving and still, of women at work in rural Vietnamese society (paddling river craft, net-mending), looking fearful, marching in demonstrations and carrying weapons. Direct links with the costumes in the first sequence are present but a complex "history" now takes precedence over "appearance," and the lyrics of traditional songs introduce an inner, experiential element to place alongside that history. Also introduced here is a silent, color close-up shot of a woman's face, which is only returned to when she begins to talk in what appears to be interview speech. A "documentary contract" is generated across the referential planes activated, however enigmatically, but the film quickly produces difficulty in spectators as they try to sustain the terms of this contract. Three main formal strategies are used to achieve this difficulty:

1. The disruption of the conventional documentary act of *knowing-by-listening* through awkward speech patterns adopted in the "interviews," multiple voiceovers from different unseen speakers, a disjunction at points between what is being said and the subtitles, and the use of large (full-screen) and rapidly scrolled segments of textual information. This requires intensive spectator work across divergent cognitive indicators.

2. The disruption of the conventional documentary act of *knowing-by-looking* through regular use of the non-naturalistic methods of extreme close-ups of the face, the mouth and the hands in the interviews (thereby disrupting the spectator's schemas for engaging with the actual interview speech). The facial portrayal (including profile shots and shots with the head turned away from the camera) is often more that of "spoken dramatic performance" than of "interviewed subject," a practice out of alignment with the traditional documentary contract. Only later in the film is this dramatic and performative mode of address seen to be appropriate in relation to the film's themes (see point 3, below).

3. The undercutting of the trust in the interview as a core means of producing knowledge in documentary, including modes of testimony, by revealing eventually that the interviews were in fact "acted" from written materials produced years before (in France) and shot in the US rather than Vietnam. In a further, unconventional move, the "actors" are then interviewed in relation to their own real lives, as well as to their responses to being filmed.

In these ways, key elements of documentary mediation, including the satisfactions of and trust placed in listening to recounted personal testimony from seen speakers, are subverted, producing a fractured experience—of the kind that Nichols (1991, pp. 257–258) discusses as the "provocations" of "unpleasure." Such dissonance may encourage the spectator to be routed into self-conscious reflection about what they are actually "warranted" by the film *to know and to feel* regarding the exotic history being presented, and to undertake revision of the schemas they started out with. During the course of the film, or even retrospectively, they might decide that a "documentary contract" is not appropriate, such is the divergence from documentary protocols, and that a shift of generic expectations is required, with appropriate adjustments to spectator frames.

This decision could be reached with various accompanying evaluations of the worth of the film and reflections on how knowing and feeling are, by contrast, so effortlessly generated by the mediations of conventional documentaries. Indeed, as indicated earlier, a possible conclusion is that the "documentary contract" is always to be treated with suspicion, and films that actively encourage this suspicion eventually reward the cognitive effort involved in watching them. However, introducing high levels of effort has its risks. As Nichols (1991, pp. 257–258) notes, "unpleasure…

can change the curious spectator into a bored one, or the paying spectator into a resentful one." As discussed above, the challenges in *Surname Viet* start at the primary levels of textual engagement. Lynn Turner (1996, p. 86) suggests that "[t]he eye and the ear are no longer as one and 'reading' the film becomes a contest of reading versus listening with the surety that, whichever is prioritized, something will be lost (and in the context of a cinematic auditorium) unlikely to be regained."

The experience of the sensory and cognitive challenge involved is well described in a posted student response:

> Was she [Trinh] trying to make us the foreigner by having all the interviewees with heavy accents? Sometimes the heavy accents were aided by the words of the women on the screen, and yet, we still struggle to listen and read. We also find that while the women are speaking, there is a translator voicing over the interview. Why does Trinh do this? Why does she choose to have them speak English and not Vietnamese? We struggle to listen to both voices as one takes over the other voice and the other fights to gain the attention back.[3]

"Struggle" can be frustrating, leading (as in the above comment) to the questioning of the filmmaker's motives, or it can be seen as part of the spectatorial labor necessary to make the film–spectator relationship work productively. An IMDb posting[4] notes how the words and images *require* activity and a sense of transnational engagement at the level of interpersonal values: "[They] require the viewer/listener to be active, to move into the text as one might in a transnational setting where communication with the speaker is valued." The phrase "move into the text" nicely captures the schema of immersive encounter being recommended here—a good example of the film's intentionality at work.

That a satisfactory understanding may not follow from one viewing alone is explicitly recognized elsewhere ("A brilliant, difficult film that repays multiple viewings"). Although repeated viewings of fiction in order to deepen its forms of satisfaction is common, the idea that a documentary might require it in order to be properly understood or even repeatedly enjoyed is a good deal rarer. *Surname Viet* can be identified as a documentary that

---

[3] See: *blogs*. https://walkerart.org/magazine/u-of-m-students-respond-to-surname-viet-given-name-nam/
(Accessed: 15 May 2018).
[4] The IMDb message boards and all postings were removed in February 2017. All comments in this chapter were gathered in 2016.

contrasts not only with mainstream work but even with those approaches taken by other kinds of "radical" (activist, critical or variously avant-garde) filmmaking. On this point, another IMDb posting remarks disparagingly: "This movie is not for those looking for the glossy, dumbed-down Hollywood documentary—if that's what you want, pass this and go to Michael Moore, choose one of his movies where the nice man will tell you what to think."

This acceptance of spectatorial work can even extend to situations where a "trick" has been played. In the case below, the trick is *Surname Viet's* "staging" of its interviews, designed to be revealed only after the spectator has been encouraged for some time to perceive them as "real." In this IMDb posting, the viewer, who had learnt in advance about the "twist" of the performed interviews, reflects on what would have happened if this had not been so and, more provocatively, on the status of the "innocent" reading that the applied schema and assignment of reference would have then produced: "The psychological impact of our expectations is intriguing in that it provides further insight into and curiosity about the film experience—if I had not known that a twist was coming... would I have digested these interviews at face value? And furthermore, what is face value?"

Questions of translation (both linguistic and in relation to cultural identity and understanding) are centrally at issue at several points in the film, as the postings themselves indicate. The expositional/argumentative work of the film, supported by archival material and varying between a personal recounting through to broader reflections on identity and geopolitics, exists side by side with sequences involving, for instance, traditional song and dance, sensuously combining rich colors and harmonious movement. The effect of such sequences is to exert an aesthetic-affective pull, taking us deeper into the "mystery" of Vietnam and its traditions. This is a beguiling sensorial trajectory in some contrast to the cognitive labor required to secure from the film reliable knowledge about this exotic world from the testimony or propositions of those who speak.

Writing in the *American Historical Review*, quite soon after the film's release, Sumiko Higashi (1990, p. 1125) asked a sharp question about the limited nature of the potential audience: "Is this film accessible to an audience that has not been schooled in theoretical debates about narratology, authorship, ethnography, documentary practice, and feminism?"

This is perhaps to see the boundaries of successful spectatorship drawn too tightly within the academy. However, it identifies the kinds of frames, abstract rather than substantive in orientation, from which a successful navigation is able to benefit.[5]

Dial H-I-S-T-O-R-Y

The second film, Johan Grimonprez's *Dial H-I-S-T-O-R-Y* (1997), routes its spectators through a flow of sequences compiled from a range of "found" sources, giving prominence to footage from television news. Widely discussed, its ostensible topic is the history of aircraft hijacking, one that connects at several points with the geopolitics of terrorism and, more broadly and loosely, with the risks and fears associated with air travel. However, its use of a very loud soundtrack and the visual energy of its diverse segments create a deliberate information overload, which reflexively drives a broader thematics—essentially a pathology of mass-media consumption. A recurrent visual feature, which becomes a trope within its discursive pattern, is shots of aircraft crashing and/or exploding, or during various stages of hijack negotiations and stand-off situations on the ground.

The film begins with a slow night-time descent through the clouds to an illuminated runway as apparently seen from a plane cockpit. Rather than watching the physical harmony of screen characters, as in the first sequence of *Surname Viet*, we are placed "inside" an experience of some uncertainty. The music is soft and comforting, suggesting a dream experience, although the male voiceover has nightmarish overtones ("Should death be a swan dive, graceful, white winged and smooth?"). As the plane lands, the cockpit is seen from the inside, disintegrating and then exploding. The explosion is then seen from outside, with the plane's fuselage torn apart, on fire and with the nose cone hurtling along the ground. Spectator subjectivity is thus shifted vigorously around, both in physical viewpoint and mood (somatic anxiety at violent dissolution being an element here).

At the end of the film comes footage of the last few seconds of the 1988 Air France Airbus disaster (not a hijacking but pilot error) at Mulhouse–Habshein airport. The elegance of the plane's apparently

---

[5] This comment raises broader questions about the skills involved in pattern-forming from avant-garde work, questions that are also relevant to the other examples. In the recent literature on the subject, see Paul Taberham (2014) for a discussion informed by cognitive theory, and David Andrews (2013) for a consideration of the issue of audience formation across changing cultural contexts.

controlled and slow descent (the intention was not a landing but a low pass over the airfield), a movement which seamlessly modulates into the horror of the crash in the woods beyond the end of the runway, provides a disturbing closure, partly echoing aspects of the opening. A loud rock-music soundtrack and montage editing add to the intensity and also to the affective disorientation of the scene.

The crash and explosion sequences provide *Dial* with a spectatorial shock-aesthetic that partly underpins but well exceeds its expositional function as an assembly of reportorial footage about hijacking, stretching through from the 1960s to the 1990s, interspersed with other materials.[6] As noted earlier, music is a strong presence throughout, regulating the tempo and tonality of events within the film. Voiceover, when it does not issue from the fragments of news reporting, is provided by two voices speaking extracts from the novels of Don DeLillo—extracts that variously provide a fragmented character-centered narrative and a set of observations about the nature of modern terror and the relationship between the novelist and the terrorist. These two modes of spoken extract—narrative and exposition/argument—variously pull the viewer, on the one hand, into the subjective and mysterious world of a personal story, one with no obvious relation to what is seen and talked about in the hijacking sequences, and on the other, into a set of sociocultural reflections working at some distance "above" the occurrences depicted in those sequences. Although very different in execution, this discursive duality, with its divergent referential planes and its shifts between the abstraction of ideas and the immediacy of the physical world, clearly has parallels with *Surname Viet*.

What spectator activity, what schematic repertoire, is required to generate an overall "sense" from *Dial* across the disparate parts of its mediating practices? Arild Fetveit (2002) offers a clear and provocative commentary on the film, situating it within his interest in the overlaps between documentary and art video/installation (the film was exhibited in galleries as well as cinemas) and what he sees as its strongly postmodernist engagement, not just with its nominal subject but with the broader theme

---

[6] Mention might be made here of the work of Adam Curtis, a British documentary filmmaker noted for his use of a wide range of images from a variety of sources to produce often bizarrely disjunctive compilations (e.g. *HyperNormalisation* 2016). However, what stops these assemblages from being "difficult" is the use of a commentary in which a clear and emphatic exposition is delivered. Spectator schemas can confidently attach to this as a core, while the richly connotative visuals and soundtrack variously modulate the overall cognitive and affective development.

of contemporary image consumption. He notes "[a]n uneasy viewing position in-between the political issues and personal disasters requiring moral response and attention, and the aesthetic discourse suspending and bracketing such attention in favour of formal features" (p. 229). Fetveit thus suggests a tension between a referential orientation and the deriving of aesthetic satisfaction.

The relation to the category of art, and to the cognitive and affective dispositions seen to be appropriate to artistic encounters, is indeed relevant. It is more pertinent here than in *Surname Viet* (where it is, nonetheless, also present) because of the overtly spectacular visual design. How do the frameworks for finding meaning and emotional investment in art differ, yet also overlap, with those applied when watching a documentary?[7]

Recognition of an "art contract" alongside any "documentary contract" does not have to block engagement, of course, but getting the two into a satisfactory schematic alignment can prove problematic, as in this IDMb post: "I get that this was made as an art installation, and that it's not always necessary for a documentary to be a huge political and sociological examination of events, but this doesn't even succeed on the terms which it itself established." Here, "art" is allowed as part of the project and a "plan" is discerned, but the film's deficit is located in a failure to carry through this plan satisfactorily. Another spectator posting on IMDb saw the "art" factor as needing to be "clicked with" if spectatorship was to be sustained. For this viewer, this had not happened, despite a few attempts:

> The problem with the film is that unless you are in the right mood to go with it it's going to be a long 68 minutes. I've started this a couple of times and to be perfectly honest I can't get more than 20 or 25 minutes into it without shutting it off. It's not bad but it's very much an art piece (it's played as an installation in museums) and unless you click with it it's something you can admire more than enjoy.

In this view, the "art" status accorded to the work positions attention to it as at least partly a matter of "taste," with associated problems in following the right schemas (the words, "the right mood," suggest that this is initially a matter of prior affective orientation).

---

[7] Here, as in passages of Surname Viet, Bill Nichols' (2001, pp. 102–105) idea of the "poetic" mode is relevant, although the widely diverse forms of figurative expressivity that this term covers prompt questions about its use in film analysis. See, for instance, Dara Waldron (2014).

Any judgment of the ethics of the film, a theme raised by Fetveit (2002), is going to turn on how the spectatorial experience places the moments of disaster in its broader scheme of viewing, as noted by another IMDb post, which claims: "While clearly this is visually captivating, there is an unpleasant sense that we're being taken on a tour of YouTube clips of death and loss rather than being given any proper analysis of events, or even a decent exposition on the supposed theme of this film." "Proper analysis" and "decent exposition" are core elements of the "documentary contract," and their short supply is seen to be compounded here by the de-referentializing of the death and loss portrayed as they become diverting "clips" within a "tour."

A "successful" viewing of the film would certainly seem to require cognitive–schematic accommodation to its aesthetic status as outside the bounds of conventional documentary, in order to find it a satisfying vehicle for affective investment within this "outer" discursive space. Engagement, then, needs to find significance beyond the immediate topic of hijacking's history, a significance lying in the broader political and cultural contexts both of terror and of media consumption, and one resourced principally through the DeLillo extracts. What level of perceived coherence might be minimally required here? Perhaps, as another IMDb posting suggests, not much: "It's all pretty scattershot as far as a coherent message [is concerned]." This would position the film not just as an "emotion machine" (Tan 1995) but as an "affective shock machine," the principal purpose of which is to disturb as much as to "say" anything.

Just how much viewers' ethical frames are effectively suspended by the sheer traumatic spectacularity of the shock process, along with any attempt to work within a scheme of assigned *reference*, is important for individual encounters with the film. The use, towards the end, of bouncy upbeat music over disaster shots and a final-credits sequence of Boris Yeltsin and Bill Clinton on a podium, holding on to one another in helpless laughter, contribute to the sense of an affective order displaced (if ironically) from any direct relationship with the disaster and death represented in the primary materials, an order which cues the viewer accordingly.

It could be claimed that whereas *Surname Viet's* project is to challenge the viewer to engage with what it wants to say about Vietnam by negotiating the contradictions and revealed artifice of its construction, *Dial* challenges the viewer with the task of turning the aesthetic intensities, mixed reportage and voiceover readings of its combinatory/associational dynamics into some broader affective pointers (not a "claim") about the "state we are in." Both films involve spectators experiencing uncertainties ("getting lost" for a while) and sharp disruptions of classical documentary schemas.

THE PRODUCTIVITY AND LIMITS OF DIFFICULTY

These two examples show documentary practices being used to present a challenge which involves the ordering of planes with widely diverse relations to reality and the bringing into coherence of propositions and arguments that are often fragmented and partial. The very idea of documentary mediation and, indeed, of spectatorship itself is subject to critical and even subversive treatment. Both examples, however, can be seen to lie right on the borders of documentary's broad and differentiated generic space (close to those limits where the category of the "essay film" is often used). Their "border" status is also, in both cases, employed within a confident critical-theoretical frame, one in which abstract ideas exert a more overt and continuous control over representation than is usual even in documentaries with radical persuasive intent.

With this in mind, it might be useful to look very briefly at two more examples of intentional difficulty in documentary, ones in which although, as above, some "blocking" or "refusal" of schematic expectations occurs, it does so within what is finally a lower order of challenge than in the previous examples.

Bondebjerg (1994) usefully develops his own account of difficulty/transgression by reference to Errol Morris's *The Thin Blue Line* (1988), one of the most widely discussed films in documentary studies, rightly identified as showing an original approach to the use of documentary visual and narrative design, but which, nevertheless, questions some dominant elements of the classical documentary protocol. Bondebjerg notes how the film invites different schemas for spectatorial engagement with the deployment of fact and fiction, and plays them off against each other (the trailer for the film speaks of it as "a new kind of murder mystery," thus avoiding the encouragement of firmly generic expectations). Different versions, sometimes part-versions, of the same crime narrative are offered, using reenactment. These have good levels of internal continuity and dramatic coherence, but they contradict each other when the attempt is made to build them into the "truth" about the murder of a policeman, which might be seen (based on confirmation of the initial documentary schema) to be the film's primary goal. It is here that Bondebjerg (1994, p. 81) observes how "the spectator is left with a lot of narrative clues and has to work hard," a process requiring "constant testing and revaluation" (p. 8).

At the same time as Morris sets up a narrative puzzle, which is partially resolved only in the closing sequences, he also quietly undermines (but, crucially, does not abandon) the indexical authenticity of the image on which much documentary premises its claims on the real. He does this by a strongly stylistic foregrounding of specific objects in close shots (in a manner not unlike the close-up shots of interviewees' faces in *Surname Viet*), thereby privileging representational form over reference and partially displacing naturalism in favor of metaphor.

There is difficulty involved here, for sure. However, one way it differs from that in the two films discussed earlier is in its scale and the amount of schematic disruption it brings. It involves pushing the spectator back from the more "comfortable" ways of looking at visual signification in documentary and, in the process, questioning these, while at the same time posing the challenge of making the flow of discrete narrative segments add up. But there still remains a lot in the film where established frames of documentary viewing, particularly in relation to dramatized modes, can provide the cognitive resources for making linkages that work.

Another example of "lower-order" difficulty is provided by Jafar Panahi's and Mojtaba Mirtahmasb's *This is Not a Film* (2011), which concerns the house arrest of Panahi in Tehran for directing films unacceptable to the Iranian state. The default sub-genre of this documentary is a "day-in-the-life" video diary, albeit one in which some scenes work as observation of a seemingly unaware Panahi performing various tasks in his flat and others as a record of his interaction and dialogue with his co-director. Panahi has the idea of describing (for the camera) the screenplay that he no longer has the legal right to make into a film, using the furniture in his flat as props (hence, the echoes of Magritte in the film's title). Viewers become involved in a multiple mediation, viewing Panahi playing himself in a film about his daily routines, which involves him in trying to create a substitute for the film he cannot make. The situation requires the spectator to be alert to paradox and contradiction, but it does so through the generation of a largely coherent "realist" frame of observation, the self-awareness of which is inflected occasionally towards direct exposition. Moreover, in some contrast with *The Thin Blue Line*, investment in the primacy of the indexical record is explicitly endorsed (whatever the ironic overtones at work) in an exchange between the two directors ("the main thing is to document").

Finally, it is significant that both *The Thin Blue Line* and *This is Not a Film*, in different ways, operate with strong narrative development, even if this development is subject to disruption. This allows, as I have indicated, a level of underlying schema continuity in story-following practice not available in the earlier examples, where narrative function is placed as subordinate to "difficult" exposition through multiple and disparate voices (including voiceovers, interviews, and literary and archival readings) and a refusal of linear development.

Documentaries of the kind I have chosen to consider clearly involve a navigational process in which "prototypes" of engagement and understanding, drawn both from more conventional documentaries and from the direct experiencing of reality, may need extensive modification and expansion, perhaps drawing on knowledge of other forms of art practice. The resultant difficulty entails spectatorial divergence in the challenge of experiencing, comprehending and interpreting the film; some spectators will respond to this challenge as a mode of stimulating and satisfying media engagement, while others will experience it as misalignment—perhaps a deficit in the filmmaking practices themselves.

Such a complex thickening of documentary textuality has not yet gained extensive hold in the more mainstream areas of production and distribution, where ideas of mediational "directness" and "clarity" (not to say "transparency") remain premium, although by no means exclusive, qualities.[8] However, within specific and independent spheres of nonfiction filmmaking culture (for example, essay films, audiovisual essays and ethnofiction), modes of portrayal that vigorously interrogate and sometimes deny documentary's possibilities for mediation continue to flourish and to find audiences.[9]

Within this chapter, I am aware that I have pursued only a few questions (sometimes begging others) in relation to a very small selection of films. However, looking at these films primarily in terms of how their difficulties are negotiated through viewing practices rather than emphasizing their formal achievements or their particular political and social purposes, as many critics and scholars have done, has seemed to open up some

---

[8] In part, this aligns such work with journalism, where—with some exceptions—modes of transparency and the "self-evident" are still dominant.

[9] The potential usefulness of combining forms of cognitive analysis with forms of spectator ethnography/biography is raised here, however problematic in research design such projects might prove to be.

promising intellectual territory. In our further understanding of the cognitive work of documentary spectatorship, I think further attention to occurrences of difficulty, including in documentaries where it is a key part of the design, will prove productive.

REFERENCES

Andrews, D. (2013) *Theorising Art Cinemas*. Austin, TX: University of Texas.

Bondebjerg, I. (1994) "Narratives of Reality: Documentary Film and Television in a Cognitive and Pragmatic Perspective," *Nordicom Review*, 1, pp. 65–85.

Bondebjerg, I. (2014) "Documentary and Cognitive Theory: Narrative, Emotion and Memory," *Media and Communication*, 2(1), pp. 13–22.

Buckland, W. (2014) (ed.) *Hollywood Puzzle Films (AFI Film Readers)*. Abingdon: Routledge.

Corner, J. (2016) "Aesthetic Experience and the Question of 'Difficulty': A Note," *Cogent Arts and Humanities*, 3(1), pp. 1–8.

Fetveit, A. (2002) *Multiaccentual Cinema Between Documentary and Fiction*. PhD thesis. University of Oslo.

Higashi, S. (1990) "Review of *Surname Viet Given Name Nam*," *American Historical Review*, 95(4), pp. 1124–1126.

Nichols, B. (1981) *Ideology and the Image*. Bloomington: Indiana University Press.

Nichols B. (1991) *Representing Reality*. Bloomington: Indiana University Press.

Nichols, B. (2001) *Introduction to Documentary*. Bloomington: Indiana University Press.

Plantinga, C. (2002) "Cognitive Film Theory: An Insiders Appraisal," *Cinémas (Journal of Film Studies)*, 12(2), pp. 15–37.

Plantinga, C. (2009) *Moving Viewers: American Film and Spectator Experience*. Oakland: University of California Press.

Steiner, G. (1978) "On Difficulty," *The Journal of Aesthetics and Art Criticism*, 36, pp. 263–276.

Taberham, P. (2014) "Avant Garde Film in an Evolutionary Context," in Nannicelli, T. and Taberham, P. (eds.) *Cognitive Media Theory*. London; New York: Routledge, pp. 214–232.

Tan, E. (1995) *Emotion and the Structure of Narrative Film: Film as Emotion Machine*. London: Routledge.

Turner, L. (1996) "Documentary Friction: Vocal and Visual Strategies in *Surname Viet, Given Name Nam*," *Parallax*, 2(2), pp. 81–93.

Waldron, D. (2014) "The Poetic Mode as Depiction," *Studies in Documentary*, 8(2), pp. 116–129.

CHAPTER 5

Docudrama and the Cognitive Evaluation of Realism

Torben Grodal

INTRODUCTION

This chapter discusses aspects of the cognitive and emotional underpinnings of viewers' experience of the "real" in audiovisual documentaries, with a special focus on docudramas. I use the term "docudrama" here to describe a film that fully or partially presents real events, using the same tools as fiction film but with the intention of providing a true picture. Docudramas, for example, use actors to portray the actual people involved and the films themselves are often scripted, in contrast to conventional documentaries, which for the most part present an unmediated photographic portrayal of reality. However, there is not always a sharp distinction between the two. In the classic documentary, *Nanook of the North* (1922), director Robert J. Flaherty asked the Inuit characters to act out different scenarios from their daily lives according to a script. To make it more "exotic," he prohibited them, for example, from using their guns in the hunting scenes, instructing them to use harpoons instead. In this sense, Flaherty's film is technically a docudrama, although most viewers at the time would have perceived it as an observational documentary. Docudramas, therefore, while laying claim to a greater degree of historical

T. Grodal (✉)
University of Copenhagen, Copenhagen, Denmark
e-mail: grodal@hum.ku.dk

© The Author(s) 2018
C. Brylla, M. Kramer (Eds.), *Cognitive Theory and Documentary Film*, https://doi.org/10.1007/978-3-319-90332-3_5

veracity, may resemble fiction genres such as historical films or dramas about everyday life. John Grierson (1966), one of the founding fathers of the documentary genre, described documentary films as "the creative treatment of actuality"; this definition appears to fit docudrama well.

Neither docudramas nor documentaries are categories with strictly necessary and sufficient conditions; they are "prototype categories" (Rosch, cited in Lakoff 1987), categories that are defined by their most prototypical specimens, without the fixed delimitations present in other categories. As such, the distinction between a documentary and a fiction film is not clear-cut (Grodal 1997, 2009): many elements of conventional fiction films, such as the use of concrete locations and certain physical actions, character psychologies or factual events, may have documentary qualities that serve as a backdrop to the drama. They may also display a high degree of perceptual realism.

Thus, the problem of realism—of deciding what can be defined as "real"—cannot be solved by linking it to a specific genre. A more productive approach is to explore the question from the perspective of the viewer. The discussion of docudrama that follows is based on an analysis of the cognitive and emotional mechanisms viewers use to evaluate the realism of the media they consume; it investigates some of the reasons why they often trust incoming information without performing a reality check to ascertain its veracity. Several of these cognitive procedures are exemplified by the reception of Stephen Frears' docudrama, *The Queen* (2006). The film portrays how the then prime minister of the United Kingdom, Tony Blair, and Queen Elizabeth dealt with the death of Princess Diana. When she heard about Diana's death, the queen's immediate reaction was to regard it as a private matter for Diana's family and of no concern to her, as the monarch, or the country at large. However, due to the popular outrage this attitude provoked, Blair decided to intervene, mediating a (radical) change in the official royal position—whether this change was genuine or not. The queen subsequently participated in the common mourning process and paid tribute to Diana in a speech on the eve of the funeral. This docudrama is a good illustration of the problems viewers face in trying to distinguish fact from fiction when confronted with a blend of dramatic reenactments and documentary footage of historical events.

CHARACTERIZATIONS OF DOCUMENTARIES AND REALITY

Many documentary theorists only approach the question of viewer experience indirectly; they tend to deal with the representation of reality by analyzing a documentary's form and production process in an attempt to discover how different types of documentaries allow for different forms (or distortions) of reality. An important contribution to this approach is Bill Nichols' (1991) typology of documentary modes: poetic, expository, participatory, observational, reflexive and performative. These modes relate to the role of the filmmaker. Do they tell the story in an expository manner, taking a God-like perspective, or do they use an observational mode, letting the images and sounds speak for themselves? Do they reflect on and represent their role as a filmmaker, in the reflexive mode, or do they reveal themselves as a participant in the film, in the participatory mode? Nichols' theory is governed by the belief that the standard expository mode of documentary may seduce the viewer into believing that the filmmaker is in possession of the absolute truth. Strongly inspired by Foucault's critique of reason as a bourgeois ideology, Nichols makes plain his preference for poetic, observational, performative and reflexive films, which, he argues, set the viewer free to experience alternative worlds, relatively unpolluted by dominant ideologies, and/or allow the director to claim personal responsibility for the film's viewpoint. However, in contrast to Andre Bazin (1967, 1972), who maintains that the medium is a true, indexical imprint of reality, Nichols acknowledges that, whatever form the documentary takes, the director will always present reality from a subjective point of view. Viewers, therefore, cannot simply rely on their own observations of the film to ascertain its veracity. Even in the observational mode, the viewer does not have uncontrolled access to reality because it is the filmmaker who chooses where to place the camera, what to select for representation and what to omit. However, it is not evident that viewers will be more careful in their evaluation of a given documentary if it is made in a participatory, reflexive or performative mode rather than an expository one; such forms might even lure them into overestimating the film's veracity. Nicholls does not articulate what processes a typical viewer might be expected to use to assess the truthfulness of a given type of documentary. Thus, his modes may be useful as tools to distinguish the different forms documentaries take, but they do not shed much light on how the viewer assesses their realism.

Whereas such approaches take the formal features of a film as their point of departure (and, for that reason, Nichols appears to exclude docudrama from his framework), others, such as that espoused by Noël Carroll (1997) and Carl Plantinga (2005), focus on the intentions of the filmmaker. For example, Plantinga discusses two definitions of documentaries, and proposes a third. The first he calls DIR (Documentary as an Indexical Record)—that is, documentary as an "indexical" imprint of reality. Plantinga convincingly argues that large parts of what are traditionally defined as documentaries are only based on indexical records to a limited degree; they include much non-indexical material, from the re-enactment of real events to voiceover commentaries and music. The second definition he calls DA or Documentary as an Assertion (of some truthful aspects of reality). Although this is close to Plantinga's (1997) earlier definition, he now argues that it is too narrow a category because a large part of the material in a documentary is not *intended* but *presented*, and visual representation is often richer in meaning than the original intention. Instead, he presents a third definition, AVR (Assertion of Veridical Representation), emphasizing that although a documentary may claim that it represents reality, it also relies on showing this reality rather than merely asserting it. Nevertheless, although such definitions may be useful in determining the intentions of the filmmaker, they do not provide adequate guidance when it comes to discovering how the average viewer discerns the truthfulness of a given documentary. The director of a film may believe they are providing a true representation but inadvertently distort reality in order to express certain meanings or elicit a particular response. A propaganda documentary or docudrama may provide a far more distorted representation of reality than many a fiction film, and the fact that the filmmaker intended it as a documentary does not help its viewers to evaluate its actual degree of veracity.

DOCUMENTARIES AND DOCUDRAMAS: THE VIEWERS' PERSPECTIVE

In contrast to the approaches outlined above, an analysis of a docudrama's realism needs to explore the sort of processes that take place in viewers' minds when watching such a film. Many of these processes are also in use when watching fiction films (Grodal 1997, 2009), although, of course, documentaries demand different cognitive and cultural capabilities because it is also essential to evaluate the films' correspondence to reality. The primary goal of mainstream fiction is to entertain, and an evaluation of its reality status is often irrelevant or even undesirable (as, for example, in science fiction or fantasy films). Documentaries and docudramas, too, need to entertain, but their main purpose is to provide information about the world; viewers are required to use many different skills, ranging from a generic understanding to specific knowledge, if they are to avoid accepting the information provided without question. This is a formidable task as the aim of a documentary is essentially to capture whatever there is to know about a certain aspect of the world—a task that would surpass anyone's capabilities. Thus, the viewer's evaluation has to be based on a combination of individual knowledge and heuristics (that is, certain internal rules and mechanisms that we use to form rapid judgments and make decisions).

Amos Tversky and Daniel Kahneman (1974), in a seminal article on heuristic methods, have established their key elements: "availability," "representativeness" and "anchoring." "Availability" means that we tend to evaluate probability on the basis of what comes into our minds at that moment: viewers of crime fiction, for example, may believe that a woman is more likely to be murdered by a perverse serial killer than by her partner or ex-partner, although in real life the latter scenario is the more statistically probable. Documentaries and newscasts tend to amplify the availability bias by focusing on interesting but atypical phenomena (such as serial killers), leading the viewer to over-evaluate, for example, the number of serial killers due to their media prominence.

"Representativeness" refers to the way in which we form judgments by means of prototypes: the idea that the majority of politicians are corrupt may be a product of the wide media availability of this trope but is not necessarily representative of politicians in general. Representativeness often involves the over-specification of prototypes. For example, we would find the statement, "Linda is a school teacher and a feminist," more probable than the more simplified "Linda is a school teacher" or "Linda is a feminist" despite the unlikelihood that increasing specification will increase probability. When watching *The Queen*, the viewer's previous knowledge of Queen Elizabeth and other royal persons will invariably be limited to public situations, usually of a ceremonial nature, and this will form their representative image of these characters. They will subsequently project this image onto their perception of these people's private behavior, to which they have little or no access, encouraging a misleading reading of the situation.

The third basic heuristic, "anchoring," is in many respects identical to what cognitive psychology calls "priming." It means that the information provided first will control, prime or anchor our understanding of what comes next. This anchoring type of agenda-setting may even allow false information to overrule our knowledge of the true information. Experiments suggest that even if participants know the right answer to a given question, they are very easily misled by false facts, especially if these false facts are repeated and/or presented in a "fluent" (easy-to-process) way (Fazio et al. 2015). In *The Queen*, Blair is portrayed from the start as a warm-hearted royalist and man of the people, a moderately specific prototype that is easy to process, and this primes the viewer's perception of his screen persona. The film omits additional aspects of his persona that may equally well be true, such as his reputation as a sly or scheming politician, although they may be part of the viewer's extra-textual knowledge, which, if mentioned, would alter their experience of the film.

There is a common presupposition that viewers who are widely exposed to media must be media-literate. However, even if it is true that they learn some basic techniques, such as understanding the conventions of flashbacks, most of the skills needed to evaluate truthfulness do not depend on media literacy but on many different cognitive competences and multidimensional knowledge about the world. Even the labels "documentary" or "docudrama" may be part of a process priming the viewer as to what to expect, as well as alluding to the filmmaker's claim to a degree of veracity. But documentary filmmakers can differ in intention, just as different subject matter can provide the viewer with different cognitive capabilities with which to evaluate the truthfulness of a film, although their evaluation may ultimately depend on their own political, social or cultural background. Generic labels are cues that prime the process of evaluating the reality status of a given film: if the label is "science fiction," the film demands alternative checking procedures to those needed if it is called "social drama" or "documentary." However, the label "docudrama" is more ambiguous: it indicates a blend of fact and fiction. Still, the prefix "docu" may nudge the viewer towards an interpretation of realism that the following word "drama" does not fully relativize.

Tversky's and Kahneman's (1974) term "anchoring" not only describes how the first information we receive tends to control our understanding of subsequent information, but also refers to the fact that priming displays a certain degree of resilience to later disconfirmation. When something has been imprinted in the long-term memory, even if it is later totally discredited, it will nevertheless continue to influence the new, truer information; "echoes" of its false claims will surround and relativize the new information (Thorson 2016). Hence, when watching a film called a "docudrama," the word "docu" may prime the viewer's perception of what are in fact highly dramatized events and lure them into presuming that most of these events possess a high degree of truthfulness.

REALITY STATUS, ACTION POTENTIALS AND PERSONAL RELEVANCE

In the first part of the mental PECMA flow (Perception, Emotion, Cognition and Motor Action) (Grodal 2009), all incoming sensory information, such as visual input, has a similar impact on our emotional experience, even if our cognitive evaluation processes indicate later that what we saw was fiction. Even when watching a fantasy film, we may be shocked by the sudden approach of a dinosaur because it is perceptually real. As Joseph Anderson (1996) argues, following James Gibson's (1979) lead, the basic composition of our brain developed long before motion pictures made it possible to simulate reality; thus, we still are prone to accept such media-borne information as true indices of real phenomena. Seeing is believing. Reality evaluation demands an active process of disconfirmation of what is not real, otherwise it will be filed in the brain as "real." Contrary to popular belief, fiction and audiovisual information do not demand a suspension of disbelief; on the contrary, all kinds of perceptual input, including fiction, demand *the suspension of belief* (Grodal 2009), otherwise the incoming information will automatically be taken as true. Whether a given film is fiction or docudrama, the viewer must constantly employ the necessary cognitive processes to assess its reality status.

When information first reaches these cognitive processes in the frontal lobes, Daniel Gilbert and colleagues argue, it is scrutinized for its reality status (Gilbert et al. 1990). The incoming information may be evaluated not as real but as memory, fantasy, sensory illusion, role play, a mental simulation or a lie, as Robert T. Knight and Donald T. Stuss (2002) illustrate. But even if at this point the incoming information is disconfirmed, it can still retain its priming/anchoring effect due to its "echoing" abilities. As the frontal lobes are the gateway to the motor system, they need to assess the quality of the information on which any subsequent action will be based. As Gibson (1979) puts it, in the context of his affordance theory, if something is real, we can act upon it; its reality status has to be

evaluated in the prefrontal cortex to prevent us acting on false information. Action here does not only refer to immediate physical action, but
also to our orientation in the world, enabling us to decide on, for example,
our political or social attitudes, as well as their corresponding actions.

As the fundamental basis of our experience of what is real lies in our
ability to interact with reality, information that demands instantaneous
action will receive more scrutiny than information that has less immediate
relevance for activity. Thus, a documentary may have different consequences in terms of viewers' future actions or potential actions: if it asserts,
for example, that New York is in imminent danger of a terrorist attack, it
will have far great relevance for viewers in New York than those viewing
the film in China, and they will scrutinize the information accordingly. If
a documentary portrays the historical events that caused the destruction of
the Roman Empire, most viewers will probably not perform a thorough
reality check because the events are in the past and have no immediate
"action potential." The past is experienced as less real than the present or
the immediate future. The feeling of "realness" is also experienced in differing degrees of intensity according to the experiences of different cohorts
of viewers. *The Queen* may not have the same action potential for an international audience as it does for a British one, especially in relation to
British general elections or attitudes towards the British monarchy. Viewers
in Britain, therefore, might be expected to perform a more thorough reality check of the film in order to seek guidance for their action potentials.

Anna Abraham and Yves von Cramon (2009) have analyzed some of
the cerebral attributes we use when experiencing reality. When we need to
interpret the reality status of certain information, two brain regions, the
anterior medial prefrontal cortex (amPFC) and the posterior cingulate
cortex (PCC), spring into action. These regions are active in the so-called
"default network" that we use, for instance, when planning future activities, and they will continuously present phenomena of particular relevance
to us. Abraham and von Cramon found that when we process media input
involving family or friends, this provokes higher brain activation (due to
the information's immediate personal relevance) than inputs involving
famous people, which has medium relevance and less activation of these
brain regions, and fictional characters, which have low relevance and consequently low activation. However, even when fictional characters have
less relevance, the emotions activated may be strong if we are engaged
with these characters or have a strong personal interest in the emotional
problem portrayed, such as dealing with the death of a loved one. *The*

Queen depicts how the death of Diana triggered a wave of grief among large parts of the British public, and the popularity of the docudrama indicates that many viewers still feel that her death, even when reenacted, is experientially real and able to activate strong personal emotions. Interestingly, in the queen's speech following Diana's death, she refers to herself as a "grandmother"—a verbal cue that her speechwriters presumably believed would activate basic cognitive networks in her audience—as part of an attempt to redeem her public persona.

Nevertheless, the cognitive and emotional relevance of memories may fade over time, whether they are personal memories or mediated ones. *The Queen*, released in 2006, deals with events that had happened only nine years earlier, and viewers (especially British viewers) at that time were still subject to a lot of information concerning the death, emanating from television, magazines and newspapers. In this sense, the memories were stored as *mediated perceptions* and *mediated knowledge*. The events in the docudrama provoked a stronger sense of their reality at the time of the film's release than they do now due to the density of the memories and associations linked to them; such memories inevitably lose some of their emotional power over time. However, the salience of the death will vary from viewer to viewer according to their personal circumstances. In the years following the release of the film, the memories about and felt reality of the events could be reactivated in viewers by the film's heavy use of archive footage gleaned from contemporary mass-media coverage: for instance, Diana (as well as other public figures such as Bill Clinton and Nelson Mandela) are often represented through archive footage—mediated images of real events. Thus, the experience of realism may be based on a perceptual realism that simulates a transparent, faithful image of the events. The use of archive footage strengthens the credibility of the staged elements of the docudrama because the actors appear to interact with the real people in the documentary footage. When the viewer sees the docudrama actors watching live television, with Clinton and Mandela talking directly to them, this has the feel of reality.

PERCEPTUAL REALISM AND MEDIATED REALISM

Even if film images do not quite have the visual resolution of the unmediated real life we see with our own eyes, modern cinema can still provide the feeling of presence. We have the sense of being close to the actors. At the time of the events portrayed in *The Queen*, the late 1990s, most viewers had an additional experience of authenticity because television was a central element in their daily lives, conveying a sense of the immediate presence of world events. In those days, before the advent of HD TV, factual reporting used a lower screen resolution. In *The Queen*, the low-resolution images (often blurred and pixelated) of the archive material contrasts with the cleaner, high-resolution dramatized images, emphasizing the documentary qualities of the film by revealing the images' source as factual televisual footage of the events, thus providing additional proof that it is a (supposedly) predominantly factual film. In an unmediated world, however, low resolution usually challenges reality status—we often experience memories or fantasies, for instance, as foggy, blurry or incomplete images that feel "unreal." Nevertheless, for viewers in 2006, although the low-resolution images may have lacked the full power of film or of reality, they still matched their daily experience of the televised reality that was one of their main sources of knowledge about the events. The 1990s TV images, therefore, still bore the mark of indexicality for a 2006 viewer. However, the fact that today's TV images have a far higher resolution could mean that our sense of perceived realism has changed and the contemporary viewer could be expected to evaluate the quality of the archive footage in *The Queen* differently.

In contrast to the archive extracts from newscasts, the dramatic sequences in the film are rendered in high resolution. The queen and the prime minister are played by actors who resemble them visually, creating a perceptual realism through physical resemblance. Many later viewers may even begin to think of the Helen Mirren character as the real image of the queen because, as mentioned earlier, the visual input is stored in the brain as "real" unless the viewer makes an active effort to question its reality. Even when seeing the actual queen, the viewer might still experience "belief echoes" that construct a picture of her out of a mix of the real queen and the actor. Also, because staged events interact with factual media in the film, the mind may unconsciously object to the interaction of "real" and "fake" images and prefer to give all the images the same reality status. This would render the film an apparently unproblematic account, whose fluency and ease of association may derail reality evaluations, as Tversky and Kahneman (1974) argue. Furthermore, the film often uses real locations or locations that most viewers will experience as real, such as the exteriors of Buckingham Palace and Balmoral Castle, which are used as establishing shots, leading the viewer to believe that the indoor scenes actually take place in these locations and not in a studio. This could be called *realism by means of metonymy* between the real events and the fictitious events.

The film's overall plot and timeline align with the historical events; however, central elements of the psychological portrayal of what went on behind the public façade are fictitious constructions whose reality status relies on the viewers' cognitive evaluations, based on *folk psychological schemas of psychological realism*. These may include personality and social-role schemas (of how a servant, a minister or a queen might behave, in both public and private). As long as the portrayal does not conflict with the viewer's psychological schemas or explicit knowledge there is no reason for a significant reality check, so even the staged events may remain filed in the brain as "real," according to the viewer's initial perceptions.

SYMBOLISM

In a secular context, the standard understanding of what is real is based on the assumption that actions are controlled by local circumstances; they are not normally linked to a transcendental causal system that implies that some metaphysical agent controls the world. Even documentaries in the poetic mode, which in principle deal with real phenomena but in a way that is associative, not based on arguments and traditional narratives, are experienced as less real (Grodal 1997, 2009). In contrast, fiction often uses transcendental "symbolic" links between different events. *The Queen*, in two interrelated instances, breaks with non-metaphysical documentary realism (the film's standard mode) and resorts to the use of highly symbolic links between different events, which imply supernatural intervention. Late in the narrative, the queen's attempts to distance herself from the pre-funeral activities become increasingly precarious; sections of the public are clearly demonstrating their deep dissatisfaction with her behavior. Against this backdrop, the queen's daily life in Balmoral suffers two major setbacks that, in the docudrama, become symbolically related to her emotional problems vis-à-vis participating in the funeral ceremonies. The first incident occurs when she is out driving in the Scottish Highlands in an off-road vehicle: as she attempts to cross a river, the vehicle breaks down. In the context of the film's narrative, this symbolizes the necessity for the queen to reassess her "journey"—that is, her previous "problematic" stance towards the funeral and the public response to Diana's death. This link between the queen's mental impasse and her immediate physical impasse implicitly suggests that some form of higher power is telling her to submit to the public pressure.

The second incident occurs when the royal hunting party sights an extraordinarily beautiful stag. They give chase but do not succeed in catching it, and a "commercial" hunting party later kills it. The death of the stag evokes sadness in the queen and, potentially, in the viewers. She visits the dead stag, a symbolic precursor to her participation in Diana's funeral. Thus, the story of the stag is clearly symbolic although the exact meaning is unclear: does it refer to the fall of greatness or to human frailty? In any case, these two events—that are probably not historical facts—are key plot points in the film, depicting experiences that are presumed to inform the queen's decision to follow Blair's advice. The film appears to suggest that supernatural forces have engineered the breakdown of the queen's car and the shooting of the stag, revealing to her the frailty of humanity and convincing her to change her mind. At this point, as a film scholar, I would doubtless start to activate my reality-checking mechanism, as the symbolic nature of these scenes conflicts with my understanding of realism—that is, it implies the presence of a metaphysical force influencing events. However, the average viewer may be lured into accepting these symbolic acts as "real" simply because they are viewing a docudrama and not using the same procedures for reality checking that they would if viewing a fiction film portraying this sort of metaphysical intervention.

RITUALS AND EMOTIONS

An important aspect of the film's claim to realism is its link to the emotion of sadness. As Nico Frijda (1988) argues, sad or painful events are generally perceived as more real than joyful ones due to the urgency of pain. Furthermore, the sadness in *The Queen* is based on one of the biggest media rituals in history, the funeral of Diana. The portrayal and evocation of rituals are very special forms of realism: rituals are part of the real world yet, at the same time, they are marked out by their unnatural, involuntary form that designates them as a-temporal or, as Daniel Dayan and Elihu Katz (1994) call them, "time-out events." These authors use Diana's wedding in 1981 as a prime example: the event contrasts with everyday reality and has a more flexible and voluntary timeline. *The Queen*'s continuous insertions of TV archive material, showing reactions from around the world, reveals Diana's funeral to be another "time-out event," when apparently whole nations abandoned their daily endeavors to follow the proceedings on television.

The classic analysis of the function of rituals is found in Emile Durkheim's seminal work, *The Elementary Forms of the Religious Life* (1915). This describes how tribal leaders use rituals evoking the supernatural to ensure the cohesion of the tribe by drawing a distinction between the sacred and the profane, and ordering submission to the sacred in the form of ritual activities. The queen's efforts to evade the British tribal ritual of the funeral of the public's symbolic representative, Diana, was seen as an avoidance of her sacred duties as head of the tribe. Rituals are derived from precautionary systems that often express themselves in meaningless behaviors, from repetitive hand-washing to social rituals, in an attempt to cope with the hazards of life (Boyer and Liénard 2006). In *The Queen*, the central event is the shared ritual of mourning, demonstrating the unity of "the people" and their shared emotions and behaviors when confronted with the fact of death. The repeated shots of grieving individuals continuously prime the audience to experience sadness. The film even mimics the ritualistic actions taking place in the funeral through constant repetition of images of people adding bouquets to the growing mountain of flowers outside Kensington Palace.

Sadness or compassion in a film lends the filmmaker and their message credibility—that is, *realism by means of moral commitment.* The viewer feels part of a ritual community; the film evokes a sense of ritualistic commitment that for a time replaces everyday realism. It implicitly argues that to object to participating in the ritual of the funeral could be perceived as a lack of moral commitment, as embodied in the "callousness" of Blair's wife, Cherie. The emphasis on the role of ritual relates to other ways in which the film tries to reconcile populism and authoritarianism: embedded in the narrative is a strong justification of the monarchy as central to British identity. In contrast to his wife, Blair appreciates the monarchy and gladly accepts the rituals surrounding his prime ministerial meetings with the queen (for example, he never turns his back on her, walking backwards as he leaves the room). In essence, he tries to reunite the rituals of "the people" with those associated with the monarchy.

DOCUDRAMA AS PROPAGANDA

The Queen was made at a time when Blair's political actions were highly controversial due to his role in the Iraq War, which many saw as acquiescing to the will of the then-president of the United States, George W. Bush (the war later proved profoundly damaging to Blair's reputation). Viewed in this context, the docudrama possesses a strong element of propaganda not only because of what it includes in its representation of the prime minister, but also by what it leaves out. It takes a radically pro-Blair attitude, portraying him as a heroic "man-of-the-people" (the film's conception of "the people" appears to reflect a right-wing populist understanding of the term). In a sense, the main enemy of the film is Cherie Blair, with her anti-royalist ideas. Blair, by contrast, wants to reunite queen and people; he never speaks of Britain as a class society. A peculiar aspect of this is the way in which the role of the prime minister (the "profane" in Durkheim's terms) is portrayed as comparable to that of the queen (the "sacred"). The queen is seen as the incarnation of the relationship between the monarchy and its people that has existed for a millennium. This is not only expressed in the way in which Blair's actions and verbal expressions illustrate his humility before the queen, but also in the way in which his private life is staged. Although, Blair at the time occupied the highest office in the land and lived in the prime-ministerial residence in Downing Street, which in many ways resembles a mansion, he is portrayed as a "commoner." Some scenes take place in either a small kitchen or an ordinary-looking sitting room, where he is shown discussing with Cherie who is going to wash the dishes—an extremely unlikely activity for a prime minister. Here, the viewer's evaluation of the reality of such a situation (and the veracity of the depiction of Blair's character) depends on their particular use of social schemas: Blair is either a "man of the people" or the "prime minister in 10 Downing Street." The heroic portrayal of Blair points not only to the dilemma that docudramas are not simply documentary records of events, but also to arguments taking place within the context of a cultural-political landscape. As a consequence, the perception of realism in the film will partly depend on the political convictions of the individual viewer, particularly as the docudrama takes a strong pro-monarchy position and, as such, could be perceived as royalist propaganda.

SUMMARY

The experience of what is real in a docudrama like *The Queen* is based on a series of different cognitive mechanisms and on the knowledge possessed by the individual viewer. Thus, it is naïve to assume that there are simple, general ways of assessing the veracity of a documentary. The exterior world does exist objectively; however, it also consists of an infinite number of facts and data, and our access to it is, on many levels, a cognitive (and emotional) construction. Our brains try to construct reality based on the facts available. In a film, these facts are sampled by the filmmaker according to a specific purpose and are processed by the individual viewer according to their cognitive capacity and personal knowledge.

This chapter only deals with a few of the facts and cognitive processes that provide the basis for evaluating the reality status of a film. The central challenge posed by documentaries is that we tend to believe incoming information unless it is actively disconfirmed, and even then it may still prime our perceptions as disconfirmation will often still allow echoes of false information to persist. Due to its perceptual realism, a documentary may appear as fact rather than a particular selection of information with a potential propaganda purpose. Furthermore, viewers often rely on prototypes and folk psychological schemas of probable behaviors and motives, and it requires an effort to perform an active scrutiny of the veracity of a documentary: messages that are easy to comprehend are easier to trust. Documentaries portray a multitude of different aspects of reality and most viewers will not have the necessary knowledge of a given set of facts to perform a reality check. They could even be misled by the triggering of emotions that are of particular relevance for them, as when the queen describes her role as a grandmother, activating a sense of trust in the audience. Documentaries also frequently attempt to also activate moral emotions, as when Blair advocates the queen's participation in the funeral ritual. Moral persuasion can make it difficult for the viewer to engage their abilities of critical evaluation.

Viewers' experience of realism and their perception of the truthfulness of documentaries and docudramas, therefore, are based on open-ended, heterogeneous procedures that are related to an individual's knowledge, cognitive skills and emotional involvement. These processes are far more complicated when viewing documentaries as opposed to fiction films, and they are strongly related to the viewer's evaluation of the film's reality status and action potentials. Docudramas, as we have seen, can be highly persuasive, especially since, as seen in the PECMA flow, incoming perceptions continue to be believed unless they are actively disproved by processes taking place in the prefrontal cortex.

REFERENCES

Abraham, A. and von Cramon, Y. D. (2009) "Reality = Relevance? Insights from Spontaneous Modulations of the Brain's Default Network When Telling Apart Reality from Fiction," *PLoS ONE*, 4(3): e4741.

Anderson, J. D. (1996) *The Reality of Illusion: An Ecological Approach to Cognitive Film Theory.* Carbondale, IL: Southern Illinois University Press.

Bazin, A. (1967) *What is Cinema? Volume I.* Berkeley: University of California Press.

Bazin, A. (1972) *What is Cinema? Volume II.* Berkeley: University of California Press.

Boyer, P. and Liénard, P. (2006) "Why Ritualized Behavior? Precaution Systems and Action Parsing in Developmental, Pathological and Cultural Rituals," *Behavioral and Brain Sciences*, 29, pp. 1–56.

Carroll, N. (1997) "Fiction, Non-Fiction, and the Film of Presumptive Assertion: A Conceptual Analysis," in Allen, R. and Smith, M. (eds.) *Film Theory and Philosophy*. New York: Oxford University Press, pp. 173–201.

Dayan, D. and Katz, E. (1994) *Media Events.* Cambridge: Harvard University Press.

Durkheim, E. (1915) *The Elementary Forms of the Religious Life.* London: George Allen & Unwin Ltd.

Fazio, L. K., Brashier, N., Payne, K. and Marsh, E. (2015) "Knowledge Does Not Protect Against Illusory Truth," *Journal of Experimental Psychology*, 144(5), pp. 993–1002.

Frijda, N. (1988) "The Law of Emotion," *American Psychologist*, 43(5), pp. 349–358.

Gibson, J. (1979) *The Ecological Approach to Visual Perception.* Boston: Houghton Mifflin.

Gilbert, D. T., Krull, D. T. and Malone, P. S. (1990) "Unbelieving the Unbelievable: Some Problems in the Rejection of False Information," *Journal of Personality and Social Psychology*, 59, pp. 601–613.

Grierson, J. (1966) "The First Principles of Documentary," in Hardy, F. (ed.) *Grierson on Documentary*. London: Faber and Faber, pp. 145–156.

Grodal, T. (1997) *Moving Pictures: A New Theory of Film Genres, Feelings, and Cognition.* Oxford: Oxford University Press.

Grodal, T. (2009) *Embodied Visions. Evolution, Emotion, Culture, and Film.* New York: Oxford University Press.

Knight, R. T. and Stuss, D. T. (2002) "Prefrontal Cortex: The Present and the Future," in Stuss, D. T. and Knight, R. T. (eds.) *Principles of Frontal Lobe Function*. New York: Oxford University Press, pp. 573–597.

Lakoff, G. (1987) *Women, Fire, and Dangerous Things.* Chicago: Chicago University Press.

Nichols, B. (1991) *Representing Reality*. Bloomington: Indiana University Press.

Plantinga, C. (1997) *Rhetoric and Representation in Nonfiction Film*. Cambridge: Cambridge University Press.

Plantinga, C. (2005) "What is a Documentary After All?," *The Journal of Aesthetics and Art Criticism*, 63(2), pp. 105–117.

Thorson, E. (2016) "Belief Echoes: The Persistent Effects of Corrected Misinformation," *Political Communication*, 33(3), pp. 460–480.

Tversky, A. and Kahneman, D. (1974) "Judgment under Uncertainty: Heuristics and Biases," *Science*, 185(4157), pp. 1124–1131.

CHAPTER 6

The Duties of Documentary in a Post-Truth Society

Dirk Eitzen

Humans need stories. This has become practically a truism among intellectuals. One finds it all over the place: in TED talks and newspaper editorials, in popular psychology and theology, in historiography and anthropology and, of course, in cognitive literary studies, such as Brian Boyd's *On the Origin of Stories: Evolution, Cognition, and Fiction* (2009). The idea has also found firm footing among contemporary documentary filmmakers.

Documentary filmmakers have been telling stories since *Nanook of the North* (1922). What is relatively new is a particular self-consciousness about storytelling as a craft. Documentary filmmakers today read screenwriting manuals, study dramatic works and deliberately borrow strategies from fiction films. Even those with experimental leanings frequently describe their work in terms of stories. For example, young filmmaker Theo Anthony (cited in Zeitchik 2017a), describing his *Ratfilm* (2017), an associational riff on rats and race in Baltimore, says, "How to we create a blueprint for ideas that can educate people and spread information around? It's films that are aware of the process, where we're not just

D. Eitzen (✉)
Franklin & Marshall College, Lancaster, PA, USA
e-mail: deitzen@fandm.edu

© The Author(s) 2018
C. Brylla, M. Kramer (eds.), *Cognitive Theory and Documentary Film*, https://doi.org/10.1007/978-3-319-90332-3_6

telling people things but giving access to tools for how to make their own stories." So pronounced is the preoccupation with stories in contemporary documentary filmmaking circles that we might well give it a name: "new documentary storytelling."

This tendency seems harmless enough, for the most part; it is just an appeal to audience interests. However, it has a disturbing resonance with another form of self-conscious storytelling that has recently taken root in the culture: fake news. On the surface, fake news and documentary storytelling do different things and stem from different impulses. Still, beneath the surface, it is quite possible that both reflect a growing disregard for truth in the wider culture—a supposed phenomenon that pundits have labeled "post-truth."

THE POST-TRUTH PHENOMENON

The Oxford English Dictionary defines post-truth as "relating to or denoting circumstances in which objective facts are less influential in shaping public opinion than appeals to emotion and personal belief." It named post-truth their 2016 Word of the Year (Oxford English Dictionaries 2016). The term has been around for a decade, but it really took off in the second half of 2016, as perplexed and alarmed journalists struggled to make sense of the rise of Donald Trump in the US and the Brexit referendum in the UK.

In fact, there is nothing new about the phenomenon. Aristotle wrote about the power of emotion to shape public opinion in his *Rhetoric*. Demagoguery, likewise, dates back to the Greeks. In American entertainment, the deliberate bending and blurring of the boundary between fact and fiction is a time-honored tradition, from P. T. Barnum's famous hoaxes in the mid-nineteenth century to reality TV today. In news journalism, Rupert Murdoch and his minions are just following a trail blazed by William Randolph Hearst and his minions a century before. While it is true that the click-bait culture of today's Internet spreads lies faster and further than ever before, the deliberate spread of false facts for personal and political ends is as old as gossip.

When journalists write about post-truth as something shocking and new, what they are really remarking on are political developments that they see as shocking and new, including the election to the US presidency of a reality-TV star with no prior political experience and a pathological propensity for lying. When journalists wish to assign blame for these developments, they invariably begin by pointing the finger at cynical or self-serving people and organizations, mostly on the political right, who deliberately manufacture and circulate false and misleading facts and stories. But what concerns them most, what prompts them to write about post-truth as opposed to just systemic lies and lying, is their discovery that many of the lies are practically impervious to fact-checking and truthful reportage. They spread like a virus that is immune to vaccines.

One possible explanation is a well-known psychological phenomenon called "confirmation bias." People tend to hear what they want to hear, believe what they want to believe, and not pay attention to or even fail to notice things that do not square with their wishes and expectations. When they do notice things that do not square with their wishes and expectations, their brain works very hard to fit these into existing frameworks of belief. Neuroscientist Drew Westen has examined how this process works in the brain by putting subjects into an fMRI brain scanner and showing them statements in which political candidates are obviously lying or pandering to their audience. In an interview with media commentator Brooke Gladstone, Weston describes what happened when people were confronted by lies from candidates they favored.

> They saw a threat, and you could see it all over their brain. Then you saw activation in the part of the brain called the anterior cingulate. It monitors and deals with conflict. So they were in conflict... [trying] to figure a way out. And then, after they had come to their conclusion that there was really no problem for their guy, you saw activation in parts of the brain that are very rich in the neurotransmitters involved in reward. These are the circuits in the brain that get activated when junkies get their fix... There was no reasoning at all going on. (Weston, cited in Gladstone 2017, p. 15)

Confirmation bias, however, is a fixed facet of human nature, so it can hardly explain the cultural shift that is taking place right now. A likelier explanation has to do with what people today want and expect from the news. Consider, for example, why so many conservatives in the US tune into right-wing commentator and media blowhard Sean Hannity. They don't watch *The Sean Hannity Show* for facts: if they wanted facts, they would check out Wikipedia or Politifact.com. They are not interested in objectivity, either: they *like* the fact that Hannity overtly takes sides. What they are most interested in is sensational tidbits that, when shared with others, cement their standing in a particular community. What they want, in a word, is *gossip*. That is why it does not particularly matter to them whether or not Hannity is telling the truth.

This casts the post-truth problem in an entirely different light. It is not primarily about lies and fake news. It is not primarily about irrational or benighted news consumers. It is most certainly not about some new cultural incapacity to conceive the difference between truth and lies, or fact and fiction. The crux of the problem is, rather, that politicized news consumers are looking to the news for something other than information or factual knowledge. They are looking to the news for social and emotional validation—the same sort of validation that people find in gossip. With gossip, who you believe depends largely upon who you trust. So it is, too, with the news. In order to be taken seriously, as more than just idle gossip or partisan propaganda, legitimate news sources like *The Washington Post* rely upon trust. They need us to believe, above all, that things they report as facts actually are facts—that they are not made up, in other words. Their editors work very hard to earn that trust. Many journalists are, therefore, deeply concerned that today's fake news erodes the public's trust in *all* news.

Critics who are concerned about what I have termed the "storytelling turn" in contemporary documentary share this anxiety. They do not have any intrinsic objection to storytelling, craft, artistry, performance, expression, subjectivity, and so on. They are not concerned to maintain some facade of objectivity, neutrality or devotion to facts. They do not even seem to be particularly worried about entertainment that deliberately blurs the line between fact and fiction, as reality TV routinely does. When they write about maintaining a line between fact and fiction in documentary, what they seem to be most concerned about is the potential for the erosion of trust in a kind of discourse that depends upon it.

New Documentary Storytelling

Many in the current generation of documentary filmmakers regard themselves as being first and foremost in the *movie* business, not the *reality* business. Reality does matter to them, but more as an impetus and raw material for their films than as something to be treated as valuable for its own sake. They see facts as useful and worthwhile, mainly as a warrant for emotional investment, although they do not have a high regard for "information" and "explanation." They make no effort to pursue objectivity, not because they perceive it as a will-o'-the-wisp, but simply because they find it uninteresting and, perhaps, somewhat authoritarian. Manipulation, craft, artistry, expression, subjectivity, storytelling, entertainment, these are not things to be avoided—for these documentary filmmakers, they are the name of the game.

I could point to countless examples. I have already mentioned Anthony. His *Ratfilm* is as much about moviemaking as it is about rats. "I'm fine with rats," he says, "[but] I could have made a film about public transportation... Anything that links places and time could have been the subject of the film. It's just a thing that has direction and momentum that you can tag along and see what it bumps into" (cited in Zeitchik 2017b). Filmmakers Jeremy Levine and Landon Van Soest describe making their 2017 observational documentary, *For Ahkeem*, in this way:

> We were talking constantly about where are the beats, where is she [the protagonist] having these turns, where's her darkest hour. We were plotting it every bit like a narrative screenplay... We are going to look at these films like *Stand by Me*... and structure our film according to what we know works. (Levine and Van Soest, cited in No Film School 2017)

In *Casting JonBenet*, a 2017 Netflix documentary about the notorious unsolved murder case of a child beauty queen, filmmaker Kitty Green presents amateur actors (from the victim's home town) auditioning for roles in a hypothetical fiction film about the incident and sharing their personal recollections of and responses to the case. "We don't consider it true crime," Green (cited in Krupp 2017) says. "I mean, it touches on true crime. And it touches on our appetite for true crime and how we're all so obsessed with it. That's sort of what we're more interested in than the case itself."

This outlook on documentary filmmaking has potential pitfalls—exploitation and deception, in particular. *New Yorker* critic Richard Brody points to *Casting JonBenet* as an example of the first. He writes:

> [The filmmaker] reduces most of the movie to stupid-white-people tricks, not because the people in the film are stupid but because [she] condenses their remarks to their catchiest, kickiest, strangest, most intimate, isolating them from their context and emphasizing their humor, their irony, their weirdness, their incongruity. (Brody 2017)

But strangeness, irony and intimate moments are the whole point of the film. They are what appeal to audiences.

As for deception, it goes without saying that documentary filmmakers routinely select, frame and edit material in ways that are largely invisible to audiences. They often stage and reorder events, too. They do all this in the interest of making engaging and compelling movies. Most of the time, viewers don't blink an eye at such manipulations; indeed, they expect them. But, occasionally, filmmakers are accused of duping audiences or playing fast and loose with the facts. One example is the sensational finale of the 2015 HBO documentary miniseries, *The Jinx*, in which accused murderer Robert Durst appears to inadvertently confess into an open mic. Subsequent investigation by journalists revealed that the filmmakers had deliberately fudged the timeline of events (Aurthur 2015). Because *The Jinx* is designed to tell a polished tale, it glosses over doubts and hides its sleights of hand. It also makes extensive use of dramatic recreations of subjects' recollections, effectively presenting them as facts. *Indiewire* critic Sam Adams (2015) writes, "There's no moral sense to [director Andrew] Jarecki's filmmaking decisions, only the desire to squeeze every last drop of conventional drama out of his material."

But audiences loved it. Over a million people watched the finale on HBO, and it generated 35,000 tweets, which were seen 11.1 million times by 2.8 million people (Kissell 2015). Thanks in part to Durst's apparent on-air confession, the series became something of a cultural sensation. That is precisely the problem, according to Adams. New distribution channels for documentary, including HBO and Netflix, strive to attract the largest possible audience and encourage documentary filmmakers to do the same. Mainstream audiences are drawn to storytelling and sensation; they are not particularly interested in reality, except as a vehicle for storytelling and sensation, as in the case of reality TV. So, documentaries like *The Jinx* step up the storytelling and sensation, audiences eat it up, and the result is a vicious cycle. The traditional concerns of documentary—in reality, knowledge and information—are being sold down the river, and the line between true nonfiction and reality entertainment is being washed away. That is Adams's concern.

Documentary filmmakers are clearly being swept along in a larger trend in the media, at least in the US. This trend has to do with deliberately appealing to the interests and desires of consumers in such things as stories, often at the expense of treating reality as intrinsically important. In the documentary domain, the forces driving the trend are largely mercantile. As documentary filmmaker Joe Berlinger reports, "I get notes from networks all the time about upping the entertainment value, upping the suspense and, you know, real life doesn't naturally fit a conventional dramatic arc, and we as makers of this kind of work are under increasing pressure to conform to the conventions of scripted television." (cited in Garfield 2015).

WHAT DOCUMENTARIES DO

Toward the end of his review of *Casting JonBenet*, Brody (2017) makes this declaration: "The essence of the modern documentary is epistemological: How do the participants—and, for that matter, the filmmaker—know what they know about the subject and about the film itself?" The root of "epistemological" is the Greek word *episteme*, which means knowledge or understanding (as opposed to *doxa*, which means opinion or belief). Brody supposes that the most important purpose of documentary—the modern documentary, anyway—is the acquisition or creation of knowledge. Documentary is fundamentally about knowing things, including how we know them. Given that purpose, the first obligation of documentary filmmakers is not to make entertaining movies but to respect reality. *Casting JonBenet*'s director, Kitty Green, is so intent on making a great movie, Brody feels, that she does not respect reality enough. In the interests of entertaining her audience, she short-changes both her subject matter and her human subjects.

Green appears to be operating according to a completely different set of assumptions. She supposes that what interests documentary viewers, and what serves them best, is not knowledge about reality per se (facts, information, evidence, and the like) but an affecting cinematic experience that makes them *feel connected* to reality. To the extent that how the film is made is important or relevant to such an experience, Green supposes that her film provides enough information for viewers to be able to figure it out on their own, so there is no particular need for self-reflexivity. Finally, she supposes that her deliberately playful and potentially confusing treatment of the boundary between fact and fiction will work to intrigue and engage viewers, thereby enhancing their interest in the film and, indirectly, in the reality that it invokes, both in its performed sequences and in its interviews.

Brody's assumptions are philosophical. They have to do with what documentary *is*, with its essential nature. That is a question that has long been of interest to scholars and intellectuals. Notably, Brody's answer to that question has much in common with what journalists see as the essential nature of the news: its first purpose is to collect and convey knowledge. If consumers treat it as entertainment or gossip, or anything other than an instrument of knowledge, they are not treating it properly. If its producers take advantage of popular interest in such things as sensation and stories for ends other than knowledge, they are doing something wrong. The cultural problem that journalists call post-truth is that a whole lot of people, consumers and producers alike, are doing things in the guise of news that news is not supposed to do. Brody would likely extend these same arguments to documentary.

Green's assumptions, in contrast, are pragmatic. They are grounded in the interests of filmmakers and audiences. They are less about what documentary *is* than about what documentaries *do*, and what documentaries do first and foremost, Green supposes, is provide a powerful viewing *experience.* They are, after all, movies. Their obligation vis-à-vis reality is to engage with it in a meaningful way, not to try to capture or convey it. For that purpose, it is the interests and expectations of viewers that are of prime importance, not the particular treatment of facts. The best documentary is the one that gives viewers the strongest sense of engagement with reality, not the one that provides the most or truest information. Any technique that works to foster a feeling of relating to reality is acceptable: storytelling, dramatization, music, whatever. The main problem with fakery or the manipulation of reality is a practical one: it can have the effect of undermining viewers' sense of engagement with reality.

With the rise of the new storytelling tendency in documentaries, Green's perspective has clearly won out. In contemporary documentaries, investigation is treated largely as a storytelling device: the promise of knowledge as a lure to viewers. What matters, in the end, is the *impression of discovery.* Just look at *The Jinx*. Even journalistic documentaries, such as the *Frontline* series on US public television, and acclaimed science documentaries, such as Fox Network's Peabody-Award winning series *Cosmos* (2014), use characters, conflict, spectacle, staging, dramatic music, and many other kinds of manipulation of reality to embed information into what are supposed to be, first of all, powerful viewing experiences.

This is nothing new, of course. Most of the documentary "greats"— Robert Flaherty, John Grierson, Robert Drew, Chris Marker, and so on and on—were consummate and deliberate storytellers, and documentary audiences have always preferred stories and sensation to information and argument. What has shifted is the way audiences and filmmakers typically conceive of the nature and purpose of documentaries. A watershed year in this shift was 1989. This was the year in which Michael Moore proved, with the theatrical release of *Roger & Me*, that documentaries could be profitable as entertainment. His film, a semi-satirical treatment of his attempts to get an interview with the then-CEO of General Motors about corporate layoffs in Flint, Michigan, received widespread critical acclaim and made nearly seven million dollars at the box office (Box Office Mojo n.d.). Still, it was famously snubbed for Oscar consideration because some claimed that it was not truly a documentary. The main reason was that it plays fast and loose with a number of facts, including making the statement that the failed Auto World amusement park in Flint was built in response to the GM layoffs, when in fact it had opened and closed well before that.

In a spirited defense of the film, critic Roger Ebert writes:

> I would no more go to "Roger & Me" for a factual analysis of GM and Flint than I would turn to the pages of *Spy* magazine for a dispassionate study of the world of Donald Trump. What "Roger & Me" supplies about General Motors, Flint and big corporations is both more important and more rare than facts. It supplies poetry, a viewpoint, indignation, opinion, anger and humor. When Michael Moore... defends the facts in his film, he's missing his own point (Ebert 1990).

Ebert's essay eloquently encapsulates the new outlook I have been describing. What is critical, Ebert suggests, is not a documentary's relationship to reality, but its relationship to its audience. Documentary is not an instrument for showing and knowing reality, it is part of a conversation *about* reality, which may take any form.

DOCUMENTARIES AND GOSSIP

The outlook of Green and Ebert is absolutely correct to this extent at least: documentaries really are no more and no less than part of a conversation *about* reality. Their images of reality are just that: images. We do not mistake them for reality. We might look to particular things documentaries show as evidence of something or other—the way prosecutors used material from *The Jinx* in the Durst murder case, for example—but that is exceedingly rare. Most of the time when we watch documentaries, we are mainly interested in the stories they tell. In terms of viewers' experience, documentaries' references to reality serve chiefly to convey relevance and import. As such, re-enactments and illustrations can work just as well as, or interchangeably with, archival materials and eyewitness accounts.

It is a puzzle, then, why people will choose to watch a long, slow documentary series like *The Jinx* for entertainment instead of a much more quickly paced, narratively coherent and intrinsically entertaining fictional crime drama like CBS's *Criminal Minds*. The answer to this puzzle, I have argued elsewhere, does not lie in any special psychological appeals that documentaries *have* as movies or stories. It does not lie in evidence, information, truth claims or anything else that they present or represent. It lies, instead, in the emotional appeals that documentaries *make* to viewers (Eitzen 2005). These emotional appeals speak to particular social dimensions of viewers' experience. In this regard, they bear a striking and illuminating resemblance to the appeals of gossip.

One of its appeals is to the viewer as a social actor. If a friend gossips to you, "Did you see that Henry got a new BMW?", the statement has more to do with your relationship with your friend and with Henry than it does with the car. It implicitly invites you to make some sort of judgment about Henry, which in turn creates a kind of alliance with your friend. *The Jinx* works in a similar way. Even though it is ostensibly about Durst—specifically, about whether or not he committed a murder—its special psychological appeal as a documentary revolves around the implied relationship between the filmmakers, their subjects and their audience. Most viewers do not know or care about Durst. Furthermore, the story that the movie tells is fairly uneventful and undramatic as stories go. What drives viewers' engagement with *The Jinx* is a sense of involvement in the shared social world that the movie invokes, especially the sense of being included in a conversation that has moral implications.

Another appeal that documentaries and gossip share is an appeal to trust the author. Whenever any discourse presents some remote state of affairs as actual, such as the phrase, "Henry got a new BMW," we have no alternative than to take it on faith. This applies to documentaries, too. In order to accept the realities they invoke as legitimate and worthwhile, we must take on faith that what they seem to show is what they actually show—that an apparently spontaneous interview is unscripted, an archival photograph is authentic, and so on. But to take something on faith does not mean to take it as a fact. Documentary viewers welcome opinion, speculation, re-enactment, continuity editing, melodramatic music, and all sorts of other contrived elements. Again, just look at *The Jinx*.

"Trust me" is an implied social pact. It has very little to do with facts per se. Consider how Donald Trump uses the phrase. It obviously does not mean "You may rely on the specific facts I'm relating here." What it means is "You can trust my *intent*; I've got your back." Whether true or false, that is the appeal that Trump makes to his followers, and it is a seductive one. Documentaries rely on the same kind of implied social pact with viewers.

Facts do matter, of course. When Trump gets them wrong, it undermines the idea that he is worthy of our trust. So it is with documentaries. This is the beef that critics have with Moore's *Roger & Me*. Again, the analogy to gossip is illuminating. If your friend speculates about how Henry was able to pay for such an expensive car, that is "just gossip." The facts are not a central concern. But what if your friend tells you, as a matter of fact, that Henry's car was a gift from his boyfriend and you later discover that the car is actually a rental? If you suppose that your friend was merely passing on hearsay, you will likely forgive the falsehood as an honest mistake. However, if you suppose that your friend deliberately made up the story in order to manipulate you, you are bound to be incensed. It is not the falsehood that matters, it is the intent. Similarly, if the reordering of events in *The Jinx* is perceived simply as an attempt to better connect with viewers, it is no big deal. But if it is perceived as cynical or self-serving, an attempt to take advantage of viewers' credulity or to drum up sensation for profit, then it is seen as a violation of the viewer's trust—the equivalent of false gossip. More important than the treatment of facts, in either case, is the social connection implied by the sharing of a viewpoint on the facts. Just like your friend's gossip about Henry's BMW, it telegraphs, "We are social allies. What I'm sharing with you is important for that reason."

This is related to a third special appeal of documentaries: they appeal to our egos. Just like gossip, they can make us feel good about ourselves by implying that we are part of a special group. We may imagine ourselves to be especially smart and sophisticated, morally superior, privy to secrets or inside information, socially privileged and exclusive, or committed to an especially worthwhile cause or belief. *The Jinx* pulls all of these emotional levers. Because it is a documentary, it appeals to us as an educated class. Because it is about crime, it invites moral judgements. Because it unfolds as a detective story, it continually discloses surprising secrets and inside information. It paints law enforcement professionals as inept, which implies a kind of political viewpoint. Also, it aired on HBO, a subscriber-only "premium" channel. All of these work to suggest, "This is an important movie *because important people watch it.*" *The Jinx* invites viewers to become part of this privileged group. Reading about the movie, or tweeting or talking about it, enhances this appeal.

Gossip has a nasty reputation. People tend to think of it as entirely harmful and evil. In fact, it has powerful positive aspects. Psychologically, it makes us feel stronger and more connected. Socially, it binds us to others and fosters reciprocity. Morally, it shapes and strengthens our sense of right

and wrong. Politically, it serves the less powerful by creating group solidar-
ity and marshalling group pressure to keep bullies and cheats in line. Much
of documentaries' power for good lies in these same positive potentials.

However, each of these positive potentials of gossip has a dark side. A
sense of moral obligation has been used to justify shunning, revenge, even
genocide. A sense of connection and belonging has been used to divide
and exclude. Special and privileged knowledge has been used to manipulate and deceive. False gossip is particularly pernicious: it creates division
and distrust, and manipulates people's allegiances and beliefs. That is what
we see happening today with fake news and the right-wing press. It is the
crux of the post-truth problem.

News is not supposed to be gossip. It is supposed to gather and dis-
seminate knowledge, based on facts. That is its first purpose. When a lot
of people treat it as gossip, this purpose is subverted, and this can have
serious negative social and political consequences. Documentaries do *not*
trade in facts in the same way that news is supposed to, by and large. Like
news, they refer to and represent situations and events that are supposed
to be real, but their power to engage and affect us revolves around social
appeals not factual information. That is how they are usually designed and
that is how they are usually perceived. In this regard, they have much
more in common with gossip than with news.

THE DUTIES OF DOCUMENTARIES

The biggest fear of post-truth catastrophists is not that people are misled
by false facts but that they may stop caring about facts altogether. To
quote media commentator Gladstone (2017, p. 47) again, "[I]t is not the
lies that pose the existential danger to democracy. It's the lying, the kind
of thoroughgoing lying that gives rise to a whole new reality or, better
still, to no reality at all." If people do not know what to believe, Gladstone
fears, they might wind up believing anything or, worse, nothing. She continues, quoting philosopher Hannah Arendt, "And a people that no longer can believe anything cannot make up its mind. It is deprived not only
of its capacity to act but also of its capacity to think and judge. And with
such a people, you can then do what you please."

Comparing fake news to false gossip helps to put Gladstone's fears into
perspective. False gossip does not make people stop caring about facts; if
it did, it would never be found out or corrected. False gossip does not
erode people's trust in their whole circle of friends, either, just in those

friends who get caught spreading it. And gossip does not in the least deprive people of the capacity to think and judge. To the contrary, a fundamental purpose of gossip is to think and judge in a social milieu. All of these things can also be said about fake news. I do not mean to suggest that it does not matter that Hannity and Breitbart News spread falsehoods; merely, that it does not turn people into sheep. The best hope for a cure for fake news lies in the fact that reality does not go away when you stop believing in it. Or when you tell a story about it. Or when you make up a spurious pseudo-reality with the intent of manipulating others. Facts have a way of asserting themselves in the end. We just need to continue to doggedly dig them up, which is what responsible journalists are doing.

But, as I have pointed out, contemporary documentaries do not operate in this realm. They do not trade in facts; they trade in stories. Their first purpose is not to impart information, it is to deliver affecting cinematic experiences. They do not reveal reality but engage in conversations about it. Their power resides not in information, it resides in appeals to viewers' social sensibilities. If social documentaries have a moral obligation, therefore, it is not primarily to dig up facts but to make socially positive appeals in a socially positive way.

Gossip is a morally messy business—what is good for the gossiper is usually not good for the gossipee. It reflects the competing interests of different groups, and which party's interests best serve the larger good is difficult if not impossible to determine. Just the same, each of the psychological appeals of gossip mentioned above implies a moral responsibility. The appeal for active social engagement implies that gossip should be relevant to its audience. The appeal for trust implies that it should be honest. And the appeal to feel like part of a special group implies that it should foster genuine community. We recognize and use these implications intuitively in judging whether gossip is good or bad. We can also apply them deliberately, to think through the moral duties of socially responsible documentary filmmakers.

Documentaries' appeal to viewers to see themselves as engaged social actors can be directed toward things that really matter or it can be diverted into mere entertainment. From this standpoint, the biggest moral problem with *The Jinx* is not that it manipulates facts but that it is largely irrelevant to viewers' lives. The same might be said of *Casting JonBenet*. Both documentaries provide enjoyable and worthwhile movie-viewing experiences but their main gratification is akin to that of snooping through somebody's dirty linen. They are no different in that regard from reality

TV. Instead of addressing topics that speak to genuine social concerns, both deliberately turn to tabloid fare as a way of drawing attention to themselves.

There are, on the other hand, countless contemporary documentaries that use the appeal of active social engagement to draw viewers' attention and concern to matters of real consequence—matters that impact people's lives. This is exemplified by two acclaimed 2016 documentaries about race: Ava DuVernay's *13th*, which makes the case that mass incarceration in the US is a modern form of slavery, and Raoul Peck's *I Am Not Your Negro*, which uses James Baldwin's words (taken from his unfinished manuscript, *Remember This House*) to explore the history of racism in the US. Both of these are examples of new documentary storytelling. That is, they are designed to be movies, first and foremost: they deliberately use compelling stories and innovative formal strategies to draw in and engage viewers. Not coincidentally, both DuVernay and Peck have a background in making fiction films.

Second, a good documentary has an obligation to be honest. That does not necessarily mean factual. An opinion can be honest. Honesty means making your meanings and intentions transparent. In his review of *Casting JonBenet*, Brody (2017) implies that the way to do this is with self-reflexivity: put your motives and methods right out there, in front of your viewers, so that they can judge them for themselves. That is no guarantee of honesty, however. A skillful filmmaker, like a skillful gossip, can use self-disclosure to create trust when trust is not genuinely deserved. Conversely, there is nothing inherently dishonest about invisibly manipulating reality in a documentary—with continuity editing, for example—if it is done for storytelling purposes and not to mislead audiences.

What matters, morally, is not the manipulation of reality, it is the manipulation of people. That is what deception does. Michael Moore's use of irony in his films is open and, therefore, honest, but his treatment of his subjects is not always so. One of many examples is the scene near the end of *Bowling for Columbine* (2002) in which Moore interviews actor and former National Rifle Association (NRA) president Charlton Heston. Moore finagles a very gracious invitation from Heston to interview him in his own home, then proceeds to bully and badger the aging and infirm actor, trying to force him to admit that, in taking part in an NRA rally in Flint, he deliberately took heartless advantage of the murder of a child that had occurred there a few weeks earlier. At the end of the scene, with a contrived reverse-angle shot, Moore holds up a photo of the child and calls after the retreating actor, "Mr. Heston, please, take a look at her. This is the girl." There is nothing dishonest about that reverse-angle shot. It is just good filmmaking. It does not abuse our trust. However, Moore did deliberately abuse Heston's trust. Maybe Heston deserved it—at least, this is what Moore implies. Moore's goal is clearly to create contempt for Heston, not understanding. This brings us to the third obligation of socially responsible documentary filmmaking.

Good gossip promotes understanding, and it does this by encouraging empathy. That is the road to genuine community. But empathy is complicated. When Moore shows the picture of the little girl who died, he is deliberately playing on our compassion for the girl in order to create disdain for Heston. He is using it to create a divided community: the little girl's family, the people of Flint and us, the viewers, on one side, and Heston and the NRA on the other. Documentaries—and stories generally—have the potential to bridge social divides. They can allow us to understand and feel for people who are different from us or who hold a different position. Smugness, self-righteousness and feelings of superiority have the opposite effect. They are the bane of empathy. Instead of working to bridge social differences, they divide people into opposing camps.

The bumbling Everyman that Michael Moore plays in his films is a cover for a sea of smugness. His films routinely work to set up the impression that *we* (the sophisticated, enlightened, elite audience of his films) are better than *they* (the unsophisticated, benighted, politically backward people on the other side of whatever issue he happens to be dealing with). This is Moore's great moral failing as a documentary filmmaker, not that he rearranges a few facts in the interest of storytelling. Consider, as an alternative, the way DuVernay treats Newt Gingrich in *13th*. Gingrich is one of the original architects of America's current political dysfunction and is, therefore, a real "bad guy" for liberals. Yet DuVernay treats him respectfully, even sympathetically. Nothing more powerfully supports her case than when he agrees with her that America's free-market fix to its mass incarceration problem has run terribly amok. Imagine how differently Moore's confrontation with Heston would have played had he taken the trouble to treat Heston in the same way.

Going Forward

Much of the discussion of the so-called post-truth phenomenon has focused on false facts. The main takeaway of this chapter, however, is that a focus on facts and whether or not they are true tends to distract from what really matters: the purpose and consequences of the discourses in which they are embedded. Take the infamous Nazi propaganda documentary, *Triumph of the Will* (1935). The facts in the film are fine. As its director, Leni Riefenstahl (1967), later observed, it shows nothing that did not actually occur. The problem with the movie is its politics. Like the giant political pageant it portrays, it was designed to glorify Nazi power and create a cult of personality around Hitler. The real problem of fake news today is, likewise, political.

The biggest danger in fake news is its antisocial tendencies. It is prejudicial and polarizing. Instead of encouraging people with different views to listen to each other, it has the effect of getting them to talk past each other. It pushes them into little, like-minded gossip bubbles. Instead of inviting them to check their worldviews against other people's and against reality, it encourages them to "go with their gut," reinforcing their prejudices and biases.

In a society in which this style of discourse runs rampant, one of the best things that a socially responsible documentary filmmaker can do is model a different style of discourse, one that is open to facts, reflects different viewpoints, and promotes empathy and understanding across social divides. The way to do that, as we learn from gossip, can be boiled down to three maxims: be relevant, be honest, and encourage understanding, especially of the socially disadvantaged. What it means to encourage understanding is pretty obvious. It usually involves stories—an area in which documentary filmmakers have a tremendous advantage over gatherers and reporters of facts. What it means to be honest, as I have pointed out, is essentially not to take advantage of people's trust. But what does it mean to be relevant? I stated previously that *The Jinx* is not relevant to viewers' lives. In fact, it tells an engaging story, deals with an actual crime and was watched by more than a million people. Is that not enough to prove its relevance?

The pragmatic orientation of new documentary storytelling—its concern to appeal to and connect with audiences—pulls filmmakers in two different directions. One is to entertain. It is obvious that if nobody watches your film, it is not going to be relevant. If nobody watches your film, you are not going to make a living as a filmmaker, either. In spite of new distribution channels for documentaries and a dramatic decline in the cost of high-quality video production, it is just as hard as ever to earn a living making documentary films. According to a 2017 report on documentary sustainability published by the National Endowment for the Arts

(NEA) in the US, 78 % of working documentary professionals say they cannot make a living making documentaries, 30 % made less than half of their salary, and another 36 % made nothing at all from their documentary work. So, naturally, the first and most compelling reason for documentary filmmakers to appeal to and connect with audiences is to make ends meet. However, the astonishing fact that 36 % of documentary filmmakers are willing to work for nothing is a strong indication of another interest of contemporary documentary filmmakers: to make a difference. Most documentary filmmakers feel called to address problems in the world, draw attention to social needs or improve people's lives. Documentary filmmaking has never been particularly profitable; a large part of what has sustained it throughout the years is the filmmakers' desire to make a difference.

The biggest challenge filmmakers face in this regard is that making a difference is a serious matter and seriousness does not play particularly well with audiences in search of entertainment. Given the choice between a trivial but entertaining reality-TV show and a relevant but serious social documentary, most people will choose the reality-TV show. That is why it is so important that contemporary documentary filmmakers craft interesting movies and relate compelling stories. The only way to expose audiences to the potential social benefits of documentaries is to woo them and draw them in. If a documentary succeeds in creating a powerful positive experience for audiences, it can help develop a taste for more such experiences. That is where the best hope for the sustainability of honest, relevant, empathetic documentary films resides. To their credit, *The Jinx* and *Casting JonBenet* both work very well toward this end, even though they are not particularly relevant to the burning issues of the day. So do Michael Moore's movies, in spite of their troubling smugness. So, my final word to any nonfiction filmmakers who may be reading this is: carry on carefully crafting stories.

REFERENCES

Adams, S. (2015) "Why Andrew Jarecki's 'The Jinx' Could Be Very, Very Bad For Documentaries," *IndieWire*, March 25 [Online]. Available at: http://www. indiewire.com/2015/03/why-andrew-jareckis-the-Jinx-could-be-very-very-bad-for-documentaries-131225/ (Accessed: June 28, 2017).

Aurthur, K. (2015) "The Holes in 'The Jinx' Might Go Deeper Than We Thought," *BuzzFeed*, March 23 [Online]. Available at: https://www.buzzfeed. com/kateaurthur/the-holes-in-the-Jinx-might-go-deeper-than-we-thought (Accessed: June 28, 2017).

Box Office Mojo. (n.d.) *Documentary Movies at the Box Office* [Online]. Available at: http://www.boxofficemojo.com/genres/chart/?id=documentary.htm (Accessed: July 13, 2017).

Boyd, B. (2009) *On the Origin of Stories: Evolution, Cognition, and Fiction.* Cambridge: Belknap Press.

Brody, R. (2017) "'Casting JonBenet': A Documentary That Unintentionally Exploits its Participants," *The New Yorker,* April 27 [Online]. Available at: http://www.newyorker.com/culture/richard-brody/casting-jonbenet-a-documentary-that-unintentionally-exploits-its-participants (Accessed: June 28, 2017).

Ebert, R. (1990) "Attacks on 'Roger & Me' Completely Miss Point of Film," *Roger Ebert's Journal,* February 11 [Online]. Available at: http://www.rogerebert.com/rogers-journal/attacks-on-roger-and-me-completely-miss-point-of-film (Accessed: July 13, 2017).

Eitzen, D. (2005) "Documentary's Peculiar Appeals," in Anderson, J. D. and Anderson, B. F. (eds.) *Moving Image Theory: Ecological Considerations.* Carbondale: Southern Illinois University Press, pp. 183–199.

Garfield, B. (2015) "Is True Crime Jinxed?", *WNYC Studios: On the Media,* March 20 [Online]. Available at: https://www.wnycstudios.org/story/true-crime-jinxed/ (Accessed: August 4, 2017).

Gladstone, B. (2017) *The Trouble with Reality: A Rumination on Moral Panic in Our Time.* New York: Workman Publishing.

Kissell, R. (2015) "Ratings: HBO's 'The Jinx' Finale Draws Over 1 Million Viewers on Sunday," *Variety,* March 17 [Online]. Available at: http://variety.com/2015/tv/news/ratings-hbos-the-TheJinx-finale-draws-over-1-million-viewers-on-sunday-1201454423/ (Accessed: July 5, 2017).

Krupp, E. (2017) "Chatting with Kitty Green, Director of 'Casting JonBenet' Documentary," *Chicago Tribune,* March 31 [Online]. Available at: http://www.chicagotribune.com/redeye/culture/ct-redeye-interview-kitty-green-director-casting-jonbenet-documentary-20170327-story.html (Accessed: 4 July 2017).

National Endowment for the Arts (NEA). (2017) *State of the Field: A Report from the Documentary Sustainability Summit,* August [Online]. Available at: https://www.arts.gov/publications/state-field-report-documentary-sustainability-summit (Accessed: August 9, 2017).

No Film School. (2017) *"For Akheem": How to Make an Authentic Movie About Someone Else's Story,* June 12 [Online]. Available at: http://nofilmschool.com/2017/06/ahkeem-interview-podcast-podcast (Accessed: June 30, 2017).

Oxford English Dictionaries. (2016) "Word of the Year 2016 is..." [Online]. Available at: https://en.oxforddictionaries.com/word-of-the-year/word-of-the-year-2016 (Accessed: June 29, 2017).

Riefenstahl, L. (1967) "Interview with Michele Delahaye," in Sarris, A. (ed.) *Interviews with Film Directors*. New York: Avon, pp. 453–473.

Zeitchik, S. (2017a) "The Director of this Movie About Rats Has Some Novel Ideas About Trump and Filmmaking," *Los Angeles Times*, March 12 [Online]. Available at: http://www.latimes.com/entertainment/movies/la-et-mn-theo-anthony-rat-film-interview-20170312-story.html (Accessed: July 4, 2017).

Zeitchik, S. (2017b) "In the Age of Alternative Facts, Decoding Truth in Documentary," *Baltimore Sun*, March 10 [Online]. Available at: http://www.baltimoresun.com/la-et-mn-true-false-documentary-trump-20170310-story.html (Accessed: July 4, 2017).

PART II

Character Engagement

CHAPTER 7

Characterization and Character Engagement in the Documentary

Carl Plantinga

Documentary filmmakers represent people, and in so doing, they *characterize* them. Through narrativization and all the filmic techniques at their disposal, they present a conception and image of the people they represent. Characterizations in documentaries come in many varieties. However, these are not merely imitations of people, not merely transparent records of *who they really are*: characterizations, whether flat or round, clear or ambiguous, are always constructions.

The documentarian films a subject, decides which of the footage to use in the finished film, and places it in a narrative (or other sort of) structure. The narration orchestrates an image-sound complex with a rhetorical purpose. The resulting representation will not be neutral but will suggest, imply, show or explicitly assert things about the person represented. Characterization is a construction because the images and sounds that represent the character are not neutral and transparent but carefully constructed and chosen to portray them in a specific way. Neither can the narrativization of those images and sounds provide a wholly objective or purely observational representation of a person: to narrativize a character in the context of a documentary, as I argue below, typically involves putting them in a moral and/or sociopolitical context that implies a favorable

C. Plantinga (✉)
Calvin College, Grand Rapids, MI, USA
e-mail: cplantin@calvin.edu

© The Author(s) 2018
C. Brylla, M. Kramer (eds.), *Cognitive Theory and Documentary Film*, https://doi.org/10.1007/978-3-319-90332-3_7

or unfavorable judgment. The necessity of selection and omission, emphasis, emplotting and point of view mean that the documentary filmmaker's
characterization of that person is a construction. That being said, this does *not* mean that documentary characterizations are fictions. Although documentaries may share some techniques of characterization with fiction film, they differ substantially in what they imply about the people they represent. The fact that documentaries, or at least prototypical documentaries, are *not* fictions raises unique ethical dilemmas about how to characterize people on screen. Although the legal parameters of informed consent may differ from country to country, many documentary filmmakers accept that it is an ethical requirement to obtain the consent of the participants whose images will appear in the film. This is in part a recognition that representing people also characterizes them, and that such characterizations have implications for their dignity, identity and right to privacy and self-determination. This chapter discusses some of the tools used by documentary filmmakers to construct characters, and the ethical obligations such characterization implies.

THE DOCUMENTARY AS "ASSERTED VERIDICAL REPRESENTATION"

The methods and ethics of documentary characterization require some background discussion of the nature of nonfiction communication. Elsewhere, I have referred to the documentary as a film of "asserted veridical representation" (Plantinga 2005, 2017). When a film is released into the public arena, it is often identified or "indexed" as either documentary or fiction (Carroll 1983; Plantinga 1997, pp. 15–25). If the film is an experimental work, or a hybrid film that straddles the fuzzy boundaries between fiction and nonfiction, then the indexing of the film will be less clear. If it is indexed as a "documentary," this implies an implicit contract between the filmmaker and the audience: the audience takes it to be a film in which the images and sounds, claims and implications are asserted to be veridical—that is, accurate or reliable guides to the film's subject. "Indexing" refers here to the identification of a film (in terms of its production, distribution and exhibition) as either documentary or fiction, and is unrelated to the term used in the philosophy of Charles Sanders Peirce and subsequent semiotic theory.

Documentaries both show and tell. First, the showing part. In the case of documentary cinematography and sound recording, it is assumed that the filmmaker has presented the film's images and sounds as reliable records of or guides to the pro-filmic event. It is as though the images and sounds are accompanied by the implicit testimony of the filmmaker that they are reliable guides to what occurred in front of the camera. They imply that an interview with a (hypothetical) deep-sea diver, for example, actually occurred in the way it appears on film, or that the noises of rioting, shouting and mayhem in the town square were recorded on location and give a sense of what the event really sounded like. Implicit in the very idea of documentary is the assertion that the filmmaker affirms the reliability of the images and sounds he or she has used. If the viewers later learn that the images and sounds were misleading, then they will assume either that the filmmaker was incompetent or dishonest, or that the film is not a documentary but propaganda or advertising—both genres of discourse that are thought to intentionally simplify, idealize, distort and fabricate. When a filmmaker presents a film to an audience as a documentary, he or she implicitly vouches for the accuracy or reliability of the images and sounds it contains. (Animated images can also be reliable guides to their subjects, but in a different way than images in traditional documentary cinematography.)

Documentaries do not merely show, however. They also "tell." The other half of the contract inherent in documentaries as "asserted veridical representations" is that whatever the propositions implied or asserted in the film, they are true reflections of the actual world. For example, when the voiceover narrator presents claims about the plight of the homeless, when parallel editing strongly implies a relationship of similarity between two events, when sober music expresses sadness or when a camera angle implies a certain perspective toward a character, the audience takes all of these as the assertion or suggestion of propositions about the world, such as "the homeless live difficult lives" or "this event is sad." Such suggestions and assertions are then subject to judgments about their truth or falsehood. Most audiences will not accept them as automatically true simply because they are asserted to be so. Yet it is the assertion of veridicality that lies at the heart of the documentary enterprise.

Nothing about "asserted veridical representation" *guarantees* that documentary films will actually be truthful, accurate or reliable. Many documentaries are in fact misleading, distorting and unreliable. This occurs because documentary filmmakers, like communicators in other media, are prone to self-deception, dishonesty, incompetence or unwitting bias, or only have access to partial truths. Nonetheless, documentaries are still presented as veridical, even if they are not actually so. This is the case even for documentaries that question the notion of accepted truth or subvert a sense of reliable testimony, as in the film *The Fog of War: Eleven Lessons from the Life of Robert S. McNamara* (2003). Although Errol Morris's film may question what Robert McNamara (former US Secretary of Defense) is saying in his interviews, the interviews themselves are presented as veridical records of what McNamara actually said. The "voice" of *The Fog of War* implies that although McNamara himself is perhaps *not* to be wholly trusted, the film's narration, on the other hand, *should* be trusted to show us what he said. The narration implies that the film is a true record of McNamara's thoughts about his activities during the Vietnam War and, through various strategies, suggests a certain perspective on McNamara.

Documentary films use their "voice" or narration to embody various degrees of confidence or assertiveness regarding what they show and tell; however, they differ in the degree to which they make claims about the people they represent. In an earlier work, *Rhetoric and Representation in Nonfiction Film* (Plantinga 1997, pp. 101–119), I make a distinction between the open and formal voices of documentary film on the basis of the degree of epistemic authority each lay claim to. This is similar to Bill Nichols' (1991) categories of "expository" and "observational" documentaries. The open voice, which I associate with direct cinema or cinema vérité, is often content merely to show, and to withhold explanations. Films using the formal voice offer more thorough explanations and come to firmer conclusions; these are either strongly implied, through various techniques of style and structure, or stated explicitly by a voice-over narrator. Thus, veridicality in the case of observational films involves less explicit telling and more showing and *implicit* telling. Without the narrator to assert propositions, the "telling" aspects of the observational film are developed implicitly through narrativization, the communicative implications of the film's style and the use of testimonies in the form of interviews.

Documentary Characterizations and Fiction

It might be tempting to say that since documentary has to construct the characterization of the people it portrays, it must be fictional, and thus there is little distinction between fiction and documentary. This would be a hasty conclusion, however. Documentary characterizations, unlike fictional characterizations, can be more or less accurate, honest and truthful regarding the particular people they represent because these characterizations are asserted veridical representations. The implicit "contract" between documentary filmmaker and audience stipulates that the film's images and sounds are presented as reliable guides to what characters actually said or did, or how they appeared. Any assertions by the voiceover narrator or implications conveyed by the narrativization or film style are asserted or implied to be truths about represented characters. The overall representation of a person in a documentary, in its totality, can be said to be its characterization of that person. Such a characterization is subject to epistemic evaluation.

I am aware that some scholars consider the word "truth" problematic—but it should not be. In fact, it is the denial of truth or truths that is especially problematic given the present political climate in the US, which has a president who disregards truth completely. I have long been an advocate for an ethical perspective on the documentary, one that insists on truth-telling and truth-showing as the central focus, and this chapter emerges from that perspective. The notion of veridicality and truth in documentary can also be defended from a philosophical perspective. Certainly, some documentaries focus on questioning rather than the kind of truth-telling we see in the expository documentary. Questioning, however, is neither epistemically neutral nor free of the assertion of propositions ostensibly believed to be truths. Questioning itself can be a form of assertion. When we question a received belief, we implicitly claim that it is uncertain, misleading, reductionist or perhaps even false. Any such claims are themselves truth claims (Plantinga 1997, pp. 219–222).

Another argument that emphasizes the distinction between characterization in fiction and characterization in documentary is that a fictional character is, of course, an imaginary being, and the fiction filmmaker has no ethical obligations to the beings they create. If I represent fictional characters as cowardly, greedy or vulgar, or as victims, felons or cheats, I do them no injustice. I cannot do wrong to fictional beings as they are not actual people. In incorporating a fictional character into my work, I may be bound by other ethical considerations of representation: that is, as an author or filmmaker, I must be sensitive to questions of stereotyping and the potential to needlessly offend members of the audience when I create fictional characters and put them into a fictional world. But those obligations are to the communities to which I distribute my film, not to the fictional character(s). Fictional characters have no rights and filmmakers have no obligations toward them.

Documentary films can be about fictional characters as well—for example, a film about the history of a comic book superhero. However, they most typically represent actual people and their broader communities. As a documentary filmmaker, my ethical obligations extend to the people whose images and recorded voices I use, whose representations become an element of my work, and to whom my documentary ultimately refers. Since the documentary filmmaker purports to represent actual people, what is implied or asserted about those people can be accurate or inaccurate, fair or misleading, presented with equanimity or as a blatant attempt at character assassination. A filmmaker cannot wrong a fictional character, but the potential to harm an actual person or an actual community is significant. Those who deny that there exist important differences between documentary and fiction films must somehow account for these differences in ethical obligations.

There remains one further objection to distinguishing between documentary and fictional characterizations. This has to do with the extent to which all people are "social actors"; indeed, both characters in fiction films and non-actors in documentaries play a role. Nichols (1991, p. 42) uses the term "social actor" to refer to people or individuals in the actual world in order to "stress the degree to which individuals represent themselves to others; this can be construed as a 'performance'." Thus, he writes, the "sense of aesthetic remove between an imaginary world in which actors perform and the historical world in which people live no longer obtains," and the "performance of social actors... is similar to the performance of fictional characters in many respects" (p. 42). Nichols seems to imply that because people often play roles in the social arena, people in documentaries are equally playing roles or "acting."

It is true that people in social environments sometimes behave in ways that suggest this, as Erving Goffman famously established in his 1959 book, *The Presentation of Self in Everyday Life*. A young woman may internalize the gender roles into which she is socialized, behaving in conventionally feminine ways in order to be accepted socially. A teenage male attending a social gathering, such as a dance or party, will often attempt to project an extrovert masculine confidence, despite feeling insecure and shy. In both cases, we could say that these people are acting a social role. Were documentary filmmakers to film the teenager's attendance at this dance, and were they both skilled enough and sensitive to the social dynamics of such a setting, part of their characterization of this teenager would include the revelation that he is playing a role. That is, if role play is a common element of everyday life, then an insightful film-maker will find a way to reveal this.

Things are different in the case of a fiction film. Take Pedro Almodóvar's *All About My Mother* (1999), for example, in which Penélope Cruz plays the role of Sister María Rosa Sanz. As a filmmaker making a fiction film, Almodóvar is not interested in examining Cruz's role play or acting; he is interested in her acting only insofar as it contributes to the successful creation of a fictional character. Thus, the fiction filmmaker uses actors to embody and portray fictional characters, while the documentary film-maker, most typically, attempts to show, assert and imply truths about actual people. While both fictional characters and people in the real world may be "social actors," only the fictional characters are performed by film actors playing fictional roles. This leaves the fiction/nonfiction distinction intact.

To Characterize or Not to Characterize? An Ethical Question

Before discussing the tools and the implications of characterization in the documentary, we should first say that the decision to either characterize or minimize the characterization of people represented in a documentary is itself an ethical question. Here I will give two examples. Some filmmakers seemingly prefer to avoid characterization as much as possible. For example, Ava DuVernay's *13th* (2016) examines the prison system in the US and its role in maintaining racial injustice. The film adopts the formal voice, in that it makes a clear argument supported by evidence. Much of this evidence comes in the form of testimony from apparent experts, interviews with people as diverse as Angela Davis and Newt Gingrich, Henry Louis Gates and Grover Norquist. What is interesting is the degree to which DuVernay resists representing the interviewees as subjectively oriented voices or as idiosyncratic, unique people. Few of the interviewees are identified, and none of them look at the camera. Instead, these sometimes anonymous talking heads look off-screen. This depersonalizes the interviews and has the effect of implying that their testimonies are all of a piece, part of an intricate, argumentative quilt that fits together with logical precision. Rendering the characterizations flat maintains a seeming objectivity. The fact that the interviewees are people with subjective opinions and complex, rounded characters is submerged by the way their testimony is fitted into a seamless argument by eliminating eye contact with the camera—and thus with the viewer. It is a common documentary convention, especially in expository and journalistic documentaries, to portray personal testimonies as strictly factual or objective. Characterizing the interviewees would have the effect of making their testimony appear subjective, so DuVernay refrains from doing this.

A different sort of issue is raised by the decision to characterize some people rather than others. Nichols (2017) takes issue with several aspects of Morris's film, *Standard Operating Procedure* (2008). Most pertinent here are his "feelings of revulsion" caused by the "complete absence of the voices of the Iraqi detainees" who were tortured by American soldiers at the Abu Ghraib prison during the Iraq War. Nichols criticizes Morris's decision to only display still photographs of the Iraqi prisoners' degradation, and not to humanize or characterize them by providing any further information or footage about who they are. The film features extended interviews with many of the guards responsible for the prisoners' torture, but gives "no voice whatsoever" to their victims (Nichols 2017, pp. 457–458). In this case, according to Nichols, characterizing the Iraqi prisoners would humanize them, while simply displaying still photos of their torture serves only to degrade them. Thus, an ethics of documentary considers not only *how* to characterize people in a film, but also *when* to characterize them.

Documentary Characterization: Flat and Round Characters

How do documentaries "show" us people and how do they "tell" us about them? We might first appeal to the common literary distinction between "flat" and "round" characters. Flat characters are uncomplicated, unchanging and characterized by only one or two traits. Round characters, on the other hand, are complex, dynamic and characterized by different, even contradictory traits, and may surprise the viewer. Unless the film is a documentary biography, it is often difficult to take the time to characterize people with such complexity that they become fully rounded characters. Thus, most documentary characterizations are flat. But are actual people ever really flat characters? And if not, under what conditions is it ethical to represent people as flat characters? This is an extremely complicated issue that demands separate treatment, and I will leave it hanging here. The question, however, does reverberate with much of what I discuss below.

To represent characters as round not only consumes much screen time, but is also difficult. Round characterization in this regard is difficult because it is more than a simple statement of fact. It might help here to separate the notion of individual facts from that of a broader truth. As Morris says of his film, *The Thin Blue Line* (1988):

> *The Thin Blue Line* has been called *Rashomon*-like. I take exception to that ... For me there is a fact of the matter, a fact of what happened on the road-way that night ... Someone shot Robert Wood, and it was either Randall Adams or David Harris. That's the fundamental issue at the center of all this. It is knowable? Yes it is. We have access to the world out there. We aren't just prisoners of our fantasies and dreams. I wanted to make a movie about how the truth is difficult to know, not how it is impossible to know. (Morris, cited in Moyers 1989)

I take Morris here to be speaking of the discovery of truths as facts— the matter of who shot Robert Wood is a matter of fact.

Characterizing a person as rounded or complex is not like discovering who committed a crime, however; it is more than the discovery of a fact or even of an accumulation of facts about a person (although that gets us part way to a round characterization). A round characterization provides a sense of a person's personality, of their deepest motivations and beliefs, of how their psychological characteristics are manifested physically in ges-ture, posture, facial expression and the grain of their voice. It provides a sense of what they think and how they think, how they interact with other people and how other people regard them. It shows us how they change over time. To accurately characterize a person as round is a remarkably difficult task. We might say of a person something like what Winston Churchill reportedly said of Russia: "It is a riddle wrapped in a mystery inside an enigma."

In *Roger and Me* (1988), Michael Moore gives many of the people represented in the film flat characterizations. He associates various officials working for the city of Flint (through "associative editing") with egre-giously awful promotional videos of the city, thus marking them as ridicu-lous. The "rabbit lady," Rhoda Britton, is shown in some scenes selling rabbits for pets or meat, and in one scene we see her butchering a rabbit. This is hardly a fully rounded characterization of Britton, but these scenes will forever characterize her in the minds of the viewers. Contrast this with the scenes of striking coal miners in Barbara Kopple's *Harlan County,*

U.S.A. (1976), where the miners and their families are treated with respect and their representations suggest their dignity as human beings. We see men, women and children at work and at play, on the picket lines and in their homes, playing and singing music, digging for coal, building props to support the mine and operating conveyor belts. What Kopple shows us are images that maintain the integrity of her subjects. The variety of activities and contexts in which she presents these people goes some way to rounding out their portraits, making them complex and multi-dimensional.

Filmmakers, however, do not always have control over how representations will be understood by the audience. Thus, some characterizations may be unintentional, in that an audience may take an image or action as emblematic of "who a person is," although the filmmaker intended no such interpretation. Thus, Moore may not have initially intended that audiences think of Britton as the "crazy rabbit lady"; nevertheless, although he was a neophyte filmmaker when he made *Roger and Me*, we might still expect him to be more sensitive to the potential harm of such a flat characterization.

As I mentioned above, attempts at complex, fully rounded characterizations most often occur in documentary biographies and in other films that expend significant energy on the representation of one or more people. These includes films that focus on a particular person or small group of people. Examples include *Don't Look Back* (1967), which follows Bob Dylan on his 1965 tour of the UK, or *What Happened, Miss Simone?* (2015), about the life of American singer, pianist and civil rights activist Nina Simone. Various of Morris's films focus on important political figures, such as McNamara in *The Fog of War* (2003) and Donald Rumsfeld in *The Unknown Known* (2013). A particularly interesting example is Todd Haynes' *I'm Not There* (2007), although this is clearly not a prototypical documentary, and many would argue that it is not a documentary at all. The film uses several different actors to portray Bob Dylan at various stages of his life and career, and its overall effect is to suggest that the human personality is protean and ultimately mysterious. The film appears to question the notion of personal identity itself, and thus the very possibility of accurate or truthful characterization.

Documentary Characterization: Character Templates

Do certain sorts of characters conventionally appear in documentary films? In other words, do documentaries present a good cross-section of the kinds of people we might meet in our everyday lives? Or do documentaries focus on people who are especially passionate, interesting, articulate or, in some other way, compelling? Do documentary filmmakers employ *a priori* templates to choose people to interview or to focus on? In a fascinating online piece published by the Tribeca Film Institute (Guerrasio 2014), documentary filmmakers are asked: "What makes a perfect documentary character?" They respond with various criteria. Jesse Moss says that he looks for "conflicted characters," who are travelling a "meaningful journey." Romona Diaz asks herself whether the people who are potential subjects for her films are fascinating, and whether the "camera loves them." Chris Hegedus and D.A. Pennebaker, who work in the direct cinema style, admit that they never know "how things will turn out," and so they reserve room for *finding* rather than choosing a character. Nonetheless, they prefer characters who are "totally passionate about what they are doing and about to risk all to pursue a dream," which suggests similarities to the goal-oriented protagonists of classic Hollywood cinema. Robert Greene says that he avoids "quirky characters" but likes characters with "layers to their personalities." While fiction filmmakers cast actors with the right qualities to play specific characters, documentary filmmakers apparently carefully choose those people who offer the right raw material to enable them to construct a fascinating and memorable character.

Documentaries filmed in the style of the formal voice and those filmed in an open-voice style differ in regard to epistemic authority and thus in the confidence with which they characterize the people that appear in the films. Biographical films using the formal voice are more likely to make firm claims about (or imply) a person's character than open-voice films. The latter are often content to show and are more hesitant to explain. For example, Edgar Morin and Jean Rouch's *Chronicle of a Summer* (1961) is content to feature interviews and other shots of the people it represents, but hesitates to draw any conclusions about them either explicitly (there is no explanatory voiceover) or implicitly (through editing or composition, for example). As with *Chronicle of a Summer*, open-voice films are also more likely to recognize some of the difficulties inherent in characterization, and thus more likely to respond by allowing the film's subject to view and comment on the footage prior to editing, offering them some measure of control over their representation. Yet no technique, reflexive or otherwise, can absolve the documentary filmmaker of the need to characterize people. No film can simply show people without implying anything about them, although DuVernay's *13th* comes close to this. *Chronicle of a Summer* portrays its characters as in some ways undefined, but also—to a certain extent—uncertain, questioning, in crisis. But here is the thing: *this is also a kind of character template*. It follows the tradition of international art cinema. David Bordwell's (2008, p. 153) description of the characters in art cinema applies well to the represented subjects of *Chronicle of a Summer*: they "lack defined desires and goals," may "act for inconsistent reasons" or "question themselves about their goals."

Documentary filmmakers may have preconceptions that guide their approach to the people who appear in their films. We have already seen that many filmmakers have a particular sort of character in mind even before the filmmaking process begins. As Brian Winston (1988) claims, the documentary "tradition of the victim" is an example of this, as is the search for the exotic "other," as in the case of the films of Robert Flaherty, with his interest in Polynesian islanders or in "Nanook" and his Inuit tribe in northern Canada. There is also what might be termed the "tradition of the villainous capitalist" seen in the films of Moore, or the "tradition of the self-deluded oddball" in the films of Morris. In characterizing people, documentary filmmakers often work with subconscious categories into which they fit such representations, as the claims of documentary filmmakers (cited above) regarding "appropriate" documentary characters make very clear.

Documentary Characterization: Character Engagement, Protagonists and Antagonists

Although we can legitimately distinguish between documentaries and fiction films in terms of characterization, the two modes do share some common techniques. In relation to fiction films, we often speak of character engagement or, in other words, the vicarious relationship between viewer and represented character. The filmmaker employs various techniques to encourage the viewer to form attitudes and perspectives towards, or antipathies and allegiances for or against, the various characters. Some journalistic filmmakers, and others such as DuVernay in *13th*, attempt to limit any sort of character engagement in the name of preserving that elusive sense of objectivity. Other documentary filmmakers, however, encourage allegiances and antipathies as a means of strengthening and providing a structure for the viewer's emotional involvement. These intended allegiances and antipathies are a primary means by which the narration of a film signals moral or sociopolitical approval or disapproval of a character. Documentary filmmakers often create protagonists and antagonists in their films, and thus character engagement is closely related to the idea of character templates. The filmmaker who exploits the creation of allegiances and antipathies most is Moore, who often casts himself as the ungainly and sympathetic protagonist on a righteous mission to confront evildoers and deliver justice. Murray Smith (1995, pp. 188–227) claims that the viewer's allegiance with a character is created in large part through moral judgment: when a viewer perceives that a character behaves morally, they are more likely to "care" or "root" for, and generally take a sympathetic interest in, the character and their circumstances and goals. In *Roger and Me*, Moore's quest is to confront Roger Smith, the chairman of General Motors, to bring him to Flint to show him the devastation that the closure of the plant has wreaked on the city. Like other well-known documentary filmmakers, including Werner Herzog and, occasionally, Agnes Varda, Moore positions himself as a subject in his films. But his portrayal of himself is hardly a neutral characterization. He becomes the sympathetic protagonist on a righteous mission, confronting powerful obstacles to achieving his goal. At the film's beginning, we learn the history of Moore's family, and even see pictures of him as a baby. Along the way, he travels through an almost surreal landscape, populated by oddballs, victims, eccentrics, celebrities and callous executives. Smith, who becomes the antagonist, is cast as the hypocritical tycoon who refuses to acknowledge the suffering caused by the actions of (what Moore casts as) his greedy corporation. In *Fahrenheit 9/11* (2004), the antagonist becomes George W. Bush, while in *Bowling for Columbine* (2002), it is National Rifle Association head and then-president, retired actor Charlton Heston.

An effective and subtle use of allegiance towards a character is found in *Murder on a Sunday Morning*, the 2002 Academy Award-winning documentary directed by French filmmaker Jean-Xavier Lestrade. The film is about the arrest and trial of a 15-year-old African-American boy, Brenton Butler, for the murder in 2000 of a tourist in Jacksonville, Florida. The prosecution's case rested in large part on the positive identification of Butler by the victim's husband and on Butler's confession, which he and his defense team claimed was coerced. Many characters are developed in the film, including the reticent Butler himself, some of the prosecuting attorneys and detectives, and the husband of the victim. The hero in the case, however, is defense attorney Patrick McGuinness, who gradually takes on the role of sympathetic protagonist, his goal being to prove that his client is innocent and that the tactics of the prosecuting attorney and his investigators are unethical, if not illegal. McGuinness gets the most screen time, and his soft-spoken intelligence and determination, together with his hard-drinking, chain-smoking demeanor, make a powerful impact. We see him in his office, in the courtroom and carting his case documents along the mean streets of Jacksonville.

Audiences are prone to grant their allegiance to McGuinness as it becomes clear that he is morally in the right, defending an innocent victim of injustice, a mere teenager without the maturity to understand, let alone fight, the charges brought against him. And like a fiction film, the viewer's allegiance with McGuinness and sympathy for Butler structure most of the powerful emotions elicited by the film. These are likely to include anger at the tactics of the prosecution and its detectives, suspense as the jury considers its verdict, welcome relief when the boy is found innocent, and admiration for McGuinness.

The fostering of allegiances and antipathies towards characters, then, is another way in which documentary filmmakers characterize the people they represent. In cases such as the films of Moore, and also Lestrade's *Murder on a Sunday Morning*, people are slotted into the roles we might expect in a well-made fiction film—as sympathetic protagonists and morally questionable antagonists. Similar techniques are used in films such as *Enemies of Happiness* (2006) and *The Eagle Huntress* (2016), both of which elicit admiration for courageous young women whose actions run counter to traditional gender roles. The generation of allegiances and antipathies towards various characters in any narrative film is a form of moral or sociopolitical judgment that is stamped on the film by the narration's implicit approval or disapproval of one or more of the characters. This is obviously an important form of characterization.

Documentary Characterization: Image and Sound

The documentary is able to characterize people like no other form of communication because it employs images and sounds. We sometimes encounter claims that film is a visual medium that relies primarily on what can be shown. This is misleading, or a partial truth at best. Of course, films communicate visually, but they also communicate aurally. Furthermore, they

rely centrally on verbal discourse (voiceover narration, intertitles, dialogue). In addition, the claims and implications of a documentary are not
made merely through images, sounds and words, but also by the organization of material through narrative, rhetorical and topical structures of
information, and editing. Thus, film is an eclectic and complex medium of
communication, combining several channels of information
simultaneously.

The cross-modal nature of filmic communication is made abundantly
clear in the use of the interview, which combines images, sounds and
words (Grindon 2007). The use of recorded images and sounds is central
to the strengths documentaries have in characterizing people. Béla Balász
(1999, pp. 306–307) notes the importance of the human face in film,
which can be displayed prominently through the close-up. The recorded
image of the face reveals the outward signs of emotion, mood, intention
and thought, and thus, Balász shows, the close-up takes the spectator from
the outer realm of broad physical space into the minute realm of physiog-
nomy and the inner world of psychology. All of the recorded images and
sounds in an interview provide visual and aural information not only about
what a person said, and not only about the face and facial expression, but
also about the gestures, postures and vocal inflections that were revealed
in the saying of it. Filmed interviews are far superior to printed interviews
in their value for characterization because they provide not only the verbal
record of the interview, but also reveal the manifold expressions of the
human body that make interpersonal communication such a rich and
vibrant text.

All things being equal, the filmed interview is a marvelous means of
characterizing people. The printed interview gives little sense of the bodily
existence of the interviewee, and next to language, the body is the richest
source of communication. The filmed interview provides hints about the
sincerity, depth of feeling, confidence and vehemence with which something is said. To use Smith's (1995, pp. 142–186) terminology with regard
to character engagement, the interview can align us with a character by
providing both "subjective access" and "spatio-temporal attachment" to
their subjectivity. The interview can also put into play processes of emotional contagion and affective mimicry (Plantinga 2009, pp. 123–136).
(These processes are precisely what DuVernay worked so hard to eliminate
in the interviews she uses in *13th*.) All things being equal, seeing and hearing the filmed interview is closer to being present at an actual interview
than reading the printed transcript. The degree to which viewers can learn

from such a filmed interview depends on their perceptiveness and ability to interpret social and bodily communication cues, as well as on the skill of the interviewer. Yet, the potential is there to mine the depths of character and personality.

Morris has worked for years to perfect the art of the filmed interview. He invented a device, the "interrotron," that provides a screen with his live video image directly below the camera, so that the interviewee appears to be speaking and responding to the camera itself. Thus, Morris can sit away from the camera and conduct the interview as though he were occupying the space of the camera. He has only gradually become interested in rounded, complex characterizations. For his initial films, *Gates of Heaven* (1978), *Vernon Florida* (1980) and *The Thin Blue Line* (1988), he interviewed a cross section of people, all of whom were connected with the particular subject of each film. Most of the interviews are relatively brief, such that the views of those involved tend to be stereotypical, sacrificing depth of characterization for an exploration, respectively, of human–pet relationships, eccentric small town America and a murder mystery. Later in his career, in films such as *A Brief History of Time* (1991), *The Fog of War* (2003), *Tabloid* (2010) and *The Unknown Known* (2013), he began to concentrate on one person (Stephen Hawking, Robert McNamara, Joyce McKinney and Donald Rumsfeld, respectively), allowing for the more full-bodied portrait that constitutes a rounded characterization.

Another tool is that hallmark of cinema vérité, observational footage, which became possible with the development of portable cameras and sound recording equipment in the late 1950s. In films of the open voice, which tend to rely on such footage and refuse the explanations of a voiceover narrator, the filmmaker is more likely to withhold explicit characterization and to rely, to some extent, on the power of the film medium to give the audience images and sounds that reveal the behavior of a person. The more the filmmaker attempts to mold viewer perceptions of character through editing, music and shot composition, for example, the further toward the formal and away from the open (or observational) voice the film moves. Albert and David Maysles followed door-to-door salesman Paul Brennan as he visited his clients, attempting to sell very expensive bibles, and the resulting film, *Salesman* (1969), provides one of the most intriguing characterizations in the history of observational cinema.

The use of such "observational" footage as a tool of characterization raises questions about the influence of the camera on the behavior of the people filmed. American documentary filmmaker Frederick Wiseman claims that the presence of the camera actually causes people to act *naturally*, while the Maysles observe that if a small film crew hangs around the film's subject for a long period of time, the novelty wears off and the subject stops paying much attention to it. Such determinations concerning the influence of the camera, however, can only be made in specific cases, in relation to the perceived intentions of the filmmaker, the subjects' perceptions of self, and the nature and context of the subject-filmmaker encounter in relation to the topic of the documentary.

These are only the most obvious techniques of characterization in the documentary. As experienced filmmakers understand, each shot composition, each edit and each camera movement also raises implications about the people being filmed. Early in his career, Wiseman was prone to flat characterizations and expressions of seeming contempt toward some of the subjects of his films, expressions that are revealed in the way his cinematographer filmed the subjects and Wiseman edited the footage. In *High School* (1968), for example, we see several scenes of teachers and high-school students in the classroom. For some reason, the cinematographer zooms in on extreme close-ups of the noses and spectacles of the some of the teachers, making them seem somewhat grotesque (as I discuss further below). In another scene, a hall monitor walks the corridors and looks through the window in a door; Wiseman then cuts to a shot of young women exercising in a gymnasium, thus suggesting that the hall monitor is leering at them. Whether the man was leering or not only Wiseman knows. The point is that the opportunities for both subtle and blatant characterizations such as these are magnified in all uses of film techniques.

THE ETHICS OF CHARACTERIZATION

We have seen that the documentary faces a paradox. On the one hand, the documentary filmmaker's characterizations are to some extent constructions: they cannot be perfectly wrought imitations or transparent records of who a person is or was. No representation could achieve that idealized goal. On the other hand, the documentary filmmaker has ethical obligations that the fiction filmmaker does not. If the characterizations in documentaries are constructions, they are still not fictions. Instead, they are bound by requirements of truth-telling and a "duty of care" toward the represented person.

What are the ethical obligations of filmmakers toward the people they represent? In my account of the documentary as a film of "asserted veridical representation," I have argued that in presenting a film as a documentary, the filmmaker implicitly asserts both that its images and sounds are accurate guides to what occurred in front of the camera and that its claims and implications are true of the actual world. Characterizations are not transparent imitations, yet they can be more or less accurate, more or less misleading. Therefore, one of the ethical obligations of filmmakers is to represent the truth, as they understand it, to the best of their ability (Plantinga 1997, pp. 219–222).

In regard to characterization, however, honesty and truth-telling are not the only ethical obligations, and moreover, they can be trumped by the duty of care. A duty of care is an ethical or legal obligation that entails that a person or organization avoids acts or omissions that can be reasonably foreseen to cause harm to others. A duty of care, as I conceive of it in relation to documentary, demands that (under most circumstances) filmmakers characterize people with care and sensitivity, granting them respect and integrity whenever appropriate and possible. (It may be the case that some people, in some situations, do not deserve such a duty of care, but I will leave that discussion for another occasion.) It is possible to present facts about people, or to display actual documentary footage and sound recordings of people, that may harm them. For example, in choosing to foreground a teacher's spectacles in extreme close-up in *High School*, Wiseman could be said to be uncharitable in his implication that the teacher is pitiable. Wiseman's teacher did actually wear spectacles, so there is a sense in which he shows us what was actually there. But why zoom in to extreme close-ups of those spectacles, making the teacher look somewhat pathetic? Why choose to include footage of the teacher that makes them look petty, mean or unintelligent, when he should have had footage that shows them in a less negative light? In this case, the footage Wiseman shows is technically accurate (the teacher in question did wear spectacles), yet in his selection and omission of footage he arguably shows the teacher in an unfavorable light, and without any motivation other than an implied moral judgment.

Suppose that the filmmaker is making a film about a living historical figure, and has gathered hours of interviews and observational footage, all of it reliable in the sense that it displays the subjects' actual behavior and what they actually said. An enormously difficult job of characterization lies ahead of the filmmaker in deciding which footage to use and how to structure it. Each selection and omission, each decision about how to organize the material, at both the local and global level, has rhetorical implications for the characterization of that person.

As I claimed in the introduction to this chapter, the tension of the prototypical documentary is that it claims to be reliable in what it records and reveals, but it is simultaneously a subjective, constructed representation. This tension has implications for documentary ethics. One ethical obligation of the documentary filmmaker is to maintain standards of accuracy and adhere to practices and representations that will not mislead viewers. The filmmaker might have other ethical obligations, however, such as a duty of care, that override the obligations of veridicality. In these cases, the filmmaker will have to weigh up the conflicting obligations. All of this leads to complex and unique ethical considerations for the documentary filmmaker.

Acknowledgments Some paragraphs in this chapter are taken from an earlier work (Plantinga 2008). The author would like to thank the editors for their insightful comments on an earlier version of this contribution.

References

Balász, B. (1999) "The Close-Up," in Mast, G., Cohen, M. and Braudy, L. (eds.) *Film Theory and Criticism: Introductory Readings*. 5th edn. Oxford: Oxford University Press, pp. 306–307.

Bordwell, D. (2008) *Poetics of Cinema*. New York: Routledge.

Carroll, N. (1983) "From Real to Reel: Entangled in the Nonfiction Film," *Philosophic Exchange*, 14, pp. 5–46.

Goffman, E. (1959) *The Presentation of Self in Everyday Life*. New York, Anchor Books.

Grindon, L. (2007) "Q&A: Poetics of the Documentary Film Interview." *Velvet Light Trap: A Critical Journal of Film and Television*, 60, pp. 4–12.

Guerrasio, J. (2014) "9 Filmmakers Tell Us What Make the Perfect Documentary Character," *Tribecca Film Institute* [Online]. Available at: https://tribecafilminstitute.org/blog/detail/9_filmmakers_tell_us_what_makes_the_perfect_documentary_character (Accessed: January 27, 2017).

Moyers, B. (1989) "Bill Moyers Interviews Errol Morris on 'The Thin Blue Line'," *Public Broadcasting System* [Online]. Available at: https://www.youtube.com/watch?v=OU4HG2QAIrI (Accessed: August 4, 2017).

Nichols, B. (1991) *Representing Reality: Issues and Concepts in Documentary*. Bloomington: Indiana University Press.

Nichols, B. (2017) "Letter to Errol Morris: Feelings of Revulsion and the Limits of Academic Discourse," in LaRocca, D. (ed.) *The Philosophy of Documentary Film: Image, Sound, Fiction, Truth.* Lanham: Lexington Books, pp. 453–458.

Plantinga, C. (1997) *Rhetoric and Representation in Nonfiction Film.* Cambridge: Cambridge University Press.

Plantinga, C. (2005) "What a Documentary Is, After All," *Journal of Aesthetics and Art Criticism,* 63(2), pp. 105–117.

Plantinga, C. (2008) "Caracterización y ética en el género documental." Translated by María Calzada and Irene De Higes Andino. *Archivos de la Filmoteca,* 57–58(1), pp. 46–67.

Plantinga, C. (2009) *Moving Viewers: American Film and the Spectator's Experience.* Berkeley: University of California Press.

Plantinga, C. (2017) "The Limits of Appropriation: Subjectivist Accounts of the Fiction/Nonfiction Distinction," in LaRocca, D. (ed.) *The Philosophy of Documentary Film: Image, Sound, Fiction, Truth.* Lanham: Lexington Books, pp. 113–124.

Smith, M. (1995) *Engaging Characters: Fiction, Emotion, and the Cinema.* Oxford: Clarendon Press.

Winston, B. (1988) "The Tradition of the Victim in Griersonian Documentary," in Rosenthal, A. (ed.) *New Challenges for Documentary.* Berkeley: University of California Press, pp. 269–287.

CHAPTER 8

The Difficulty of Eliciting Empathy in Documentary

Jan Nåls

INTRODUCTION

Eliciting audience empathy is one of the most sought-after objectives of documentary filmmakers—and one of the hardest to achieve. In recent years, empathy has emerged as a key concept in the understanding and construction of documentary narrative. As documentary film producer Tabitha Jackson (cited in Curtis 2014) states: "There are incredibly important stories to be told, and injustices to be highlighted. A documentary camera is a kind of empathy machine. A documentary can put you in someone else's shoes." However, it appears that eliciting empathy with screen characters is one of the most challenging tasks a documentary filmmaker can face, and although many filmmakers display a well-meaning desire to create films that evoke an empathetic response, they frequently fail in the attempt. This chapter examines the gap between authorial intention and audience impact as exemplified by two contemporary South African documentaries, *Miners Shot Down* (2014) and *I, Afrikaner* (2013), both of which pursue the goal of empathy for social, cultural and activist reasons. The choice of these films was informed by their strong

J. Nåls (✉)
Arcada University of Applied Sciences, Helsinki, Finland
e-mail: jan.nals@arcada.fi

© The Author(s) 2018
C. Brylla, M. Kramer (Eds.), *Cognitive Theory and Documentary Film*, https://Doi.org/10.1007/978-3-319-90332-3_8

135

sociocultural agendas and their stated intent to reach a wider audience outside South Africa, their country of origin. Documentary has the potential to express a sense of common humanity, one based on the arousal of empathy with characters from different cultures and social contexts. This chapter explores, both from an academic and from a film-practice perspective, how and why the films in these two case studies do not realize this potential, and what can be learnt from their shortcomings.

The potential for documentary filmmakers to fall prey to the fallacy that audience responses automatically match their intentions can be verified theoretically, as well as confirmed through my own experience with teaching documentary practice. From a theoretical perspective, this fallacy implicitly presumes that what Stuart Hall calls the "dominant-hegemonic" construct of the audience viewing position is the norm in filmmaking. This is predicated on the receiver interpreting the meaning of a message in the exact way the sender intended—that is, the encoding matches the decoding. However, as Hall (1980, p. 136) notes, the act of viewing involves several reading positions, and "decodings do not follow inevitably from encodings." Similarly, Vivian Sobchack (1992) argues that film is a dialogue between the filmmaker and the spectator, since both are viewing subjects. She claims that the film experience is an interplay or "commutation" between the authorial expression of the filmmaker's perception and the spectatorial perception of that expression (p. 35). As this is not a symmetrical relationship—the filmmaker's and the spectator's perception will only converge to a varying degree—Sobchack warns against the conflation of authorial expression and audience perception, an assumption that mistakenly holds that the locus of perception lies solely within the text (p. 16).

These theoretical observations are supported by my personal experience as a lecturer in documentary practice. I have been researching and advocating for empathy in documentaries for the better part of ten years; however, both I (as a supervisor) and my students (as filmmakers) have frequently fallen short of our intentions—a retrospective insight gained through a process of critical reflection in the teaching-learning context. This quandary was palpable when I coordinated (and taught on) a recent transcultural documentary film exchange program between Finland, South Africa and Ghana. Its aim was not only to produce a practical outcome,[1] but also to enhance cultural understanding through the use of

---

[1] This outcome was the "Documentary and Diversity" exchange programme, funded by the North South South Exchange (NSSE). This scheme, devised by the Finnish Foreign Ministry, aims to enhance cultural understanding and build academic networks linking Africa and Europe.

documentary as a method of inquiry. The frustrations and joys of the practical side of documentary filmmaking highlighted the challenges involved in creating a sense of empathy in a transcultural setting, especially in a postcolonial and social-activist context in which eliciting empathy with the screen characters is not just a challenge but a necessity.

In the two case studies discussed here, the filmmakers' intentions and their films' shortcomings, in terms of evoking audience empathy, is explored in a two-stage process. This involves first evaluating empirical data related to the films' distribution context and then using a cognitive analysis of the film text to hypothesize the "actual" impact on the spectator. The first stage (collating the empirical data) reveals that both films, *Miners Shot Down* and *I, Afrikaner*, have the intention of eliciting character empathy within a sociocultural context—the former in relation to social activism and the latter in relation to undoing cultural stereotypes. The filmmakers openly proclaimed their objectives in interviews and written statements, but these goals are also manifest in paratexts, such as the films' trailers, posters and press kits. The second stage of the analysis uses Amy Coplan's (2011) model of high-level empathy, in conjunction with appraisal theory (Wondra and Ellsworth 2015) and theories of characterization, to perform a textual analysis. The results appear to partly contradict the authorial intentions, revealing that the films' failure to establish empathy is mainly due to the following factors:

1. The filmmakers favor rational argumentation and sociocultural contextualization over the sort of emotional argumentation that potentially encourages empathy.
2. They neglect important elements of characterization, in particular the establishment of character motivation in relation to their goals or objects of desire.

My aim is not to discredit these two important and (in many ways) affecting films, or their creators, but rather to raise critical awareness of the tension between the filmmakers' intentions and the audience response, thus generating knowledge about the relationship between narrative empathy and authorship that could prove of benefit to scholars, practitioners and educators alike. Having seen many examples of flawed narratives and character portrayals in the pedagogic as well as the professional filmmaking sphere, I deliberately chose to analyze films that only partially fail to achieve their purpose—a somewhat unusual endeavor in the field of documentary film studies, but nonetheless an insightful one.

MINERS SHOT DOWN

Miners Shot Down (2014) is a documentary by writer/director Rehad Desai and writer/producer Anita Khanna, produced by Uhuru Productions, a South African company, in collaboration with various European and Japanese broadcasters (IKON, SVT, YLE, DR TV, RTS, NRK and NHK). The film gives an account of one of the most dramatic and traumatic events in contemporary South African history. Its press release summarizes the story as follows:

> In August 2012, mineworkers in one of South Africa's biggest platinum mines began a wildcat strike for better wages. Six days later, the police used live ammunition to brutally suppress the strike, killing 34 and injuring many more. Using the point of view of the Marikana miners, *Miners Shot Down* follows the strike from day one up until the culminating massacre, showing the courageous but isolated fight waged by a group of low-paid workers against the combined forces of the mining company, Lonmin, the ANC government and their allies in the National Union of Mineworkers. (Miners Shot Down 2017)

Since its release, the film has achieved a significant amount of international exposure and critical success, winning an International Emmy Award for Best Documentary in 2015.

Sometime before the massacre took place, the filmmakers were in the process of making an activist film about climate change for COP 17, the United Nations Climate Change Conference in Durban, when they were approached with a request to make a film about mining in South Africa. Khanna (cited in Frassinelli 2016, p. 423) recalls the start of the process, when they decided to focus on characters rather than solely on facts and arguments: "We were looking for a story with characters. We wanted to find a story that would work in a film. We didn't just want to go somewhere and talk about the issues." Similarly, the director, Desai (cited in Leiman 2014), told an interviewer that they wanted to engage an international audience by telling a powerful story: "Listening and telling stories is a human need, they help us make sense of ourselves and our wider world. This was a big story that needed to be accessible not only to all South Africans but the wider world." In another interview, Desai asserted that their goal was to use the power of the film to provoke a reaction in the viewers and inspire them to act:

That's the power of film: to put it all together in a story form, characterise the subjects, humanise the victims, provide the necessary context. And then you know their side of the story. You can make people complicit, and in making them feel complicit in the story, you get a willingness to act on it. (Desai cited in Frassinelli 2016, p. 425)

The aim of the filmmakers was to tell the miners' side of the story and thus elicit empathy for them amongst a global audience. The latter comment from Desai, however, suggests a parallel and perhaps contradictory agenda: the filmmakers were seeking to shock the audience into feeling complicit in the massacre by inducing a sense of guilt, based on an assumption that the viewers' position (in terms of ethnicity, race, culture and social class) is one of power and privilege in relation to that of the miners. These different intentions are evident in the film's three promotional posters, which mediate the miners' point of view from different perspectives. One depicts a demonstration of mineworkers, where the group is uniform in both size and appearance. The second also shows a demonstration but with a specific individual in the foreground, implying that this is perhaps the main character with whom audiences can empathize. The third simply depicts a pair of shoes. These belong to a faceless miner, devoid of identity, who lies dead on the ground. As their interviews suggest, the filmmakers' main objective was to "use the miners' point of view," "to tell their side of story," in order to encourage audience members to empathize with the mineworkers, arousing in them a desire for social activism.

Empathy is one of the primary ways in which we emotionally engage with one another in daily life, and film scholars agree that this emotional engagement also occurs with characters in screen narratives (Livingston and Plantinga 2008, pp. 102–103). Coplan (2011, pp. 4–5) argues that high-level empathy depends on three stages: affective matching, other-oriented perspective-taking and clear self–other differentiation.

"Affective matching" indicates that we have managed to match another individual's emotion or affect; "other-oriented perspective-taking" then allows us to imagine ourselves in another's situation, evaluating it from their perspective; finally, "clear self-other differentiation" enables us to engage on a deep level with the other, while preventing us from losing sight of where the self ends and the other begins. Without differentiation, we run the risk of failing to empathize; instead, we become enmeshed in our emotions and let our imaginative process become "contaminated" by our self-perspective, ending up with an emotional simulation that does not in fact replicate the experience of the other (Coplan 2011, p. 16). In relation to the second stage, appraisal theories argue that emotional experience is based on an observer's evaluative interpretation (or appraisal) of another's particular situation, and this is the crucial determinant of the observer's vicarious emotional experiences, including that of empathy (Wondra and Ellsworth 2015, p. 418). Empathy presupposes that the observer's appraisal equals that of the subject (p. 424). Thus, if the filmmaker wants to elicit empathy with screen characters, it is vital that they ensure the thorough characterization of their subjects and the concretization of their subjects' circumstances.

Richard Dyer and Paul McDonald (1998, pp. 104–113), in their analysis of the "novelistic conception of character," provide examples of some relevant aspects of characterization. Believable novelistic characters possess traits such as particularity, interiority, roundness, development and motive—in effect, the opposite of stereotypes, which produce flat, prototypical characters who generally function through one main character trait that appears impervious to change. Whether stereotypical traits are positive or negative, a viewer is less likely to engage emotionally with a character who does not reveal new traits or have a goal or object of desire that triggers their development. In contrast, rounded characters are defined by a multiplicity of traits that form a complex whole (p. 105). A rounded character is predisposed to invite empathy since multiple character traits are likely to evoke associations in viewers which activate emotional responses corresponding to the emotions displayed by the screen character.

Miners Shot Down begins with a voiceover by Desai, stating that the events at Marikana shook him "to the core." What ensues is a story that tries to discover who was responsible for the killings. This dramatic question helps to establish a narrative situation, and the film follows the sequence of events to the very end, when the 34 miners are killed by the police. The film does not have a single main character but, instead, features a unified group of striking mineworkers. However, Coplan's empathy model requires affective matching with the mental state of another individual, and this is partly inhibited in the film by its collectivizing effect. For example, at the beginning, we are introduced to three miners who are named individuals (two of them, Tholakele Dlunga and Mzoxolo Magidiwana, are interviewees, and the third, Mgcineni Noki, is one of the victims). However, Dlunga and Magidiwana are identified as "strike leaders"; they advance the narrative in their *collective* function as participants and eyewitnesses but (crucially) not as actual *individuals* who are affected by the events. The film denies us insight into the mental state of any individual miner, whether visually or recounted through interviews. Both Dlunga and Magidiwana are shown giving interviews after the event, but they do not reveal their emotional state before, during or after the strike and the massacre. Indeed, they express no emotion other than a sustained anger at the perceived injustice—at one moment, Magidiwana waves his finger at the camera in fury. Affective matching with the miners is therefore difficult since emotions are repeatedly toned down in favor of rational arguments, factual information and the fixed emotion of collective anger against the establishment. This apparent focus on accounts of the event and of social injustice in lieu of personalized stories also inhibits other-oriented perspectives, as personal situational cues are omitted. Magidiwana, for example, was permanently disabled when he was shot by the police, but this fact is never revealed in the film; he is denied the opportunity to display his feelings about the implications of his disability.

Interestingly, however, the film meets Coplan's third criterion of self–other differentiation. Most of the time, the miners are portrayed from a relative distance as a uniform group, all displaying congruous character traits, as well as possessing similar social and ethnic identities. Nevertheless, fulfilling this criterion alone is not enough to generate empathy, and it contradicts Dyer's and McDonald's concept of "rounded characters," which is an essential prerequisite for the understanding of multilayered individuals.

In term of goals, the miners share a common objective at the start of the film: higher wages. Later in the narrative, this is reduced to the goal of talks with the management, and later still, to mere survival. Paradoxically, although they must continuously face different levels of conflict, the miners are not shown as changing or developing during the narrative. This is partly because the film does not pursue individual stories and goals; when instances of development do occur, they do so in a collective fashion. Furthermore, the specific motive for the miner's actions remains unclear. Their "macro motive" is the pursuit of more pay to alleviate their poverty (which is made plain through their general appearance and their overall working conditions), but there are no "micro motives" that reveal what is at stake for individuals, such as how their precarious circumstances specifically affect them and their families. The plot also lacks a set-up or igniting incident—an event that disrupts the status quo of the main characters—to account for even the collective developments, since we are thrust into the middle of the dramatic narrative as it begins to unfold. This way, the socio-historical gravitas and the political and social implications of the event are once again foregrounded at the expense of individual stories.

As mentioned earlier, the miners' on-screen characters are determined by the fact that they belong to a particular profession.[2] As such, they display several congruous traits, such as courage, passion, powerlessness, hope and despair, but these are portrayed as collective characteristics. They are all uneducated and illiterate, to give one example, which makes it far harder for them to reach their goals. In one poignant scene, the miners are given a written message from the management, but the miner who receives the message cannot accept it as he cannot read. No one comes to his aid—no one else can read either.

It is interesting to note that, perhaps inadvertently, the film portrays the miners' adversaries with more individual roundness and narrative development. For instance, billionaire businessman, Cyril Ramaphosa[3] is portrayed as the central culprit, the man who is possibly to blame for urging the police to act so forcefully against the striking miners. At the same time, he is the only character in the narrative to undergo any sort of meaningful change, even if he is given much less screen time than the miners themselves. The director of the mining company explains his earlier admiration for Ramaphosa, who was formerly the leader of the mineworker's union under the apartheid regime and a close associate of Nelson Mandela, but who has apparently been corrupted by wealth and power, and is now acting against the interests of those he used to represent. Purely in terms of narrative exposition, this example of characterization renders Ramaphosa the character in the film with the highest potential for empathy—an outcome that is unlikely to have been the conscious aim of the filmmakers given the content of their publicity statements.

Nevertheless, the film does contain occasional scenes that carry the potential for empathy. One such scene shows AMCU[4] leader, Joseph Mathunjwa, breaking down in tears when he recalls the brutal events and his inability to stop the tragedy. This allows for temporary affective matching and other-oriented perspective-taking, while maintaining a clear self-

[2] This approach to narrative echoes that of Sergei Eisenstein (1969), who chose to use specific categorical "types" to represent entire social classes or interests in his films, which feature class struggles.

[3] Cyril Ramaphosa was elected president of the African National Congress (ANC) in December 2017 and president of South Africa in February 2018.

[4] The Association of Mineworkers and Construction Union.

other differentiation. The problem is that Mathunjwa is not one of the miners, and our empathy is steered temporarily towards a minor character who represents institutions and interests that lie outside the central narrative thread. All in all, there are significant barriers preventing spectatorial empathy with any one of the group of miners at the center of the unfolding narrative, in sharp contrast to the filmmakers' stated intentions.

I, Afrikaner

The documentary, *I, Afrikaner* (2013), similarly explores some of the deep divides in South African society but this time from the perspective of characters belonging to the Afrikaner minority. The film is directed by Annalet Steenkamp and produced by South African companies Go Trolley Films and Film Shebeen. Its press kit offers the following synopsis:

> *I, Afrikaner* is an intimate family saga, following four generations of South African Boers as they grapple with their identity as white farmers in a post-Apartheid South Africa, where land ownership is highly contentious, and violence and racism are endemic. Blacks and whites live largely segregated lives, and the farmers—who still constitute the propertied and employing classes—experience a growth of violent murders, which threaten their way of life. (Steenkamp 2017)

The director stated her intentions in a press release: "With *I, Afrikaner* I look behind stereotype to delve underneath my contentious skin and reflect on the intimate lives that are dear to me: the four generations of my Boer family" (Steenkamp 2017). She continues that there is a need for an "honest" film about the Afrikaner dilemma. Her intention to pursue an "honest" (and "intimate") approach is evident from the poster of the film, as well as from its press material: the poster depicts Steenkamp's grandmother asleep in in bed, while the press kit contains photographs of some of the characters in the film, often in a private space, such as their home or backyard, or in a public space but caught engrossed in private emotions, when attending a funeral, for example, or embracing a child in church. The intention of the director is to bring the characters as close as possible to the audience, to put the viewers in their shoes, in order to elicit empathy with them. This strategy is also present in the film itself, which constantly uses extreme close-ups of the characters, their objects and their everyday actions, alternating with wide shots of the dry and largely empty landscape they inhabit.

I, Afrikaner does not have one obvious main character; rather, it features a range of characters—all part of the four generations of Steenkamp's family. Her grandfather and grandmother feature only at the beginning and end of the film, but their circumstances change during the story: the grandmother moves away from the family farm while her husband passes away. However, the film does not portray the characters changing as persons; their traits remain fixed. One character who is different in this regard is Shanel, the director's niece, who undergoes a transformative change during the narrative. She is also (together with her grandmother) the character most regularly shot in close-up, as she slowly reveals her inner self. Steenkamp herself is present only at the very beginning of the narrative and does not undergo any significant character development on screen. Thus, since the director is a distanced, intra-diegetic narrator rather than the main narrative character, it is Shanel who emerges as the character with the most potential for eliciting empathy.

Shanel is a rounded character. She displays traits such as kindness, independence, generosity, self-confidence, self-doubt and courage, and she states her object of desire very clearly: she wants Afrikaners and black South Africans to live in peace with each other in a more equal society in which resources are distributed more evenly. The tangibility of her object of desire, however, is not apparent: it is hard to know when or how her dream of peace will be fulfilled. Thus, Shanel is constructed as a character who believes in the future. But this hope is challenged when a neighbor and close friend is murdered. This event provokes a dramatic change in Shanel: she no longer wants to visit her black friends and stays alone at home, refusing to interact with anyone, not even the filmmaker. She is transformed from an active, hopeful character into a passive, despairing one. The last shot of Shanel, however, shows her singing an emotional song in a school performance. She is smiling and seems to have regained a little of her hope and trust in the future, although whether this is the case remains somewhat ambiguous. In any case, she is portrayed throughout as a complex character, particularly as her family background and the attitudes of her close relatives make it hard for her to reach her object of desire: a peaceful relationship between Afrikaners and black South Africans.

Despite this, in terms of empathy, the overall characterization in the film is flawed: not even Shanel, the most developed character, fulfills the different aspects of characterization cited by Dyer and McDonald (1998). For example, Shanel's motives remain unclear: why does she wish for a peaceful solution when everyone around her—be it her family or other members of the Afrikaner community—believe in defending their own interests, often with violence? Shanel is an outsider in this respect, but we are not given access to the reasons why she has adopted this position. Hence, our understanding of her character is undermined, and any potential sense of empathy is further diminished by the fact that she is just one of several characters featured. The others share similar flaws in their on-screen portrayal as the motives behind their actions remain equally hidden. The narrative also fails to establish an igniting incident that would mark the beginning of the story and perhaps the establishment of motive. As viewers, it is hard for us to appraise Shanel's or any other characters' situation in the way they understand it themselves; this means that, according to appraisal theory (Wondra and Ellsworth 2015), our empathy is diminished.

I, Afrikaner does, however, display an abundance of emotional scenes. In one, Hester, the directors' grandmother, speaks with tears in her eyes about leaving the farm where she has spent the past 40 years. In another scene, Shanel cries as she recounts her family's racial prejudice. These and other scenes may fleetingly invite affective matching, as advocated by Coplan (2011)—viewers may be inclined to recognize the emotions (such as sadness or anger) on display—but they do not necessarily provide for other-oriented perspective-taking since the narrative situations remain unresolved and unclear. For this reason, even though *I, Afrikaner* features one rounded individual, Shanel, who undergoes meaningful change, her actions are more likely to invite sympathy than empathy. Suzanne Keen (2006, p. 209) summarizes the difference between the two emotions: she describes empathy as "feeling-with" ("I feel what You feel. I feel Your pain.") as opposed to sympathy or "feeling-for" ("I feel a supportive emotion about Your feelings. I feel pity for Your pain.") Thus, sympathy may be a type of *engagement* but, unlike empathy, it is not a type of *identification*.

Although the reasons for individual characters' actions remain obscure, the collective reasons for their suffering are clear: the looming presence of violence, caused by South Africa's social and ethnic divisions. Other collective conflicts include the harsh economic realities of their lives, the challenges of the natural environment (for example, the wild animals) and the threat of robbers. The film, however, does not show any instance of conflict between individuals; the Afrikaners are never portrayed in direct conflict with one another or with characters outside of the family. Shanel mentions that she disagrees with the rest of her family on many issues, but any individual conflicts or clashes she might experience as a result are not depicted. Fear and hatred are often touched upon as generalized emotions representing wider social and ethnic conflicts, and although these conflicts also represent obstacles to Shanel's desire for peace between the different ethnic groups, the narrative mainly treats them as collective concerns. In a similar way to *Miners Shot Down*, the film favors the construction and exposition of shared contextual concerns that account for deeply rooted social conflicts. While these explain the overall situation of shared suffering, the motivations for the individuals' actions, based on their appraisal of this situation, are omitted, and the potential for arousing empathy is diminished.

CONCLUSION

This chapter has proposed the narrative generation of empathy as a conceptual framework for the discussion of authorial intent and its hypothesized effects on documentary audiences. In contrast to the declared intentions of the filmmakers, the two films discussed here fall somewhat short in the construction of empathy, both in terms of characterization and narrative situation. *Miners Shot Down* favors rational argument and shies away from showing its characters' emotional states. The miners are portrayed throughout as a uniform group and no individual emerges with whom viewers could empathize. The only character who is represented as a rounded individual, and who experiences the sort of meaningful change that potentially could elicit empathy, is blamed for sanctioning the massacre. By contrast, *I, Afrikaner* does not shy away from showing its characters as individuals in intimate moments and in varying emotional states. Nevertheless, in both films, most of the characters have minimal character traits and do not undergo any meaningful personal development. In addition, neither their personal narratives nor their motives and goals are revealed, and this impairs the ability of the audience to form the sort of appraisal that could generate an emotional response and, ultimately, lead to empathy.

However, in both films, there is no lack of sociocultural and political contextualization, conforming to at least some of the filmmakers' stated aims of encouraging political activism and social awareness. The reasons for the characters' suffering are clearly illustrated by the corresponding abundance of scenes of shared conflict; however, this contextualization is achieved at the expense of individual character development, which largely precludes identification through empathetic engagement. In a sense, the characters are left hanging in an intricately contextualized story world; they are disempowered by being denied a rounded individuality.

The resulting lack of empathy renders it highly questionable whether the activist and awareness-raising aims of the films have been actually achieved, despite the richness of their contextualization. But whether this is the case or not, the filmmakers' overall aim of encouraging audiences to identify with the screen characters is unlikely to have been fulfilled.

Although the "why" of the suffering is clearly present in both films, what is lacking is an attempt to expose the "why" of the characters' existence and agency in relation to that suffering. The reasons behind this are perhaps linked to the extent of the polarization that not only marks South Africa's political history but also its current political situation. On visits to the country with other Western filmmakers and film students, I have observed that the differences between ethnic and racial groups inevitably come to the fore in any discussions; politics is ubiquitous and individuals seem to construct their identities around ethnicity, race and political affiliation. This holds true for many South African filmmakers as well, who tend to represent individuals' behavior as determined by their affiliation to larger groups, thus placing flat characters in complex contexts. Arguably, the opposite is true for Western filmmakers, who tend to favor individual stories that portray rounded characters in flat or generic contexts lacking social and cultural depth. Perhaps documentary filmmakers who want to elicit empathy *and* expose sociocultural issues need to strike a balance and include both the "why" of suffering and the "why" of character. In order to empathize with the other, it is not enough to observe a character suffering or to understand the global reasons behind it, we also need to understand the reasons behind the actions they take (or their refusal or inability to act) as a consequence of that suffering.

REFERENCES

Coplan, A. (2011) "Understanding Empathy: Its Features and Effects," in Coplan, A. and Goldie, P. (eds.) *Empathy: Philosophical and Psychological Perspectives.* Oxford: Oxford University Press, pp. 2–18.

Curtis, S. (2014) "Championing Documentary as an Empathy Machine: Tabitha Jackson Joins the Sundance Institute," *International Documentary Association: Documentary Magazine* [Online]. Available at: http://www.documentary.org/magazine/championing-documentary-empathy-machine-tabitha-jackson-joins-sundance-institute (Accessed: September 2, 2017).

Dyer, R. and McDonald, P. (1998) *Stars.* 2nd edn. London: British Film Institute.

Eisenstein, S. (1969) *Film Form: Essays in Film Theory.* New York: Harcourt.

Frassinelli, P. P. (2016) "The Making and Political Life of Miners Shot Down: An Interview with Rehad Desai and Anita Khanna," *Communicatio: South African Journal for Communication and Research,* 42(3). pp. 422–432.

Hall, S. ([1973] 1980) "Encoding/Decoding," in Centre for Contemporary Cultural Studies (ed.) *Culture, Media, Language: Working Papers in Cultural Studies, 1972–79.* London: Hutchinson, pp. 128–138.

Keen, S. (2006) "A Theory of Narrative Empathy," *Narrative*, 14(3), pp. 207–236.

Leiman, L. (2014) "Director Rehad Desai Talks about the Making of the Documentary Miners Shot Down," *Between 10and5: The Creative Showcase* [Online]. Available at: http://10and5.com/2014/09/01/director-rehad-desai-talks-about-the-making-of-the-documentary-miners-shot-down/ (Accessed: September 2, 2017).

Livingston, P. and Plantinga, C. (eds.) (2008) *The Routledge Companion to Philosophy and Film.* London: Routledge.

Miners Shot Down (2017) *Miners Shot Down* Press Kit [Online]. Available at: http://www.minersshotdown.co.za/press-kitdate (Accessed: September 2, 2017).

Sobchack, V. (1992) *The Address of the Eye: A Phenomenology of the Film Experience.* Princeton, NJ: Princeton University Press.

Steenkamp, A. (2017) *I Afrikaner* Press Kit [Online]. Available at: http://www.iafrikanerfilm.com/presskit.html (Accessed: September 2, 2017).

Wondra, J. D. and Ellsworth, P. C. (2015) "An Appraisal Theory of Empathy and Other Vicarious Emotional Experiences," *Psychological Review*, 122(3), pp. 411–428.

Fake Pictures, Real Emotions: A Case Study of *Art and Craft*

Aubrey Tang

INTRODUCTION

This chapter investigates the function of morally ambiguous characters in documentary film; it argues that such characters can persuade viewers to renegotiate their moral values, transcend the differences between authenticity and replica, and transgress established social boundaries. It takes, as a case study, *Art and Craft* (2014), a documentary directed by Sam Cullman and Jennifer Grausman, and co-directed by Mark Becker, which chronicles the life of Mark A. Landis, an American art forger living in Laurel, Mississippi. The film is analyzed using an interdisciplinary methodology, drawing first on a textual analysis of Landis's highly particularized screen character, which is then examined in the light of cognitive theories on the construction and perception of fictional characters in film and literature, alongside a discussion of the related moral implications. Psychological considerations of "affect" are used to frame a close reading of empirical data relating to the reception of the film, including 130 online messages, six pieces of journalistic literature, four film festivals/screenings reports, as well as the hundreds of letters and gifts mailed directly to

A. Tang (✉)
University of California, Irvine, Irvine, CA, USA
e-mail: aubrey.tang@uci.edu

© The Author(s) 2018
C. Brylla, M. Kramer (eds.), *Cognitive Theory and Documentary Film*, https://doi.org/10.1007/978-3-319-90332-3_9

Landis.[1] There is a strong correlation between Landis's screen persona and his perceived persona in real life—he is presented more as an unconventional "philanthropist" than a devious criminal.[2] Viewers' sympathetic responses and transgressive emotions generally follow a similar trajectory in documentaries and fiction films; however, as this study of *Art and Craft* shows, documentaries can provide alternative routes to emotional engagement, due to the genre's special relationship with reality.

Art and Craft focuses on Landis's life, and mainly takes place in Laurel, from around 2011 to 2014. A single white man in his late fifties, who suffers from mental illness, Landis made a hobby out of creating fake masterpieces and donating them to small museums, mainly in the American South, over a period of nearly three decades. Because the paintings were donated, the museums made relatively little effort to authenticate them—unlike the artworks they purchase, which they subject to a rigorous authentication process. As a result, Landis's mischief went unnoticed until Matt Leininger, the registrar of the Oklahoma City Museum of Art at the time, discovered that some of the donated works were forgeries. Although Leininger was instructed by his employer to disregard the whole affair, he continued his investigation into Landis outside working hours, even going so far as to warn other curators, the FBI and the media. In fact, Leininger became so obsessed that, even after the museum was forced to fire him, he continued to pursue his quest to bring Landis to justice. Landis, however, was never arrested. Uninterested in financial gain, he never sold his artworks, only donated them. Furthermore, he paid for his own travel to the museums, so his escapades were all undertaken at his own expense (they were funded by an inheritance from his late mother, his late father's US Navy pension and his own disability benefits from the federal government).[3] He also waived his entitlement to the tax write-offs that accompany

---

[1] The 130 internet messages mentioned in this chapter were shown to me by Landis in confidence. For reasons of privacy, I can neither make concrete references to individual letters nor disclose the names of or personal information about their senders.

[2] Based on my personal interactions with Landis, I can confirm his philanthropy. When helping me gather the sample fan messages, he seemed more concerned with the benefits I would derive from this study than his own self-interest. His thoughtful and caring demeanor towards me revealed an altruism that may explain his practice of creating art forgeries for donation rather than financial gain.

[3] The information about Landis's sources of income is not clearly conveyed in the film, but was later specified by the filmmaker and a journalist. See Sam Cullman (2015) and Alec Wilkinson (2013).

donations. As a result, although the museums were led to believe that the artworks were genuine, the FBI's Art Crime Team deemed Landis's behavior lawful (that is, in accordance with US legislation) since it involved negligible financial loss. Despite Leininger's efforts to expose him in the media, some institutions—unaware of the story—continued to accept Landis's artworks. The deception only came to an end in 2011, when the *Financial Times* ran an exposé of Landis which was picked up by the global media, and the museums finally began to turn him away.

AN UNCONVENTIONAL ART FORGER: MARK LANDIS

Art and Craft's depiction of Landis creates a highly unconventional screen character, utterly distinct from the characterization of art forgers in most fiction and documentary films. The film brings to light the unusual nature of his real-life circumstances, helping explain his motivation and persona, as well as the public reaction to him. For example, Landis's motivation differs from that of other forgers: he is not interested in money, he harbors no resentments and he is not an egoist. *Art and Craft* eschews narration; however, it makes clear through its interviews with various museum professionals that Landis always donated his forged artworks. This posits a particularly unconventional scenario, since the production of most, if not all, counterfeit art is financially motivated. In addition, while forgers of artistic masterpieces generally seek notoriety or pursue other such narcissistic goals, the audience can clearly see that Landis is not motivated by any egotistical considerations. For instance, the film includes an interview with John Gabber, a *Financial Times* journalist, who speaks of calling Landis again and again, ringing his doorbell and waiting for hours outside his apartment in hope of an interview; Landis never answers the phone or opens the door. Gabber recalls that when Landis finally consented to meet him, the first thing he told him, after admitting to his forgeries, was that he was worried he would become too well-known and would not be allowed into a museum ever again. As he has no interest in money or fame, Landis's character leaves the audience with a sense of moral confusion. While forgery is generally considered immoral, its immorality is located in the act's intent: the desire for money, vengeance, fame or simply to feed the forger's ego. The film essentially renders Landis's character morally ambiguous as he is motivated by none of these things.

Landis's screen persona also contrasts dramatically with that of other art forgers in other respects: they are often portrayed as confident, anti-establishment, even heroic figures, while Landis has an extremely idio-syncratic personality—frail, mentally ill, humble but charming in a peculiar way. The film opens with this bald, pale, soft-spoken 59-year-old, with a slightly crooked posture, walking through the parking lot of an art supply chain store. His clothes appear outdated and oversized, and his demeanor is distant—he seems oblivious to his surroundings. This immediately sub-verts the image of the typical, self-confident, provocative art forger nor-mally encountered in fiction films, or even in documentaries about such infamous forgers as Elmyr de Hory in *F for Fake* (1973) or Wolfgang Beltracchi in *Beltracchi: The Art of Forgery* (2014). Instead, the audience sees Landis wandering along the aisles of the store, looking for discounted picture frames. All the while, the scene is accompanied by a score inspired by 1940s Big Band music. This somewhat discordant and non-diegetic music suggests that this is a man out of sync with the present day. Later, we see him going to a follow-up appointment at a mental health facility, and we discover that he was diagnosed as schizophrenic at the age of 17, and has been living alone since his mother's death two years previously.

Besides being disconnected from and overlooked by society, Landis possesses another quality atypical of art forgers: humility. While other forgers commonly boast of their skills and techniques, Landis appears unassuming, despite the fact that he has successfully fooled professionals in dozens of museums. When asked how he managed this, he casually explains that he creates the paintings while sitting on his bed watching TV, using photocopies, pencils, paints, glue, instant coffee, cheap picture frames and pieces of wood bought from a home improvement store. His relative carelessness over his choice of materials is in stark contrast to the attitude of most art forgers, who take pride in verisimilitude and obsess over every detail, using old canvases and paints that are free of any new chemicals. Landis, however, sees replicating artworks as a rather trivial activity, never spending longer than an hour on each piece (Wilkinson 2013). He also denies that he is a "real artist," claiming to be a hobbyist who likes creating arts and crafts. As art historian Noah Charney (2012, p. 69) affirms, "[h]e has none of the passive-aggression and rash bravado of renowned art forgers like Eric Hebborn, Hanvan Meegeren, or Elmyr de Hory." Landis's humility about his talents makes him stand out in the popular discourse about narcissistic art forgers such as Beltracchi, who claims that he can successfully fake any masterpiece (that is, he can paint as well as any of the original old masters) (*Beltracchi* 2014). All portrayals of Landis in *Art and Craft* seem to suggest that he is an ordinary, lonely old man, forgotten by society, a social type we encounter in most American neighborhoods but generally ignore.

The initial mainstream coverage of Landis exemplifies his unconventional character. The film reveals that the publicity was at first entirely negative: it shows some early footage from Local News 12 WKRC-TV in Cincinnati, Ohio, in which Landis is reported as a conman on the loose. Landis was also portrayed as a demonic imposter by other local TV channels, such as Local News KATC-TV3 in Lafayette, Louisiana in 2010, although this is not included in the film (Motifman 2010). In 2011, one of the most authoritative national newspapers in the US, *The New York Times* (Kennedy 2011), represented Landis as a cunning criminal, who had managed to deceive museum professionals and evade an FBI agent. And immediately after the release of *Art and Craft* in 2014, National Public Radio (NPR) and *The Washington Post* described him as "odd" and "awkward" (Blair 2014; Merry 2014), and a follow-up *New York Times* article referred to him as downright "creepy" (Holden 2014). In the film, the curatorial circle holds an equally negative view of Landis: two museum professionals describe him as "quirky" and "eccentric." Although the audience later sees Landis acknowledged as a talented artist at a Cincinnati art exhibition, public opinion at this point was overwhelmingly negative— an atypical response to either a fictional or documentary portrayal of an art forger. Historically, the public's fascination with art forgery as a spectacle has been fed by fiction films, documentaries and television. Inspired by elements of thriller, mystery and true-crime genres, these portrayals usually involve a mixture of enigma and heroism, echoing the motifs found in classical Hollywood heist films. Art forgers are typically depicted as intelligent, charismatic and talented; they are considered heroic outlaws and are rarely presented as demonic in the way Landis was initially portrayed by the popular media. In this respect too, he is a decidedly unconventional figure.

CHARACTER PARTICULARITY AND AMBIGUITY

Art and Craft has created a character that disrupts the prototypical relationship between plot, character and scenes found in traditional biographical documentaries. Although it relates to fictional narratives, Patrick Colm Hogan's (2010) character typology can also be applied to documentary. He explains that as a story is constructed, its plot, characters and scenes inform each other's development (pp. 136–137). Thus, a typical art forger narrative has a crime story (plot) and an art forger (character) who creates counterfeit art and hoodwinks the professionals in one or more museum/ gallery/art auction settings (scenes). Of these three components, Hogan argues, the characters possess a disproportionate importance in terms of how they affect the scenes and the plot (pp. 138, 142). Thus, particulariz- ing the prototypical characters is a reliable means of particularizing an entire narrative. While *Art and Craft* still features the prototypical structure of art forgery narratives, such as the fake artefacts, the museums, the likable pro- tagonist (Landis) and the unlikeable official antagonists (Leininger and the other museum professionals), Landis's unusual character effectively particu- larizes the film's narrative despite its prototypical structure.

One example of this is a scene in which Landis meets with the staff of a nearby museum, spinning them a yarn about a nonexistent deceased sister who owned an authentic painting that he now wants to donate. As in *F for Fake* and *Beltracchi*, the concrete locations or "crime scenes" where the forgeries are disseminated (streets, auction houses, art fairs and museums) are prototypical for this kind of narrative. But Landis's self-effacing and diffident persona, which becomes evident as he speaks to the museum staff, stands in direct contrast to de Hory's and Beltracchi's stance, render- ing the narrative function of these crime scenes particular rather than pro- totypical. A similar example can be found in the scenes showing the creation of the forgeries: while de Hory and Beltracchi adopt a typical attitude of pride and self-congratulation towards their meticulously per- formed work, Landis nonchalantly creates his forgeries while sitting on his bed watching TV. Therefore, although *Art and Craft* incorporates proto- typical scenarios, Landis's idiosyncratic character alters the viewer's expected perception of them. The plotline and scenes are dictated by his particular character, and the narrative develops coherently around him rather than being molded by a prototypical narrative template.

The effect of this character particularization on the film's audience is one of surprise and fascination. Prescriptive characterization necessarily entails predictable plotlines and scenes; non-prescriptive characterization suggests unpredictability. Characters who do not conform to the predict- able plotlines in which they are embedded intrigue the viewer as they have no way of knowing what to expect from the narrative or how to explain the characters' paradoxical traits. Landis simultaneously conforms to and defies the prototypical characterization of an art forger: he is shown as the paradoxical composite of a petty criminal who cons people into accepting forgeries and a philanthropist with a strong code of moral conduct who donates his art to the public,[4] thus creating a morally ambiguous but appealing character. Evidence of this can be found in the journalistic litera-ture, audience responses at screenings and online messages from fans, all of which confirm the largely positive impact of the film on Landis's public persona.

Alec Wilkinson (2013), for example, wrote an article about Landis in *The New Yorker*—one of the most perceptive, well-researched and positive biographical accounts in popular discourse. Wilkinson's detailed account portrays Landis as a multidimensional subject, and he supports this por-trayal with contextual facts and background information. The art-and-lifestyle magazine, *Paste*, also made it clear that "[a]lthough we know that what Landis is doing is fraudulent, we can't help but like the guy" (Ziemba 2014). Other film and arts-related journalistic outlets (Meier 2014; Goldstein 2014; DeFore 2014; Hohenadel 2014), including *Hyperallergic*, *Artspace*, *Hollywood Reporter* and *The Eye* (*Slate*'s design blog), all expressed a more positive recognition of Landis than the general news media. This far-reaching impact was due, not least, to the wide distribu-tion of the film: it was released on DVD, made available on numerous video streaming services (YouTube, iTunes, Amazon, Google Play, Vudu) and broadcast on PBS. The overwhelmingly positive audience response to Landis has subsequently extended to his life off-screen. He has attended numerous screenings with the documentary crew, including those at pres-tigious film festivals, such as AFI Docs and Tribeca, and universities in the Southern states (of the US), including Emory University, as well as a screening hosted by the National Alliance on Mental Illness (NAMI), a nonprofit mental health organization (Landis 2016; Mark Landis Original 2014). At these events, he appeared to be appreciated and celebrated by journalists and live audiences alike (FlyingOverTr0ut 2014; Loll 2016). After meeting Landis at a university screening, one student even asked him to adopt her as his honorary granddaughter—a request he accepted with pleasure (Landis 2016).

Other signs of this fascination with Landis can be seen in the plethora of messages and gifts he has received. A friend he met while filming built

---

[4] Landis repeatedly explains his personal ethics in the film by quoting verbatim from pre-1970s films and TV series. He says that he lives by "the code of *The Saint*," meaning one should be as ethical as Simon Templar, the Robin Hood-type hero of the show. However, he laments that ethical behavior never pays off in modern society, as Finch, the protagonist of the 1967 Hollywood musical, *How to Succeed in Business Without Really Trying*, discovers.

him a website that allows fans to send him messages and place orders for commissioned artworks (Mark Landis Original 2014). Landis continues to receive hundreds of messages from the film's multinational audiences—and to reply to every single one (Loll 2016; Landis 2016). For this chapter, I studied 130 of these messages and observed the following most common recurring themes: the audience is sympathetic to Landis; they find him inspiring; and they want to establish a benevolent personal relationship with him. One fan invited Landis to his wedding, while others have offered to be his friends, asked to meet him, and offered him gifts or material resources, such as meals, drinks or studio space. He has also received over one hundred commissions for artworks (Loll 2016), as well as a large amount of traditional mail, including greeting and gift cards (Landis 2016).

This positive reception is clearly a direct result of the film, since (as related earlier) museum curators nationwide and the major US media outlets had previously expressed unquestionably negative opinions of Landis. The audience's acceptance of a morally ambiguous character can be explained by exploring the appeal of similar characters encountered in fiction. Murray Smith (2011) argues that an audience finds it much more psychologically feasible to engage with a character who displays morally ambiguous behavior if it does not appear to incur any costs in real life. Analyzing the character of mafia boss Tony Soprano in the TV series *The Sopranos* (1999–2007), Smith states:

> This source of appeal is likely to be much more salient and powerful in the context of fictional engagement, where the imagined pleasures and benefits of such behavior do not have to be set against any real costs (i.e. worries about the potential harm that such agents of "rogue power" might inflict on oneself and those one cares about) … [C]ontemplating the actions of Soprano in the imagination simply is not the same, in all respects, as encountering the actions of a real equivalent to Soprano. (Smith 2011, p. 80)

Hence, the determining factors in whether an audience experiences a positive emotional response to a character are the real consequences rather than the actual nature of the character's moral flaws. Landis's flaws, serious as they are, cause no real harm: he donates his forgeries without hope of financial gain and (from a legal perspective) has committed no crime. Thus, the audience finds it acceptable to like him as a character and perhaps even feel a sense of moral allegiance towards him.[5] However, while the audience's evaluation of "real costs" in relation to character engagement operates in a similar way in both fiction and documentary, it should be noted that documentary characters can provide viewers with an opportunity to actualize the costs of their engagement in a way that fictional characters cannot.

Moreover, Landis's non-prescriptive, particularized character provides an avenue for the viewers' imagination and fantasy; although he disrupts conventional expectations about the *prototypical* art forger, this does not necessarily mean that he cannot, as an *archetypical* character, offer them the same imaginative pleasure and satisfaction. The distinction between prototypes and archetypes is sometimes overlooked, but arguably the notion of prototype is more descriptive of the narrative structure, while the archetype is more descriptive of the psychological structure of a character. Theoretically, in the analysis of characters, prototypes and archetypes can (and often do) overlap, but their emphases are different. While both prototypes and archetypes refer to types/patterns of characters, archetypes are specifically associated with the Jungian psychoanalytic concept of a "collective unconscious" that extends beyond the individual. Archetypes are recurring characters and motifs that are conceived instinctually; they exist in all epochs and all cultures (Davis et al. 1982). They reveal universal concerns, processed by the hard-wired parts of the human psyche, such as a caring mother's love for her child. As Henry Bacon (2009, p. 80) puts it, archetypes are "crystallizations of near-universal ways of responding to basic psychological concerns on an imaginary level, free of the restraints of the real world." In this regard, although structurally divergent from the conventional characterization of an art forger, Landis does function as a quintessential archetype—as a "Robin Hood-of-the-art-world" character.

This function can be explained through the archetypes' aptitude to fuel our fantasy. Bacon (2015, p. 17) argues that archetypes are instrumental in connecting with the viewers' "fantasies of physical prowess or exceptional professional, social, or sexual competence... [in] a situation onto which [they] can project a fantasy aspect of [themselves]." When watching

---

[5] The audience referred to here is the primary audience of the film—the average spectator. Museum professionals, on the other hand, may perceive that Landis has caused them real harm, potentially threatening the reputation of their institutions. Arguably, they comprise a smaller, secondary audience, which is a lot less likely to find Landis appealing.

an archetypical screen character, viewers can "fantasize about what [they] are going to do, what [they] would like to do, and even what [they] cannot possibly do" (p. 17). Further, archetypes facilitate a kind of "symptomatic [audience response] in the form of fantasies with intertwined psychological and social references," projecting our "hopes and frustrations, dreams, and anxieties" (2009, p. 80). So, on a symbolic level, Landis's harmless exploit of creating forged artworks and successfully donating them as authentic artefacts offers the audience the fantasy of fighting global capitalism and its commodification of art.

In *Art and Craft*, this symbolism is emphasized, for example, in the scene where Landis creates an artwork on his bed, in front of the TV, while explaining how he started his "hobby." A sequence of shots showing him putting on a pair of gloves, sawing a wooden board and taking some supplies out of a plastic bag is immediately followed by the well-choreographed sequence of a shoot-out in the classic Western playing on his TV. This montage suggests to the audience that instead of shooting opponents, Landis's way of getting back at the society that has disenfranchised him is to create forgeries. Instead of guns, his weapons are gloves and art supplies. These images provide the viewers with the archetypical ingredients with which to create an "art world's Robin Hood" fantasy—an heroic, individual rebellion—thus vicariously satisfying their desire to strike at the capitalist commodification of art. After all, art today is viewed by its wealthy buyers as a financial investment, a tool to diversify portfolios in the hope of withstanding market changes (Goetzmann 1993), as well as a means of generating undeserved amounts of even greater wealth. This fantasy can also be linked to an anti-establishment dream of economic and social justice, since the donated forgeries appear to disrupt belief in the authenticity of some museum collections, however futile Landis's actions may actually be in this respect.

TRANSGRESSIVE EMOTIONS

The viewers' fascination and willingness to engage with Landis's character occur not only on a narrative and symbolic level, but also on an emotional one, eliciting powerful transgressive emotions that contradict established moral values. For instance, while all Landis's fan letters express sympathy toward him, several representative online messages demonstrate that, for the viewers of the film, his character transcends the difference between real and fake. Some fans suggest that it does not matter whether the pictures he creates are real or fake as long as he can feel free to paint whatever he wants. Most of the messages do not clarify what they mean by this, failing to specify, for instance, whether they refer to displaying forgeries in the home or whether they condone exhibiting them in a museum. Many messages use encouraging phrases, such as "keep doing what you're doing" and "stay true to yourself," along with numerous virtual hugs. These recurring themes clearly indicate a sense of compassion: viewers prioritize this sympathetic character's personal freedom and mental wellbeing over an adamantine ontological distinction between real and fake—a dichotomy that is as predominant in today's materialist Western culture as it has been in documentary studies in relation to the authenticity of images and sounds.

In a study analyzing viewers' transgressive emotions and their capacity for disrupting moral orthodoxy, E. J. Horberg and Dacher Keltner (2007) state that viewers' intuitive emotions relating to moral allegiance constitute low-level cognition but also a response to social inequality. Such "moral emotions" rarely comprise rational thoughts alone; instead, they are "a complicated combination of principled reasoning, emotion, and perspective taking" (pp. 155–156). One key moral emotion is "compassion." This is capable of reconfiguring moral judgments by confronting them with other moral distributional principles: when someone feels compassionate, they feel sympathy and may be spurred into performing a benevolent act to alleviate another's suffering, even if this act violates their moral principles (pp. 164–165). Compassion is thus "closely related to issues of harm, need and helping" (p. 164). Considering the severely deprived nature of Landis's life, his social reality, compassion appears the best way to describe the type of transgressive emotions his character elicits in the film's audience.

One example is the scene where Landis explains why he smokes. He recalls that when he went into the emergency room to throw up after being given his psychiatric medication, he remembered that the characters in the classic films he watches on Turner Classic Movies (TCM) always light up a cigarette when they need to calm down, and so he tried smoking. After we see him taking out different prescription bottles of Lorazepam (an anti-anxiety drug), he continues to ramble on about his feelings—his worries about being labeled an art forger, of becoming known as a crook and a drinker, like his father—as he paces up and down. Shortly afterwards, the camera accompanies him to a follow-up appointment at the clinic, where a medical assistant records his weight, which is very low (120

1b) despite the fact that he is wearing a heavy winter jacket. She chats with him about common medical topics, such as his appetite, and we discover that although Landis has told her that his mother has passed away, the assistant appears to have forgotten and asks how she is doing. Since this woman is possibly one of the few people Landis sees on a regular basis, we understand from this encounter both that he is very lonely and that people generally pay little attention to him. Although not happy about the assistant's question, he appears to take no offense and remains calm. Afterwards, the scene changes to Landis's dimly lit bedroom, full of art books, art supplies, paintings and a pile of laundry. His TV is on and he is dipping Melba toast into a tub of spread. He then explains the reason behind his addiction to "philanthropy": when donating a forged artwork, he is—for once—able to enjoy a moment when people are nice to him.

Scenes like this clearly convey Landis's painful lack of human interaction and his simple wish to feel connected to the world; he seems isolated and forgotten by society. Having no financial or institutional ambitions, Landis's loneliness is strangely compelling. In the eyes of a compassionate viewer, this makes him a character truly deserving of support, forgiveness and kindness. His moral flaws, which incur no harm, can be forgiven, and moral boundaries can be reconfigured.

CONCLUSION

This chapter uses Landis to illustrate how a morally ambiguous character can elicit a powerfully sympathetic audience response, provided that there are no real-life costs. The highly unusual, paradoxical nature of his character invites the viewers to connect and engage because they experience fascination and compassion. It also provides them with an avenue for imagination and fantasy, demonstrating how ambiguous characters can elicit transgressive emotions, which in turn can effectively transform the viewers' moral bearings. The emotion of compassion, in particular, does not operate in terms of rational moral evaluations; rather, it is intuitive and altruistic. These mechanisms operate whether the characters belong to a documentary or a fiction film. However, because documentary characters are empirical subjects that exist in a common social reality that the viewers share, their access to these characters and the way they evaluate the liabilities involved in the characters' actions differ from those of fictional characters. Nevertheless, the outcome—renegotiated moral boundaries— is comparable.

REFERENCES

Bacon, H. (2009) "Blendings of Real, Fictional, and Other Imaginary People," *Projections*, 3(1), pp. 77–99.

Bacon, H. (2015) *The Fascination of Film Violence*. Basingstoke: Palgrave Macmillan.

Blair, E. (2014) "'Art & Craft' Explores How One Forger Duped More Than 45 Museums," *National Public Radio (NPR)*, September 27 [Online]. Available at: http://www.npr.org/2014/09/27/351738720/art-craft-explores-how-one-forger-duped-more-than-45-museums (Accessed: September 15, 2016).

Charney N. (2012) "Lessons from the History of Art Crime: Mark Landis: The Forger Who Has Yet to Commit a Crime," *Journal of Art Crime*, 7, pp. 69–70.

Cullman, S. (2015) *Open Mind Panel Discussion, 'Art and Craft'* [Public talk to The Friends of the Semel Institute for Neuroscience & Human Behavior, University of California, Los Angeles], May 29.

Davis, R. A., Farrell, J. M. and Matthews, S. S. (1982) "The Dream World of Film: A Jungian Perspective on Cinematic Communication," *The Western Journal of Speech Communication*, 46(4), pp. 326–343.

DeFore, J. (2014) "Art and Craft: Film Review," *The Hollywood Reporter*, May 7 [Online]. Available at: http://www.hollywoodreporter.com/review/art-craft-film-review-702147 (Accessed: September 15, 2016).

FlyingOverTr0ut (2014) *Interview with Mark Landis of "Art and Craft" at AFI docs 2014.* Available at: https://www.youtube.com/watch?v=auVnb86Iiqw (Accessed: September 15, 2016).

Goetzmann, W. N. (1993) "Accounting for Taste: Art and the Financial Markets Over Three Centuries," *The American Economic Review*, 83(5), pp. 1370–1376.

Goldstein, A. M. (2014) "Art Forger Mark Landis on How He Became an Unlikely Folk Hero," *Artspace*, December 27 [Online]. Available at: http://www.artspace.com/magazine/interviews_features/qa/mark-landis-interview-52568 (Accessed: September 15, 2016).

Hogan, P. C. (2010) "Characters and Their Plots," in Eder, J., Jannidis, F. and Schneider, R. (eds.) *Characters in Fictional Worlds: Understanding Imaginary Beings in Literature, Film, and Other Media*. Berlin: De Gruyter, pp. 134–154.

Hohenadel, K. (2014) "How One of the Most Prolific Known Forgers in Modern History Faked Great Works of Art," *The Eye: Slate's Design Blog*, 18 September [Online]. Available at: http://www.slate.com/blogs/the_eye/2014/09/18/mark_landis_documentary_art_and_craft_offers_a_behind_the_scenes_look_at.html (Accessed: September 15, 2016).

Holden, S. (2014) "For This Con Artist, No Crime That Pays: 'Art and Craft,' About a Donor of Faked Paintings," *The New York Times*, September 18 [Online]. Available at: http://www.nytimes.com/2014/09/19/movies/art-and-craft-about-a-donor-of-faked-paintings.html (Accessed: September 15, 2016).

Horberg, E. J. and Keltner, D. (2007) "Passions for Justice," in DeCremer, D. (ed.) *Advances in the Psychology of Justice and Affect*. Charlotte, NC: Information Age Publishing, pp. 155–172.

Kennedy, R. (2011) "Elusive Forger, Giving but Never Stealing," *The New York Times*, January 11 [Online]. Available at: http://www.nytimes. com/2011/01/12/arts/design/12fraud.html?pagewanted=all&module=Sea rch&mabReward=relbias%3As&_r=0 (Accessed: September 15, 2016).

Landis, M. (2016) Telephone Conversation with the Author, September 14, 2016.

Loll, C. (2016) Telephone Conversation with the Author, September 13, 2016.

Mark Landis Original (2014) *Mark Landis* [Online]. Available at: http://mark-landisoriginal.com/ (Accessed: September 15, 2016).

Meier, A. (2014) "A New Documentary for the Forger Who Infiltrated America's Art Museums," *Hyperallergic*, September 26 [Online]. Available at: http:// hyperallergic.com/151678/a-new-documentary-for-the-forger-who-infiltrated-americas-art-museums/ (Accessed: September 15, 2016).

Merry, S. (2014) "'*Art and Craft*' Movie Review: Making Forgeries, but Few Friends," *The Washington Post*, October 20 [Online]. Available at: https:// www.washingtonpost.com/goingoutguide/movies/art-and-craft-movie-review-making-forgeries-but-few-friends/2014/10/02/01e2e5a0-47e5-11e 4-b72e-d60a9229cc10_story.html?utm_term=.9c570f6602c0 (Accessed: September 15, 2016).

Motifman ([1960] 2010) *Art Fraud Story* [Online] Available at: https://www. youtube.com/watch?v=zIrjAKUBNLY (Accessed: September 15, 2016).

Smith, M. (2011) "Just What is It That Makes Tony Soprano Such an Appealing, Attractive Murderer?" in Jones, W. E. and Vice, S. (ed.) *Ethics at the Cinema*. New York: Oxford University Press, pp. 66–90.

Wilkinson, A. (2013) "The Giveaway," *The New Yorker*, August 26 [Online]. Available at: http://www.newyorker.com/magazine/2013/08/26/the-giveaway (Accessed: September 15, 2016).

Ziemba, C. N. (2014) "*Art and Craft*," *Paste*, September 24 [Online]. Available at: https://www.pastemagazine.com/articles/2014/09/art-and-craft.html (Accessed September 15, 2016).

CHAPTER 10

Engaging Animals in Wildlife Documentaries: From Anthropomorphism to Trans-Species Empathy

Alexa Weik von Mossner

Wildlife documentaries are a highly popular genre of nonfiction film. Not only are they a staple of TV programs around the globe, but several of the most successful theatrically released documentaries in recent years—from *Winged Migration* (2001), directed by Jacques Perrin, Jacques Cluzaud and Michel Debats, to *Chimpanzee* (2012) by Alastair Fothergill and Mark Linfield—also fall into this genre. This enduring popularity suggests that there is something about wildlife film that speaks to us, despite being (or perhaps because it is) often devoid of human characters. In part, this may be explained by well-tried modes of storytelling that are in no way exclusive to the genre. As Stephen Rust (2014, p. 227) reminds us, "familiar tropes and patterns such as the hero story, Darwinian survival plots, and sentimental human treatments of nonhuman family life have long been used to shape the narrative structures of films about such diverse animals as lemmings, dolphins, and dung beetles." As an ecocinema scholar, Rust is appropriately critical of such "anthropomorphic projections" of human storylines onto nonhuman lives because they fail to acknowledge the existential otherness and independent agency of nonhuman creatures. And

A. Weik von Mossner (✉)
University of Klagenfurt, Klagenfurt, Austria
e-mail: Alexa.WeikvonMossner@aau.at

© The Author(s) 2018   163
C. Brylla, M. Kramer (Eds.), *Cognitive Theory and Documentary Film*, https://doi.org/10.1007/978-3-319-90332-3_10

yet, as every wildlife filmmaker will confirm, they are a vital component of the genre. Regardless of whether a dung beetle could actually be expected to embark on a heroic journey, filmmakers will often look for that journey in the hours and hours of footage they have produced. If they are lucky, they will find it, and thus get that much closer to selling their film to a distributor, a TV station and, ultimately, to an audience that is looking for an emotionally satisfying viewing experience.

However, while the anthropomorphic projection of human storylines onto nonhuman lives is an important component of the narrative structure of wildlife film, it cannot alone explain the popularity of the genre. Ecocritic Bart Welling (2014, p. 82) reminds us that what we feel when we watch wildlife films "does not just depend on techniques employed by filmmakers to promote superficial anthropomorphism or to tap into our innate drive to make sense of the world by comparing animal physiology and behavior to our own." If we really want to understand the affective appeal of documentaries featuring animals, he argues, then we must pay attention to the ways in which they "provide viewers with heavily mediated but potentially transformative modes of access to the emotional lives of our nonhuman kin" (p. 82).

In this reading, it is not only crude anthropomorphic personification that allows us to relate to nonhuman protagonists, but also *a shared biology* that enables us to cognitively read the emotional expressions of other animals' bodies, while at the same time sharing their affective states on the subconscious level through emotional contagion, affective mimicry and other processes of embodied simulation.

Welling's (2014, p. 82) ecocritical observations take their cue from Torben Grodal's (2009) biocultural approach to film, but they "expand the biocultural frame of reference to encompass the more-than-human emotional landscape in which human emotions originally developed, along with the range of animal feelings to which our emotions are intimately related." This chapter, in turn, takes its cue from Welling to bring the discussion back to cognitive film theory and the question of what happens to nonfiction character engagement when the character in question is an animal. The first section draws on ecocriticism, affective neuroscience, cognitive film theory and cognitive ethology (the study of animal minds) to examine our engagement with nonhuman characters on film, paying attention to different modes of anthropomorphism and their relationship to trans-species empathy. The second section applies this theoretical framework to selected scenes from two wildlife films—*Winged Migration* and *Chimpanzee*—and relates it to issues of indexicality. In this context, it addresses a question that should concern not only ecocritics but also cognitive film scholars with an interest in documentary films: does it make any difference to our emotional engagement if we believe the animal and its surrounding storyworld to be *factual* as we do when watching a wildlife film?

FEELING ANIMALS: A COGNITIVE APPROACH TO NONHUMAN CHARACTER ENGAGEMENT

Viewers' cognitive and affective relationships to film characters have been a central concern of cognitive film theory almost from its inception. "Our propensity to respond emotionally to fictional characters," writes Murray Smith (1995, p. 1), "is a key aspect of our experience and enjoyment of narrative films." Such observations, which are similarly discussed by several scholars in this volume, do not only pertain to fictional characters but are also relevant for our engagement with factual protagonists as well. Moreover, as scores of ecocritics have argued, it is a fallacy to assume that characters must be human, or even be *like* humans, to engage human audiences (Armbruster 2013; Burt 2002; Pick 2011; Welling 2009; Welling and Kapel 2012). Given this insight, the question is whether it is the anthropomorphic projection of human characteristics onto nonhuman actors alone that enables us to care for cinematic animals or whether we also respond directly to them on the affective level across species boundaries. There is no doubt that when animals are "cast" as "protagonists" and thus become characters that drive a story, they are often heavily anthropomorphized. In fiction films, this is even true on the level of performance, since their animal protagonists tend to undergo extensive training before the camera rolls, teaching them to perform physical expressions that viewers can easily understand and interpret. Documentaries rarely use trained animals, but anthropomorphism can also be located on the level of storytelling and of filmic production more generally.

A significant part of this anthropomorphism is, in fact, unavoidable. Welling reminds us that:

> [Film is] by its very nature a superficially anthropomorphic technology, since it captures selected scenes from the visual and aural commons that all seeing and hearing organisms can perceive, albeit in different ways, and translates them into a medium that only humans and very few other animals can make sense of. (Welling 2014, p. 83)

The same is true on the level of narrativization and storytelling. Jesús Rivas and Gordon M. Burghardt (2002, p. 10) note that anthropomorphism is the inevitable "default condition of the human mind," and that our comprehension of other beings and our environments more generally is therefore inescapably colored by the specific sensual, affective and cognitive apparatus of our species. When we tell a story about an animal's perceptions, thoughts and feelings, we cannot help but do so from our own limited human perspective, regardless of the medium we use. Philosopher Thomas Nagel (1974, p. 436), in his article "What Is It Like to Be a Bat?" famously argues that we experience insurmountable difficulties when trying to understand the subjective experience of a bat because "bat sonar… is not similar in its operation to any sense we possess, and there is no reason to suppose that it is subjectively like anything we can experience or imagine." The cognitive apparatuses of bats and humans, Nagel suggests, are simply too different to allow for a true understanding of the animal's subjective experience. By the same logic, it would also be difficult to make a wildlife film about a bat that truly captures and communicates that experience of the world, which is so utterly different from ours. No matter how hard we try to do the animal justice, we will always represent and understand it in human terms.

Yet, despite these cognitive and technological limitations, the filmic depiction of nonhuman characters does not automatically have to lead to what primatologist Frans De Waal (2001, p. 71) calls the 'bambification' of animals, a form of romanticization that obfuscates the reality of animal behavior and animals' actual cognitive and affective capabilities. Ecocritic Greg Garrard (2012, p. 155) uses the label "crude anthropomorphism" for such unduly romantic and, in the end, deeply ignorant and insensitive depictions of animal others. Like De Waal, he distinguishes crude anthropomorphism from its "more sophisticated, critical forms," and names as a prime example of the former the false assumption that the pulled-back corners of a dolphin's mouth are the equivalent of a human smile, signaling happiness (p. 155). Ironically, however, this simplistic anthropomorphic misinterpretation has "helped to propel [this] animal to the status of culture hero" (p. 155). In Louie Psihoyos's Academy Award-winning documentary, *The Cove* (2009), former dolphin trainer Ric O'Barry emphasizes the disastrous implications of this misinterpretation for the hundreds of thousands of "happy" cetaceans that have been put to work in media productions like the TV-series *Flipper* and in marine shows around the world, calling the dolphin's smile "nature's greatest deception." In perhaps an attempt to defend his past occupation as an animal trainer, O'Barry shifts the blame to "nature," as if nature was an intentional agent that deliberately deceives humans about the true state of affairs. However, it is not nature but the human perceiving agent that first makes the attributional mistake and then exploits it for commercial entertainment. Welling (2009, p. 56) provocatively calls such crudely anthropomorphic depictions of dolphins and other animals a form of "ecoporn" because they enable—and in fact encourage—a dominant, pleasure-taking and objectifying gaze on the "animal other" that is accompanied by an utter disregard for its actual nature and needs.

It is not only ecocritics, however, who are wary of such ignorance and disregard. Ethologists, too, have problematized crude, unreflective and chauvinistic versions of anthropomorphism and have argued that researchers have an obligation to reflect on their sensual and cognitive biases. Rivas and Burghardt (2002, p. 11) suggest: "Although it is true that we will never fully appreciate how another animal experiences the world, by doing our best to accomplish this through applying critical anthropomorphism, including the full range of available scientific data, we will get closer to understanding the life of the animal." Critical anthropomorphism, in this definition, is acting against bambification by showing awareness of the inevitable anthropocentric bias of our interpretation, while at the same time using scientific knowledge to put ourselves "in the animal's shoes." Such deliberate employment of cognitive trans-species empathy is important since, as research in the field consistently suggests, we tend to drastically underestimate the mental capacities of animals, as well as their abilities to feel, express and communicate their cognitive and emotional states to other agents (Bekoff et al. 2002; Bekoff 2003; Berns 2013; De Waal 2009). Marc Bekoff (2007, p. xviii) remembers that, when he started his work in the 1970s, "researchers were almost all skeptics who spent their time wondering if dogs, cats, chimpanzees, and other animals felt anything." Today, the situation is reversed, with the paradigm shifting to such an extent "that the burden of proof now falls more often to those who still argue that animals don't experience emotions." Fieldwork in cognitive ethology, founded by the zoologist Donald Griffin in the early 1980s, has greatly contributed to this paradigm shift, which prompts us to understand nonhuman animals as sentient others who have emotions, thoughts, beliefs, rationality and consciousness. The corresponding lab work, conducted by affective neuroscientists such as Jaak Panksepp (1998) and Gregory Berns (2013), complements field research by giving us a better understanding of animal minds and brains.

From the perspective of ecocriticism and cognitive ethology, then, the bambification of nonhuman animals by crude anthropomorphism is problematic because it directly contributes to a deep-seated misunderstanding of the lives of their actual counterparts. Nevertheless, if we find such crude forms of anthropomorphism in a great variety of popular films, it is because they are so very effective in engaging viewers. The unabashed projection of human characteristics and human drama onto nonhuman protagonists in both fiction and nonfiction film allows for the same modes of recognition, alignment and allegiance that Smith detects in viewers' relationships to human characters. Recognition, as Smith (1995, p. 82) puts it, is the "spectator's construction of the character: the perception of a set of textual elements, in film typically cohering around the image of a body, as an individuated and continuous human agent." The agent does not have to be human, however. Viewers can also recognize a nonhuman body as a character if the narrative elements cohere sufficiently around it. And once they have recognized the animal as character, they can also be aligned with that character and encouraged to build moral allegiance to it.

Alignment, Smith explains, "describes the process by which spectators are placed in relation to characters in terms of their access to their actions, and to what they know and feel" (p. 82). Allegiance, by contrast, "depends upon the spectator having what she takes to be reliable access to the character's state of mind, on understanding the context of the character's actions, and on having morally evaluated the character on the basis of this knowledge" (p. 84). Arguably, it is allegiance that is most heavily influenced by crudely anthropomorphic storytelling techniques. As long as the animal character behaves very much like a human, and viewers have no trouble accessing und understanding their thoughts and emotions, it will be very easy for them to form strong emotional and moral allegiances. This can perhaps be most easily grasped when we think of the crudely anthropomorphized heroes of Disney animation films, from *Bambi* (1942) to *The Lion King* (1994) and beyond. It is just as true, however, for documentaries featuring untrained wildlife as part of a larger story about maturation, affection or simply survival. One of the most notorious examples is Luc Jacquet's blockbuster documentary *March of the Penguins* (2005), which frames the social lives of penguins in terms of the human nuclear family. Noël Sturgeon and Douglas Kellner are two of many critics who have chastised Disney for choosing to follow 'a standard anthropomorphic script' (Sturgeon 2009, p. 120) that uses animals 'for the purposes of constructing conservative ideological machines' (Kellner 2010, p. 77) while downplaying or ignoring outright their actual behavior and social dynamics.

The worldwide success of *March of the Penguins* demonstrates how easy it is for humans to get emotional about animals that seem to behave like (idealized) humans. And yet, the question looms large whether it is *only* such crude anthropomorphic projections that enable us to feel with and for animals in film. Carl Plantinga (2009) argues that viewers' empathetic and sympathetic responses to screen characters are solicited by a range of filmic techniques, among them the use of close-ups that allow for emotional contagion through affective mimicry. He explains:

> [A]ffective mimicry is generated by the grain of the voice, subtle inflections of tone and cadence, facial expressions, gestures and postures. Affective mimicry results from the spectator's experience of photographic and aural representations of the human body and voice. We are a species of mimics, and various sorts of motor mimicry strongly affect spectators without them being consciously aware of it. (Plantinga 2009, p. 114)

Neuroscientist Vittorio Gallese (2014, pp. 3–4) explains such 'mimicking' in terms of embodied simulation, which he defines as "a non-conscious, pre-reflective functional mechanism of the brain–body system, whose function is to model objects, agents and events." In the context of this chapter, it is important to note that such processes of embodied simulation do not necessarily stop at species lines. Research in "trans-species psychology" (Bradshaw and Watkins 2006), which pushes for a "cross-species understanding of empathy" (Panksepp and Panksepp 2013), shows that the physical display of internal emotional states can be contagious not only within but also *across* species boundaries, regardless of anthropomorphism. This is evidenced in a study conducted by Franklin et al. (2013), which used fMRI to examine neural responses in (human) participants when presented with pictures of suffering humans and pictures of suffering dogs. The authors found "that viewing human and animal suffering led to large overlapping regions of activation previously implicated in empathic responding to suffering, including the anterior cingulate gyrus and anterior insula" (p. 217). The results of the study indicate "that there are many overlapping [brain] regions in humans' empathic responses to viewing animal and human suffering, particularly in areas classically associated with empathic response" (p. 225).

These scientific observations suggest that there is more to our emotional engagement with animal characters in documentaries than crude anthropomorphic projection. Considering trans-species empathy allows us to see that we do not necessarily have to project human qualities onto nonhuman creatures in order to feel for them; we are biologically equipped to automatically feel—*across* species lines—with and for the (nonanthropomorphized) animals we encounter in real life and in cultural texts. This may explain the emotional response that Dirk Eitzen (2005) reports in "Documentary's Peculiar Appeals" as a result of watching a suffering dog in Robert Gardner's documentary *Forest of Bliss* (1985). Eitzen writes that seeing the dog being attacked relentlessly "by a pack of more-robust dogs" was "practically unbearable. I was literally nauseated. I wanted to turn away" (p. 183). He explains his physical response to the documented dog attack as follows:

> When I see a dog that is being attacked cringe before the fangs of its attackers, I cringe, too—not outwardly perhaps, but at least in those parts of my brain that know from experience what it feels like to cringe before a physical threat. This triggers a rush of adrenaline. It is partly what accounts for my extreme discomfort. It is partly why I feel such strong sympathy for the victim. (Eitzen 2005, p. 190)

What Eitzen describes here is a process of embodied simulation leading to affective empathy, empathic distress, and then to sympathy and moral allegiance. Important to the argument here is the fact that this visceral response is not cued by a crudely anthropomorphic framing of the dog by the filmmakers, as in the case of *March of the Penguins*. Like the subjects in the study by Franklin et al., who did not have any narrative context when reacting to the images of suffering dogs, Eitzen's response is an immediate and involuntary process of embodied simulation as he "cringe[s] too" and feels the dog's distress in his own body and mind.

Eitzen's visceral empathic response to the dog fits perfectly not only with the results of the fMRI study, but also with psychologist Martin Hoffman's account of the relationship between *empathic distress* and *prosocial action*. Hoffman (2000, p. 16) writes that the experience of empathic distress when watching another creature suffer often leads to the activation of preexisting "moral principles" and, ultimately, to bystander guilt, which in turn is a strong motivator for helping behavior. Eitzen (2005, p. 190) offers some anecdotal evidence for the involvement of such moral principles when he suggests that his visceral response to the dog may have been mediated by his general sympathy for "underdogs" and intensified by his cognitive understanding that he was watching a nonfiction film. Both observations are important. Eitzen does not differentiate between human and nonhuman underdogs (in fact, the very term "underdog" clearly has its roots in the observation of animal behavior). It may be tempting to explain his attitude in terms of crude anthropomorphic projection (and the blunt ascription of human characteristics to a nonhuman entity), but it seems more pertinent here to attribute it to a recognition that underdogs exist in *both* human and canine communities, and that this is therefore something the two species share. His second observation about the importance of the documentary format leads us to the question of whether there is anything "peculiar"—to use Eitzen's term—in our emotional response to representations of animals that we believe to be factual because we are watching a *documentary* film.

THE PECULIAR APPEALS OF WILDLIFE DOCUMENTARY

As many contributors to this volume observe, drawing a clear line between fiction and documentary formats is not always easy, which is one of the reasons why many theoretical concepts can be applied to both modes of film. Noël Carroll (1996, p. 286) argues that "the distinction between nonfiction and fiction was never really based on differences in formal techniques" because "when it comes to technique, fiction and nonfiction filmmakers can and do imitate each other, just as fiction and nonfiction writers can and do." The decisive factor for viewers, Carroll (1996, p. 287) suggests, is that films come labeled or indexed either as fiction or nonfiction, and we (as viewers) therefore expect a certain kind of film when we buy a ticket to see it. Both Plantinga and Eitzen have picked up the issue of indexicality; however, whereas Plantinga (cited in Eitzen 1995, p. 95) claims that how a film is indexed becomes a "property or element of the text within its socio-cultural milieu," Eitzen takes the opposite stance, arguing that it is up to the viewer to decide *when* a film is a documentary. In Eitzen's (1995, p. 98) view, a simple question—"Might it be lying?"— determines the nature of a film in the eyes of a viewer as only documentaries can "lie" in the sense of departing from the actual state of affairs they claim to represent. Eitzen later zooms in on the affective dimension of this question when considering his own response to the suffering dog in *Forest of Bliss*.

Even in a fiction film, seeing an event like this would be profoundly disturbing. Seeing it in a documentary, I found it practically unbearable... And yet, because this was a documentary, I felt an even stronger compulsion to watch. Even more than that, I wanted to intervene. I wanted to pick up a rock and throw it at the dogs that were so viciously attacking one of their own kind. (Eitzen 2005, p. 190)

If we tie this response back to the question "Might it be lying?", the answer is, "Yes, it *might* be lying," because—unlike a fiction film—the documentary claims to represent the actual world. However, few viewers will question the veracity of a documentary until they have reason to do so, and they will assume, as Eitzen does here, that the suffering of the dog was *real* at the time of filming. "When documentaries... produce strong responses," he argues, "there is something special, something uniquely compelling and affecting, in their impact" (p. 190). This *something* is directly related to our cognitive understanding that what we see has actual consequences in the real world. What is so painful about watching the represented dog suffer is the belief that the end credits will contain no disclaimer that "no animals were harmed during the making of this movie." The awareness that the dog really *did* suffer, and that its expression of fear and pain were caused by real fear and pain, is what triggered not only trans-species empathic distress in Eitzen, but also bystander guilt and an inclination to intervene.

Building his argument on the insights of both ecological psychology and cognitive science, Eitzen (2005, p. 183) claims that the viewer's assumption that what happens in a documentary really *did* happen in actual life (as opposed of it just being pretense, as in the case of fiction) is what makes it "consequential" in the eyes of that viewer. And it is the viewer's belief in the *actuality* and *consequentiality* of the depicted events that leads to the peculiar emotional appeal of documentary film. This, to no small degree, explains why some people (myself included) find it nearly unbearable to keep watching when animals get killed and eaten in wildlife documentaries. Welling (2014, p. 86) gives the example of the documentary film, *Winged Migration*, in which "one of the film's hard-working avian subjects is shown grounded with a broken wing on an African beach, desperately trying to escape a horde of hungry crabs." Contrary to the argument that any empathic responses to that sight are solely anthropomorphic projections, he asserts that "[h]umans share enough innate dispositions with birds—such as the fear of being eaten—to justify the observation that the terror we may experience on viewing this scene is grounded in biology, and not simply a by-product of certain cultural anxieties" (p. 86). In other words, rather than cognitively projecting human feelings onto the bird, viewers are able to share the bird's actual terror through affective processes of emotional contagion.

This is an interesting extension of Eitzen's argument: wild birds are not a companion species in the way domesticated dogs are, yet Welling (2014, p. 86) suggests that, as viewers, we can and will feel with the bird on a deeply visceral and highly emotional level. And for those who still need convincing, he recounts the subsequent shot in the film which shows "the crabs swarming over and devouring... something", and then adds that the filmmakers confess in a DVD interview that the devoured object was, in fact, not the injured bird but "a dead fish, and that they had actually rescued the ... bird from the crabs." This little anecdote is fascinating for two reasons. First, it seems to suggest that the filmmakers themselves felt too much trans-species empathy with the bird to just go on filming its death (as many wildlife filmmakers would). Second, the stab of pain and pity that some viewers will feel at the sight of the "dead bird" is actually triggered by successful staging and fakery. In Eitzen's terms, this is a moment when the film "lies" about the actual state of affairs, since the bird was not truly eaten.

Arguably, such moments of "lying" in a documentary are unethical, but as several studies on wildlife film have shown (Bousé 2000; Chris 2006; Mitman 2009; Rust 2014) various forms of staging and manipulation are quite common in the genre in order to provide engaging experiences for viewers. Environmental historian Gregg Mitman (2009, p. 121) writes that the producers of Disney nature documentaries regularly put animals in controlled conditions to facilitate the shooting process and obtain the desired shots. Prominent examples include award-winning nature cinematographers Alfred and Elma Milotte, who "had no qualms about using a wire-cage enclosure with a glass barrier separating a coyote and a beaver to obtain footage of the two animals in the same frame while shooting scenes for *Beaver Valley*", a 1950 documentary directed by James Algar for Disney's popular *True-Life Adventures* series. "Such staging," Mitman explains, was considered "a legitimate film technique, provided that the scene was true to events either documented or deemed plausible by naturalists in the field" (p. 121). That this somewhat loose approach to filmic authenticity still prevails in the twenty-first century is evidenced by a more recent Disney documentary—Alastair Fothergill's and Mark Linfield's

Chimpanzee—in which not one but several young chimps impersonate the film's protagonist Oscar.

Since *Chimpanzee* is indexed and marketed as a nature documentary rather than a fiction film, we might once again consider this a case of "lying" because the base assumption of viewers will likely be that the protagonist they are aligned with throughout the narrative is always one and the same. They are also likely to assume that this protagonist is identical with a real-life chimp named "Oscar", who indeed did (as he does in the film) lose his mother at a young age and was later adopted by the male leader of the group. This assumption of authenticity and consequentiality is, as Eitzen claims, an important factor in viewers' emotional response to the depicted events in a documentary film, and it also plays a central role in the development of moral allegiance to the nonhuman protagonist. Reviewers have lauded *Chimpanzee* for its stunning cinematography and many deeply touching moments which, not by coincidence, come with countless close-ups of Oscar's face. Like *March of the Penguins*, *Chimpanzee* certainly uses a good deal of crude anthropomorphism in the construction of a familiar storyline that leads from happy childhood, through abandonment and near-death, to finally the life-saving adoption and happy ending. However, we must also turn our attention to the many moments in the film in which there is simply no need for crude anthropomorphism since trans-species empathy allows viewers to feel along with little Oscar in the ways outlined by both Franklin et al. and Eitzen. The close-ups of Oscar's face—and his body language more generally—allow for both the cognitive attribution of a state of mind and more visceral embodied simulation processes such as affective mimicry. When Oscar is happy, we are likely to feel the same, and when his body position and facial expression show fear, we tend to feel afraid. In the latter case, we probably also feel a strong desire to intervene and save the little guy from starvation.

In his review of the film for *Newsday*, Rafer Guzman (2012) displays both his emotional engagement and his moral allegiance to the chimp when he writes that "Oscar's family... coldly reject[s] the newly orphaned chimp. The images of little Oscar growing thin and tick-bitten with no one to feed or groom him are heartbreaking". While such moments would also be touching in a fiction film, there is a qualitative difference to the viewer's response because they assume that these things did *really* happen to Oscar during principal shooting. And so, it perhaps is not surprising that the documentary's May 2013 release in Germany ignited a public controversy, focused on its claim to factuality, after it became known that the character Oscar was not identical with the actual Oscar, and was in fact "played" by several young chimpanzees. People complained that they had been lied to by the film. The director, Fothergill (cited in von Leszczynski 2013), reacted to the criticism by admitting that the filmmakers "constructed it to a certain extent," but he insisted that "it's not a fake. It is a true story." He admitted that in addition to using several chimps to portray Oscar, events did not happen in exactly the same chronological order as presented in the film, nor did they all take place in the same location, but suggested that he really had intended to make a feature film with a true background because people "want a strong story. They want strong characters" (cited in von Leszczynski 2013). It seems that—much like the producers of a fiction film—the filmmakers simply put the needs of the story above the need for factuality.

The trouble with *Chimpanzee*, then, is in part the fact that it was indexed and marketed by its production company as a documentary, leading spectators to view it as such. While it is safe to assume that they would also have empathized with little Oscar had they believed they were watching a fiction film, their belief in the film's factuality led them to feel duped when they learnt of its staged nature, precisely because their feelings had been "peculiar" in the sense outlined by Eitzen (above). This also makes clear that anthropomorphic storytelling techniques can hinge on many different levels of the cinematic representation of animals, modulating the moments of trans-species empathy we might feel for nonhuman characters in myriad ways. Like Fothergill, Swiss primatologist Christophe Boesch (cited in von Leszczynski 2013), a scientific consultant for *Chimpanzee*, has insisted that "the film is true from a scientific point of view" because it depicts behavior that "corresponds to that of the chimpanzees of the Tai National Park", where the narrative is set. Similar things could be said of much of fiction, however. Thus, at least as a documentary, *Chimpanzee* is (strictly speaking) a film that lies in terms of its factual indexicality.

CONCLUSION

In this chapter, I have suggested that research in cognitive ethology and affective neuroscience can help explain why we respond empathically not only to the heavily anthropomorphized animals we find in Disney animation and related forms of fiction, but that our biological makeup also allows us to empathize on an affective and involuntary level with actual and un-anthropomorphized animals. The producers of wildlife films and other documentaries featuring animals rely on these cognitive and affective abilities in viewers when showing close-ups and other shots that communicate animal emotions. In addition, they often use crudely anthropomorphizing storytelling techniques, which suggest that animals not only have similar needs but also the same hopes and goals as humans. They do so because they want their films to be commercially viable—and, as many cognitive film scholars have argued, emotionally engaging films tend to be the most successful at the box office.

However, there is frequently a further, more altruistic motivation behind the creation of emotionally engaging animal stories. Wildlife filmmakers often want to raise awareness for the species they depict, and they sometimes go so far as to tie their films to specific conservation projects. This is even the case with highly commercial films such as *Chimpanzee*. During its opening week, Disney donated 20 cents of every *Chimpanzee* ticket sold to the Jane Goodall Institute for the "See *Chimpanzee*, Save Chimpanzees" program, later extending the campaign into the second weekend (Horon 2012). And even if the effects are not quite as immediate and tangible, wildlife films may contribute to raising awareness. Welling (2014, pp. 86–87) speculates that *Winged Migration*'s "mesmerizing formation shots" and fascinating insights into the lives of migrating birds "can be productively extrapolated to our everyday interactions with birds... and nonhuman beings in general" and thereby "mitigate" our relationship to the more-than-human world. While they always run the risk of turning into ecoporn and bambification, wildlife documentaries can, nevertheless, help us gain a better understanding of what it is like to experience the world through a different set of senses, and can remind us (both on the cognitive and the visceral level) that conscious, thinking and feeling beings deserve to be treated with more respect.

What such documentaries also offer is a different perspective on cognitive approaches to film characters. To date, such approaches have been deeply anthropocentric, in the sense that they tend to be concerned first and foremost with human characters. While Eitzen's analysis of his reactions to the documentation of a suffering dog demonstrates that there have been some productive observations on viewer engagement with animals, they seem to be almost coincidental. My concluding suggestion is, therefore, that cognitive film theory has not yet given enough thought to animal characters more generally, but particularly to the *actual* nonhuman protagonists of documentary films that engage viewers across species lines.

REFERENCES

Armbruster, K. (2013) "What Do We Want from Talking Animals? Reflections on Literary Representations of Animal Voices and Minds," in DeMello, M. (ed.) *Speaking for Animals: Animal Autobiographical Writing*. New York: Routledge, pp. 17–33.

Bekoff, M. (2003) *Minding Animals: Awareness, Emotions, and Heart*. New York: Oxford University Press.

Bekoff, M. (2007) *The Emotional Lives of Animals: A Leading Scientist Explores Animal Joy, Sorrow, and Empathy—And Why They Matter*. Novato: New World Library.

Bekoff, M., Allen, C. and Burghardt, G. (eds.) (2002) *The Cognitive Animal: Empirical and Theoretical Perspectives on Animal Cognition*. Cambridge: MIT Press.

Berns, G. (2013) "Dogs Are People, Too." *The New York Times*, October 5 [Online]. Available at: http://www.nytimes.com/2013/10/06/opinion/sunday/dogs-are-people-too.html?_r=0 (Accessed: September 10, 2016).

Bousé, D. (2000) *Wildlife Films*. Philadelphia: University of Pennsylvania Press.

Bradshaw, G. A. and Watkins, M. (2006) "Trans-species Psychology: Theory and Praxis," *Spring Journal*, 75, pp. 69–94.

Burt, J. (2002) *Animals in Film*. London: Reaktion Books.

Carroll, N. (1996) "Nonfiction Film and Postmodernist Skepticism," in Bordwell, D. and Carroll, N. (eds.) *Post-Theory: Reconstructing Film Studies*. Madison: University of Wisconsin Press, pp. 283–305.

Chris, C. (2006) *Watching Wildlife*. Minneapolis: University of Minnesota Press.

De Waal, F. (2001) *The Ape and the Sushi Master: Cultural Reflections of a Primatologist*. New York: Basic Books.

De Waal, F. (2009) *The Age of Empathy: Nature's Lessons for a Kinder Society*. New York: Three River Press.

Eitzen, D. (1995) "When is a Documentary? Documentary as a Mode of Reception," *Cinema Journal*, 35(1, Autumn), pp. 81–102.

Eitzen, D. (2005) "Documentary's Peculiar Appeals," in Anderson, J. T. (ed.) *Moving Image Theory*. Carbondale: Southern Illinois University Press, pp. 183–199.

Franklin, R. G., Anthony, J. N., Baker, M., Beeney, J. E., Vescio, T. K., Lenz-Watson, A. and Adams, R. B. (2013) "Neural Responses to Perceiving Suffering in Humans and Animals," *Social Neuroscience*, 8(3), pp. 217–227.

Gallese, V. (2014) "Bodily Selves in Relation: Embodied Simulation as Second-Person Perspective on Intersubjectivity," *Philosophical Transactions of the Royal Society B*, 1–10 [Online]. Available at: http://rstb.royalsocietypublishing.org/content/369/1644/20130177 (Accessed: September 10, 2016).

Garrard, G. (2012) *Ecocriticism: The New Critical Idiom*. 2nd edn. New York: Routledge.

Grodal, T. (2009) *Embodied Visions: Evolution, Emotion, Culture, and Film*. Oxford: Oxford University Press.

Guzman, R. (2012) "*Chimpanzee* is Compelling and Cute," *Newsday*, April 18 [Online]. Available at: http://www.newsday.com/entertainment/movies/chimpanzee-is-compelling-and-cute-1.3669064 (Accessed: September 10, 2016).

Hoffman, M. (2000) *Empathy and Moral Development: Implications for Caring and Justice*. Cambridge: Cambridge University Press.

Horon, S. (2012) "Disney Extends 'Chimpanzee' Donations," *Global Animal*, April 27 [Online]. Available at: http://www.globalanimal.org/2012/04/27/disney-extends-chimpanzee-donations/73107/ (Accessed: September 10, 2010).

Kellner, D. (2010) *Cinema Wars*. Oxford: Blackwell Publishing.

Mitman, G. (2009) *Reel Nature: America's Romance with Wildlife on Film*. Seattle: University of Washington Press.

Nagel, T. (1974) "What Is It Like to Be a Bat?," *The Philosophical Review*, 83(4), pp. 435–450.

Panksepp, J. (1998) *Affective Neuroscience: The Foundations of Human and Animal Emotions*. New York: Oxford University Press.

Panksepp, J. and Panksepp, J. B. (2013) "Toward a Cross-species Understanding of Empathy," *Trends in Neuroscience*, 36(8), pp. 489–496.

Pick, A. (2011) *Creaturely Poetics: Animality and Vulnerability in Literature and Film*. New York: Columbia University Press.

Plantinga, C. (2009) *Moving Viewers: American Film and the Spectator Experience*. Berkeley: University of California Press.

Rivas, J. and Burghardt, G. M. (2002) "Crotalomorphism: A Metaphor for Understanding Anthropomorphism by Omission," in Bekoff, M., Allen, C. and Burghardt, G. M. (eds.) *The Cognitive Animal: Empirical and Theoretical Perspectives on Animal Cognition*. Cambridge, MA: MIT Press.

Rust, S. (2014) "Ecocinema and the Wildlife Film," in Westling, L. (ed.) *The Cambridge Companion to Literature and the Environment*. Cambridge: Cambridge University Press, pp. 226–239.

Smith, M. (1995) *Engaging Characters: Fiction, Emotion, and the Cinema*. Oxford: Oxford University Press.

Sturgeon, N. (2009) *Environmentalism in Popular Culture: Gender, Race, Sexuality, and the Politics of the Natural*. Tucson: University of Arizona Press.

Von Leszczynski, U. (2013) "Film *Chimpanzee* Leads to Questions Over the 'Truth'," *Gulf Times*, May 19 [Online]. Available at: http://www.gulf-times.com/story/353179/Film-Chimpanzee-leads-to-questions-over-the-truth (Accessed: September 10, 2016).

Welling, B. H. (2009) "Ecoporn: On the Limits of Visualizing the Nonhuman," in Dobrin, S. and Morey, S. (eds.) *Ecosee: Image, Rhetoric, Nature*. Albany: SUNY Press, pp. 53–77.

Welling, B. H. (2014) "On 'The Inexplicable Magic of Cinema': Critical Anthropomorphism, Emotion, and the Wildness of Wildlife Films," in Weik von Mossner, A. (ed.) *Moving Environments: Affect, Emotion, Ecology, and Film*. Waterloo: Wilfrid Laurier University Press, pp. 81–101.

Welling, B. H. and Kapel, S. (2012) "The Return of the Animal: Presenting and Representing Non-Human Beings Response-ably in the (Post-)Humanities Classroom," in Garrard, G. (ed.) *Teaching Ecocriticism in Green Cultural Studies*. Basingstoke: Palgrave Macmillan.

PART III

Emotions and Embodied Experience

CHAPTER 11

Collateral Emotions: Political Web Videos and Divergent Audience Responses

Jens Eder

During the last decade, the landscape of audiovisual media has fundamentally changed. Online video has become a medium of its own, no less important than cinema or television. In this medium, various new documentary forms are emerging, and even more traditional forms are functioning differently in their digitally networked environments. Particularly interesting is the case of political web videos and the diverging emotions they elicit. As per definition, political emotions are connected to the conflicting concerns of different groups engaged in societal struggles. Many videos address such concerns, trigger clashes between collective emotions and exert persuasive power. Current debates highlight the ethical and political issues at stake: participation or propaganda, visibility or surveillance, dignity or defamation. Many of these issues depend crucially on filmmakers' affective strategies and viewers' responses.

Turning to the example of WikiLeaks' harrowing video *Collateral Murder* (2010), this chapter explores the question of how divergent affective responses to documentary web videos can be explained. Every day on Facebook, YouTube or Twitter we see viewers' reactions diverge, yet there are no comprehensive explanations of this as yet. This chapter, therefore, suggests a preliminary explanation of divergent responses by considering

J. Eder (✉)
Film University Babelsberg KONRAD WOLF, Potsdam, Germany

© The Author(s) 2018   183
C. Brylla, M. Kramer (eds.), *Cognitive Theory and Documentary Film*, https://doi.org/10.1007/978-3-319-90332-3_11

the characteristics of: (1) web video as a medium; (2) documentary as a genre; (3) film's affective structures; and (4) viewers' social dispositions. Its argument is based on an understanding of documentaries as "asserted veridical representations" (Plantinga 2005) and of emotions/affects as psychophysical processes interconnecting perceptual and cognitive appraisals, bodily arousal and behavioral tendencies (Moors 2009).

I will argue for the following theses: first, online video is a new audiovisual medium with specific characteristics that influence documentary practice and bring forth new documentary forms. Second, some characteristics of documentary web videos contribute to both a particular visibility and a striking divergence of audience responses—including various unintended "collateral" emotions (e.g. Dillard and Nabi 2006, p. 130). Third, to explain this divergence we need theories of emotion elicitation that systematically describe the interplay of audiovisual structures and viewers' dispositions. Drawing on my previous work (Eder 2008, 2017), this chapter offers a model that allows us to track the affective experiences of different groups of viewers to the nodes where their reactions diverge, and to provide reasons for their divergence in today's media environments.

Nonfiction Web Videos: Considering Medium and Genre

During the last decade, the audiovisual environment has changed profoundly. Arguably, online video has become an audiovisual medium of its own, a "socially realized structure of communication" (Gitelman 2008, p. 7), defined by its prototypical constellation of digital technologies, organizations, forms, conventions and practices. Production is characterized by low costs, ease of use, lack of professional filters and new possibilities for co-creation and remediation, all of which contribute to the huge variety of professional and non-professional user-generated and user-collected content. Distribution is networked, algorithmic, less restricted by gatekeepers, potentially global and permanently accessible. Reception is characterized by usually small, often mobile screens, by higher degrees of distraction, but most of all by new possibilities for interaction and participation: videos are collected in channels, liked, commented upon, re-edited and spread across platforms, sometimes entering other media. In fact, online video has developed into the largest field of audiovisual production and distribution, and it is growing rapidly (e.g. Meeker 2016).

In this media environment, various new nonfiction forms, such as vlogs or mashups, are emerging. While most videos are short unedited recordings that do not qualify as documentary films, social media also contribute to the unimaginable variety and reach of documentaries (Nash et al. 2014). Some of these, like *Under the Dome* (2015), get more than 100 million views globally in just a few days. Others explore the possibilities of the medium in innovative ways: for example, interactive documentaries or crowdsourced creative commons films, such as *Preempting Dissent* (2014), which sometimes blur the boundaries between fiction and nonfiction, activism and art, or film and game. Yet, even more conventional "webdocs" and mobilization films like *Kony2012* (2012), which emulate classical documentary forms, are shaped by their new contexts of production, distribution and reception. They are made for the Web 2.0 and anticipate their viewers' follow-up interactions (by using viral strategies, for example).

The medial characteristics of web video influence viewers' emotions in various ways. On the one hand, videos are often watched on small screens, over short time-spans and in distracted states of mind, which presumably leads to less intense responses than in movie theaters. On the other hand, videos are embedded in multimodal "webspheres" with specific affordances (Brügger 2010), and many become meaningful elements of networked interactions. When they are watched, liked, shared or commented upon, they become parts of their viewers' public self-expression, construction of identities, and struggle for attention and social capital (Sundar et al. 2015). This tends to intensify emotional involvement and evoke additional emotions related to the viewers' own identities and actions, especially to social emotions like pride or shame.

These affective tendencies of the medium meet the most general tendencies of the genre. Documentaries share some affective structures with fiction films (Bondebjerg 2014). However, as "asserted veridical representations" (Plantinga 2005, p. 114), they invite the audience to accept their images, sounds and statements as reliable sources for *concrete beliefs* about the persons, objects and events they represent. On the one hand, this claim of veridicality constrains filmmakers' possibilities for shaping viewers' emotions (for instance, by inventing fantastic events). On the other hand, it brings forth a "concrete continuity between ourselves and the world on the screen" (Gaines, cited in Smaill 2010, p. 5). This perceived continuity tends to make us feel that: (1) the represented events have consequences in our shared reality (Eitzen 2005); (2) our own concerns may be affected by them; (3) we have some agency or moral responsibility towards them; and (4) we can expect veracity from the filmmakers. Taken together, this not only saturates viewers' "witness emotions" (Tan 1996) with a feeling of "realness," but also fosters additional self-, group- or interaction-related emotions—for instance, fear about our fate, guilt about our non-assistance or outrage about deceitful filmmakers. This general tendency of the genre is reinforced by the above-mentioned tendency of online video: the users' sense of agency and identity in a public space of networked interaction. In other words, documentary web videos make us feel like we should act, and their digital environments offer immediate possibilities to act. If and how these tendencies are realized depends on many factors: for instance, they take different shapes in the various kinds and modes of documentary (Bondebjerg 2014; Brinckmann 2014; Nichols 2010; Smaill 2010; Weik von Mossner 2014). Moreover, their realization depends on the viewers' dispositions—for example, their closeness to the represented events. Studies on nonfictional television indicate, for instance, that most viewers are hardly moved by representations of distant suffering in the news but some viewers are, and that longer documentaries elicit stronger emotions (Scott 2014).

The combined medial and generic tendencies of documentary web videos contribute to a spectatorship divergence that surfaces most strikingly in political conflicts. Politics—the public discussion and regulation of common affairs—is a conflictual process because the various social groups in or across societies have different interests, power and status (Celikates and Gosepath 2013). The possibilities of including user-generated footage (from witnesses, for example), circumventing gatekeepers and reaching global and niche audiences on a small budget, have proven particularly attractive for less powerful groups. This has contributed to the emergence of several new genres of activist videos, partly based on earlier traditions of "committed documentaries" (Waugh 2011) but adapting the practices of political documentation, education, commentary, mobilization and self-representation to the new media environment (Askanius 2014; Mateos and Gaona 2015; Presence 2016). Their forms range from "strategic impact documentaries" (Nash and Corner 2016) to citizen journalism, "artivist" videos, and grassroots productions serving the aims of group connection and self-expression. In the context of the research project, *Video Activism 2.0* (Eder et al. 2016), I study the affective strategies of activist videos in, for instance, presenting evidence, narrating stories or developing arguments (Eder 2017). As they are made by citizens, groups or NGOs who oppose the dominant politics, most of these videos are highly controversial and evoke diverging political emotions in different audience groups.

COLLATERAL MURDER AND THE DIVERGENCE OF VIEWERS' RESPONSES

A particularly instructive example of an activist video is WikiLeaks' *Collateral Murder*, released on April 3, 2010 on the organization's own website and shared widely on various platforms. The production and global distribution of the video would not have been possible without the features of the new media environment. The 18-minute film consists predominantly of edited footage from the targeting system of a US attack helicopter during the Iraq War in 2007. The US army had kept the footage secret until it was leaked by whistleblower Chelsea (then Bradley) Manning and digitally reconstructed and edited by WikiLeaks members. The footage shows how the helicopter crew kills several Iraqi citizens and two Reuters photojournalists in a public square in Baghdad. Exchanging cynical remarks about their victims, the crew continues the assault even when a minivan arrives and unarmed men attempt to rescue the only survivor. After the attack, ground forces arrive and find two injured children in the van. The edited video explains these events by sparse textual inserts. The leaked footage is framed by a prologue introducing the killed journalists and an epilogue exposing the cover-up by the military and inviting viewers to support WikiLeaks. On the WikiLeaks website, *Collateral Murder* is accompanied by an unedited version of the footage and additional information such as transcripts of the soldiers' radio messages.

At the time of writing, the edited video has been watched nearly 15.8 million times on YouTube alone, and it has triggered furious debates. YouTube's commentary thread contains more than 80,000 statements (some of them pages long), mostly expressing antagonistic emotions and providing us with clear indicators of some of the viewers' responses. Here is a choice of examples (using original spelling):

1. Eleanor Carter: This is fucking sickening. What bastard high school dropouts my country puts on the battlefield—no worse—above the battlefield with cowardly Apache helicopters who are trigger happy and don't even care that they just killed a dozen civilians just to kill 1 guy who they weren't even sure had a weapon.

2. Edward Kirkhope: This is despicable. They completely lied that they had seen guns. Killing people helping the injured. Then killed children.
3. Jake Luxford: This gives me so many chills.
4. Jesse James: This is a terrible and sad outcome but every journalist knows the danger when you enter this type of environment, this could happen... This is war.
5. Geek Krew (wwllhero9): I found it kind of badass and funny tbh. They deserve it for every american life theyve taken.
6. Peter Martin: Its hard not to get sick watching this massacre. Anyone who sees this blood lust and defends it on patriotic grounds would need to get psychiatric treatment. I honestly never thought that it was possible to exterminate human beings and glory in it, revel at the 'dead bastards', laugh at the dead and the dying and now I know, it's very possible. ... So, clearly the United States is a cesspool of human waste and it represents a serious threat to humanity. It's semi-literate president Bush with his British counterpart Tony Blair will rot in hell I hope ... Perverts!
7. Lisas Corner: The world and its people are horrible ... nobody even got into jail for that ... only the person who made it public ... humans are unfair assholes who only care about them selfes ... I hate the U.S.A. fuck you.
8. Amber Dahlem: We wonder why everyone hates us. Lets piss off a country, then kill them all, then rebuild them at tax payer money. Wow we suck as a nation.
9. Paul G (Paulie): It's pretty sad to see all the hate against every single American ... As an officer in the U.S. Army, it is always hard to read and see what really went on in Iraq. It is definitely difficult to see a video like this. ... It is truly unfortunate that the actions of some detestable military personnel from the United States made all of us look bad. ... I can't apologize for an entire Army and can't speak for all the terrible things that our members have done, but I still am sorry to people who have actually felt the negative effects due to our intervention. ... we are coping too. I will continue to love America and defend it in the military, but I hope that our country doesn't spiral into the wrong and evil direction again.
10. Miguel Mota (Moogs): Great video, just like in *Call of Duty*.

Of course, this is only a minuscule sample of commentaries by English-speaking users who felt strongly enough to be moved to comment, but it suffices to demonstrate the extreme divergence of explicitly expressed emotions. As a first step in the analysis, we can distinguish at least four different kinds of responses, according to their object:

1. Many viewers express *event- and actor-related emotions* that probably were also intended by WikiLeaks: shock, horror and disgust over the events, compassion for the victims and moral outrage over the soldiers' actions (as in examples 1–3). Contrary statements, however, indicate sympathy with the soldiers, satisfaction with the strike and even glee over the killing of alleged 'terrorists' (as in 5). Some commentators also adopt a smug attitude of fatalistic sobriety ("this is war," example 4).
2. Quite a few viewers express *emotions related to their own self and group identities* (as in 6–9). Some US citizens speak of collective shame and guilt, others are proud of their country's military power. Some people from other countries express their hatred toward the US or a desire for revenge. Often, such group-related emotions are connected with anticipations of the *possible consequences of the video* (as in 9), such as concern about the image of the US or fear of retaliation.
3. Further emotions are related to the *producers and distributors of the video*: for instance, admiration for WikiLeaks, compassion for the jailed whistle-blower, Manning (as in 7) or, on the contrary, contempt for them.
4. A final group of reactions is characterized by an amoral, voyeuristic attitude of enjoying *the video as an artefact offering a fictionalized spectacle* (in 10 this is marked by the intertextual comparison). It is unclear what exactly such comments express: sarcasm, a lack of empathy, a struggle to cope with the disturbing content, or feelings of superiority by provoking others.

Below, I will suggest how these (and further kinds of responses) can be systematically described and explained. For now, the examples simply demonstrate how viewers' actual responses to political web videos often diverge significantly. The easy accessibility, dynamic spread, transcultural distribution and private reception of online videos mean that their audiences are usually much more fragmented and heterogeneous than the audiences of theatrical films. Many video producers target several groups of viewers at once, *intending* to evoke divergent affective responses. For instance, the so-called Islamic State's videos aim not only to evoke shock, horror and anxiety in the enemy's public (Rieger et al. 2013), they are also designed to elicit pleasurable feelings of power, pride and malicious glee among the perpetrators and their followers, submissive admiration in rival factions, and outrage among the adversary's elites. However, even if homogeneous responses are intended, as is the case with *Collateral Murder*, conflicts between political identities and interests will invariably lead to diverging emotions. This is enhanced by the medial and generic characteristics of online videos, which stimulate self- and group-related emotions in spaces of public interaction. The anonymity and spontaneity of expression on social media platforms reduce social pressures to conform to emotional norms, thus encouraging a divergence of expression which, in turn, may feed back into the affective experience itself.

EXPLAINING DIVERGENT RESPONSES: THEORIES AND THEIR VIEWERS

The case of *Collateral Murder*, and countless other comments on social media, illustrate the general observation that online videos regularly elicit widely diverging emotional responses. To explain this divergence, theories of spectatorship and emotion are challenged to account more systematically for differences in at least three respects: media and their genres, affects and viewers' dispositions.

1. *Media/genres*: Most current theories of spectatorship focus on feature films in the movie theater, but they fail to acknowledge the affective specificity of other audiovisual genres and media (for example, the spreadability and asserted veridicality of nonfiction videos in the social web).
2. *Affects*: Most theories focus on event- and actor-related emotions (the first group of responses to *Collateral Murder*), but do not consider the full range of affective responses (for example, emotions directed at the viewers themselves, the filmmakers or other contextual aspects).
3. *Viewers' dispositions*: Most theories focus on intended, hypothetical or ideal spectators, or on a film's "invitation to feel" (Smith 2003, p. 3), but tend to neglect viewers' social identities and political interests in specific contexts.

Scholars from empirical reception studies (e.g. Barker 2012) have repeatedly criticized film theories for neglecting the variety of spectators' responses; cognitive approaches in particular have been accused of being blind to sociocultural differences (e.g. Hake 2012, p. 19). However, phenomenological, psychoanalytical and Deleuzian theories also concentrate on hypothesized viewers watching feature films in the movie theater. And even cultural studies approaches, in the tradition of Stuart Hall (1980), lack adequate theoretical models to examine the reactions of different audience groups. To explain the responses to *Collateral Murder*, for instance, it would not be sufficient to distinguish between "dominant, negotiated and oppositional readings" that depend on viewers' race, class, gender or sexual orientation.

In the following analysis, I draw on my previous work (e.g. Eder 2008, 2017) to provide some theoretical tools and indicate how cognitive-perceptual theories could take on the challenges mentioned above. Based on multidimensional network theories of emotions (Keil and Eder 2005; Moors 2009; Grodal 2009; Smith 2003), I understand preconscious "affects" and conscious "emotions" as the poles of a continuum that includes any psychophysical processes characterized by the coordination of perceptual or cognitive stimulus appraisals, bodily arousal, action tendencies, expressive and instrumental behavior, and (often) subjective feelings. Different emotions or affects are specified by their patterns of those interrelated processes.

Films can be seen as constellations of *affective cues*—from perceivable pictures to abstract arguments—with the potential of intersubjectively eliciting certain affects and emotions (Smith 2003; Feagin 1996, p. 171). The specific constellation of cues in space and time can be called the film's *affective structure* (Tan 1996; Smith 2003). Affective responses are elicited when cues interact with the viewers' *affective dispositions*, the bodily and mental structures that make them react in typical ways to certain kinds of stimuli (Persson 2003; Feagin 1996, p. 172). Dispositions range from the architecture of the brain to specific personal concerns, and from the universal to the cultural, social, individual and situational. Broadly, then, relations between films and affects can be explained on the basis of the following formula:

Films' structures + viewers' dispositions = viewers' affective responses

Thus, the most general question for theories of film and affect is the following: what affective cues evoke what responses in viewers with what dispositions?

So far, cognitive theories have focused mostly on general or universal dispositions—for instance, common structures of the body and brain, evolutionary adaptations, general appraisal factors, the need for control or cross-cultural moral intuitions. However, the example of *Collateral Murder* shows that dispositions that lead to systematic *differences* between viewers' responses are of equal importance. To identify the most important dispositions, film theorists could take advantage of the wide range of research undertaken in the social sciences. I can only offer a brief selection of relevant concepts here.

The only concept that cognitive theorists seem to have taken up so far is Jonathan Haidt's (2012) idea of *moral emotions*, governed by intuitive concerns about care, fairness, loyalty, authority or purity. Haidt claims that the relative weight of these concerns already differs between political groups: liberal viewers who value *care* might pity the victims, while conservative viewers who value *loyalty* might sympathize with the perpetrators from their own faction. Morality, however, is too narrow a frame, and it can be influenced by other social concerns. Many of the diverging responses to *Collateral Murder* could, rather, be framed as *political emotions*: that is, social emotions caused by interrelations between and inside political groups, including nation states, parties or groups in civil society (Clarke et al. 2006; Nussbaum 2013). Political emotions may be other-centered (for example, care, hate or fear) or self-centered (for example, pride, guilt or shame). As *social emotions*, many of these result "from real, anticipated, recollected, or imagined outcomes of social relationships," in terms of power and status (Kemper 1978, p. 43), which may conflict with morality or override it. Moreover, political emotions are *intergroup emotions* that "arise when people identify with a social group and respond emotionally to events or objects that impinge on that group" (Smith and Mackie 2008, p. 428; Scheve and Ismer 2013). In media psychology, this is discussed under the heading of "social identity theory" (e.g. Trepte and Loy 2017). Recurring patterns of conflict between groups lead to corresponding patterns of emotion, to specific distributions of sympathy, antipathy or empathy across in-groups and out-groups. From this perspective, political documentaries can be seen as tools that can be used to not only trigger and distribute intergroup emotions or to build (imagined) communities, but also exclude others from those communities. Viewers react to the perceived group memberships and relationships of producers, distributors and audiences, and especially to developments relevant to their own groups' power or status.

In the case of *Collateral Murder*, many of the differences between viewers' affective responses could be explained by referring to moral, social, political and intergroup frames that position the viewers along antagonistic lines. Which dispositions are relevant will depend not only on the represented act (the helicopter attack), but also on the act of representation (the leaking of classified footage). We may assume that the following dispositions play a central role: national identities as citizens of the US, Iraq, or allied or neutral countries; professional identities as soldiers or journalists; political orientations as leftist or rightist, liberal or conservative, hawk or pacifist, and proponents or opponents of digital leaks. We may further assume that the represented events will be framed differently depending on how these groups' relations, power and status are concerned. For instance, US viewers who strongly identify with their nation will tend to sympathize with the soldiers and block empathy with the victims in order to keep their group's perceived power and status intact.

Importantly, such dispositions and consequential emotions can be activated not only by the represented events but also by the act of representation. For instance, US right-wingers will tend to hate WikiLeaks for disseminating *Collateral Murder* and fear consequential damage for their in-group. Many viewers will see themselves not as impartial observers but as enemies in an uneven power structure. This tendency will be increased by nonfiction-based beliefs that the events actually happened, as well as medium-based assumptions of interacting in an anonymous web environment that facilitates enlightenment as well as manipulation. But to explain how viewers' dispositions lead to specific emotions and to develop hypotheses that can be tested by empirical methods (Reinhard and Olson 2016), we need to know more precisely how viewers' dispositions interact with film's affective structures.

FILM'S AFFECTIVE STRUCTURES: FOUR LAYERS OF SPECTATORSHIP DIVERGENCE

Many aesthetic and psychological theories distinguish between several structural levels of artworks or related audience experiences (e.g. Persson 2003; Bordwell 2008). A triangulation of such theories has led me to describe the affective structures of films as composed of four layers that correspond to viewers' sensual, cognitive and affective processing of certain kinds of cues: "forms," "worlds," "meanings" and "reflections" (e.g. Eder 2008, 2017). These layers are interconnected by bidirectional reception processes (bottom-up/top-down), so that any layer may influence the others.

1. *Forms:* The mostly preconscious perception of audiovisual signs (forms, colors, sounds or patterns, rhythms, movements) triggers *perceptual affects and moods* even before any objects are recognized. This level is addressed when we speak of "sad" hues, "beautiful" forms, "nervous" rhythms, and so on. It dominates in abstract films and grounds the following layers of experiencing representational films. Film theories struggle to describe this level of sensual experiences with concepts like "direct affect" (Plantinga 2009, pp. 117–120), "basic aesthetic effects" or "feelings of intensity" (Grodal 2009, p. 272).

2. *Worlds:* Above the threshold of object recognition, viewers re-create a film's represented world by developing mental models of spaces, characters and events. This evokes a whole range of *representational* or *diegetic emotions:* desire for knowledge, control and orientation in time and space; sympathy or empathy with represented persons and groups; emotional side-taking in their conflicts; curiosity, suspense and surprise about actions and events; situational feelings of hope, joy, and so on. Most theories focus on this level, on a film's "referential meaning" (Bordwell 1989), characters" "situational meaning structures" (Tan 1996) or the embodied simulation of action (Grodal 2009). On this level, factual and fictional world-representations tend to generate different kinds of emotions because of their different relations to viewers' lifeworlds.

3. *Meanings:* Viewers regularly search audiovisual forms and worlds for higher-level, general meanings. This includes the processes of sense-making, thematic comprehension, inference, association and abstraction (Bremond et al. 1995), often by interpreting formal motifs or elements of the represented world as secondary signs (symbols, metaphors, allusions) that express something else. By way of this, viewers understand overarching themes, messages and arguments, "explicit or implicit meanings" (Bordwell 1989) or "meta-perspectives" (Grodal 2009). These higher-level meanings are felt: they evoke various *thematic emotions* related to the viewers' own

worldviews—for instance, forms of "eudaimonic" "appreciation" (Oliver and Bartsch 2010). Fiction films also transmit general messages that concern real-world issues. In documentaries, however, such messages are more often the contentious result of political rhetoric, which tends to make viewers aware of the next level.

4. *Reflections*: Beyond intended meanings, viewers regularly reflect on their own current communicative context when watching a film or video. They criticize a film's lack of authenticity or admire its aesthetic design ("artifact emotions") (Tan 1996), scrutinize the filmmakers' intentions and the film's "symptomatic meanings" (Bordwell 1989), enjoy feelings of participating in a public communication (Grodal 2009, p. 274), anticipate impacts on other audiences, reflect on their own responses and feel meta-emotions like pride in their ability to empathize (Jäger and Bartsch 2006). Such affective responses may be called *reflective emotions*, as they presuppose reflections about the elements, causes and consequences of the current process of communication. Such emotions may be triggered by the film's forms, worlds and meanings, but also by contextual or paratextual information such as titles, credits, self-references and posters. Most theories only touch upon selected aspects of this important layer of affective cues, but it can be more comprehensively described by using the concept of mental *context models of discourse* (van Dijk 2008). Context models represent all the relevant aspects of "communicative episodes in which we participate" (p. 130): the spatiotemporal and medial settings; the participants, including the producers, oneself and other users; and the communicative events and textual elements. All these aspects can trigger certain kinds of emotions. The rhetorical mode of political documentaries regularly calls viewers' attention to the filmmakers who try to persuade them, as well as to the possible results of this attempt. In the case of political web videos, it becomes crucial that viewers react to the perceived group memberships, intentions and relationships of producers, distributors and audiences, and especially to consequences relevant to their own groups' power or status. Often, viewers become angry with politically opposed filmmakers or sympathize with filmmakers fighting for a mutual cause.

With each layer, the specific system of affective cues can be described in more detail by using aesthetic, rhetorical and other concepts. To ignore certain layers in theory or analysis is problematic, as they are interconnected and nested in complex ways. In the temporal flow of watching films, their affective impulses interact: for instance, a shocking action may be downplayed by gentle forms or stressed by unpleasant ones. There is a certain bottom-up drift: to infer general messages, viewers have to understand represented worlds, and to do that, they have to perceive audiovisual forms. As the layers become more cognitively complex, the probability that the affective responses of different groups of viewers diverge also increases. Perceptual affects like the startle response (layer 1) are hard to avoid, and bodily responses to images of mutilation are hard to control (layer 2). In contrast, higher-level moral responses to persons, meanings or communicative situations are much more dependent on the viewers' group attitudes and ideologies. This is especially important in the case of political videos. But the bottom-up drift does not exclude top-down influences; on the contrary, if viewers doubt the filmmakers' credibility (layer 4), for example, they may also respond differently to the represented events (layer 2) or even lose the desire to invest perceptual attention (level 1). The interaction between all four layers means that film theories may not ignore any of them.

COLLATERAL MURDER AND COLLATERAL EMOTIONS

By reconstructing how a film's affective structures interact with viewers' dispositions (bottom-up as well as top-down), the conceptual tools outlined above can be applied to explain divergent responses to controversial videos like *Collateral Murder*, including various kinds of "collateral emotions" (Dillard and Nabi 2006).

Viewers enter the reception process with various paratextual information from different websites and with diverging dispositions and anticipations (curiosity about the leak, fear of learning ugly things about their in-group, and so on) that inform their viewing experience. On this basis, they perceive the *forms* of the video, which are mainly characterized by blurred, grey figures that frustrate precise object recognition, by monotonous static noises, cold voices, sudden changes of volume and perspective, and by slow, lingering or prowling camera movements. For most viewers, these cues will elicit tense, nervous feelings and dreary, unpleasant moods, which underlie the whole experience and stress the gruesome action (for example, the sudden noise when the helicopter shoots will startle most viewers).

In terms of the *represented world*, we can also expect certain commonalities. All viewers observe an act of deadly violence. Most will feel suspense as to how it unfolds and will respond with some degree of horror and fascination at perceiving the carnage from a distance, without hearing the victims' cries or seeing their pain in color and close-up. More specifically, viewers react to the unequal conflict between helpless victims who are visible but inaudible and powerful soldiers who are audible but invisible. *Collateral Murder* forces viewers into the soldiers' *perceptual* perspective but suggests an *evaluative* perspective that is contrary to their cynical remarks. For example, the prologue has already introduced the killed Reuters employees as likable colleagues and fathers. By way of such strategies, the video aims to distribute sympathy and antipathy across the conflict constellation.

Whether this aim is actually achieved, however, depends on the viewers' dispositions and their acceptance of the video as a truthful documentary. If viewers with common moral intuitions believe that the attack happened as represented, their emotions will include constellations of shock and disgust about the events, compassion for the victims, outrage towards the perpetrators and sympathy for the benefactors trying to rescue the wounded (comments 1–3, above). In some cases, such emotions will be tempered by a contemplative or fatalistic sobriety (comment 4). Some viewers, however, watch the whole video as if it were fictional, adopting an amoral aesthetic attitude and enjoying the spectacular attack with voyeuristic pleasure (comment 10).

These emotions match Boltanski's (1999) famous model of responses toward distant suffering: pamphleteering, philanthropy, sublimation and solitary enjoyment. But other reactions escape this model and are contrary to intended responses: some viewers express spite towards the victims, sympathy with the soldiers and satisfaction with the strike (comment 5). They believe that the attack happened, but not as represented by WikiLeaks, and see the victims not as innocents but as armed "terrorists" who "deserve it". This obviously changes their moral appraisals and resulting emotions. But from a standpoint of common morality, this would still not justify the expressed satisfaction. After all, the helicopter crew deride and kill maimed people crouching on the ground, which disturbs even viewers who are themselves US soldiers (comment 9). The satisfied responses of other viewers can only be explained by extreme nationalist, pro-war dispositions and by their stance toward the filmmakers (layer 4)—they hate and distrust WikiLeaks, and do not *want* to believe the video (see below).

This also concerns the next layer of cues, the general *meanings* of the video. The title *Collateral Murder* already suggests an explicit message: what we are observing is not an accident but murder, the military has lied about it and those responsible should be prosecuted. Moreover, the attack stands for the behavior of the US army in general. Implicitly, the video suggests that this war crime is not the only one, and demands that further massacres be prevented. These messages build on explicit statements, as well as the evidential rhetoric of the audiovisual material. Responses towards these statements are partly independent from reactions to the represented events: viewers may believe that the murderous attack really happened, but that it is a rare exception, or they might doubt the documentary's veracity but still think that the US Army deserves this kind of criticism. In any case, the general meanings concern the larger social groups many viewers are related to in some way: journalists, Iraqi citizens, the US and its military. Therefore, this layer of cues will often trigger emotions influenced by the viewers' relations to these groups. For example, many US citizens feel collective shame and guilt, or anger towards their own group (comments 6–9), while political opponents, journalists or Iraqi citizens might feel outrage, hate or contempt for the US military or the US in general. In contrast, others from the pro-war, pro-US camp will feel offended by the message, become angry or react with defiance, reinterpreting the events as expressing a general message about the military prowess of the US.

Their anger may extend from the message to its sender, thus reaching the next layer of communicative *reflections*, stimulated by the viewers' contextual models. Again, social dispositions, genre and medium influence this layer of emotions, based on the viewers' reflections about the filmmakers, the video itself and its possible impact on other audiences. Strikingly, many of the emotions expressed in the comments are related to the producers and distributors of the video. Depending on the viewer's in-group and political stance, emotions either take the form of admiration for WikiLeaks, Julian Assange (its founder) and Manning (for example, comment 7), or hate and contempt for these "traitors". The comments on *Collateral Murder* show that many US viewers worry about the possible consequences of the video for their in-group, fearing retaliation or damage to the image of US soldiers (as in comment 9). Further reflective responses concern the video itself, its form and its relation to documentary norms. At the time, many US right-wingers have expressed anger at the "manipulative" video, while some leftists have deplored its populist design, which has made it easier to brush aside as mere propaganda.

This provisional analysis already indicates how the growing complexity of appraisal processes, as well as the relevant dispositions of each layer, contribute to increasingly divergent responses. We can assume that

WikiLeaks primarily addressed critical Western viewers with the aim of stimulating intra-group criticism through emotions like collective guilt and moral outrage at in-group perpetrators. These intended responses can be frequently found in the commentaries. Most interesting, however, is the case of pro-war, right-wing US viewers. The video's represented events and its messages conflict most strongly with their dispositions, causing cognitive dissonance and threatening their in-groups with a loss of power and status (such as damage to reputation and self-image, or judicial and political consequences for the military).

Genre and medium enhance this threat: the documentary mode discloses visible evidence. The medium makes this evidence widely available in interactive webspheres that offer further information (for example, about the army's attempts to hide the footage or WikiLeaks' spectacular coup in making it public). The commentaries indicate that, in order to escape the threat and other unpleasant feelings, pro-war viewers take the following options: (1) relativizing guilt by stressing commonalities with the victims ("we are coping too," comment 9); (2) generalizing the perpetrators' behavior as common practice ('this is war', comment 4); (3) fictionalizing the evidence ("just like *Call of Duty*," comment 10); or (4) doubting the represented evidence, the message and the veracity of the filmmakers (layers 2, 3 and 4). In all these cases, social dispositions and reflective emotions act as top-down influences on lower layers of affective responses—for example, by changing the moral appraisal of the perpetrators and blocking empathy with the victims. Compassion, guilt and group-related anxiety can then be converted into anger about deceitful, traitorous filmmakers—a maximal divergence from intended responses. Such kinds of political emotions may also have contributed to the fact that a majority of US mass media downplayed the evidence of the leaked footage (Christensen 2014).

To conclude, the example of *Collateral Murder* demonstrates that affective responses to political videos diverge so strongly because viewers' dispositions, the tendencies of the documentary genre, the characteristics of online video as a medium and the four layers of filmic cues interact in influencing viewers' affective processes. This chapter has offered some conceptual tools that can be used to take these aspects into account. Starting from the question of how divergent affective responses to documentary web videos can be explained, I have argued for the following theses: the medial characteristics of online video bring forth new documentary forms and contribute to a strikingly visible divergence of audience responses on social media platforms, especially in the case of political web videos that express the contentious interests of social groups. To explain this divergence, we need theories that systematically describe the interplay of audiovisual structures and viewers' social dispositions, and that make it possible to track the experiences of different groups of viewers to the nodes where their affective responses diverge. In building such theories, film studies can benefit from recent research in the social sciences. This would be a relevant endeavor, as many ethical and political issues that trouble today's societies also depend on filmmakers' affective strategies and viewers' responses.

Acknowledgements I would like to thank Katja Crone and the editors of this volume for their helpful comments.

REFERENCES

Askanius, T. (2014) "Video for Change," in Wilkins, K. G., Obregon, R. and Tufte, T. (eds.) *The Handbook of Development Communication and Social Change*. Hoboken, NJ: Wiley.

Barker, M. (2012) "Crossing Out the Audience," in Christie, I. (ed.) *Audiences: Defining and Researching Screen Entertainment Reception*. Amsterdam: Amsterdam University Press.

Boltanski, L. (1999) *Distant Suffering: Morality, Media, and Politics*. Cambridge: Cambridge University Press.

Bondebjerg, I. (2014) "Documentary and Cognitive Theory: Narrative, Emotion, and Memory," *Media and Communication*, 1(1), pp. 12–21.

Bordwell, D. (1989) *Making Meaning: Inference and Rhetoric in the Interpretation of Cinema*. Cambridge, MA: Harvard University Press.

Bordwell, D. (2008) *Poetics of Cinema*. New York: Routledge.

Bremond, C., Landy, J. and Pavel, T. (eds.) (1995) *Thematics: New Approaches*. New York: State University of New York Press.

Brinckmann, C. N. (2014) *Color and Empathy. Essays on Two Aspects of Films*. Amsterdam: Amsterdam University Press.

Brügger, N. (2010) *Website Analysis: Elements of a Conceptual Architecture*. Aarhus: The Centre for Internet Research.

Celikates, R. and Gosepath, S. (2013) *Politische Philosophie*. Stuttgart: Reclam.

Christensen, C. (2014) "Collateral Murder and the After-Life of Activist Imagery," *Medium*, April [Online]. Available at: https://medium.com/@ChrChristensen/collateral-murder-and-the-after-life-of-activist-imagery-3fc2accd82bb (Accessed: March 21, 2016).

Clarke, S., Hoggett, P. and Thompson, S. (eds.) (2006) *Emotion, Politics and Society*. Basingstoke: Palgrave Macmillan.

Dillard, J. P. and Nabi, R. (2006) "The Persuasive Influence of Emotion in Cancer Prevention and Detection Messages," *Journal of Communication*, 56, pp. 123–139.

Eder, J. (2008) *Die Figur im Film. Grundlagen der Figurenanalyse*. Marburg: Schüren Verlag.

Eder, J. (2017) "Affective Image Operations," in Eder, J. and Klonk, C. (eds.) *Image Operations: Visual Media and Political Conflict*. Manchester: Manchester University Press.

Eder, J., Tedjasukmana, C. and Hartmann, B. (eds.) (2016) *Video Activism 2.0 between Social Media and Social Movements* [Online]. Available at: http://videoactivism. net/en/ (Accessed: March 20, 2016).

Eitzen, D. (2005) "Documentary's Peculiar Appeals," in Anderson, J. D. and Anderson, B. F. (eds.) *Moving Image Theory*. Carbondale: Southern Illinois University Press.

Feagin, S. (1996) *Reading with Feeling: The Aesthetics of Appreciation*. Ithaca, NY: Cornell University Press.

Gitelman, L. (2008) *Always Already New: Media, History, and the Data of Culture*. Cambridge, MA: MIT Press.

Grodal, T. (2009) *Embodied Visions: Evolution, Emotion, Culture, and Film*. Oxford: Oxford University Press.

Haidt, J. (2012) *The Righteous Mind: Why Good People are Divided by Politics and Religion*. London: Penguin.

Hake, S. (2012) *Screen Nazis: Cinema, History, and Democracy*. Madison: University of Wisconsin Press.

Hall, S. (1980) "Encoding/Decoding," in Hall, S., Hobson, D., Lowe, A. and Willis, P. (eds.) *Culture, Media, Language*. London: Hutchinson.

Jäger, C. and Bartsch, A. (2006) "Meta-Emotions," *Grazer Philosophische Studien*, 73, pp. 179–204.

Keil, A. and Eder, J. (2005) "Audiovisuelle Medien und emotionale *Netzwerke*," in Grau, O. and Keil, A. *(eds.) Mediale Emotionen. Zur Lenkung von Gefühlen durch Bild und Sound*. Frankfurt am Main: Fischer.

Kemper, T. D. (1978) *A Social Interactional Theory of Emotions*. New York: Wiley.

Mateos, C. and Gaona, C. (2015) "Video Activism: A Descriptive Typology," *Global Media Journal*, Special Issue, 1–25 [Online]. Available at: http://www. globalmediajournal.com/open-access/video-activism-a-descriptive-typology. php?aid=62532 (Accessed: March 13, 2016).

Meeker, M. (2016) "Internet Trends 2016. Code Conference," *Presentation Slides*, 1 June [Online]. Available at: http://www.kpcb.com/internet-trends (Accessed: March 13, 2016).

Moors, A. (2009) "Theories of Emotion Causation: A Review," *Cognition and Emotion*, 23(4), pp. 625–662.

Nash, K. and Corner, J. (2016) "Strategic Impact Documentary: Contexts of Production and Social Intervention," *European Journal of Communication*, 31(3), pp. 227–242.

Nash, K., Hight, C. and Summerhayes, C. (eds.) (2014) *New Documentary Ecologies: Emerging Platforms, Practices and Discourses*. Basingstoke: Palgrave Macmillan.

Nichols, B. (2010) *Introduction to Documentary*. 2nd edn. Bloomington: Indiana University Press.

Nussbaum, M. C. (2013) *Political Emotions: Why Love Matters for Justice*. Cambridge: The Belknap Press.

Oliver, M. B. and Bartsch, A. (2010) "Appreciation as Audience Response: Exploring Entertainment Gratifications beyond Hedonism," *Human Communication Research*, 36(1), pp. 53–81.

Persson, P. (2003) *Understanding Cinema: A Psychological Theory of Moving Imagery*. Cambridge: Cambridge University Press.

Plantinga, C. R. (2005) "What a Documentary Is, After All," *Journal of Aesthetics and Art Criticism*, 63(2), pp. 105–117.

Plantinga, C. R. (2009) *Moving Viewers: American Film and the Spectator's Experience*. Berkeley: University of California Press.

Presence, S. (2016) "Reel News in the Digital Age: Radical Video-Activism in Britain," In Molloy, C. and Tzioumakis, Y. (eds.) *The Routledge Companion to Film and Politics*. London: Routledge.

Reinhard, C. and Olson, C. (2016) *Making Sense of Cinema: Empirical Studies into Film Spectators and Spectatorship*. London: Bloomsbury.

Rieger, D., Frischlich, L. and Bente, G. (2013) *Propaganda 2.0: Psychological Effects of Right-Wing and Islamic Extremist Internet Videos*. Köln: Luchterhand, BKA.

Scheve, C. V. and Ismer, S. (2013) "Towards a Theory of Collective Emotions," *Emotion Review*, 5(4), pp. 406–413.

Scott, M. (2014) "The Mediation of Distant Suffering: An Empirical Contribution Beyond Television News Texts," *Media, Culture & Society*, 36(1), pp. 3–19.

Smaill, B. (2010) *The Documentary: Politics, Emotion, Culture*. Basingstoke, Hampshire: Palgrave Macmillan.

Smith, E. R. and Mackie, D. M. (2008) "Intergroup Emotions," in Lewis, M., Haviland-Jones, J. and Barrett, L. F. (eds.) *Handbook of Emotions*. 3rd edn. New York: Guilford Publications.

Smith, G. M. (2003) *Film Structure and the Emotion System*. Cambridge: Cambridge University Press.

Sundar, S., Jia, H., Waddell, T. F. and Huang, Y. (2015) "Toward a Theory of Interactive Media Effects (TIME)," in Sundar, S. (ed.) *The Handbook of the Psychology of Communication Technology*. Hoboken, NJ: Wiley-Blackwell.

Tan, E. S. (1996) *Emotion and the Structure of Narrative Film: Film as an Emotion Machine*. Mahwah, NJ: Lawrence Erlbaum.

Trepte, S. and Loy, L. S. (2017) "Social Identity Theory and Self-Categorization Theory," in Hoffner, C. and Roessler, P. (eds.) *The International Encyclopedia of Media Effects*. Hoboken, NJ: Wiley.

Van Dijk, T. A. (2008) *Discourse and Context: A Sociocognitive Approach*. Cambridge: Cambridge University Press.

Waugh, T. (2011) *"Show Us Life": Toward a History and Aesthetics of the Committed Documentary*. Metuchen, NJ: Scarecrow Press.

Weik von Mossner, A. (ed.) (2014) *Moving Environments: Affect, Emotion, Ecology, and Film*. Ontario: Wilfried Laurier University Press.

CHAPTER 12

Slow TV: The Experiential and Multisensory Documentary

Luis Rocha Antunes

In his essay, "Documentary and Cognitive Theory: Narrative, Emotion and Memory", Ib Bondebjerg (2014, p. 14) illustrates how cognitive film theory can help reveal the narrative and emotional levels of the documentary genre, arguing that "the link between narrative, emotion and memory" in documentary film is "central for our understanding of who we are, for our understanding of how mediated visual material and forms of representation influence our mind and body". Bondebjerg's is one of the few approaches to documentary film that specifically locates itself in the field of cognitive film theory. However, despite his assumption that narrative and emotional resonance are essential prerequisites for most documentaries, the emergence of a new documentary genre called "slow TV" reveals the existence of other experiential aspects that lie beyond these two dimensions, while still remaining within the scope of cognitive film theory.

In this chapter, I examine two multi-hour documentary films produced by Norwegian public broadcaster, NRK, which fall under the label "slow aesthetics", a concept that is delineated more fully below. Whether this type of film features human characters or not (as in the case of the films studied here), slow aesthetics is distinguished by a lack of character development and an absence of related emotional cues. Arguably, slow films

L. R. Antunes (✉)
Augusta University, Augusta, GA, USA

© The Author(s) 2018
C. Brylla, M. Kramer (eds.), *Cognitive Theory and Documentary Film*, https://doi.org/10.1007/978-3-319-90332-3_12

offer a high degree of experientiality at the level of such perceptual senses as the vestibular (the sense of orientation and balance related to our navigation in space) and thermoception or sense of temperature. However, although I focus predominantly on these two non-traditional senses, since they are the primary experiential stimuli in the two case studies, I also make cross-modal references to the traditional senses of sight and hearing, the two essential inputs for filmic experiences. By examining the nature of experientiality and multisensoriality in slow-TV documentaries, my main goal is to show that cognitive film theory can be productively applied to levels of human experience that go beyond the dimensions of narrative and emotion.

Cognitive film theory has shown that our minds are strongly predisposed towards narrative structures and that "certain emotional structures … are triggered when we are confronted with stories, images and human interaction" (Bondebjerg 2014, p. 15). But how do we assess the cognitive importance of documentaries that possess hardly any narrative constituents and no salient emotional cues? In my book, *The Multisensory Film Experience: A Cognitive Model of Experiential Film Aesthetics* (Antunes 2016a), I point to how cognitive film theory's lack of a clear conceptual distinction between such fundamental concepts as embodiment and affect has resulted in the over-generalized categorization of the film experience as composed solely of emotions and narrative. As a consequence, the different levels of cinematic experience that fall outside the discussion on the five classic senses have been neglected—one of the most relevant of these being perceptual experience, which takes place across a number of other senses. Another reason for this neglect is the difficulty of conceiving that an audiovisual medium such as film is capable of eliciting perceptual experiences (other than those of vision and sound) without direct sensory stimulation or the character projection and neural mirroring that some cognitive film scholars have argued are prerequisites (Antunes 2014, 2016a).

The following examination of the vestibular sense in *Bergensbanen: Minutt for Minutt (The Bergen Train: Minute by Minute)* (NRK 2009)[1] and thermoception in *Nasjonal Vedkveld (National Wood [Fire] Night)* (NRK 2013)[2] has the advantage that since these films contain hardly any

---

[1] Available online at: https://tv.nrk.no/program/prho63004009/bergensbanen-minutt-for-minutt (Accessed: April 2, 2017).
[2] Available online at: https://tv.nrk.no/serie/nasjonal-vedkveld (Accessed: April 2, 2017).

direct human presence, the analysis cannot be based on characters and ideas of projection or neural mirroring. The organic nature of the pro-filmic materiality in these documentaries allows us to explore a conception of film ecology in which landscape and nature are not simply represented audiovisually, but also generate the perceptual experiences that provide these films' primary cinematic appeal. Over a number of hours, the films present material worlds as a perceptual cinematic experience; they seek to explore the experiential nature of orientation and balance (the vestibular sense) and temperature (thermoception) rather than concepts of sublimity or beauty—that is, romantic cultural constructions of landscapes and nature. Thus, slow TV documentaries can be used to explore the sensory dimensions of film within the eco-documentary framework, implying the primacy of the viewer's engagement with the sensory modalities of land-scape and nature rather than the primacy of narrative comprehension, emotional salience, moral and ethical considerations, or the acquisition of knowledge.

Although this chapter focuses on perceptual experience, it does not exclude the potential for emotion, narrative or hermeneutics. However, these higher levels of cognition are not the entry points for slow docu-mentaries, and the focus here on sensory experience is not only due to the (arguably intrinsic) nature of the first film's slow train trip and the second film's experience of watching a wood fire burning in a fireplace, but also because it is a way of re-centering the argument, addressing cognitive film theory's lack of attention to perceptual experience in documentary film. The fact that this analysis focuses mainly on perceptual levels of experience (low-level cognition) should not preclude but, rather, act as a spur to future research on high-level cognition such as emotional understanding, narrative comprehension and thematic interpretation using either a bot-tom-up or top-down approach. Examining nonfiction film through the lens of "slow aesthetics", in which narrative and emotion are seemingly absent, can bring new perspectives to documentary film theory's classic discussions on the concepts of truthfulness, objectivity and reality. These concepts are generally connected to documentary's capacity to manipulate our point of view through narrative techniques that lead us to believe in a specific fact or elicit our empathy with or sympathy for a character or nar-rative event, resulting in an emotional response. The interplay of these character-led and plot-led concepts has been at the core of discourses on the rhetorical, representational and ethical nature of documentaries. From this perspective, it is important that cognitive (as well as general documentary) film studies also examines the spectatorial experience of slow documentaries, despite their apparent lack of characters, narratives and emotions.

These considerations lead us to the historical inception of cinema itself. Early forms of film, from Edison's to the Lumière Brothers', display scenes of realism embedded within experientiality, where perceptual experience is perhaps more salient than any narrative (these early films often have no more than one event) or emotion (they frequently show scenes of daily life with no intrinsic emotional impact). These early forms of so-called "actuality film" have also been labelled a kind of "cinema of attractions" (Gunning 1990), due to the primacy of their experiential appeal over that of narrative and emotion. The fact that the actuality film depicting scenes of everyday life relates to experientiality more than to narrative or emotion might at first glance be a reason to think of these images as documentary records of reality. However, documentary cannot be defined by experientiality alone: a fiction film will also have layers of experientiality, just as a documentary will also have layers of narrative and emotion. Although experientiality does not play a primary role in the ontological discussion of what documentary is and how we define it, it can—as in the case of slow TV—create a spectatorial sense of *experiencing reality as it is*, a sense that the images we see are objectively recording and documenting an aspect of the real world. However, as the following analysis reveals, this supposed reality is not as objective as might first appear: the viewer's experience of these slow documentaries is subject to a certain perceptual manipulation, including the filmic mediation of long takes and (predominantly) wide shots.

Furthermore, although these slow films are generally accepted as documentaries, due to their apparently neutral representation of reality without the potentially manipulative presence of narrative or emotional cues, the truth is that they appear to play the role of (experiential) entertainment more often associated with fiction film—that is, they primarily engage our senses rather than informing us. They may still educate the viewer about the Norwegian rail network or how to tend an open fire, but this takes place in an experiential rather than an expository way. In a sense, although these slow films do not appear manipulative in terms of narrative or emotion, they are still constructed, albeit in the realm of the senses. Although they give the impression of being pure documentaries—for example, objectively recording aspects of the landscape—they actually comprise a form of highly constructed reality and are arguably even more subjective than impressionistic or reflexive documentary forms. Slow-TV documentaries are of a different nature to the early actuality films. This is due to their historical context. They are films born in the digital age, emerging out of the time-extending potential of digital recording technologies, and are the result of the possibilities this raises for contemplative forms of filming, in which a camera can be left to film for a long period without the need for maintenance or adjustment. They are the result of affordable, lightweight equipment that allows the recording of pictures and sounds over long time spans, thus challenging the classic concepts of the documentary form and raising questions that could not be anticipated by the early actuality films.

The concept of slowness is generally examined at the levels of form (a reduction in pace, for instance) and narrative (a minimal storyline). However, on an experiential level, slow films are usually energetic and proactive in terms of their intense appeal to our perceptual systems (Antunes 2016a). The NRK's series of long, continuous, multi-hour documentaries—ranging from a train ride and a voyage by ship to a knitting session—may be minimal (and indeed slow) in terms of narrative, but they are extremely energetic on an experiential level. The concept of cinematic slowness is complex and difficult to define in absolute terms as it depends on specific layers of textuality and spectatorship, and not all of these will necessarily match the film's measured pace. My examination of *Bergensbanen* and *Nasjonal Vedkveld* implies a critical reflection on this filmic concept. For example, contrary to the conventional assumption that a leisurely pace results in diminished experientiality, slow narratives may well elicit energetic sensory responses. This should not only help us to understand the multisensorial and experiential levels of documentary film, which have yet to be explored by cognitive theory, but also to map the relationships between some of the dimensions that define slow cinema. The methodology I adopt in the following pages involves the sort of micro-textual analysis and close reading that are essential to assessing the intricate, experiential nature of these documentaries.

ECO-DOCUMENTARY: CONSIDERATIONS ON THE CONCEPT OF ECOLOGY

Although the concept of ecology is commonly associated with the natural environment and especially with human beings' relationship to it, this analysis uses the concept in its more general sense (as applying to any

environment) in order to investigate its material cinematic nature in relation to human perception. This broadly aligns with James Gibson's (1966,
1986) notion of "cognitive ecology". Gibson's work on perception and
cognition in the field of cognitive ecology, and the studies of cognitive
psychologists Julian Hochberg and Virginia Brooks (1978), have laid the
foundations for cognitive film theory and given rise to ecological perspectives on film that are based on an understanding not of ecology's cultural
and ethical aspects but of the way human perception constructs the material world of a film (Hochberg 1978, 1986; Hochberg and Brooks 1978;
Anderson 1996). Thus, the focus of an ecological approach in cognitive
film theory is not so much on what is represented in a film, its content or
themes, but on the dynamic perceptual relationship between the film's
spectators and the material world they construct out of what the filmic
world affords them—this includes the influence of the film's style, the
mediation of its characters (where there are any) and their own capacity to
draw inferences by mining different layers of knowledge.

The starting point of this analysis is the experiential nature of the slow-
TV documentary. In eco-cinema, this carries many possibilities for
meaning-making and is central to the development of the genre. Helen
Wheatley (2010) has produced a rich portrait of slow TV's different forms,
referring to it as a "geographic genre" and "spectacular television", and
tracing its different potentialities in terms of genre, reception and cultural
value. The possibilities lying ahead of slow TV are tremendous given the
current digital paradigm of production and distribution, where new technology such as mobile action cameras and drones offer novel ways of capturing the environment and streaming channels afford new ways of content
distribution, rendering it possible to give viewers sensory information
alongside the audiovisual content. This includes such extra-filmic information as temperature, GPS coordinates and air pressure. Furthermore, there
is the ever-evolving reality of TV technology, with new high-definition
screens, which are often used, as Wheatley points out, in the way that artists' canvases hung on walls were used historically.

The issues of experientiality that slow TV has brought to the fore relate
to ecology not simply as a theme with ethical implications but as an idea
of nature as defined by the perceptual and material relationship between
human beings and their environment. Wheatley believes that slow TV
involves the kind of contemplative engagement more commonly associated with fine art and photography, and she contrasts this with theories of
the distracted or "sit-forward" viewer. As such, slow TV is at odds with

"theories of television's distracted viewership [that] understand television as anti-spectacular" (Wheatley 2010, p. 238). Slow TV has, thus far, pre-supposed an absence of screen characters, and for that reason it is an inter-esting alternative to the type of documentary based on narrative and emotions; however, it represents a challenge for film cognitivists, who appear to struggle with the idea that elements of cinematic perception can fall outside the notions of projection and mirroring. Slow TV is a form of pure cinematic experientiality—in William Boddy's and Lynn Spigel's words (cited in Wheatley 2010, p. 241), a form of "armchair travel", where "the outside world [comes] into the private home." Although there is some notion of contemplation involved, slow TV is arguably not the same as the concept of "window shopping" (Friedberg 2006; Elsaesser and Hagener 2009), a term that conveys a sense of passive observation or voyeurism; rather, it involves an active, rich participation in sensual experi-ence—experientiality in its full sensory range—involving full physical, sen-sory engagement. This contrasts with Finn Arne Jørgensen's (2014, p. 97) analogy of the mediated experience of a train trip, in which "[t]he land-scape of train travel is not experienced directly on the body, but through a window." The metaphor of the window does not apply here, for the rea-son that it is grounded exclusively in visual conceptions of cinema. We *look* through a window (Friedberg 2006; Elsaesser and Hagener 2009); we *experience* through a film.

BERGENSBANEN/THE BERGEN TRAIN: A VESTIBULAR FILM EXPERIENCE

Bergensbanen: Minutt for Minutt (2009) is a train journey that is filmed simultaneously by three cameras mounted in the front of the train, one looking straight ahead and the other two pointing to each side at 45-degree angles. The three camera views are assembled like the panels of a triptych and the film pans from one panel to another. A further camera films the show's presenter, inside the train, and archive footage and songs are inserted in the parts of the film when the train enters a tunnel and the screen goes dark. Although, out of the three cameras at the front of the train, the central one is the most oriented on the vestibular sense, all three provide a sensation of movement and vestibular navigation.

The navigational experience of the train ride plays with a number of vestibular elements that contradict the idea that such a journey could be monotonous. This cinematic exercise offers a multitude of navigational possibilities that constantly engage our vestibular sense. For instance, when the track bifurcates, we are unsure which one the train will move onto: although there is a single track for most of the way and its direction is not surprising (it can be seen from some distance), in some parts of the ride (when travelling through stations, for example), we are suddenly confronted with multiple tracks. Another moment that can cue an embodied response is when the sun hits the camera directly, dazzling the viewer; we may reposition ourselves physically in an attempt to see the way ahead, only to realize that moving will not change our visual field. This response is, in itself, a reminder that our vestibular sense is at work even though we are static, sitting in front of a screen (although the same would be true even if we were not). The sunlight can also give us a general sense of geographical direction: for example, when the train is at first travelling into the sun, then during the journey, the sun moves to the right, then behind the train, then back to the right again—something we can tell by noticing the shadow cast by the train. Because we know that the sun moves from south-east to south-west, if we are travelling from the west (Bergen) to the south-east (Oslo), we are able to estimate our approximate geographical trajectory by checking the time of day at each of the trip's segments.

However, besides these inferential elements, there are more direct cues that encourage vestibular engagement by hooking our attention onto the navigational view provided by the moving train. For example, if the train is travelling at a relatively fast pace, it is not unusual for our survival instinct to come to the fore, forcing us to keep our eyes on the visual field. Also, the sense of motion and forward movement can trigger a basic perceptual interest, as these are not just general measurements of our visual field but are distributed in a complex way across different viewing perspectives and according to the spatial depth of the objects we are seeing. For instance, the rail tracks immediately in front of the train seem to move at a faster speed than those further away, and the landscape nearer the train appears to move past us more rapidly than the landscape in the distance or in front of us. The mental snapshots we make of the journey map the differences in movement and compel us to construct a sense of visual depth using the three-dimensional cues. The complexity of this experience is a result of the navigational cues of speed and direction; therefore, they are not exclusively visual but contain a vestibular component. The fact that our vestibular sense is tuned to the navigational experience charges the film with experiential richness, and this has the potential to transform (at least for some spectators) a slow film into an intense one, converting it into a primarily sensory rather than narrative or emotional experience.

Evidence that the experience of this train trip is not just visual but also vestibular is offered by an analysis of the concrete elements of the film and of our visual–vestibular interactions at the neural and physiological levels. In some of the tunnels, we sometimes experience an illusion that reveals the ongoing interaction between the visual and vestibular senses. If we enter a tunnel that immediately curves to the right, we sometimes see a lighted sign on the right-hand side of a central axis. In the cases in which we are unaware that the train is no longer travelling straight ahead, we will fail to understand that although the light appears on the right-hand side of the frame, it is actually on the left, from a spatial perspective. This means that when the train passes the sign, it changes from the right to the left-hand side of our visual field. When this happens, our vestibular sense will reinterpret the information and readjust the navigational coordinates and the position of our bodily reference points as we view the film. As a result of this readjustment, we may experience the sensation of a sudden shift to the right-hand side. A similar visual–vestibular interaction takes place when we see a white light on the central axis of the frame and interpret it as the end of the tunnel, due to the contrast in color temperature with the lights on the tunnel's sides. When the white light approaches and, instead of expanding in size in front of us, shifts (as a result of the visual coordinates) to the side of the tunnel opposite the other yellow lights, our vestibular system readjusts our body-center coordinates and sense of navigational direction. We may also experience the visual–vestibular illusion that our body is shifting the navigational direction.

These concrete examples highlight the way visual–vestibular interactions create vivid sensations. They also show that what we see is not just visual but vestibular too, and our experience of *Bergensbanen* is not just eye- but body-centered. These illusions reveal that all our senses are engaged with the film. Research on visual–vestibular interactions provides abundant evidence that what we call "seeing" is not just a visual but a multisensory experience (Antunes 2016a). The most obvious evidence is the so-called vestibular ocular reflex (also known as VOR), which is a kind of eye movement that compensates for the movements of our head, giving us the illusory experience of a stable external world. A perhaps more pertinent case of visual–vestibular interaction is the so-called "train illusion" or "vection"—the sense that we are moving, despite being stationary, because a large proportion of our visual field is in motion. This highlights that there is not only a connection between sight and the vestibular sense (equivalent illusions and values have been studied for aural–vestibular interactions), but there is also a level of embodiment, of actual physical implications for our experience of self-motion, when we encounter audiovisual-mediated content with no direct vestibular input.

The bottom line is that a viewer of *Bergensbanen* will be engaged through their vestibular sense in a way that is articulated with sight and hearing, rendering the film a multisensory and experiential activity in spite of the fact that the medium offers only audiovisual stimuli. Besides the vestibular illusions of self-motion, such as the train illusion, and the direct connection between sight and the vestibular sense through VOR, there are other points of connection between the vestibular sense and other sensory systems. These are the neural connections in the brain, especially at the level of the *superior colliculus* (SC), a neural area of complex multisensory integration (Antunes 2012, 2016a, b). Although all the senses interact with one another, the vestibular sense, due to its influence on the SC, has particular multisensory importance (Brodal 2010; Angelaki and Cullen 2008). It may seem puzzling to think that our body actually engages in navigational activities even when we are seated. However, that is only because we think of body positions such as posture as static, whereas, at a vestibular level, there are no neutral or disconnected positions and even postural adjustment is a proactive and dynamic kind of motor action. Thus, the common-sense notion that *sitting* means *to be still* should give way to an awareness that even the most apparently neutral body position has a navigational nature.

The active and dynamic vestibular processes give experientiality its salience, and its multisensory nature renders the train ride an immersive experience, not in the traditional sense of immersion in a filmic narrative nor even in the sense of immersion in an art installation with multisensory (not just audiovisual) stimuli, but in the most purely perceptual sense. It also shows the potential of a level of perception that escapes the domain of meaning-making through higher cognitive factors such as narrative comprehension and emotions. However, this perceptual sphere is not a reductive aspect of cinematic experience: experientiality is also capable of creating meaning and is not without cognitive significance (Antunes 2016a). Rather, it represents a cinematic alternative to more conventional narrative forms and the primary value given to emotion and character engagement. *Bergensbanen*, for instance, is a film of pure contemplation, of dynamic experientiality, that dispenses with many of the conventional layers of film such as character engagement and emotion, yet nevertheless contains a strong appeal to the senses, inviting cinematic immersion. This is corroborated by such films' popularity with and positive responses from general audiences. Furthermore, this is a cinematic form with great potential for research in the field of conceptual metaphor theory (Fahlenbrach 2016), particularly in the domain of spatial metaphors (Lakoff and Johnson 1980), as it offers the opportunity to map experiential and multisensory metaphors. As conceptual metaphor theory has demonstrated, higher meanings can be inferred from matters of experientiality, such as the vestibular-related metaphor of mental relationship as a spatial relationship (Antunes 2016b).

One example of an experiential metaphor is the use of "flatness." As well as the *directional* component of our vestibular experience of film, *Bergensbanen* has the component of *balance*, and together these constitute what we understand as the vestibular sense. This ensures that we have an extremely flat and stable kind of experience, derived from the stability of the body of the train itself. This is in contrast to vestibular experiences in other films, in which we experience stability but not flatness (for example, *This is Cinerama!*, 1952) or instability and bumpiness (for example, Gus Van Sant's *Gerry*, 2002). But our vestibular experiences are never neutral and even an experience of flatness is permeated by a sense of balance. *Bergensbanen* may offer a sense of stability and flatness but there are, nonetheless, proactive and dynamic elements in the vestibular experience. Having said that, the train ride in *Bergensbanen* is not entirely flat or stable: there are subtle descending or ascending motions, and we sometimes experience a sense of instability when the train shifts between tracks or follows accentuated curves in the track. Most of the time, however, it is a pleasurably smooth and stable navigational experience. Although it is beyond the scope of this chapter, the examination of this particular experience in relation to higher cognitive dimensions (for example, interpretation or cultural schemas) may well yield interesting results.

The role of sound may be subtler than that of vision in *Bergensbanen*, but it is still influential and adds to the multisensory nature of our vestibular experience of the film. This is exemplified when the train enters a tunnel: we have only minimal visual inputs, such as the lights flashing past on the walls, but we become very aware of the sound of the train on the track. This is amplified to the maximum when the track curves, since the rotational energy of the train creates stronger vectors of force on the metal of the track, increasing attrition and raising the volume of the sound. In this case, we can use the volume as a directional referent, one that is especially useful given that we have little if any visual input. This means that sound can have a spatial and directional role that compensates for our lack of vision.

NASJONAL VEDKVELD/NATIONAL WOOD NIGHT:
A THERMOCEPTIVE FILM EXPERIENCE

Nasjonal Vedkveld (2013) comprises a single shot, lasting more than two hours, of a wood fire burning in a fireplace. It uses only one camera to give a view of the interior of the fireplace, just inside the surrounding stone frame, a relatively close framing that creates a sense of physical proximity to the fire's thermoceptive cues. The view of the fire can be mapped as different thermoceptive areas, with different scales of heat radiating across the spatial coordinates, along its vertical and horizontal axes as well as its depth. The heat is given a material configuration through audiovisual cues, mainly in relation to its impact on the burning wood. For instance, some of the logs are flaming brightly, some have become smoldering black charcoal and some have disintegrated into white ash, while others are still unaltered by the heat. Then there is the arrangement of the logs and the direction of the flames: knowing that heat travels upwards, we can infer that the heat will be more intense on the ends of the logs pointing upwards. This is one of the ways in which we can spatially map the heat from the fire.

Although a two-hour film of a fireplace might seem an odd concept, the abundant temperature cues offering complex sensory information of a thermoceptive nature makes this slow film extremely rich on an experiential level. *Nasjonal Vedkveld* offers a dynamic and varied amount of stimuli: for example, we know that the logs that are smoking will soon start to burn—it indicates that their temperature is rising and they are hotter than the logs without smoke. Another set of cues is offered by the spectrum of colors to which we assign thermoceptive meaning: bright red, black, white and brown not only indicate approximate temperatures but also function as a kind of thermoceptive timeline. These colors indicate the material state of the wood and represent the marks left on it by the temperature— black implies that only part of the material has been burnt, whereas white indicates that it has been completely burnt and its carbon has been transformed.

However, we not only draw disembodied perceptual inferences through mapping the colors associated with temperature and noting the temporal changes in the material state of the wood (as well as the spatial thermoceptive coordinates), we also potentially experience motor responses of a thermoceptive nature as we watch the film. These responses reveal two things: one is the embodied level of cinematic thermoception that lies beyond

mere visual perception; the other is the multisensory capacity of audiovisually mediated content to affect our experience as spectators. There are
many potential sensations and responses that occur during the viewing of
the film that illustrate this—for example, we may rub our hands together
as if in front of a real fire or check on our own thermal comfort. Added to
this is the visual movement of the changing shape of the flames and the
different gradients of red blooming in the smoldering ashes, as well as the
sparks and smoke. If we are immersed in the filmic experience, sparks fly-
ing towards the camera provoke a startled motor response, or we reposition ourselves according to our visual perception of higher or lower
temperatures.

Thermoception can be audiovisually represented in many ways; however, in *Nasjonal Vedkveld*, it is not merely represented as an audiovisual
element but also shapes the audiovisual stimuli too, as when the heat
waves subtly distort the image (just as when we see heat rising from the
surface of a road), while the soundtrack is filled with noise of cracking
wood. Heat becomes physical by impacting the film itself and shaping its
materiality; it is like a thermoceptive breeze with both a visual representation and an aural rhythm with sonic resonance. We can hear the sounds of
the different flames, one higher, another lower. Then there is the constant
hum of the burning logs and the sound of the heat cracking the wood.

Thermoception in this film is not only composed of low-level perceptual elements but also of higher experiential dimensions, revealing that
there is room for causal expectations and meanings in its perceptual experience. For instance, as the fire burns lower, we expect either that someone
will add more logs or the fire (and the film) will come to a natural end.
There is, in some way, a sensory goal determined by the thermoceptive
dynamics of the fire and the changes in the material world of the film, just
as narrative comprehension has related goals and schemas (Bordwell
1985). The goals in the two slow documentaries analyzed here are of a
similar nature: that is, they are related to the meaning-making that the
perceptual experience prompts in the viewer. We also experience "micro-
climaxes" as we watch these films: for example, when we anticipate that
one of the logs will break apart—which indeed does happen (at minute
14:26), causing radical changes in the disposition of the fire. These sensory segments of expectation are sometimes underscored by the musical
track playing in the background: for example, when it coincides with the
sudden changes in the fire's configuration. We can also, on a higher perceptual level, use thermoception to infer information about the material

L. R. ANTUNES

state of the fire that we would not otherwise know through visual information alone. This is the case when we see smoke coming through a tiny
hole in a log, indicating the heat inside. Without the knowledge of what
the smoke represents in this context, we would not know what was happening inside the log as it is visually inaccessible. Although the mental
stimulus of the smoke is visual, it is nevertheless of a thermoceptive nature,
indicating the material state of the wood. Expectations about a less specified and more general temperature are also possible: for instance, when
more logs are added to the fire and it flares up, we assume a general rise in
the temperature of the room.

In addition to these experiential meanings, there may well be an additional layer of cultural meanings. For example, the fire could be seen to
embody a sheltered, comfortable domestic space, in contrast to relatively
harsh outdoor conditions, while the logs could embody the activity of
woodcutting. Again, however, an analysis of these is beyond the scope of
this chapter.

Just as there is on-screen movement in *Bergensbanen*, there is also, sur-
prisingly, movement in *Nasjonal Vedkveld*. This is experienced through
the material transformation of the logs and the impact of temperature on
the direction of the smoke. In a sense, the film also offers a case of landscape transformation through the energy dynamics of the set—that is,
through the changes in the disposition of the logs and in the fire's material
state. This form of thermoceptive landscape is a spatial as much as a temporal dimension of the film. As the film unfolds, we become aware of a
general increase in the temperature of the environment around the fireplace, which is linked to an awareness of time passing. The longer we
experience the fire, the higher our general awareness of the rising temperature, because our thermoceptive awareness of heat has been reset at the
start of the film. In a similar way to the landscape experience in
Bergensbanen, with its micro-cycles and perceptual segments created by
the alternation between stationary moments (when the train pulls into a
station and comes to a halt) and movement, *Nasjonal Vedkveld* also carries
a sense of micro-cycles, generated by our inference of the temperature,
which falls as the wood turns to ash and then rises again as more logs are
added to the fire.

Although thermoception is a sensory modality that is inherently tied to
human perception, there is hardly any human presence in *Nasjonal
Vedkveld*; however, it still shapes the film and our experience of it. This
clearly shows that a film needs neither narrative nor emotional cues (in the

conventional sense of characters performing actions) in order to be considered a full-blown cinematic experience. The human presence is minimal, briefly glimpsed when someone's hands reach out to toast a marshmallow, add more logs or re-adjust their position on the fire. When this happens, the inferences we make from the thermoceptive cues and the perceptual affect we experience as a result of the film's style (its camera positioning, framing and sound design) are all intensified and focused on the thermoceptive impact on the unseen body behind the hands. Arguably, at this particular moment in the film, we project or mirror thermoception through the mediation of a human presence—that is, we experience emotion via association and situational context. However, in the rest of the film, thermoception is only present at the level of the organic materiality of its setting, and there is no projection or mirroring in relation to the human body.

CONCLUSION

This chapter has demonstrated that, from a spectatorial point of view, the experience of slow aesthetics appears direct and immediate, in line with the Bazinian definition of realism. At the same time, the interaction of film form and perceptual mechanisms comprises a highly mediated experience, which has ecological advantages. One of the attributes of the audiovisual film medium is the way it "align[s] the rhythmic nature of our perception with 'the thread of the world' and places us in a time window that offers motor action without fatigue, danger without damage, and mood alignment without self-judgment" (Antunes 2012, p. 524). The ecological advantages of mediated experiences have more power if the definition of film perception is taken beyond the limitation of a sense-to-sense correspondence to encompass an audiovisual medium that gives us access to the elements of a multisensory experience, including temperature and movement, without the risks we would incur if we were in direct contact with the actual sensory energy of these modalities. This idea of cinematic experientiality as a full-blown multisensory experience with embodied perception goes far further than the cognitive ecology of Gibson (1966, 1986), Hochberg (1978, 1986) and Hochberg and Brooks (1978), who assume that film perception is limited to sight and hearing. As this analysis of *Bergensbanen* and *Nasjonal Vedkveld* has shown, slow TV represents a challenge to cognitive film theory since the ecology of cinematic perception takes us beyond narrative, emotion and the senses of sight and hearing. Furthermore, these two documentaries also question the concept of "slowness" in film: although they adhere to the stylistic and narrative premises of slow cinema (long takes and minimal or nonexistent narrative), they also contain experiential riches.

Acknowledgements I would like to acknowledge that part of the research for this chapter was made during my time as a Visiting Researcher at the University of Texas in 2016/2017. I would also like to thank the editors of this book, Catalin Brylla and Mette Kramer, for their valuable feedback and encouragement, and Amy Antunes for her assistance with the editing of this chapter and her encouragement.

REFERENCES

Anderson, J. (1996) *The Reality of Illusion: An Ecological Approach to Cognitive Film Theory.* Carbondale, IL: Southern Illinois University Press.

Angelaki, D. E. and Cullen, K. E. (2008) "Vestibular System: The Many Facets of a Multimodal Sense," *Annual Review of Neuroscience*, 31, pp. 125–150.

Antunes, L. R. (2012) "The Vestibular in Film: Orientation and Balance in Gus Van Sant's 'Cinema of Walking'," *Essays in Philosophy*, 13(2), pp. 522–549.

Antunes, L. R. (2014) "Neural Correlates of the Multisensory Film Experience," in Grabowski, M. (ed.) *Neuroscience and Media: New Understandings and Representations.* New York: Routledge, pp. 46–60.

Antunes, L. R. (2016a) *The Multisensory Film Experience: A Cognitive Model of Experiential Film Aesthetics.* Bristol: Intellect Books.

Antunes, L. R. (2016b) "Identity as a Walking Experience: Multisensory and Experiential Metaphor in Film," in Fahlenbrach, K. (ed.) *Embodied Metaphors in Television and Video Games: Cognitive Approaches.* New York: Routledge, pp. 234–247.

Bondebjerg, I. (2014) "Documentary and Cognitive Theory: Narrative, Emotion and Memory," *Media and Communication*, 2(1), pp. 13–22.

Bordwell, D. (1985) *Narration in the Fiction Film.* London: Methuen.

Brodal, P. (2010) *The Central Nervous System: Structure and Function.* Oxford: Oxford University Press.

Elsaesser, T. and Hagener, M. (eds.) (2009) *Film Theory: An Introduction Through the Senses.* New York: Routledge.

Fahlenbrach, K. (ed.) (2016) *Embodied Metaphors in Film, Television, and Video Games: Cognitive Approaches.* New York: Routledge.

Friedberg, A. (2006) *The Virtual Window: From Alberti to Microsoft.* Cambridge, MA: MIT Press.

Gibson, J. (1966) *The Senses Considered as Perceptual Systems.* Boston: Houghton Mifflin.

Gibson, J. (1986) *Ecological Approach to Visual Perception.* New York: Lawrence Erlbaum.

Gunning, T. (1990) "The Cinema of Attraction: Early Film, Its Spectator, and the Avant-Garde," in Elsaesser, T. (ed.) *Early Cinema: Space Frame Narrative.* London: British Film Institute, pp. 56–62.

Hochberg, J. (1978) *Perception.* Englewood Cliffs, NJ: Prentice-Hall.

Hochberg, J. (1986) "Representation of Motion and Space in Video and Cinematic Displays," in Boff, K. R., Kaufman L. and Thomas, J. P. (eds.) *Handbook of Perception and Human Performance. Vol. I. Sensory Processes and Perception.* New York: Wiley, pp. 22–64.

Hochberg, J. and Brooks, V. (1978) "Film Cutting and Visual Momentum," in Senders, J. W., Fischer, D. F. and Monty, R. A. (eds.) *Eye Movements and the Higher Psychological Functions.* Hillsdale: Lawrence Erlbaum Associates, pp. 293–313.

Jørgensen, F. A. (2014) "The Armchair Traveler's Guide to Digital Environmental Humanities," *Environmental Humanities*, 4, pp. 95–112.

Lakoff, G. and Johnson, M. (1980) *Metaphors We Live By.* Chicago: University of Chicago Press.

Wheatley, H. (2010) "Beautiful Images in Spectacular Clarity: Spectacular Television, Landscape Programming and the Question of (Tele)visual Pleasure," *Screen*, 52(2), pp. 233–248.

CHAPTER 13

Toward a Cognitive Definition of First-Person Documentary

Veerle Ros, Jennifer M. J. O'Connell, Miklós Kiss,
and Annelies van Noortwijk

Subjective and Personal Tendencies in Documentary Films

Contemporary documentary practice is witnessing a predominant trend, in which films abandon the longstanding ideal of objectivity in favor of more diverse and subjective perspectives on reality. From bold new uses of reenactment and performance, as seen in *Episode III: Enjoy Poverty* (Renzo Martens 2008) and *A Strange Love Affair with Ego* (Ester Gould 2015), through creative and playful editing of home-video and archival footage, as in *Tarnation* (Jonathan Caouette 2003), *I for India* (Sandhya Suri 2005) and *Heart of a Dog* (Laurie Anderson 2015), to the recent wave of animated documentaries, such as *Persepolis* (Marjane Satrapi 2007), *Waltz with Bashir* (Ari Folman 2008) and *Crulic: The Path to Beyond* (Anca Damian 2011), many contemporary documentaries seem to opt out of the idea of 'capturing reality' with a camera in favor of extensive formal experimentation and the creative, liberal and imaginative expression of subjec-

V. Ros (✉) • J. M. J. O'Connell • M. Kiss • A. van Noortwijk
University of Groningen, Groningen, The Netherlands
e-mail: v.ros@rug.nl; j.m.j.oconnell@rug.nl; m.kiss@rug.nl; a.van.noortwijk@rug.nl

© The Author(s) 2018   223
C. Brylla, M. Kramer (eds.), *Cognitive Theory and Documentary Film*, https://doi.org/10.1007/978-3-319-90332-3_13

tive memories and experiences. Central to this development are a reevaluation of the documentary subject and a blurring of boundaries between subject and filmmaker. This convergence of positions has led to the emergence of the 'first-person' documentary, a growing and diverse set of films in which the roles of filmmaker and subject coincide (Lebow 2012). While examples of subjective and autobiographical documentaries can be found among the oeuvres of experimental filmmakers as far back as the 1940s (e.g. Maya Deren's 1943 *Meshes of the Afternoon*), it was only with the enthusiastic reception of a more recent wave of first-person films like *Wide Awake* (Alan Berliner 2006), *Arirang* (Kim Ki-duk 2011) and *Cameraperson* (Kirsten Johnson 2016), that a widespread, fundamental shift towards the increasing use and scholarly appreciation of subjective and personal perspectives in documentary could be noticed (Bruzzi 2006; Renov 2004; Rascaroli 2009; Lebow 2012). This development, in turn, has contributed to a shift in our understanding of documentary film's central truth claim.

The idea that photographic and filmic images contain "traces" of historical or actual reality (Bazin 1960; Barthes 1981) has long been thought of as central to documentary's defining quality as a "document" of historical reality (Currie 1999; Nichols 1991)—a mode of thinking that corresponded closely to the aims of the Direct Cinema movement, which pledged to observe the world with seemingly as little intervention as possible. This paradigm of a quasi-unmediated view of the world proved untenable in the face of arguments concerning the inherently constructed nature of representations, which have been given additional momentum by the current digitization and virtualization of visual media (Rombes 2009). Recent documentaries abandon this referential claim altogether by utilizing formal techniques, such as reenactment, animation, digital-image manipulation and associative montage, asserting their authenticity through different means instead. In response, documentary theory has shifted its focus towards the reappreciation of elements previously thought of as marginal to documentary practice, such as performativity (Bruzzi 2006), subjectivity (Renov 2004; Rascaroli 2009) and self-representation (Lane 2002; Lebow 2012). While this has led to an understanding of documentary as something more dynamic, diverse, subjective and performative than previously assumed, a side-effect is that the boundaries between documentary and fiction film appear to have become ever more nebulous. In spite of this development, the cognitive distinction between fiction and nonfiction remains of crucial importance to human communication

(Bondebjerg 2014b, p. 39). Thus, it has become necessary to ask how, under this new practical and theoretical paradigm, viewers continue to make that distinction in first-person documentary.

Our aim here is to investigate how a method of cognitive poetics—"an interdisciplinary approach to the study of literature [and film] using the tools offered by cognitive science" (Tsur 2008, p. 1)—could contribute to a more refined understanding of documentary in general, and first-person films in particular, by taking into account the dynamic interplay between a film's formal properties, its social context and the mental processes of a hypothetical viewer. After providing a brief survey of existing theoretical approaches to subjective tendencies in documentary and their current limitations, we present the process by which viewers distinguish documentary from fiction film as an act of cognitive framing: the selection of a set of preexisting expectations on the basis of the recognizable aspects of a situation (Minsky 1975, p. 1). We then demonstrate how the selection of the documentary frame is dependent on an interplay of cues that can be found in the textual (formal and stylistic) and contextual (intertextual and paratextual) elements of a film with the real-world knowledge of the viewer. From this perspective, first-person documentary could be understood as a sub-frame of the documentary frame, which allows for greater degrees of subjectivity and experimentation and comes with its own unique set of viewer expectations and emotional affects. Through the example of a scene from *Cameraperson* (Kirsten Johnson 2016), we show how the foregrounding of a filmmaker's personal, affective involvement with the content of a scene can act as a cue for the selection of this sub-frame. Existing at the intersections of personal memory and historical fact, these documentaries confront their viewers with a variety (and often a contradictory combination) of framing cues, challenging elementary processes of meaning-making and inviting viewers to share empathically in personal, subjective perspectives.

Defining First-Person Documentary

The emergence of the diverse and heterogeneous group of films we refer to as "first-person documentaries" has been addressed from several theoretical angles, but providing a clear definition for it has so far proven difficult. What complicates matters is that it encompasses an incredibly diverse set of practices and techniques, and traverses several documentary sub-genres, making it particularly problematic to delineate on the basis of formal or contextual properties alone (O'Connell 2015, p. 21). Perhaps as a consequence of this diversity, several different labels circulate, each focusing on a related but at times distinct set of practices, such as performative documentary (Nichols 2010; Bruzzi 2006), autobiographical documentary (Renov 2004; Lane 2002), personal cinema (Rascaroli 2009), essay film (Corrigan 2011) and first-person documentary (Lebow 2012).

Bill Nichols (2010) defines this set of films as "performative documentary" to set it apart from five previously defined modes of documentary: namely, the poetic, expository, observational, participatory and reflexive modes. The performative mode, he writes, underlines "the complexity of our knowledge of the world by emphasizing its subjective and affective dimensions" through "the free combination of the actual and the imagined" (p. 202). While this description seems to fit the current wave of first-person documentaries, a problem arises when we take into account Stella Bruzzi's (2006) differing, more elaborate interpretation of performativity. Bruzzi bases her understanding of documentary performance on Judith Butler's *Gender Trouble* (1990) and J.L. Austin's *Philosophical Papers* (1970). By focusing on documentary's function as "utterances that simultaneously both describe and perform an action" and taking identity into account as a matter of communication, she complicates Nichols' fixed, categorical employment of the term (p. 48). Moreover, Bruzzi argues for the central role played by performance in all forms of documentary. Indeed, as sociologist Erving Goffman (1959) argues, almost every instance of human interaction has elements of conscious and unconscious role play that are similar to the staging of a play, and it is hard to see why acting in front of a camera (even if the character role one plays is oneself) should be any different. Bruzzi (2006, p. 13) proposes to analyze documentary as "a perpetual negotiation between the real event and its representation," claiming that both viewers and filmmakers are perfectly aware of the impossibility of a purely "objective" representation of reality (p. 7). Her suggestion, therefore, is to treat every documentary as an act of performance—but therein lies the problem with the term for our investigation. If performativity is an unavoidable part of documentary practice, it ceases to function as a defining quality of the particular (first-person) group of documentaries we are attempting to delineate.

Michael Renov (2004, pp. 44–45) applies the terms "autobiographical documentary" and "new autobiography" in his description of the current trend of recent subjective documentaries, suggesting that these terms may encompass various related autobiographical modes, from "essayistic" films to "the confessional mode" and "domestic ethnography." As John Corner (2006, p. 128) states, "Renov's explorations into the documentation of the self extends our sense of documentary's metaphoric range and its continuing depictive potential." However, central to all these modes of filmmaking is "the activity of self-inscription" (Renov 2004, p. 106), rather than the side of documentary reception we wish to investigate.

Moving away from the focus on subjective documentary as a means of authorial expression, Laura Rascaroli (2009) distinguishes two dominant trends within the larger field of subjective documentary films—"personal cinema" and "the essay film." She defines the essay film as a form of self-expression that is usually subjective but need not necessarily be autobiographical. By contrast, "personal cinema" is always autobiographical, distinguishing the two forms on the basis of the kind of commitment they ask of their viewer (pp. 14–16). Although many "personal films" take the shape of a series of deeply personal reflections, this intimate mental world is opened up for the viewer, resulting in a shared autobiographical text (p. 118). Similarly, Timothy Corrigan (2011) categorizes different essay film modes: Interview, Travel, Diary, Editorial and Refractive Cinema. Reality, however, is more complex—essay films are often quite slippery and overlapping, mixing multiple modes. Acknowledging this, Corrigan (2011, p. 8) states he believes "this overlapping is partly to do with the 'unmethodical method' that, according to Adorno, is the fundamental form of the essay and helps explain one of the central paradoxes and challenges of the essay: It is a genre of experience." As is the case with Rascaroli's endeavors, Corrigan's work is a valuable step towards positioning essayistic film in film history by acknowledging its dialogical interpersonal dimensions instead of viewing it mainly as a means of "personal" expression—a welcome change of perspective. However, neither author provides a more specific take on how such viewing dynamics may come about.

Documentary theory has clearly moved beyond the assumption that in order to convey an authentic representation of real events, a film must strive for objectivity. Central to these approaches appears to be a match of two (formerly held to be incompatible) concepts: subjectivity and documentary. It is from the intriguing interplay of these two forces that a form of cinema emerges that is especially challenging to earlier theories of documentary, and it is this broader category of subjective documentaries that our definition should seek to address. We are interested in films that provide a personal, subjective perspective on real situations or events, a perspective that results in stylistic divergence from the traditional formal conventions of documentary film. This broad and varied group of films is best encompassed in Alisa Lebow's definition of first-person films:

> First person films can be... autobiographical in full, or only implicitly and in part. They may take the form of a self-portrait, or, indeed, the portrait of another. They are, very often, not a cinema of 'me', but about someone close, dear, beloved or intriguing, who nonetheless informs the filmmaker's sense of him or herself. They may not be about a person, self or other, at all, but about a neighborhood, a community, a phenomenon or event. The designation 'first person film' is foremost about a mode of address: these films 'speak' from the articulated point of view of the filmmaker who readily acknowledges her subjective position. (Lebow 2012, p. 1)

This definition is broad enough to include all documentaries that provide personal, subjective perspectives on real events. Furthermore, Lebow's definition implies a specific emotional affect that many scholars suggest is a defining property of this type of documentary: that of a temporary empathic 'merging' of the perspectives of viewer and filmmaker. What is lacking, however, is a specification of how exactly this sense of immersion in a subjective, personal perspective arises. Therefore, the question remains: what combination of textual, contextual, paratextual and/or real-world properties leads viewers towards the perception and appreciation of a documentary as a first-person documentary?

DOCUMENTARY AS A COGNITIVE FRAME

Over the past twenty years, cognitive approaches to film studies have grown to such an extent that they now occupy a prominent position. Although, until recently, most of the attention has been directed towards fiction film, some scholars have argued convincingly for the potential of a cognitive approach to documentary (Eitzen 1995; Currie 1995; Plantinga 1997; Smith 2003; Tsang 2011; Bondebjerg 1994, 2014a, b, among others). This chapter taps into that potential by investigating how first-person documentary could be defined as a cognitive frame that comes with its own set of evaluative criteria and emotional affects.

One of the earliest proponents of the idea that documentary cannot be defined solely on the basis of its formal properties was Dirk Eitzen (1995). Arguing against the notion that documentary can be defined as a stable category, Eitzen claims that "documentary must be seen ... not as a kind of text but as a kind of 'reading'" (p. 82).[1] He suggests that viewers are guided in their interpretation of films by elements of a film's formal properties or context. Such "situational cues" can either take the form of explicit verbal labels (such as explanatory title sequences, program notes in a TV guide, and so on) or the more ephemeral form of references to familiar historical events or the cinematic conventions of a certain type of documentary (p. 95). Eitzen sketches here the basics for a cognitive, reception-based approach to documentary, in which the focus is shifted from defining documentary as a stable—objective and text-immanent— category to a more dynamic question of how viewers actually distinguish documentaries from fiction films.

The notion of "frames" invoked by Eitzen is central to understanding the reception of documentary from a cognitive perspective. Frames, in general, can be understood as sets of expectations that we may project onto a situation (in the case of documentary, the encounter with a "medial performance") in order to make sense of it (Minsky 1975, p. 1). Frame theory stresses that "framing" is a cognitive and interpretive activity in which we are constantly engaged; "frames" form the meta-conceptual structures that guide our interpretation and enable signification (Wolf 2006, pp. 4–5). Cognitive frames, then, can be defined as inherited and culturally acquired mental organizing principles that regulate interpretation by guiding expectations and focusing attention on the potentially significant elements of a situation, which are determined on the basis of the outcome of similar past experiences (Goffman 1974). In cinema, the selection and appropriation of a frame depends on elements of a given audiovisual simulation and its context, which signal its expected pertinence, thus triggering a response: viewers utilize their preexisting real-world and medium-specific knowledge to structure incoming information, to regulate their own expectations and, ultimately, to evaluate an experience. This suggests we could define documentary as a cognitive frame, a specific set of expectations that can be applied to film on the basis of its adherence to culturally established formal conventions (which may change as our visual culture develops) and the ways in which it is framed socially and contextually (which may also change as documentary constantly acquires new social functions). This definition enables us to place the

---

[1] For a similar claim, presented from a phenomenological perspective, see Vivian Sobchack's (1999) article, "Toward a Phenomenology of Nonfictional Film Experience."

attribution of documentary value on the side of reception without succumbing to the notion that the choice to view a film as a documentary is purely subjective or arbitrary.

In a similar line of thinking, Ib Bondebjerg (1994, p. 74) draws on Marvin Minsky's (1975) concept of the "frame" (noting its clear similarity with Goffman's use of the term) to suggest that documentary can be understood as a prototypical structure that comes with its own set of default assumptions, which help us to "reason, generalize and to predict, foresee or deduct what may happen or has happened" in a given situation. Drawing on Wolfgang Iser's (cited by Bondebjerg 1994, p. 83) idea that a fictional discourse depends on a set of conventions that are "shared by the author and the audience and understood as such," Bondebjerg suggests that our framing of nonfictional film and television, likewise, depends on a similar "communicative contract" between filmmaker and viewer (p. 84). He outlines four pragmatic dimensions upon which this contract rests: the institutional dimension (the sociological, cultural structure of the viewing experience); the intertextual dimension (the textual, cultural and psychological aspects of a genre, oeuvre or otherwise related group of films); the experiential dimension (based on knowledge, attitudes and concepts acquired through our interaction with the world); and the situational dimension (the concrete time and place of the viewing experience) (p. 84). Thus, Bondebjerg treats the documentary frame as something that does not arise exclusively from a viewer's personal experiences but is equally a product of institutional forces, social conventions and commonly shared beliefs and values.

If documentary is indeed best understood as a cognitive frame, we should next inquire on which factors of a film's presentation and context do viewers base their selection of a frame. On the one hand, Eitzen (1995, p. 95) suggests that situational cues guide viewers towards the documentary frame, but his list of examples of cues remains rather sketchy. On the other hand, the four dimensions outlined by Bondebjerg more accurately expose the complex interplay of factors that influence our reading of a film, but render it difficult to isolate the specific, individual elements of a film's text or context that guide viewers toward the documentary frame. We suggest a middle-way and more pragmatic approach that distinguishes between three primary "levels" at which framing cues may be found to operate: (1) the formal/textual level, (2) the contextual/paratextual level, and (3) the real-world referential level. Rather than treating these three levels separately from the cognitive dimensions of documentary, we view them as the three primary sources of "input" for the universal cognitive process of framing. While watching a film, a viewer's cognition draws on the cues (potentially) available on all three of these levels in order to determine the (apparently) appropriate framing for a film:

1. *Formal and textual framing cues* are found in elements of a film's formal—stylistic and narrative—presentation. The example that Eitzen (1995, p. 91) uses of a "jiggly" camera is an illustration of a formal/textual cue, an aesthetic convention that is associated with a certain type of documentary filmmaking. It is important to note, however, that formal conventions are not necessarily adhered to by all documentaries, and that they can also change over time or be exploited by fictional films in the service of their ambitions for realistic representation (the diegetic use of hand-held cameras in Eduardo Sánchez and Daniel Myrick's 1999 film, *The Blair Witch Project*, is an example of this).
2. *Contextual and paratextual framing cues* can be found in the programming of film festivals, trailers, TV guides, DVD covers, VOD info blurbs, reviews, posters and promotional websites. The context of a film's release often plays a critical part in how it is received; films are marketed to a target audience and specific elements of their narrative might be highlighted as important. Many first-person documentaries are excellent examples of the potential for contextual framing to override the viewer's evaluation of a film on the basis of its formal properties.
3. Finally, *real-world referential framing cues* originate from what we already (might) know of the real-world situation that is represented in a documentary before engaging with it on any level. According to Torben Grodal (2009, pp. 255–256), "our knowledge modifies our experience of realism. ... There is thus a potential conflict between the kind of realism established by perception and that established by knowledge." Thus, while many documentaries employ techniques that would seem to counter the establishment of perceptual realism (that is to say, an uninhibited, embodied immersion in the cinematic world), knowing the fact that they represent objects and events known to actually exist in the real world may, nevertheless, act as a powerful cue to establish a sense of *factual realism*.

This brief outline is, of course, far from exhaustive, but it could potentially serve as the basis of a structured analysis of the framing process.

Eventually, one of the aims of a cognitive approach to documentary should be to specify the most significant cues that lead viewers towards the framing of a film as a documentary and to reveal their interplay by showing how they may modify, strengthen or contradict each other. This project lies beyond the current scope of this chapter. Instead of further specifying and theorizing these levels, let us now consider how, within this model, first-person documentary could be defined as a sub-frame of the documentary frame, corresponding to a specific configuration of formal/textual, contextual/paratextual and real-world referential cues.

Framing First-Person Documentary

First-person documentaries present an interesting case for this model as they challenge the formal conventions of traditional documentary, providing their viewers with various cues that do not automatically fit the documentary frame. As noted earlier, many first-person documentaries abandon the indexical claim of observational documentary in favor of new, experimental forms of representation. This raises the question of how, in spite of such formal innovations, viewers still come to frame these films as documentaries. As further noted, first-person documentary has a specific affective dimension that sets it apart from the traditional documentary norm and enables an empathic merging of the perspective of the viewer with that of the filmmaker. Two experiential properties appear to be essential to our selection of the first-person sub-frame: on the one hand, an awareness of watching a representation of historical or actual reality, and on the other, an awareness that this representation is "filtered" through the subjective perspective of the filmmaker. To show how such an awareness could be established, we will briefly sketch how, on each of the three levels outlined above, framing cues could lead viewers to experience a film as *both* a nonfictional representation *and* a subjectively filtered narrative.

On level (1), the *formal/ textual level*, first-person documentaries divert from the familiar conventions of observational documentary by employing a wide variety of anti-mimetic techniques of representation, ranging from animation (for example, *Persepolis, Waltz with Bashir, Crulic: The Path to Beyond*) to digital-image manipulation, collage and associative montage (for example, *Tarnation; Heart of a Dog*), performative reenactments (for example, *A Strange Love Affair with Ego*) or even the use of sculptural art (for example, Rithy Panh's 2013 *The Missing Picture*). According to Grodal (2009, p. 250), our sense of perceptual realism depends on a combination of "perceptual specificity" and "familiarity," both which may be hampered by the stylistic techniques utilized in first-person documentary.

Techniques like animation and reenactment reduce the sense of realism; that is to say, they restrict the representation's optical fidelity and block the viewer's access to the perceptual specifics of the historical or actual events represented. Furthermore, such techniques break away from the "familiar" documentary genre conventions—although viewers may, of course, become familiar with them in time, to the point where they solidify into new conventions. Grodal suggests that "our intuitive sense of objectivity or subjectivity depends on the issue of control rather than on whether something is evaluated as real or not in an absolute sense" and that this feeling of "control" depends on the extent to which a filmic representation supports our motor actions (p. 230). Simply put, the more straightforwardly "mimetic" a filmic representation is, the more it allows for an embodied immersion in the filmic world and the more objective it will seem on a perceptual level. First-person documentaries tend to utilize elements of overt stylization that disrupt the viewer's sense of perceptual realism and act as clear cues to frame them as subjective narratives. Furthermore, formal/textual cues may come in the form of overt acknowledgments of the subjective perspective, such as a voiceover speaking in the first person or the overt presence of the filmmaker as an on-screen character (such as Renzo Martens in *Episode III: Enjoy Poverty* or Kim Ki-duk in *Arirang*).

As demonstrated below, however, cues at both the contextual/paratextual level and the real-world referential level provide the viewer with clear indications that, although the perspective provided by the film may be subjective, the events represented are nonfictional. Thus, while these documentaries may forfeit their claim to perceptual specificity and its associated sense of indexicality, the events and phenomena they represent are still specific and real—that is to say, as far as viewers can determine, given the extratextual cues that are available to them. Much of this estimation depends on the subject matter's "familiarity" (to use Grodal's term again); lacking concrete evidence, humans are hard-wired to give greater credence to stories that correspond with what they already know.

At level (2), the *contextual and paratextual level*, first-person documentaries seem to be surrounded with framing cues that emphasize their status both as nonfictional narratives and as artworks that reflect a personal vision. Contextually, most first-person documentaries are categorized and indexed very clearly as documentaries, whether through their programming (for example, their inclusion in film festivals such as the International Documentary Film Festival Amsterdam) or labeling as "documentary" (for example, on movie review websites and databases such as the Internet Movie Database). At the same time, however, reviews tend to indicate the intimate subject matter of the film and emphasize the role of its creator as an individual with personal preoccupations who, due to a close relationship with the subject, is uniquely qualified to share their subjective perspective on it. Examples of this phenomenon abound, from the advertising of the recent documentary *Heart of a Dog* as a film by "acclaimed musician and performance artist Laurie Anderson" (Movieclips Film Festivals & Indie Films 2015), through the descriptions of *A Strange Love Affair with Ego* as filmmaker Ester Gould's "personal quest" to understand her sister Rowan (IDFA 2016), to Roger Ebert's (2003) review of *Tarnation* as an example of "intensely personal and subjective autobiographical filmmaking." The marketing and critical reception of these films clearly seeks to frame them as performative artworks that reflect the unique, subjective perspectives of their visionary creators.

Finally, on level (3), the *real-world level*, viewers tend to have limited access to specific, factual knowledge of the situations that first-person documentaries represent. As many first-person documentaries deal with personal histories, family histories and other subjective histories that do not (yet) form a part of established, common historical knowledge, viewers often have little choice but to accept the documentary as their only window onto the reality of the represented situation. Nevertheless, those elements of a first-person documentary that do correspond to the specific or general real-world knowledge available to the viewer act as powerful cues to frame the film as a documentary. For example, the inclusion of several historical BBC television broadcasts, including an interview with the former British prime minister, Margaret Thatcher, lends Sandya Suri's autobiographical family memoir, *I for India*, a strong connection with known historical reality.[2] When we apply Grodal's criteria of cinematic realism to this film, the inclusion of such highly specific, recognizable fragments of evidently nonfictional material reinforces the sense of realism of the entire

---

[2] It is worth keeping in mind how much of our knowledge of history is mediated and may be subject to various degrees of manipulation, so that "historical reality" in this context must be taken to mean a commonly agreed-upon understanding of historical events rather than a literal record of them.

documentary, while the less specifically recognizable elements of the documentary correspond to familiar tropes of family dynamics, diaspora and racism. This mix of perceptual specificity, recognizability and general familiarity is what lends the film its strong sense of factual authenticity, in spite of the subjective perspective it represents.

In summary, we hypothesize that the selection of the first-person documentary frame depends on a combination of: (1) textual/formal cues that elicit a sense of overt subjectivity; (2) contextual cues that emphasize a film's status as personal cinema; and (3) contextual cues and correspondences with real-world knowledge that affirms its status as nonfiction. The application of the "first-person documentary frame" may thus be described as the result of a complex framing process, a hermeneutic negotiation between cues that elicit a strong sense of subjectivity and cues that lead the viewer to frame this experience as still belonging to the realm of documentary film. Based on existing definitional attempts of first-person documentaries, we furthermore hypothesize that the first-person documentary frame comes with its own set of expectations and emotional affects. It is likely that viewers evaluate first-person documentaries on the basis of their *emotional authenticity* rather than their *factual reliability*.

THE AFFECTIVE DIMENSIONS OF THE FIRST-PERSON FRAME IN KIRSTEN JOHNSON'S *CAMERAPERSON*

Film viewing is an embodied activity, and the emotions experienced when watching films closely resemble those experienced in real-life situations (Grodal 2009; Plantinga and Smith 1999; Plantinga 2009; Bondebjerg 2014a). Framing, as a cognitive activity, profoundly affects the experiential "stakes" of a situation. For example, we evaluate a scene depicting violence or torture very differently when we know it to be actuality, not fiction. Considering that the neural architecture that governs our emotions developed at a time when fictional representations did not yet exist and "all incoming data were essentially true" (Grodal 2009, p. 185), these differences in evaluation can only be explained as the result of the application of an "as-if" frame (Bondebjerg 1994, p. 73) at a higher-order cognitive level. This fictional frame can provide a measure of relief when we are confronted with extreme scenes. Although they may still affect us deeply, we can comfort ourselves with the knowledge that they are "just pretense." Likewise, when our awareness of a documentary's subjectivity causes us to apply the first-person sub-frame to it, this also comes with its own unique set of affective implications.

Emotions such as care and empathy, which originally developed in relation to the care of newborn infants (Lambert 2012), are conspicuously triggered by many films (Grodal and Kramer 2010, pp. 20–22). Our ability to feel empathy for others has extended from parental love to include friends, relatives and group members over the course of our evolutionary history (Churchland 2011). Evidence from empirical studies suggests that empathy and bonding do not stem from selfless altruism but continue to depend on a sense of kinship or "oneness," the sense that another person is "of the same stuff" as ourselves (Maner et al. 2002).

The classical observational mode of documentary presentation does not lend itself well to the establishment of an empathic relationship between documentary subject, filmmaker and viewer. While such documentaries may play upon the emotions of their viewers in powerful ways, they aim to present perspectives that, at least, seem impartial and objective. Hence, a great deal of effort is devoted to purposefully obscuring the fact that the perspective given on a situation is unavoidably shaped (at least in part) by the personal fascinations, concerns and prejudices of the filmmaker.

In first-person documentary, the borders between these three agents are more diffuse: not only do the roles and interests of filmmaker and subject frequently coincide, but viewers are also invited to share in this perspective, to make it their own. By emphasizing subjective experiences and feelings, first-person documentaries shift the focus of their viewers from the factual details of the situation that is represented (which, being specific and clearly different to our own, is something we can more easily distance ourselves from) towards its emotional dimensions, which are universally human. This effect does not come about spontaneously; rather, it should be understood as the result of a complex (and to some extent calculated) interplay of framing cues provided at the contextual/paratextual, formal/textual and real-world referential levels.

In the case of *Cameraperson* (2016), the contextual framing cues are provided by the film's website, where we find the following brief synopsis: "Exposing her role behind the camera, [director] Kirsten Johnson reaches into the vast trove of footage she has shot over decades around the world. What emerges is a visually bold memoir and a revelatory interrogation of the power of the camera." These lines explicitly foreground the idea that the film presents its author's critical reflection on her own creative process.

The term "memoir," moreover, suggests that an extensive degree of access to the personal memories of the author will be provided, and this will help us construct her as a character we can come to understand and empathize with. Furthermore, we are provided with compelling reasons to want to immerse ourselves in her perspective: the material in the film is described as a "trove of footage," presented in a "bold" and "revelatory" manner. As such, the framing cues provided here in just a few words are already sufficient to make us aware that this film presents its creator's subjective perspective rather than an objective or impartial one, and that we are meant to empathize with this perspective.

On the formal/textual level, *Cameraperson* consists of a combination of documentary footage, shot in diverse locations around the world over the course of Johnson's career as cinematographer, and more personal 'home movie' material, centered around her children and her mother who suffers from Alzheimer's. While some of the repurposed material originates from documentaries shot in a rather straightforward observational style, it takes on a more subjective character in this particular juxtaposition. Specific choices in editing explicitly foreground the filmmaker's presence as both observer and participant in the scenes that are shown. For example, we are frequently made aware of the filmmaker's presence behind the camera through vocal interjections and adjustments to the camera settings. Loosely centering its structure on the themes of birth, life and death, the dialectical montage of the film establishes interesting links between the personal "home video" material and the preexisting material shot for other documentaries, revealing the personal in the universal, and vice versa.

The film includes a number of scenes with intense emotional content, such as a conversation with survivors of war and ethnic cleansing in Bosnia and Herzegovina and an interview with a boy who was handicapped, and lost a friend, in a land-mine accident. Such negative emotions are balanced with pleasant scenes, like one of children playing in a garden. Viewers are given little indication of the intended connections between the scenes other than their loose organization around the film's central themes. As a result, the focus of their attention shifts from the construction of the film's central argument or narrative to the specific way of looking and the universal emotions it represents.

At the real-world referential level, the fact that the film is largely made of documentary footage, and includes no animated or otherwise stylized sequences, provides its viewers with a high degree of perceptual specificity, heightening its sense of realism. Through its explicit references to known historical events, such as the war in Bosnia and Herzegovina (or, conversely, the absence of any scenes depicting fantastical, surreal or otherwise non-natural content), further asserts its status as a piece of nonfiction. This framing additionally enhances the film's emotional impact, making it impossible to distance oneself from the events that are represented by viewing them as "just pretense."

The combined effect of these contextual, formal and real-world referential cues is clearly witnessed in one of the film's most emotionally charged moments. In this scene, we witness how a midwife struggles to get a newborn infant to take its first breath. Most of the factual details of this situation are omitted. We are given the name of the hospital and the city but not told why the filmmaker is documenting this birth, who the mother is, or any other circumstances. The absence of a soundtrack and the panicked questions of the filmmaker enhance the tension of the scene and act as powerful emotional cues to activate feelings of fear, panic and distress in the viewer (Smith 1999). Naturally, the newborn infant presents a suitable target for our instinctive tendency to care for the lives of our offspring. Although the child is not ours, we may fear for its life as if it were. Simultaneously, we are cued to feel with the filmmaker, who, rather than keeping an objective distance, reveals her own emotional stake in the scene through her interjections. Although she does not appear within the frame, her nervous questions from behind the camera reveal the ambiguity of her presence as both observer and potential actor. We ask ourselves—as she does—at what point should she stop filming and try to help. Johnson eventually does intervene, going around the hospital in search of an oxygen supply, with little success. After what seems an eternity, the midwife succeeds in getting the child to take its first breath, but whether it will survive the effects of its prolonged asphyxiation without an oxygen mask remains an open question.

While it could be argued that the emotional content of this scene is so powerful that it would trigger a strong emotional response regardless of its presentation, it is easy to see how the first-person sub-frame adds an additional degree of closeness to our empathic involvement. By putting its viewers explicitly in the shoes of the filmmaker, with whom the contextual framing has already prepared us to empathize, the film lets us experience these events from her subjective perspective. This immersion is further enhanced by our shared feeling of the lack of any power to meaningfully intervene, resulting in a shared feeling of helplessness. The way in which this scene cues us not only to *feel for* its subject but to also *feel with* the filmmaker seems to momentarily erode the boundaries that normally exist between these three agents. Had the same scene been accompanied by a voiceover or intertitles providing additional contextual information, these would have cued viewers to engage higher-order cognitive processes and reduced its emotional immediacy. In its current presentation, the scene illustrates the potential of first-person documentaries to immerse viewers in the subjective perspective of their authors and to trigger strong feelings of empathy for people who are not part of our immediate family circle or tribe, foregrounding the universally shared emotional dimensions of situations.

Concluding Remarks

First-person documentaries push the boundaries of creative liberty within the documentary frame, employing a wide range of techniques (reenactment, digital-image manipulation, collage, montage, animation) and materials (archival footage, photographs, stock footage, citations from other films, reenacted scenes, controversial material) to tell stories about real events from highly subjective—personal—perspectives. We can witness a corresponding shift in focus in recent documentary studies, as scholars relinquish the idea of defining documentary as a stable category, or as the immanent quality of a set of films, and define it instead as a mode of reception or cognitive frame (Eitzen 1995; Bondebjerg 2014a). However, much work remains to be done in detailing the exact criteria that govern the selection of this frame of reception, as well as the specific expectations and emotional affects it raises, and that is precisely the contribution that a cognitive approach to documentary could supply.

When documentary is defined not as a text-immanent quality, but rather as a set of expectations and forms of knowledge that functions as a suitable frame for the viewer to potentially assign to a film, and when it can evolve dynamically in relation to changing conventions, it becomes clear how techniques such as re-enactment, animation and montage have been part of the documentary tradition from its very outset, despite the fact that such techniques would appear, on the surface, to divert from documentary's referential ties to historical reality. Indeed, the first-person subframe reveals the malleability of the documentary frame by utilizing formal techniques that seem to contradict classical notions of documentary as being factual and argumentative. When we embrace the idea that documentary may encompass a diverse set of sub-frames, each of which comes with its own unique set of evaluative criteria and emotional affects, we can understand the foregrounding of subjective experiences that we see in recent first-person films as another stage in documentary's ongoing project of authentically representing the world we inhabit. Seeking to immerse their viewers in the personal perspectives of their authors, these films foreground emotional content over factual information and make bold use of unconventional techniques of presentation. In doing so, the first-person documentary frame further challenges conventional ideas of what a documentary should or should not be, and demonstrates the merits of a cognitive approach to the field.

REFERENCES

Austin, J. L. (1970) *Philosophical Papers.* 2nd edn. Oxford: Clarendon Press.
Barthes, R. (1981; 2010) *Camera Lucida: Reflections on Photography.* New York: Hill and Wang.
Bazin, A. (1960) "The Ontology of the Photographic Image," *Film Quarterly,* 13(4), pp. 4–9.
Bondebjerg, I. (1994) "Narratives of Reality: Documentary Film and Television in a Cognitive and Pragmatic Perspective," *Nordicom Review,* 1, pp. 65–85.
Bondebjerg, I. (2014a) "Documentary and Cognitive Theory: Narrative, Emotion and Memory," *Media and Communication,* 2(1), pp. 12–21.
Bondebjerg, I. (2014b) *Engaging with Reality: Documentary & Globalization.* Bristol: Intellect.
Bruzzi, S. (2006) *New Documentary.* 2nd edn. London; New York: Routledge.
Butler, J. (1990) *Gender Trouble: Feminism and the Subversion of Identity.* New York; London: Routledge.
Churchland, P. S. (2011) *BrainTrust: What Neuroscience Tells Us About Morality.* Princeton, NJ: Princeton University Press.
Corner, J. (2006) 'The Subject in Documentary', *Screen,* 47(1), pp. 125–128.
Corrigan, T. (2011) *The Essay Film: From Montaigne, After Marker.* Oxford: Oxford University Press.
Currie, G. (1995) *Image and Mind: Film, Philosophy, and Cognitive Science.* Cambridge: Cambridge University Press.
Currie, G. (1999) 'Visible Traces: Documentary and the Contents of Photographs', *Journal of Aesthetics and Art Criticism,* 57(3), pp. 285–297.
Ebert, R. (2003) Review of *Tarnation* [Online]. Available at: http://www. ebertfest.com/six/tarnation_review.htm (Accessed: December 21, 2016).
Eitzen, D. (1995) 'When is a Documentary?: Documentary as a Mode of Reception', *Cinema Journal,* 35(1), pp. 81–102.

Goffman, E. (1959) *The Presentation of Self in Everyday Life*. New York: Anchor Books.

Goffman, E. (1974) *Frame Analysis: An Essay on the Organization of Experience*. New York: Harper and Row.

Grodal, T. (2009) *Embodied Visions: Evolution, Emotion, Culture, and Film*. New York: Oxford University Press.

Grodal, T. and Kramer, M. (2010) 'Empathy, Film and the Brain', *Semiotic Inquiry*, 30, pp. 19–35.

IDFA (International Documentary Filmfestival Amsterdam) (2016) Review of *A Strange Love Affair with Ego* [Online]. Available at: https://www.idfa.nl/nl/tags/project.aspx?id=0EB122D3-2D7D-474F-9AFE-25948DD336E8 (Accessed: December 21, 2016).

Lambert, K. (2012) "The Parental Brain: Transformations and Adaptations," *Psychology & Behavior*, 107(5), pp. 792–800.

Lane, J. (2002) *The Autobiographical Documentary in America*. Madison: University of Wisconsin Press.

Lebow, A. (2012) *The Cinema of Me*. London; New York: Wallflower Press.

Maner, J. K., Luce, C. L., Neuberg, S. L., Cialdini, R. B., Brown, S. and Sagarin, B. J. (2002) "The Effects of Perspective Taking on Motivations: Still No Evidence for Altruism," *Personality and Social Psychology Bulletin*, 28(11), pp. 1601–1610.

Minsky, M. (1975) "Framework for Representing Knowledge," in Winston, P. (ed.) *The Psychology of Computer Vision*. New York: McGraw-Hill.

Movieclips Film Festivals & Indie Films (2015) *Heart of a Dog* Official Trailer 1 [Documentary Movie HD] [Online]. Available at: https://www.youtube.com/watch?v=v37BnyHefnY (Accessed: 21 December 2016).

Nichols, B. (1991) *Representing Reality*. Bloomington: Indiana University Press.

Nichols, B. (2010) *Introduction to Documentary*. 2nd edn. Bloomington: Indiana University Press.

O'Connell, J. M. (2015) *Traversing the Divide: Cognitive Approach to the Dialogical Nature of First Person Documentary*. Groningen: University of Groningen.

Plantinga, C. (1997) *Rhetoric and Representation in Non-fiction Film*. Cambridge: Cambridge University Press.

Plantinga, C. (2009) "Emotion and Affect," in Livingston, P. and Plantinga, C. (eds.) *The Routledge Companion to Philosophy and Film*. London; New York: Routledge, pp. 86–96.

Plantinga, C. and Smith, G. M. (1999) *Passionate Views: Film, Cognition and Emotion*. Baltimore, MD; London: The John Hopkins University Press.

Rascaroli, L. (2009) *The Personal Camera*. London: Wallflower Press.

Renov, M. (2004) *The Subject of Documentary*. Minneapolis: University of Minnesota Press.

Rombes, N. (2009) *Cinema in the Digital Age*. London: Wallflower Press.

Smith, G. M. (1999) "Local Emotions, Global Moods," in, Plantinga, C. and Smith, G. M. (eds.) *Passionate Views*. Baltimore, MD: John Hopkins University Press, pp. 103–126.

Smith, G. M. (2003) *Film Structure and the Emotion System*. Cambridge: Cambridge University Press.

Sobchack, V. (1999) "Toward a Phenomenology of Nonfiction Film Experience," in Gaines, J. M. and Renov, M. (eds.) *Collecting Visible Evidence*. Minneapolis: University of Minnesota Press, pp. 241–254.

Tsang, H. (2011) "Emotion, Documentary and Van der Keuken's *Face Value*," *Studies in Documentary Film*, 5(1), pp. 17–30.

Tsur, R. (2008) *Toward a Theory of Cognitive Poetics*. Sussex: Sussex Academic Press.

Wolf, W. (2006) "Introduction: Frames, Framings and Framing Borders in Literature and Other Media," in Wolf, W. and Berhhart, W. (eds.) *Framing Borders in Literature and Other Media*. Amsterdam: Rodopi, pp. 1–40.

CHAPTER 14

The Communication of Relational
Knowledge in the First-Person Documentary

Mette Kramer

In his work, *The Subject of Documentary* (2004), Michael Renov reflects on the subjective turn in documentary film that began in the 1980s. According to Renov, the mushrooming of first-person, often autobiographical documentaries should be understood as a response to the social, cultural and political changes that took place between the 1960s and 1970s. He points to the rise of the women's movement and the youth rebellions as significant factors in the shift of subjectivity and performativity—previously only expressed by avant-garde filmmakers and video artists—into the realm of documentary film. The turn from the political to the personal, which was enabled by contemporary technical advances, became, in Renov's (2004, p. xvi) words, "a tool for coupling liberatory public testimony and private therapy." Today, at a time when "identity politics has become increasingly prevalent in the decades since the dissolution of movement or class-based political struggle" (2008, p. 48), it finds expression in many different media forms and formats.[1] These sorts of

---

[1] See Ib Bondebjerg's (2016) article, "Den subjective dokumentar," exploring media in this sense.

M. Kramer (✉)
University of Copenhagen, Copenhagen, Denmark
e-mail: mettekramer@mail.dk

© The Author(s) 2018   243
C. Brylla, M. Kramer (eds.), *Cognitive Theory and Documentary Film*, https://doi.org/10.1007/978-3-319-90332-3_14

documentaries enact "a politics of the body (the guts, the bowels, the balls) rather than of the mind." Renov (2004, p. 174) notes that "[i]n these films and tapes (increasingly the latter), subjectivity is no longer constructed as "something shameful"; it is the filter through which the real enters discourse, as well as a kind of experimental compass guiding the work towards its goal as embodied knowledge."

Bill Nichols describes his perception of performative documentaries in a similar way:

> [They] bring the emotional intensities of embodied experience and knowledge to the fore rather than attempt to do something tangible. If they set out to do something it is to help us sense what a certain situation or experience feels like. They want us to feel on a visceral level more than understand on a conceptual level. (Nichols 2017, p. 151)

However, what is missing from these descriptions of the role of the first-person documentary in our culture and history is an account of the sort of "knowledge" this type of film embodies and communicates in affective and cognitive terms. This chapter, however, is not intended as a critique of these authors (two of the most prominent voices in contemporary documentary theory); rather, it builds on their work by shedding new light on this type of documentary film and the kind of knowledge it communicates (for better or worse) using the theoretical perspective afforded by the "affective turn" that took place in the humanities and social sciences in the mid-1990s. This refers to the growing tendency to embrace the emotions and to theorize and analyze a range of fields using affect theory and related empirical research, a reflection of the scientific world's increasing interest in embodiment and affective processes (Gregg and Seigworth 2010).

Thus, in the following study, after looking briefly at the theoretical literature on first-person documentaries (particularly Anne Jerslev's (2002) important work on the "intimate" type of first-person documentary), I apply social-cognitive theory to the genre, using an attachment-theory and infant-developmental-research framework. I analyze how the schematic structures of the intimate first-person documentary tap into (and add to) "implicit and explicit relational knowledge" (Lyons-Ruth et al. 1998) by drawing upon the embodied reality that is enacted emotionally and cognitively, and explore how relational schemas play a role in both the director's communication and regulation of attachment emotion and the viewer's response. To narrow the focus, I concentrate on two films: the main case study is Swedish director Linda Västrik's *Pappa Och Jag* (*Father and I*) (1999), but I also look at the documentary *Family* (2001) by Danish directors Phie Ambo and Sami Saif.

THE FIRST-PERSON DOCUMENTARY FILM, COGNITIVE FILM THEORY AND INFANT DEVELOPMENTAL RESEARCH

As Alisa Lebow (2012) argues, "first-person documentary" is an umbrella term, capable of incorporating documentary films with different yet over-lapping focal points. Some scholars analyze the first-person film from the perspective of autobiography (Renov 2004), some take performance (Nichols 1991) and/or subjectivity (Renov 2004) as their concern, and some study this type of film from the perspective of the director as they confront significant others and negotiate personal family dynamics. In the latter case, theorists use such labels as "domestic ethnography" (Renov 2004), while the more exclusive term "intimate documentary film" (Jerslev 2002) is used to describe those films in which the director's optic is focused primarily on one significant other—these could be seen as a sub-category of the domestic ethnographic documentary.

In the "intimate" first-person documentary, the autobiographical element is always the primary focal point, as the director's personal search to find and/or get to know a missing or unfamiliar significant other occupies center stage. Accordingly, the director looks back at their past, using home videos and family photos, and often engages in an on-screen confrontation with the significant other in order to convey a sense of social and emotional interaction. *Pappa Och Jag* is one such intimate film. Here, the young director, Linda Västrik, quizzes her "pappa" (who was absent during most of her childhood) about whether or not he is her biological father. She is insistent in her search for answers, whether behind or in front of the camera, pleading with her parents, in particular her father, to assume the adult responsibility they should have accepted years ago by submitting to a parental DNA test. In the other case study, *Family*, which falls under the rubric of domestic ethnography as its theme is the wider topic of family dynamics and insecure attachment, the filmmaker, Sami Saif, searches for his absent Yemeni father. His co-director and girlfriend, Phie Ambo, guides him from behind the camera in his quest to figure out where his father went after he left his wife and abandoned Sami and his older brother, Thomas.

Despite covering the same territory—the directors' relational bond/s—the films present two different intersubjective perspectives. In the case of *Pappa Och Jag*, the viewpoint is a single one (Linda's view of her father), while *Family* operates with a double intersubjective focus as Phie is both the camerawoman and part of the narrative: she addresses interpersonal matters with Sami, as well as sharing her perspective of her boyfriend with the viewer. Even though the two films overlap thematically, the strategies the directors employ to communicate their interaction with their "attachment figures" vary greatly. Whereas *Pappa Och Jag* uses observational documentary with a distinctive visual style, *Family* mixes observational documentary with lyrical, dramatized passages, thus underlining the broad differences in thematic and formal orchestration that exist within the genre.

First-person documentaries about significant others are relational journeys. For Linda, the journey began in infancy, when her parents divorced. When she turned 12, she stopped trying to contact her father as he failed to respond to her letters or phone calls; however, it is evident that she has never achieved a sense of closure. In contrast, Sami postponed his journey until four years after his older brother, Thomas, had committed suicide and his mother had died from alcoholism—tragic events that underscore a similar need for emotional closure over paternal loss. The type of documentaries described here share with fiction films, in particular with romances and melodramas, certain overarching universal themes, such as the formation, loss or recuperation of social attachments (Kramer 2007; Grodal and Kramer 2014). As I argue elsewhere (Kramer 2010), these films fall into the category of "attachment films." In such a film, the scenario most likely to elicit a response is one in which the viewer can relate to the character's desire to form a social bond or their emotional struggle after the loss of such a bond. From the perspective of cognitive film theory, the films' social-emotional arena of loss and gain represents a form of "mammalian attachment," embodying ecologically valid scenarios that have the potential to attract the viewer's attention and engage them in the narrative. We recognize basic social emotional responses and actions in ourselves and in (fictive as well as real) others when the meaning these create within our brain triggers our embodied emotions.

A film's thematic relevance for the viewer, therefore, can be found in their own embodiment of emotional responses. We are biological organisms with brains that have evolved to respond functionally to the potential for action in our surrounding environment. Attachment, along with its associated emotions, is motivated by the potential for a substantial mammalian reward, and a film will often exploit its understanding of this to ensure it arouses this universal emotional receptivity. In filmic attachment, the viewer's emotions are enhanced by different plot constructions that embody the characters' needs as they are placed in different situations. These run the gamut of emotional responses, from joy, love and excitement, through sadness, mourning and tenderness, to disappointment, anger and despair. In short, across both the domains of documentary and fiction film, the theme of attachment can be orchestrated and molded according to the vision of the director, the actors' ability to portray this vision, the film's script and the surrounding sociocultural trends (Kramer forthcoming). Although relative, the difference between fiction and documentary attachment films can be found in their orchestration of the relational material and in the viewer's evaluation of the film's reality (Grodal 2009).

In first-person documentary films like *Pappa Och Jag* and *Family*, the subjectivity of attachment is communicated directly as the content is based on independent acts consisting of the director's ongoing interaction with the attachment figure (the father) through interviews and/or a reconstruction of the past by way of family photos and home videos. Arguably, the tone of this type of film is set by its staging, direction and the different emotional modalities (of humor in *Family*, of anger and despair in *Pappa Och Jag*) that convey the filmmakers' subjective experience and memory of their emotions, which they retrieve through their interaction (as an adult) with their attachment figure.

Jerslev (2005, p. 113) notes that, in an intimate film such as *Family*, "to a certain extent there is no anterior life that has been destroyed by the presence of the camera... the camera is part of Sami's reality and subjectivity." With the camera serving as an "extension to the director's body" (Jerslev 2002), it is as if the viewer needs the "virtual performance" (Nichols 1991) it embodies—so common in this type of film—in order to come to some sort of understanding of the nature of the director's attachment bond. When Nichols (1991), in contrasting the performance of fiction and documentaries, coined the term "virtual performance," he was referring to the ordinary person's "everyday presentation of self." He may also have been alluding to the work of sociologist Erving Goffman (1959), who believed that social life itself is a discourse since we are always actors performing on the stage of society. According to Nichols (1991, p. 122), virtual performance "presents the logic of actual performance without signs of conscious awareness that this presentation is an act." Here, it is important to note—even if Nichols does not use this perspective—that characters in the first-person documentary can show different degrees of self-consciousness in relation to their performances, and that the fascination and the realism of the first-person documentary lies in the viewer's experience of these more-or-less conscious acts. Linda's on-going confrontation with her father is painful to watch precisely because the viewer is seeing an independent actor placing herself in a real-life traumatic situation in which she is not always aware—or has chosen not to be aware—of the consequences of her own performance. The unbearable feeling of watching actions that, in the words of Dirk Eitzen (2007), are "consequential" in real life, gives the first-person documentary its "peculiar" appeal.

However, as a cognitive film scholar with an interest in infant developmental research, I believe there is an additional element that can help clarify the inherent difficulties a documentary director faces when performing themselves, and explain the fascination this type of film holds. Documentaries like *Family* and *Pappa Och Jag* owe their attraction to the universal relevance of attachment needs, and their building blocks are the on-screen interactions between the director and the attachment figure. The viewer is witnessing unique moments that echo and embody previous interactions, transmitted by the director's "embodied relational knowledge." In other words, by presenting reiterated enactments between the director and their attachment figure, these films provide viewers with unique intersubjective experiences or, as developmental psychologist Daniel Stern (1985) describes them, relational schemas of "being with."

Interpersonal processes often operate in a paralinguistic and non-verbal fashion originating in the relational experiences of the individual with their caregiver(s). These memories are stored in the procedural memory system during the formative stages of an infant's ontogeny—that is, they are part of our implicit "relational knowledge" (Lyons-Ruth et al. 1998). Relational knowledge is a dual system: whereas implicit relational knowledge operates from birth and is automatic and typically beyond conscious recall (although therapy can potentially render such experiences available), explicit relational knowledge refers to declarative, symbolic, imaginary representations of how it is to "be with" someone, and are conscious experiences. The factually based material of the first-person documentary film (for instance, the reality of Linda's relationship with her father) relies on the director's subjective experience of implicit and explicit schematic knowledge, which they communicate to the viewer by capturing on screen both their present and derived experiences of their relationship with their attachment figure. This type of film typically presents its audience with what could be referred to as a model scenario of the insecurity that arises from the mixed emotions of anger and despair that build up when social and emotional attachment bonds are not met, mutually agreed upon or repaired. How the model scenario plays out, however, depends on the director's vision of the film and their stylistic mastery—in particular, their deeper knowledge of the effect of their own performance, how aware they are of their emotions, actions and reactivation of past emotions (especially those tied to unconscious implicit relational knowledge), and how they choose to frame their characters, including their own.

Thus, I argue in this chapter, on the basis of an analysis of *Pappa Och Jag* and *Family*, that the way a director chooses, consciously or unconsciously, to orchestrate their real-life material is grounded in their relational knowledge and the degree to which they are aware of their own performance. This will play a significant role in the film's communication of emotion, and consequently will determine the viewer's experience, particularly the degree to which they empathize with the character.

ATTACHMENT THEORY AND *PAPPA OCH JAG*

The following analysis of *Pappa Och Jag* focuses on attachment theory and social-cognitive schema theory. The goal is to explore the extent to which relational schemas are at work in the film and the benefit we can derive from using attachment theory and the theory of social-cognitive schemas to describe the director's embodied relational knowledge, as well as the viewer's experience of the film's orchestration of its material. At the end of the chapter, the example of the film, *Family*, affords an alternative view of how a director can choose to orchestrate and communicate the self within a scenario of insecure family dynamics.

The relevance of attachment security was established by John Bowlby's (1969) seminal research into attachment as a universal adaptation that has evolved to protect and aid the core mammalian interests crucial to our self-preservation and survival. There is abundant evidence to suggest that the evolutionary development of the attachment between a caregiver and an infant, which also serves to cement the bond between a male and female parent in order to ensure the health of the infant, has been co-opted to also serve adult attachment needs. Thus, throughout evolution, attachment has functioned as an adaptive system that provides the immature, defense-less human animal with protection, and this behavior has been carried over to adulthood, motivating us to bond with each other. According to Bowlby (1969), attachment is characterized by four behavioral features, manifest as actions directed towards the attachment figure: proximity-maintenance; a pattern of separation distress when the attachment figure is unavailable; secure-base behavior; and safe-haven behavior. The need for proximity to the caregiver, such as that shown by Linda and Sami, not only serves as a biological survival system, ensuring safety in the face of threats, but also plays a behavioral role in the physiological and psychological emotional regulation of the relationship between the parent and the infant. Similarly, secure-base behavior describes how the infant seeks its caregiver (its "safe haven") after exploring its surroundings; when the mother is absent, the infant responds via an array of emotional reactions signifying distress, including anger, despair and (later) detachment. These common psycho-logical mechanisms are replicated in adult relationships when we experi-ence separation and bereavement (Bowlby 1973).

Armed with the phone as a surrogate for emotional contact with the absent parent or as a research tool for unearthing answers about the past, both Linda and Sami undergo the phases of attachment behavior described above in their search for the truth about their fathers. Linda's mother, despite her inconsistencies, has provided her daughter with an adequate safe haven, although Linda has not at this stage attained emotional solace. She is emotionally over-aroused and seems incapable of separating herself from her own attachment despair—which is especially communicated in her implicit relational knowledge—in order to rise to the challenge of looking at herself from the outside (Høgel 2003), nor has she succeeded in detaching herself from her father, despite the fact that he does not appear to want a relationship with his daughter. It seems that her relational knowledge about her father has not achieved the necessary state of reflec-tion to transform him into a fully rounded character; instead, on-screen, Linda gives the impression of being self-absorbed. In an article in Swedish newspaper *Dagens Nyheder*, she writes:

> I regard the film as an exploration of the experiences of the first generation of children of divorced parents, and the damage the parents have done to us. My father's actions are so very concrete. They are obvious, and it is easy to see how the power is distributed. There are other ways, however, of denial that are harder to see. (Västrik 2000, my translation)

The question, however, is whether the responsibility for providing Linda with answers about the identity of her biological father should rest entirely with her (real/step) father. The film graphically communicates the dysfunctional relationship between father and daughter; in particular, it represents Linda's normative quest to ensure that her father assumes paternal responsibility, despite the fact that he possibly has multiple reasons for behaving in the way he does. For instance, if he is Linda's stepfather, he might have had less interest in taking up his paternal responsibilities after the divorce from her mother, and even if he is her real father and responsible for neglecting his daughter, it could be that he feels unable to respond to her emotional needs as he is still consumed by his own primitive emotions arising from the break-up of his marriage. His behavior on-screen could also be a sign that he is uncomfortable with the camera and the whole filmic set-up.

The filmmaker conveys her subjective experience of her relationship with her father from the film's outset. In the prologue, she provides information about her upbringing: she speaks to the camera about how her parents separated when she was four and how she has not had contact with her father since, due to his refusal to respond to her letters and calls. We then see Linda filming her father, who has apparently agreed to appear in the film (although he later withdraws from the project). She questions him as he sits on a sofa in front of the camera in a number of consecutive scenes that take place in his apartment. He is evidently ill at ease in this situation, particularly when faced with the issue of his fatherhood. Linda (who is off-screen) asks him whether he questions his paternity and, if so, will take responsibility, with her mother, for finding out if he truly is her father. In reply, however, he insists on talking around the subject; sometimes he tells Linda he will help with her project and at other times he avoids the subject altogether, possibly projecting his insecurities onto Linda by questioning her to "find out who it is I'm speaking to"—for example, asking her who her favorite film director is, as though this were of any relevance at this stage of the relationship. His behavior could be a sign of avoidance or merely his form of psychological defense in the verbal boxing match with his daughter. Linda's answer to his question ("Fassbinder") feels more like a counterattack, given Fassbinder's portraits of human emotion. When Linda requests that her father takes off his shirt so they can observe their possible physical resemblance, he protests that he does not want the viewers to see his stomach—clearly, this is a reasonable objection, as most people would not want an audience to see them half-naked. Linda, on the other hand, is more comfortable with the presence of the camera and clearly is the mature party in the relationship when it comes to asking relevant questions about fatherhood. Yet, when she appears in front of the camera to compare her shoulder bones with those of her father, it becomes clear that she is no longer just the film director but is also re-inhabiting the child Linda, and re-experiencing her implicit relational knowledge of her father's lack of paternal care.

Goffman (1959) speaks of two levels of communication in social life, one being interpersonal communication. In the case of *Pappa Och Jag*, an understanding of this level illustrates how Linda's implicit relational knowledge is communicated non-verbally without any conscious emotional regulation. Goffman distinguishes between expressions that are "given" and expressions that are "given off." Whereas the former includes the voluntary body language we display to others, the latter are involuntary expressions arising from emotional processes. In the film, we witness the formal presence and conscious performances of Linda and her father, such as the father's refusal to take off his shirt and his dislike of the whole filmic project, but mostly we experience (through our own bodies) the slow drip of emotion seeping from both characters. Throughout the scenes with her father, Linda's tense off-screen voice communicates anger; even more significantly, when she appears in front of the camera her muscles are tensed, she clenches her teeth and her body appears to respond as though she is preparing to fight. Her father, on the other hand, shows his frustration a number of times by biting his lip, taking deep breaths, laughing nervously and turning away from the camera. The scenes in the apartment communicate the pair's overall, generalized interaction. Linda could have placed herself and her father in any other situation and, if the subject matter was still his paternity, the emotions communicated would doubtless have fallen into the same category of anger and (later) despair on Linda's part, and frustration, anger and avoidance on the part of her father. This would be the case not only because of her father's continued avoidance of the subject, but also—importantly—because of Linda's appearance of being emotionally overwhelmed and her apparent high susceptibility to distress, as well the fact that her father evidently feels exposed to what seems to be his daughter's desire for revenge for the damage she believes he has caused her.

The matter of his paternity is an unresolved issue that undoubtedly has shaped Linda's perception of her father. Consequently, she has placed her father in an emotional situation that communicates his attachment to her from her perspective. She shows her father's parental style by positioning the camera in front of him whenever he is confronted with a subject he wants to avoid or appears uncomfortable with. Nevertheless, this begs the question of whether Linda orchestrates the scene in this way because this is how she sees her father or because she wants the viewer to regard him in a certain light. There are always two sides to relational dyads, and an observant viewer will notice that the director not only frames the dysfunctional father–daughter relationship, but also positions herself (throughout the film) at the margins of the frame, thus representing either her own emotional instability or the way she has been pushed aside by her father. The narrative form and stylistic arrangement work in tandem to highlight Linda's sense of despair, a point the film repeatedly reiterates by returning to the same scene several times, with the only change being Linda's questions, which evoke in her father the same sort of evasive and awkward answers. The filmmaker seems determined to present the camera as an all-observing and, naively, neutral (see, e.g., Høgel 2003) means of communicating her subjective experience of her father, which embodies her explicit relational knowledge, devoid of reflection as to how she herself implicitly contributes to the father–daughter conflict.

The apartment scenes are followed by one that reveals Linda's sadness as she cries into the phone while speaking to her mother. Briefly, before making the call, she fiddles with the camera (at the time, her father is not visible); a moment later, while Linda is on the phone, a background image of her father appears, combing his hair in the bathroom, seemingly unconcerned that his daughter is so distraught. Clearly, the director has positioned the camera so that her father can appear in the background, while she places herself at the far end of the frame. The scene between Linda and her father, and the staging of her separation distress, is replayed towards the end of the film when it becomes evident that he has once again failed to repair their relationship. We learn that Linda has paid for the DNA test herself, yet her father does not believe that the DNA copy she gives him is genuine; he wants the original. This again frustrates Linda, until her mother offers her some solace, at which point the film ends.

Schemas and Working Models of Relational Knowledge

As should be clear from the contributions to this volume, a cognitive film theory perspective presupposes an overlap between the mental capacities we use in everyday life and the ones we use when watching fiction and documentary films (Grodal 2009; Bondebjerg 1994). As David Bordwell (1985, pp. 36, 167) argues, we should differentiate the "realistic" motivations and schemas we form on the basis of our experiences and the outcome of our everyday interpersonal occurrences from film's "generic motivation and conventions"; the latter are based on motivations and expectations that typically appear in certain genres of film (Branigan 1992). Our schemas of people and/or groups we have never experienced in real life can easily be formed through the media.

The reception studies conducted by Birgit Höijer (1992a, b) (see also Bondebjerg 1994) suggest that viewers of both fiction films and documentaries use a range of schemas across the different genres, including universal, cultural and personal schemas. These are linked to what Höijer (1992a) calls "experience spheres": that is, the universal schemas but also the personal experiences about oneself in relation to others in social contexts that viewers project onto both real and fictive agents. Social psychologist Mark Baldwin's (1992) concept of "interpersonal/relational schemas" is a useful analytical tool here. Baldwin emphasizes the importance of relationship schemas, which are activated and shaped according to the experiences we have in both the real and the mediated online world. The term refers to the integration of the internalized self with others, along with our regular personal interactions. Accordingly, we may have a "self-schema" (for example, of vulnerability or security), "schemas of others" (for example, as rejecting or accepting us) and a "script" of the interaction and communication between the self and the other (for example, "if I show the other that I'm sad, she/he will reject/accept me") (Baldwin 1992). Linda's schema of herself, and of herself with others, embody her former experiences of vulnerability: she is accustomed to and expects rejection from her father but has not found any solace in the fact that she recognizes this experience, and so she keeps returning to the scenario of rejection with mixed feelings, possibly in the hope of a happy ending. In this social cognitive view, relational schemas are formed on the basis of repeated interactions with others in the social world and are derived from conditioning and associative processes. Relational schemas work like other schemas (Fiske and Taylor 1984): they influence information processing in interpersonal circumstances. In a documentary film, they not only operate as input for the director in implicit and explicit ways, but also guide the viewer's interpretations and expectations based on their prior schematic knowledge (Kramer forthcoming).

Relational schemas are closely related to "internal working models"—a term coined by Bowlby (1973), who was among the first to acknowledge that children construct models of themselves in relation to their surroundings. These are representational structures of the self as it interacts with others, thereby conforming to theories of attachment interactions that predict the future patterns of relationships (Hazan and Shaver 1987). Mary Ainsworth's (1978) research and clinical practice, which has since been verified empirically, suggest that infants develop internal working models based on their "attachment styles," which they carry over into their adult lives. An attachment style is "the systematic pattern of relational expectations, emotions, and behaviors that results from a particular history of attachment experiences" (Schachner et al. 2005, p. 143). It is likely to follow the individual into his or her adult experiences of attachment, although as we mature we are capable of revising our relationship portfolio in light of new experiences. Both Bowlby and Ainsworth also assume that infants' internal representations of the outer world and how flexibly they respond to situations in their external environment depend on their attachment styles: secure, avoidant, ambivalent or disorganized (Ainsworth et al. 1978). An infant's attachment style originates in their relationship with their parent, with "secure attachment" being the most common. Here, the parent demonstrates responsible and emotionally regulated caregiving, as well as empathetic responses, endowing the infant's representation of the self with a secure identity and confidence in the availability of the caregiver—a security that Linda has possibly never felt. For example, an infant's reactive cry and their separation anxiety are adaptive responses likely to ensure its survival if their needs are met by a responsive caregiver (or in subsequent adult relationships). As mentioned earlier, when absent from its mother, an infant exhibits a significant array of emotional reactions: separation distress, despair and, eventually, detachment. If these emotional cues are not regularly met with responsive care—that is, if a parent avoids their responsibility or is incapable of regulating the infant's emotions, or if their response is ambivalent, as in the case of Linda's father—the child is likely to develop a poorly regulated attachment style, unless it is successfully regulated at a later stage in life.

Once an experience has been repeated several times, it is then stored in the brain, often as an unconscious memory, and is likely to be reactivated by similar tactile, acoustic and/or perceptual cues. A young child, in its first years of life, will develop a system of unconscious schematic processing. Thus, a mother's or father's facial expressions of joy, anger or sadness will give rise to an automatic schematic processing that becomes embedded as attachment behavior and implicit relational knowledge (Schore 1999).

Evidently, Linda is responding to her surroundings in a way that is primed by unconscious expectations of her father's behavior derived from past experience—that is, her generalized schematic representations translate into a sense of how it is to "be with" her father. Arguably, the director, in her on-screen interaction with her attachment figures, is reconstructing and reliving these relational moments as she seeks to communicate to the viewer how she experiences her relational world. In this way, Linda and her father (and her mother, for that matter, although Linda's relationship with her commands less attention) are performing roles as social actors by replaying and responding to a model scenario of their previous and present life, or what Stern (2000) calls a "RIG" (Repeated Interaction that has been Generalized).

Interpersonal schemas about relationships are mediated in films by various means: relational messages can be communicated verbally or non-verbally and framed by what could be called "attachment intensifiers." As Jerslev (2002) argues, intimate first-person documentary films take advantage of various "strategies for closeness" by using different ways of conveying relational intimacy. In the sofa scenes in *Pappa Och Jag*, the non-verbal signals, derived from the implicit relational knowledge that Linda directs towards her father and in response to him, suggest that her ambivalent attachment to him—her anger and resentment, even disgust, when he touches her shoulder bones, for example—has not been emotionally regulated, even in her adult life. Overall, in allowing us to witness Linda's poorly regulated attachment bond, the film pushes at the boundary at which the private becomes too personal. While Linda is filming herself in close contact with the object of her ambivalence, she appears incapable of distancing herself from her own presentation as a character; it is difficult to recognize when she is performing and when her genuine self takes over. As a result, in the most intense scenes between father and daughter, the viewer is placed in a position in which they oscillate between embodied empathy with Linda and a more nuanced, disengaged and controlled assessment of the situation (the extent to which they do so will also depend on the viewer's own emotional regulation capacities, as well as their ability to read what lies behind Linda's and her father's embodied signals). Disengagement, however, is probably not what the director intended when she put herself in front of the camera.

By contrast, in *Family*, the dramatization of the real material and the dual focus on the attachment bond work to regulate Sami's on-screen emotional response to his loss. Here, lyrical sequences with symbolic meaning create a break in the emotional intensity, allowing the viewer space for higher cognitive reflection on what they have seen. For Sami, the search to find his father is performed in a reluctant "avoidant attachment" style, but with a humorous tone that provides some relief from the painful story about an absent father and the loss of a brother, giving the viewer time to relate to Sami's feelings. In the film's most significant attachment scene, where Sami manages to speak to members of his extended family over the phone, using the pretense that he is an airline pilot as an alibi for tracking down his father, we never actually get to see the father. Instead, we directly witness Sami's "attachment wound" and his implicit relational knowledge as his face cracks in despair, allowing us the space to feel the trauma he has been through, losing his father, mother and brother. However, in communicating Sami's distress, the film never places the stress on his trauma; it conveys his relational knowledge in a controlled way. The manner in which he behaves in various scenes throughout the film, resorting to excuses and bad jokes to avoid confronting his past, lying about his brother's suicide, gives a sense of how he has learnt to cope with the situation. He lies repeatedly when confronted with the emotional turmoil of the aftermath of his family disaster, but his clown-like behavior, albeit dysfunctional, creates a positive viewing distance that is also communicated by the camera's two positions. Behind the camera, Sami's kind yet insistent girlfriend, Phie, enacts Bowlby's "safe haven," which Sami needs if he is to confront his past. Overall, the film manages to fulfil its project of repairing Sami's past in an emotionally functional way, as communicated by its humorous tone—or at least that is the impression we are given. When the father finally calls his son, Sami's face lights up and his endearing laughter fills the room, despite the suffering he has been through. Although Sami never meets his father, he bonds with a half-brother he never knew he had and with whom he shares an absent father. The film suggests that, through this new connection, Sami has become capable of soothing his attachment wounds and finally accepting his relationship with his father, as well as his brother's death.

In contrast, Linda's confrontational style has no filter. She attacks her father on-screen, creating an intense energy that makes it difficult for the viewer to empathize with her, a point that is underscored by the film's style, which works in tandem with the content to create a visualization of her despair. Both Linda and Sami come up against the closed environment common to insecure attachment in which the dyadic communication has never been repaired by the parent. The films provide the viewer with routes to relational knowledge of insecure attachment narratives and offer schemas of ways of "being with" an absent or emotionally absent significant other. Yet the manner in which the different directors choose to cope with the situation, and to orchestrate and communicate their attachment bonds on film, creates two opposite coping strategies and viewer experiences.

In this chapter, I have argued that the first-person documentary's many modes and diverging and overlapping focal points render it difficult to define. I have demonstrated, however, using developmental psychology and attachment theory, that the schematic structures operating in both intimate and domestic ethnographic first-person documentaries draw on "implicit and explicit relational knowledge" (Lyons-Ruth et al. 1998). As relational knowledge arises from the director's own embodied reality and regulation of attachment experiences, enacted emotionally and cognitively on screen, this is likely to influence the viewer's experience of the film and their engagement with the characters. This offers a new theoretical perspective that could prove vital to the further investigation of relational first-person documentaries.

Acknowledgements I would like to thank Ib Bondebjerg and Torben Grodal for their comments during the development of this chapter.

REFERENCES

Ainsworth, M., Blehar, M., Waters, E. and Wall, S. (1978) *Patterns of Attachment: A Psychological Study of the Strange Situation*. Mahwah, NJ: Laurence Erlbaum Associates.

Baldwin, M. (1992) "Relational Schemas and the Processing of Social Information," *Psychological Bulletin*, 112(3), pp. 461–484.

Bondebjerg, I. (1994) "Narratives of Reality: Documentary Film and Television in a Cognitive and Pragmatic Perspective," *Nordicom Review*, 1, pp. 65–87.

Bondebjerg, I. (2016) "Den subjective dokumentar," July 5 [Online]. Available online at: https://ibbondebjerg.com/2016/07/05/den-subjektive-dokumentar/ (Accessed: May 22, 2017).

Bordwell, D. (1985) *Narration in the Fiction Film*. Madison: University of Wisconsin Press.

Bowlby, J. (1969) *Attachment and Loss, Vol. 1: Attachment.* New York: Basic Books.

Bowlby, J. (1973) *Attachment and Loss, Vol. 2: Separation.* New York: Basic Books.

Branigan E. (1992) *Narrative Comprehension and Film.* London; New York: Routledge.

Eitzen, D. (2007) "Documentary's Peculiar Appeals," in Anderson, J. D. and Anderson, B. F. (eds.) *Moving Image Theory: Ecological Considerations.* Carbondale: Southern Illinois University Press, pp. 183–199.

Fiske, S. T. and Taylor, S. E. (1984) *Social Cognition.* New York: Random House.

Goffman, E. (1959) *The Presentation of Self in Everyday Life.* Harmondsworth: Penguin Books.

Gregg, M. and Seigworth, G. J. (2010) *The Affect Theory Reader.* Durham, NC: Duke University Press.

Grodal, T. (2009) *Embodied Visions: Evolution, Emotion, Culture, and Film.* New York: Oxford University Press.

Grodal, T. and Kramer, M. (2014) "Film, Neuro-aesthetics and Empathy', in Lauring, J. O. (ed.) *An Introduction to Neuroaesthetics: The Neuroscientific Approach to Aesthetic Experience, Artistic Creativity, and Arts Appreciation.* Copenhagen: Museum Tusculanum, pp. 139–158.

Hazan, C. and Shaver, P. (1987) "Romantic Love Conceptualized as an Attachment Process', *Journal of Personality and Social Psychology*, 52(3), pp. 511–524.

Høgel, J. (2003) "Nærvær og distance," October 17 [Online]. Available online at: http://www.ekkofilm.dk/artikler/naervaer-og-distance/ (Accessed: May 10, 2017).

Höijer, B. (1992a) "Socio-Cognitive Structures and Television Reception," *Media, Culture and Society*, 14, pp. 583–603.

Höijer, B. (1992b) "Reception of Television Narration as a Socio-Cognitive Process: A Schema-Theoretical Outline," *Poetics*, 21(4), pp. 283–304.

Jerslev, A. (2002) "Den intime dokumentar," *Kosmorama*, 48, pp. 229, 40–68.

Jerslev, A. (2005) "Performativity and Documentary: Sami Saif's and Phie Ambo's *Family* and Performativity Performative Realism," in Jerslev, A. and Gade, R. (eds.) *Interdisciplinary Studies in Art and Media.* Copenhagen: Museum Tusculanum Press, pp. 85–116.

Kramer, M. (2007) "Film, følelser og kognition,|" in Skov, M. and Jensen, T. W. (eds.) *Følelser og kognition.* Copenhagen: Museum Tusculanum Press, pp. 243–262.

Kramer, M. (2010) "The Embrace of Mother Nature: Appraisal Processes and the Regulation of Affect in Attachment Genres', *New Review of Film and Television Studies*, 8(4), pp. 412–435.

Kramer, M. (forthcoming) *Social Attachment on the Screen: Affect, Cognition and Film.* New York: Bloomsbury.

Lebow, A. (2012) *The Cinema of Me: The Self and Subjectivity in First Person Documentary*. London: Wallflower Press.

Lyons-Ruth, K., Bruschweiler-Stern, N., Harrison, A., Morgan, A., Nahum, J., Sander, L., Stern, D. and Tronick, E. (1998) "Implicit Relational Knowing: Its Role in Development and Psychoanalytic Treatment', *Infant Mental Health Journal*, 19(3), pp. 282–289.

Nichols, B. (1991) *Representing Reality: Issues and Concepts in Documentary*. Bloomington: Indiana University Press.

Nichols, B. (2017) *Introduction to Documentary Film*. Bloomington: Indiana University Press.

Renov, M. (2004) *The Subject of Documentary*. Minneapolis: University of Minnesota Press.

Renov, M. (2008) "First-Person Films: Some Theses on Self-Inscription," in Austin, T. and de Jong, W. (eds.) *Rethinking Documentary: New Perspectives, New Practices*. New York: Open University Press, pp. 39–50.

Schachner, D. A., Shaver, P. R. and Mikulnicier, M. (2005) "Patterns of Non-verbal Behavior and Sensitivity in the Context of Attachment Relationships," *Journal of Non-verbal Behavior*, 29(3), pp. 141–169.

Schore, A. N. (1999) *Affect Regulation and the Origin of the Self: The Neurobiology of Emotional Development*. Hove: Psychology Press.

Stern, D. N. (1985) *The Interpersonal World of the Infant: A View from Psychoanalysis and Cognitive Development*. New York: Basic Books.

Stern, D. N. (2000) *Spædbarnets interpersonelle verden*. København: Hans Reitzels Forlag.

Västrik, L. (2000) "Uppgörelse med filmens hjälp. Pappa och Jag. Berättelsen om Linda Västrik og hennes far visas på dokumentarfilmsfestivällen," *Dagens Nyheder*, March 14 [Online]. Available at: https://www.dn.se/arkiv/kultur/uppgorelse-med-filmens-hjalp-pappa-och-jag-berattelsen-om-linda-Västrik-och-hennes-far-visas-pa/ (Accessed: February10, 2017).

PART IV

Documentary Practice

CHAPTER 15

A Social Cognition Approach to Stereotyping in Documentary Practice

Catalin Brylla

Beth Haller (2010, p. 27) explains that Western societies are mass-mediated, and "their citizens understand 'reality' through personal experience and mass media information." This means that if we have no lived interactions with(in) a particular community, our understanding of that community is, to a large degree, formed by the social stereotypes disseminated across different media, especially nonfiction media. However, as stereotypes are hardwired cognitive mechanisms that enable social comprehension and interaction, it would be counterproductive to attempt to make a general case against them. Hence, in this chapter, the concept "stereotype" is used to refer specifically to those filmic representations that perpetuate hegemonic ingroup/outgroup binaries, contributing to the maintenance of detrimental social boundaries between communities. The particular binary of abled *vs.* disabled—the focus of my current film practice—is the subject of the chapter's case study.

This discourse on stereotypes, which is situated at the intersection of social cognition and cultural studies, is concerned with the formation of "otherness." According to Richard Dyer (2006, p. 355), this represents a form of boundary maintenance using the "fixed, clear-cut and unalterable" representations attached to those excluded by society's normative

C. Brylla (✉)
University of West London, London, UK

© The Author(s) 2018
C. Brylla, M. Kramer (eds.), *Cognitive Theory and Documentary Film*, https://doi.org/10.1007/978-3-319-90332-3_15

rules. Known as the "outgroup homogeneity effect," these stereotypes are fuelled by undifferentiated categorical perceptions of outgroup members (Moskowitz 2005, p. 459), deemed "abnormal others," and are the pre-requisites for the formation of prejudice and the enactment of discrimination (e.g. Nelson 2009; Kite and Whitley 2016). For instance, Susan T. Fiske et al. (2002, pp. 895–896) have shown that non-disabled people tend to hold paternalistic prejudices towards disabled people, shaped by stereotypes of perceived inferiority, low status, incompetence and pitiful-ness. There is an obvious link between such social stereotypes and how disabled people are generally portrayed in nonfiction media: as Dyer (2002, p. 1) reminds us, the way social groups are treated in real life is a direct consequence of their media representation. Furthermore, these ste-reotypes can also inform the self-esteem, self-perception and self-identity of members of the stigmatized outgroup (Zhang and Haller 2013, p. 322), with a consequently detrimental impact on their cognitive and social per-formance due, for example, to long-term stress arousal (Schmader et al. 2008).

Stereotypes in films are formed and perpetuated through the specific configuration of popular narrative formulas and categorical sociocultural schemas. However, equipped with this knowledge, documentary practi-tioners can create films that have the capacity to collectively *re*configure such stereotypes and reduce the perception of the categorical other's "abnormality." Such research-led, critical practice shows that cognitive models can help filmmakers make conscious (rather than intuitive) deci-sions about representation, narrative structuring and the use of audiovi-sual aesthetics—decisions that are informed by an understanding of their film's possible social implications. It also highlights the need for cognitive scholars to abandon the assumption of a universal audience and instead critically engage with the particular social contexts that frame the con-struction and reception of documentary films.

With this in mind, this chapter first briefly establishes the folk-psychological mechanisms spectators and filmmakers share, and which are apparent in the narrative formulas widely disseminated by documentary filmmaking textbooks. This provides a valuable insight for film practitio-ners and teachers of film production into how common narrative and character schemas can potentially lead to, as well as result from, the forma-tion of stereotypes that create harmful ingroup/outgroup divisions. This general hypothesis is then tested by analyzing a range of mainstream documentaries that depict blind people according to schematic narratives and character roles, with the conclusion that the frequent application of coherent *narrative* stereotypes of characters with visual disabilities leads to *social* stereotypes that "other" blind people. These become ossified as a divisive abled/disabled binary in spectators' schematic dispositions. Finally, the chapter demonstrates how this meta-practice knowledge has informed my own filmmaking, most particularly in relation to my documentary, *The Terry Fragments* (2018), featuring a blind painter. The film exemplifies the ways in which I strive to reconfigure the narrative and, by implication, social stereotypes of blindness.

FROM FOLK PSYCHOLOGY TO NARRATIVE AND SOCIAL STEREOTYPES

Filmmakers and spectators share the same mechanism of schema formation and the same need to construct and comprehend narratives because they also share an inherent "folk psychology." This is defined by the philosophy of mind and cognitive science as a hardwired cognitive disposition that propels us to automatically turn to everyday knowledge to "predict and explain the behavior of others" (Currie 2004, p. 108). The universal human need to make sense of the thoughts, feelings and actions of others manifests itself in the construction of narratives (Hutto 2007, p. 45). Film is one of the cultural artefacts that shapes and is shaped by this inbuilt narrative practice,[1] which is why the study of film reveals shared interpretations, experiences and dispositions, comprising what Carl Plantinga (2011, p. 30) calls, the "filmmaker–audience loop". This loop accounts for the fact that, on the one hand, an audience is able to understand a film narrative, and on the other, a filmmaker can heuristically predict an audience's response. Although the inextricable relationship between filmmakers, films and spectators has been widely discussed in cognitive film studies (albeit predominantly in terms of fiction films), there is still a lacuna in the discourse, as Plantinga (2009, p. 257) points out, when it comes to the understanding of how folk psychology informs spectator demographics and identity politics, and—particularly relevant in the context of this chapter—how it can result in averse social implications through the formation and use of stereotypes.

---

[1] For a detailed account of how folk psychology operates both in real life and in film, see Per Persson (2003, pp. 161–246).

Documentary filmmaking textbooks are rich repositories of folk-psychological mechanisms and their role in the conception of schematic film narratives and the representation of real-life characters. These norma-tive mechanisms have the potential to perpetuate outgroup stereotypes that, as will later become apparent in the analysis of films about blindness, cultivate the social boundary between "us" (the abled) and "the others" (the disabled). Some of the most popular textbooks include: *Documentaries: And how to Make Them* (Glynne 2008); *Directing the Documentary* (Rabiger 2004); *Documentary Storytelling* (Bernard 2007); *Creative Documentary: Theory and Practice* (de Jong et al. 2012); and *Documentary Editing* (Everett 2010).[2] Although their pedagogical value is indisput-able—they enable the acquisition of filmmaking skills that help streamline the production process and create narratives that resonate with main-stream audiences—these books lack both sociocultural contextualization and any critical consideration of the potential such skills hold for social "othering." In short, they fail to actively encourage the practitioner to critically assess the given narrative and aesthetic formulas.

The central tenet of these texts is the creation of empathy and character-related emotions. For instance, Sheila Curran Bernard (2007, p. 27) argues that a documentary should tell "a story for greatest emotional impact and audience participation." Similarly, Michael Rabiger (2004, p. 135) declares that "documentary should act on our hearts, not on our minds alone … It exists not just to inform us about something but to change how we feel about it too." These emotions should be evoked through a character-centered narrative that makes the audience "draw dif-ficult conclusions about motives and responsibilities, and takes us along as accomplices in a painful quest for truth" (p. 11). According to Karen Everett (2010, pp. 68–87), a plot journey has to start with a life-altering conflict (the "inciting incident") that upsets the character's world at the beginning of the narrative, guaranteeing that the audience empathizes with the character and feels motivated to follow him or her through their difficult journey towards a final denouement. Evidently, the emphasis is on creating an empathic emotional response to the characters by encouraging the viewer to fully comprehend and experience their motivations, behavior and psychological development in the context of the film's goal-driven

---

[2] This selection of titles is only indicative and is based on their recurrence on the reading lists of undergraduate and postgraduate documentary practice courses, as well as being fre-quently recommended within the wider documentary filmmaking community.

narrative. These types of narratives, therefore, operate according to folk-psychological principles, which, according to Plantinga's filmmaker–audience loop, resonate with universal audience schemas.

In order to universalize character behavior and motivations in a variety of circumstances and so facilitate the generation of empathy, these textbooks recommend the clear exposition of easily recognizable, comprehensible and emotionally experienceable character traits and constellations (e.g. Everett 2010, p. 91; de Jong et al. 2012, pp. 119–129; Rabiger 2004, p. 229), drawing from a pool of stock characters. This renders the strategies for character-led documentary narratives virtually identical to the ones used in fiction screenwriting (or in telling stories through any type of medium), as Henry Bacon's description of stock characters suggests:

> Stock characters, by definition, exist in a ready-made form in a shared cultural sphere. In an individual film they are elaborated by a few character traits... Their motivations are self-evident... At its most simplistic the mere recognition of a stock character is sufficient to explain a certain type of behavior. Transtextual motivations reign. (Bacon 2011, p. 42)

When it comes to the representation of people from particular social groups, the constant deployment of stock characters can shape the audience's long-term mental representations of the real world and even change their general beliefs toward these groups (Polichak and Gerrig 2002, p. 92). In such cases, narrative schemas directly link to corresponding social schemas. Thus, Patrick Colm Hogan (2015, p. 335) warns that the use of simplified, categorical identities (that is, stereotypes) to represent people deemed to belong to outgroups increases group division and fosters discrimination. In addition, the evocation of a generic ("universalized") empathy does not, as filmmakers often assume, automatically deconstruct hegemonic ingroup/outgroup relations, but can result in either "failed" empathy without any real-world effects or "false" empathy that relates more to the imagination of the ingroup spectator than to the outgroup character (pp. 340–341).

The knowledge obtained through a critical cognitive study of filmmaking textbooks, therefore, can help the filmmaker adjust their deployment of established craft skills. The following case study, taken from my own film practice, illustrates this by first examining common stereotypes of blindness in other documentaries and then analyzing how this has informed my attempt to reconfigure these stereotypes through my own documentary films.

NARRATIVE AND SOCIAL STEREOTYPES OF BLINDNESS

Documentaries depicting blind people generally adhere to folk-psychological narrative formulas: they usually aim to engage the viewer with the emotional world of their characters, prompting the audience to empathize with them by experiencing a narrative journey in which the disability is the narrative force that drives the plot. The most popular formula is the "supercrip" journey found in *Blindsight* (Lucy Walker 2006), *High Ground* (Mike Brown 2012) and *Victory over Darkness* (Donny Eichar 2008). The "super cripple" (or "supercrip"), as Colin Barnes (1992, p. 12) explains, is a stereotype that assigns superhuman, almost magical abilities to disabled people, in order to elicit respect from the non-disabled.

Blindsight tells the story of the attempt by six blind Tibetan teenagers to climb a mountain in the Himalayas. At the beginning, the film establishes that many Tibetans consider blindness a curse, and this immediately sets up the characters' primary narrative goal of overcoming the social stigmatization they suffer in their community. The seemingly impossible physical journey represents a parallel spiritual process of transformation, at the end of which the characters feel themselves validated as members of society. A very similar storyline occurs in *High Ground*, where eleven war veterans with different mental and physical injuries—one was blinded by a bomb—also climb a mountain in the Himalayas. The blind character, Steve Baskis, grows increasingly more confident throughout the journey, especially when moving through rough terrain. Meanwhile, in *Victory over Darkness*, the heroic struggle to overcome physical impairment and gain social acceptance is performed by five blind athletes competing in the Ironman Triathlon. All three plots place the blind characters in initial character schemas: each are beset by some form of conflict-laden predicament (such as trauma, exclusion or bitterness) which impels them to take a physical or mental journey of transformation. By the end of the journey, they have overcome their initial predicament (Pointon 1997, p. 87). Following the narrative conventions, the initially precarious character schema progressively and cathartically changes during the journey into its positive binary opposite, the "supercrip" stereotype.

Another popular narrative template focuses on the tragic progression of blindness, as seen in *Notes on Blindness* (Peter Middleton and James Spinney 2016), *Going Blind* (Joseph Lovett 2010) and *Across Still Water* (Ruth Grimberg 2015). In these films, characters who have begun to go blind or who are partially sighted attempt to come to terms with the inevitable deterioration of their vision. For example, in *Notes on Blindness*, the main character, John Hull, describes in a voiceover the physical effect of his loss of vision, especially the fact that he can no longer see his wife and children but still retains a visual memory of their physical appearance. Later, his wife explains how Hull's loss of sight has impaired their relationship, as *his* lack of the ability to "see" and *her* lack of the ability "to-be-seen" have had a negative impact on their affective interpersonal experience. His emotional decline, losing himself in "loneliness and nothingness" and "a sense of impending doom," is finally transformed as Hull comes to terms with his blindness and learns to consider his "new" life as a cathartic rebirth.

Similarly, *Across Still Water*, depicts John Chapman's initial fear of his impending blindness (particularly in relation to his ability to pursue his hobby of night fishing), which is encapsulated in his reluctance to use a cane and a guide dog. By the end of the film, however, Chapman not only accepts his condition but also indicates that he will continue fishing, a determination that is underlined when he lands a large carp. Meanwhile, the autobiographical *Going Blind* establishes filmmaker Joseph Lovett as a man who also dreads the loss of vision and the way the deterioration of his sight is severely impacting his physical activities, such as cycling and, by implication, filmmaking. However, after learning more about his condition (glaucoma) and meeting a variety of visually impaired people, who describe how they have learnt to overcome daily obstacles, he adopts a more positive attitude towards living with blindness. All three films essentially end with the archetypical death and rebirth theme found in numerous Western literary works (e.g. Bloom and Hobby 2009).

Narrative arcs, such as those of the "supercrip" and the "tragic journey," are consciously constructed by filmmakers through a careful selection of what events to film, how to film them and in what order to edit them, according to the array of folk-psychological narrative conventions mentioned above. For example, the plot template of problem–intensification–climax–resolution (Bernard 2007, p. 28; Rabiger 2004, p. 80) is prevalent, as is the carefully plotted progression of obstacles in order to create a dramatic arc. This narrative tension between the character's aims and their ability to overcome the obstacles in their path is seen as a prerequisite if the audience is to identify with the characters (de Jong et al. 2012, p. 124): it ensures that viewers feel they have access to the characters' minds, understanding their thoughts and motivations, experiencing corresponding emotions and empathizing with their screen personas. However, the generated empathy represents Hogan's notion of a "false" schematic empathy, evoking a paternalistic sense of pity and inspiration among ingroup members, which technically transforms the intended empathy into sympathy.

Thus, from a social perspective, the main problem with these films is the use of blindness as the key constituent and driving force for the narrative "supercrip" and "tragic character" stereotypes, which is why they rapidly turn into socially othering stereotypes. For instance, *Notes on Blindness* makes little reference to Hull's distinguished academic career or his books on religious education, and when it does refer to these accomplishments, it consistently links them to his blindness. Indeed, the character's religiosity is portrayed as the vehicle for a cathartic process whereby he is able to come to terms with his deteriorating vision. This predominant focus on his disability sacrifices other aspects of Hull's life, the addition of which would have turned him into a more rounded character, one that would not fit so easily into the supercrip or tragic-journey schemas.

Disability scholars have long lamented that fiction and documentary films featuring blind characters do not portray the diversity, complexity and ambiguity of individual character traits (Schillmeier 2006; Badia Corbella and Sánchez-Guijo Acevedo 2010) but instead focus on the convenient narrative of blindness. Disabled film characters in general are one-dimensional and function only through their impairment. As such, the use of disability as a major character trait, plot device or atmosphere is a lazy shortcut for writers and filmmakers who wish to draw the audience into the story (Shakespeare 1999, p. 165) by instrumentalizing what appears to be the most obvious hardship or area of conflict in the characters' lives, thus conforming with the advice proffered by the filmmaking textbooks. The disability becomes, according to David Mitchell and Sharon Snyder (2000, p. 59), a "surface manifestation of internal symptomology" that stands for the equally abnormal subjectivity of the individual.

This emphasized abnormality or deficiency and its resulting supercrip and tragic-journey schemas function as a direct antithesis to the non-disabled norm in society, highlighting the loss or lack of a particular ability and establishing a binary of "us" (seeing) *vs.* "them" (blind) (Markotić 2008, p. 7). This attests to the cognitive attributes of stereotypes as rigid, simple and homogenous, and to their role in perpetuating the maintenance of ingroup/outgroup boundaries. In the specific case of blindness, this boundary is of an ableist nature, one that regards blind people as inferior, less socially capable and pitiable, instilling a paternalistic prejudice.

From a film-practice perspective, however, the question remains as to how this knowledge has aided my own filmmaking practice in its attempt to represent blindness without resorting to conventional disability stereotypes. The film analyses above illustrate how blind people are, to a large degree, reduced to their disability and placed within schematic narratives with the aim of eliciting the viewer's empathy. Since, from a social-cognitive perspective, stereotype-inconsistent information can undermine stereotyping (Moskowitz 2005, pp. 481–482), one solution would be to maintain schematic empathy-driven narratives but shift the focus away from disability. This would have the advantage of bypassing disability stereotypes while providing the audience with an engaging documentary that still resonates with universal folk-psychological schemas. One such example is *Dina* (Antonio Santini and Dan Sickles 2017), which uses the narrative of a romantic comedy to depict the lives of Dina Buno and Scott Levin, who each have varying degrees of intellectual disability; the film culminates in their wedding day.

However, there are potential risks with such an approach. Firstly, the disability is deliberately relegated to the background and the characters' similarities with non-disabled people are emphasized. This "normalization"—another (though less frequent) disability stereotype—is problematic as it tends to deny the existence of ableist prejudice and discrimination, and skates over aspects of victimhood, trauma or burden (Pointon 1997, pp. 89–90). Secondly, such narratives are often carried by inspirational and overly positive plots that make the audience feel "nobly uplifted, even ethically superior, for 'supporting' what is in effect a blatantly over-sweetened version of life with disability as concocted by a community that cannot countenance physical imperfection except in certain sanctioned and saccharine forms" (Riley 2005, p. 71). Thirdly, categorical identities based on simplistic and minimal definitions of outgroup members (whether they normalize the disability or present it as a deviant spectacle) can promote further divisiveness because they increase the perception of schematic outgroup homogeneity, in contrast to the ingroup, which is perceived as more non-schematic and heterogeneous (Moskowitz 2005, p. 59; Dyer 2006, p. 355).

A more reliable way of preventing disability stereotypes is to shift from "categorical" to "practical" identity representation—a socially coordinated complex identity that is, at the same time, individually unique

(Hogan 2015, p. 335), acknowledging the presence of both personal and collective character traits in the individual. Essentially, categorical identities are deductive and prescribed, while practical identities are inductive and grounded. This strategy also addresses the lack of diverse and multilayered (rather than universalized) portrayals of disabled people. If reiterated frequently enough in nonfiction media, this defiance of existing disability stereotypes and refusal to meet certain schematic expectations may well lead viewers to the perception of a more heterogeneous outgroup, and may even begin to gradually reduce the averse social divisions that are currently manifest in paternalistic prejudice and discrimination towards the disabled community.

An Alternative Narrative of Blindness

My documentary, *The Terry Fragments*, illustrates the use of practical identity representation and the reduction of schematic narrative scenarios as major filmmaking strategies. The film depicts the everyday life of Terry, a blind painter, using narrative fragmentation: it juxtaposes related and unrelated events, in which the disability itself is neither foregrounded nor relegated to the background but is simply *there* as a tacit part of the character's quotidian existence. Narrative fragmentation usually results in what Bill Nichols (1981, p. 211) terms "mosaic narratives," in which the "whole is not organized as a narrative but more poetically, as a mosaic; only the parts have a diegetic unity." Greg Smith (2007) analyses the way this type of narrative structure is employed (as an alternative to a folk-psychological plot) in *The Aristocrats* (Paul Provenza 2005), a documentary film in which the same joke is repeatedly performed and interpreted by different comedians. He observes that its episodic structure focuses on self-enclosed fragments, each of which are singular moments that highlight the performative act itself without setting up any character development or cause-and-effect (or question-and-answer) chains, thus undermining any narrative impulse towards forward progression or the infamous 'narrative arc' (pp. 87–88).

The Terry Fragments also uses this sort of episodic structure to portray the protagonist's life through a collage of incomplete vignettes that appear in no apparent order, such as Terry labelling his CDs or pouring his traditional evening whiskey. The only chronological string of events is that which portrays him at different stages of working on a painting; however, as the painting process is almost incidentally intertwined with other quotidian episodes and is also open-ended (the audience never sees the finished painting), there is no overall goal-driven character trajectory. Together with the randomness of the different fragments, this strategy precludes the formation of formulaic plots and schematic event scenarios, such as the inciting incident, which functions as a jump-start to a goal-driven journey, or the denouement at the end of that journey. By implication, this also precludes the audience perceiving the character in a fixed schematic role or categorical identity; instead, the film mediates Terry's multilayered and ambiguous practical identity, which is in itself a negotiation of different identities based on the separate scenarios in each scene: skilled painter, philosopher, musician, blind man, hermit, misanthrope or bitter man (because of his blindness), as well his girlfriend's jovial partner.[3] Of course, the cognitive processing of such personalities and scenarios also require the viewer's deployment of a range of folk-psychological character and event schemas, even certain stereotypes (for example, Terry as the "eccentric artist"), within the individual fragments. However, these operate at a micro-narrative (scene) rather than macro-narrative (plot) level, and this helps disperse generic empathic responses and character schemas. In other words, by the end of the film, the viewer should have a multilayered impression of Terry that does not easily match the narrative or social character schemas that operate in common portrayals and perceptions of blindness.

The narrative fragmentation was a particular challenge during the editing process, as my paradoxical objective was to make the narrative appear like a chaotic muddle of arbitrary scenes by using certain systematic principles. This was largely facilitated by my adoption of the neurocognitive model of "event segmentation," which describes how we process the fluctuating sensory information we encounter in daily life and give it meaning by separating the continuous flows of related or unrelated events into small segments that are specific and defined (Tversky et al. 2008, p. 436). This segmentation operates through the cognitive recognition of event boundaries, which are "points of perceptual and conceptual changes" that bracket together events of relative stability (Swallow et al. 2009, p. 236). In *The Terry Fragments*, this stability is accomplished by ensuring

---

[3] Seung-jun Yi's *Planet of Snail* (2011) is a rare example of a documentary about a blind character that also uses narrative fragmentation, resulting in a multilayered practical identity portrayal. The main character is portrayed as a poet, a theatre actor, a deaf–blind man, and a loving husband and good-humored partner.

that most episodes are coherent in terms of space, time, aesthetic treatment (for example, cinematography and editing) and general theme. Consequently, almost all the scenes resemble self-contained short films with, to use Nichols's (1981) term, a strong "diegetic unity."

Nevertheless, according to the 'event segmentation' model, the events must not only be intrinsically coherent but also extrinsically disparate in order for a segmentation to appear in the first place. Hence, in *The Terry Fragment*'s narrative scenes, it was only possible to convey the sense of a series of disparate fragments following one another by creating a strong contrast and avoiding causal links between the episodes. The contrast is evident in scene length, themes, the characters' clothing, the weather, filmic aesthetics, rhythm and mood. The segmentation effect is reinforced by titles dividing the episodes, which laconically signpost their content (for example, "Pouring Whiskey" or "Painting 1").

One example can be found in the "Still Life" scene, which is directly followed by the "Writers' Club 1" scene. The "Still Life" scene is composed of long static shots of objects in Terry's home during the daytime. The mood is neutral, and the absence of any characters creates a period of "dead time," which potentially triggers disparate reflections in the viewer—speculation about the objects in the scene or absent characters, self-reflection, symbolic interpretation, metaphorical associations, anticipation of future scenes or recollection of past ones (several seen objects reference earlier scenes). By contrast, the "Writers' Club" scene, which takes place at night in someone else's home, is highly dynamic and verbally busy; it involves a range of participants and conveys a positive mood, due to the constant humorous exchanges about literary genres and story ideas. The audience collectively experiences the characters' conversations without being given time to reflect on or interpret them. In addition, the filmic style contrasts the obviously hand-held shots in this scene with the static tripod shots in the previous one. Further contrasts include the time of day, the different domestic spaces and the opposing themes of non-speaking material objects *vs.* verbalized stories. There is also no causal progression between the two scenes, and there is a stark change in the mode of spectatorial address: the "Still Life" scene, a montage of empty spaces accompanied by non-diegetic music, express a high degree of authorship, whereas the "Writers' Club" scene is purely observational, without any apparent authorial intervention.

This seemingly unsystematic oscillation between different aesthetics, diegetic content and modes of address reflects the uniqueness of each moment and the randomness of the narrative fragments (even if there are recurrent motifs and loose subplots, such as the painting process). The audience simply cannot predict what comes next, and the coherence of potential folk-psychological plot trajectories and character schemas is counteracted, as is the formation of generic documentary modes or genres that rely on the spectator's deployment of intertextual schemas of narrative and aesthetics. Thus, the reconfiguration of such a range of cognitive schemas is potentially conducive to reconfiguring disability stereotypes. This hypothesis is not least supported by the viewer's activation and acquisition of knowledge through the episodic structure of the film. Narrative comprehension relies on the activation of two types of past knowledge structures: "generic knowledge" and "episodic knowledge" (Grasser et al. 2002, p. 244). Generic knowledge is based on schematic scripts and stereotypes, both of which are informed by the past consumption of folk-psychological narratives, while episodic knowledge is based on individual episodes experienced in the past at a particular time and place. Hence, a narrative comprising unique, momentary experiences without a generic plot structure activates episodic knowledge and impedes the activation of generic knowledge. It also prompts spectators to acquire new episodic knowledge that is largely devoid of disability-related schemas, and this may inform how they experience documentary films featuring similar (blind) characters in the future.

FINAL REFLECTIONS

This chapter proposes that the documentary filmmaker should be alert to the schematic dispositions embedded in their own practice and in their intended target audience, and consciously and critically reflect on the social implications of their filmmaking choices. Basically, filmmakers need to be aware of how folk psychology works and what its pitfalls are. Teachers of film production, too, need to understand folk psychology and the way its mechanisms govern ubiquitous storytelling formulas, in order to critically frame the craft knowledge found in textbooks. This does not mean that these formulas should be subverted; rather, they should be adjusted in relation to the desired audience experience or social impact. This approach may help filmmakers to *avoid* certain stereotypes, *use* certain stereotypes deliberately (for example, for specific activist purposes) or tell stories that *depart* from particular stereotypes while using other stereo-typical schemas that resonate with mainstream audiences.

The balance between reconfiguring stereotypes and using stereotypes that will resonate with a wide audience is a high-wire act. The prevalence of folk psychology and stereotyping embedded in filmmaking textbooks, filmmakers and audiences attests to the fact that they are essential, hardwired mechanisms that enable us to interact in the social world. Even the practice of maintaining ingroup/outgroup divisions—which are not always hegemonic divisions—is a hardwired strategy that results in a variety of benefits, such as the solidification of ingroup identity. These divisions are also intricate and relative, as every group holds its own stereotypes between different subgroups, and an outgroup will also hold certain stereotypes towards the ingroup, which reverses the ingroup/outgroup relationship. The main point is that social-cognitive schemas are fundamental to our existence, and completely deviating from them in film narratives may deter a mainstream audience. What the filmmaker needs to take into consideration, however, when adhering to mainstream narrative strategies, is the potential for detrimental social consequences. Ableist (social and narrative) stereotypes of the disabled, for example, strongly indicate the existence of prejudices that in the real world compromise accessibility, opportunities, social support and adequate medical care for disabled people.

On a final note, the type of research-led film practice advocated here is beset by theoretical hypotheses, combined with heuristic and intuitive decisions; spectatorship is theorized and inferred but not empirically verified. From an independent filmmaker's perspective, an experimental verification (for example, through an audience research study) would prove unpragmatic and is not common practice, although anecdotal indications of audience reception can emerge, for example, during previews and Q&As following cinema screenings. Nevertheless, the critical framing of film practice through the flexible adoption of cognitive spectatorship models is still more expedient than "blindly" following textbook conventions.

Acknowledgements I would like to thank Carl Plantinga, Torben Grodal and Mette Kramer for their valuable feedback during early drafts of this chapter.

REFERENCES

Bacon, H. (2011) "The Extent of Mental Completion of Films," *Projections*, 5(1) [Online]. Available at: http://berghahnjournals.com/view/journals/projections/5/1/proj050104.xml (Accessed: September 16, 2017).

Badia Corbella, M. and Sánchez-Guijo Acevedo, F. (2010) "The Representation of People with Visual Impairment in Films," *Journal of Medicine and Movies*, 6(2), pp. 69–77.

Barnes, C. (1992) *Disabling Imagery and the Media: An Exploration of the Principles for Media Representations of Disabled People*. Krumlin: The British Council of Organisations of Disabled People and Ryburn Publishing.

Bernard, S. C. (2007) *Documentary Storytelling: Making Stronger and More Dramatic Nonfiction Films*. 2nd edn. Boston: Focal Press.

Bloom, H. and Hobby, B. (eds.) (2009) *Rebirth and Renewal*. New York: Bloom's Literary Criticism.

Currie, G. (2004) "Cognitivism," in Miller, T. and Stam, R. (eds.) *A Companion to Film Theory*. Oxford: John Wiley & Sons, pp. 105–122.

De Jong, W., Knudsen, E. and Rothwell, J. (2012) *Creative Documentary: Theory and Practice*. Harlow: Pearson.

Dyer, R. (2002) *The Matter of Images: Essays on Representations*. 2nd edn. London: Routledge.

Dyer, R. (2006) "Stereotyping," in Durham, M. G. and Kellner, D. (eds.) *Media and Cultural Studies: Keyworks*. Oxford: Blackwell, pp. 353–365.

Everett, K. (2010) *Documentary Editing*. New Doc Editing [Online]. Available at: http://newdocediting.com/documentary-editing/ (Accessed: March 13, 2012).

Fiske, S. T., Cuddy, A. J. C., Glick, P. and Xu, J. (2002) "A Model of (Often Mixed) Stereotype Content: Competence and Warmth Respectively Follow from Perceived Status and Competition," *Journal of Personality and Social Psychology*, 82(6), pp. 878–902.

Glynne, A. (2008) *Documentaries: And How to Make Them*. Harpenden: Creative Essentials.

Grasser, A. C., Olde, B. and Klettke, B. (2002) "How Does the Mind Construct and Represent Stories?," in Green, M. C., Strange, J. J. and Brock, T. C. (eds.) *Narrative Impact: Social and Cognitive Foundations*. Mahwah, NJ: Lawrence Erlbaum Associates, pp. 229–262.

Haller, B. A. (2010) *Representing Disability in an Ableist World: Essays on Mass Media*. Louisville: Advocado Press.

Hogan, P. C. (2015) "The Psychology of Colonialism and Postcolonialism: Cognitive Approaches to Identity and Empathy," in Zunshine, L. (ed.) *The Oxford Handbook of Cognitive Literary Studies*. New York: Oxford University Press, pp. 329–346.

Hutto, D. D. (2007) "The Narrative Practice Hypothesis: Origins and Applications of Folk Psychology," in Hutto, D. D. (ed.) *Narrative and Understanding Persons*. Cambridge: Cambridge University Press, pp. 43–68.

Kite, M. E. and Whitley, B. E. (2016) *Psychology of Prejudice and Discrimination*. New York: Routledge.

Markotić, N. (2008) "Punching Up the Story: Disability and Film," *Canadian Journal of Film Studies*, 17(1), pp. 2–10.

Mitchell, D. T. and Snyder, S. L. (2000) *Narrative Prosthesis: Disability and the Dependencies of Discourse*. Ann Arbor: University of Michigan Press.

Moskowitz, G. B. (2005) *Social Cognition: Understanding Self and Others*. New York: Guilford Press.

Nelson, T. D. (ed.) (2009) *Handbook of Prejudice, Stereotyping, and Discrimination*. New York: Psychology Press.

Nichols, B. (1981) *Ideology and the Image: Social Representation in the Cinema and Other Media*. Bloomington: Indiana University Press.

Persson, P. (2003) *Understanding Cinema: A Psychological Theory of Moving Imagery*. Cambridge: Cambridge University Press.

Plantinga, C. (2009) "Spectatorship," in Livingston, P. and Plantinga, C. (eds.) *The Routledge Companion to Philosophy and Film*. New York: Routledge, pp. 249–259.

Plantinga, C. (2011) "Folk Psychology for Film Critics and Scholars," *Projections*, 5(2), pp. 26–50.

Pointon, A. (1997) "Disability and Documentary," in Pointon, A. and Davies, C. (eds.) *Framed: Interrogating Disability in the Media*. London: British Film Institute, pp. 84–92.

Polichak, J. W. and Gerrig, R. J. (2002) "'Get Up and Win!'—Participatory Responses to Narrative," in Green, M. C., Strange, J. J. and Brock, T. C. (eds.) *Narrative Impact: Social and Cognitive Foundations*. Mahwah, NJ: Lawrence Erlbaum Associates, pp. 71–96.

Rabiger, M. (2004) *Directing the Documentary*. 4th edn. Boston: Focal Press.

Riley, C. A. (2005) *Disability and the Media: Prescriptions for Change*. Hanover: University Press of New England.

Schillmeier, M. (2006) 'Othering Blindness: On Modern Epistemological Politics," *Disability & Society*, 21(5), pp. 471–474.

Schmader, T., Johns, M. and Forbes, C. (2008) "An Integrated Process Model of Stereotype Threat Effects on Performance," *Psychological Review*, 115(2), pp. 336–356.

Shakespeare, T. (1999) "Art and Lies? Representations of Disability on Film," in Corker, M. and French, S. (eds.) *Disability Discourse*. Buckingham: Open University Press, pp. 164–172.

Smith, G. M. (2007) "*The Segmenting Spectator: Documentary Structure and The Aristocrats*," *Projections*, 1(2), pp. 83–100.

Swallow, K. M., Zacks, J. M. and Abrams, R. A. (2009) "Event Boundaries in Perception Affect Memory Encoding and Updating," *Journal of Experimental Psychology: General*, 138(2), pp. 236–257.

Tversky, B., Zacks, J. M. and Hard, B. M. (2008) "The Structure of Experience," in Shipley, T. F. and Zacks, J. M. (eds.) *Understanding Events: From Perception to Action*. New York: Oxford University Press, pp. 436–464.

Zhang, L. and Haller, B. (2013) "Consuming Image: How Mass Media Impact the Identity of People with Disabilities," *Communication Quarterly*, 61(3), pp. 319–334.

CHAPTER 16

A Cognitive Approach to Producing the Documentary Interview

Michael Grabowski

Several chapters in this book address how audiences perceive, empathize with and understand those who are presented in documentaries, including how documentaries portray people as characters, the emotional connections that are generated between documentary participants and viewers, and how viewers evaluate the "realness" of a documentary story. These are all important questions, but they fall within the domain of the documentary as a completed artefact, a product already produced that generates meaning as it is consumed. They address questions about reception.

In this context, it is also important to keep in mind that documentaries are *made*. When planning for a documentary production, I am concerned with a different set of questions: for example, how to gather the raw materials to construct a complete narrative, how to arrange those elements to generate a story that reflects participants' experiences, and the compromises I have to make in order to complete the project without losing the core of its vision.

Traditionally, producers have answered these questions by means of convention and experience. Documentary crews share techniques, discuss production practices and watch other works in order to develop styles that

M. Grabowski (✉)
Manhattan College, Bronx, NY, USA
e-mail: michael.grabowski@manhattan.edu

© The Author(s) 2018
C. Brylla, M. Kramer (Eds.), *Cognitive Theory and Documentary Film*, https://Doi.org/10.1007/978-3-319-90332-3_16

serve their story. Conventions become established because they are effective; however, as media evolve, conventions must as well. In the course of working for more than 25 years in news, documentary, and reality and fiction production (first as a sound recordist, videographer, editor, director and producer, and more recently as a story consultant to broadcast, cable and streaming networks and programs), I have sought explanations for why these conventions work and how I should modify my own techniques as I tell stories in new media environments. I have found that cognitive film theory offers a path to understanding not only how we perceive stories but also how to tell them effectively.

This chapter examines one component central to most documentaries: the interview. Although they may be used in different ways, documentary interviews are so ubiquitous that producing them occurs without much thought into why they work the way they do. What follows is not a definitive examination of documentary production, but I describe some conventional production processes used in professional film and television shoots. In particular, I examine three types of interview setups and discuss how cognitive theories like Torben Grodal's PECMA flow model, embodied simulation and the perception of facial expressions can help explain why these conventions work. Finally, I conjecture how new media environments are reshaping these conventions and how cognitive theories can inform documentarians on how to effectively adapt their production practices.

THE PECMA FLOW, EMBODIED SIMULATION AND REALISM

Grodal's (2009) PECMA flow model explains that viewers experience film narratives using perceptual, emotional, cognitive and (largely suppressed) motor action systems. According to this model, emotions generated by perceptions are "action potentials," shaped by cognition and memory to either engage or suppress actions in order to respond to these perceptions. He bases this theory in evolutionary and cognitive psychology, arguing that film takes advantage of a nervous system that has evolved in the service of primates' survival and reproduction in their natural environment. The processing flows both top-down and bottom-up in this model, connecting perceptions to memories, schemas and action potentials.

This flow taps into a social basis of emotion that has evolved to predict the mental state of an observed other. Vittorio Gallese and Michele Guerra (2012) argue that film engages the human mirroring system to generate an embodied simulation of observed actions. They reference the neural correlates in the parieto-premotor cortical regions of the brain as a part of the mirroring system to show that viewers simulate observed characters' emotions, movements and actions using their own embodiment and mental states. Viewers empathize with characters through the mimicry of facial expressions and body movements on a pre-cognitive level, which can sometimes generate emotions at odds with the cognition of the narrative (Plantinga 2009; Smith 1995). Thus, embodied simulation can produce less sophisticated, automatic and involuntary responses—Elaine Hatfield et al. (1994) refer to this as "emotional contagion." The observation of another's facial expression and body movements produces a simulation in the observer that can be used to assess the emotion of the observed, predict future action and prepare an action response.

Both fiction and documentary films, Grodal (2009) argues, use the interplay of perceptual and categorical realism to associate what viewers see on screen with their observations of and interactions with the real world. According to Grodal, perceptual realism relies on the representation of images and sounds that mimic the natural world in such a way that they create specific indexical relationships to their real-world counterparts, while categorical realism produces abstract representations of the real world that share schematic mental features. However, documentaries also use what he calls an "imperfect perceptual realism" to assert the reality of a story (pp. 251–264). Handheld camera moves, muffled audio and image artefacts, or what I call "artefacts of recording," communicate that the footage has been gathered and presented without manipulation. Thus, documentaries establish their realness by presenting recordings of people and spaces that highlight features that can be recognized as a part of the natural world and by implying (via genre, titles, narration, sound bite/B-roll formal structure, recording artefacts and intertextual elements of publicity, distribution and marketing) that what viewers are watching is a documentation of an observed reality.

While the PECMA flow model and embodied simulation seek to explain how audiences experience audiovisual content, it can also inform documentarians how to produce the content used to construct the observed narrative. A fundamental building block of documentary is the interview, and this can take several forms. Whether it is a conversation between an on-screen interviewer and participant, a participant in a single shot with an off-screen interviewer, or a form of self-interrogation in which the participant addresses viewers directly, the interview provides oral information for the narrative while presenting facial expressions and body movements that provide salient embodied and affective information for, and generate automatic responses from, the viewers.

COGNITIVE THEORY AND INTERVIEW SETUPS

More so than fiction-film production, creative roles in documentaries are often blurred between director, producer, editor, videographers and researchers. While a single person may be solely responsible for some personal documentaries, in other productions producers may conduct interviews, videographers may choose how to frame interviews, editors may have more influence over how sound bites from interviews are used and researchers may identify people to interview. Moreover, using archival footage in documentaries means filmmakers have no control over the creation of some footage. When referring to the documentary director or producer, I am generalizing the roles that may be shared by two or more people or fulfilled by a single person. However, I limit my discussion of the interview to footage gathered by the producer, the director or their crew.

As producers plan for and conduct interviews to use in a documentary, they have several related but distinct concerns: choosing participants to interview, motivating them to share stories that will become part of the documentary narrative, and capturing the interview in a way that will be most effective in conveying that narrative. Their goal is to produce footage for editors to use in constructing a narrative; in pursuit of that goal, they perform (with the participants) in an interpersonal discourse that is influenced by the production environment in which the conversation takes place. Thus, cognitive film theories that are used to understand the interaction between the finished documentary and its viewers can also guide directors when setting up environments and engaging participants, in order to produce footage that enlists viewers' perceptions.

Participants may experience a wide variety of encounters with a documentary crew. Person-on-the-street (or *vox populi*) interviews are spontaneous and have little prior knowledge of the participant, while seated interviews often involve research and pre-interviews with participants to prepare for the interview itself. Technically, productions range from webcam footage to high-resolution cinema cameras, lights, audio-processing equipment and elaborate sets. Interviews may take place in a studio or on location in an interior or exterior space. In this chapter, I examine three different types of interview setups: EFP, ENG and direct-address interviews.

EFP Interviews

The electronic field production (EFP) setup requires a fixed location. Figure 16.1 shows how the lights, camera and microphone encompass the interview participant. The camera is mounted on a support, sometimes a crane or jib arm, but most often a tripod or pedestal. The interviewer sits as close to the axis of the camera lens as possible, so that both of the participant's eyes are visible in the image. Ideally, the camera uses a medium telephoto lens (100 mm in a 35 mm format) to produce a natural-looking face: a wider lens unnaturally elongates facial features, while a longer lens flattens the face. A larger monitor displays the shot for the crew to inspect. Several lights illuminate the subject and setting; diffusion filters are often installed to create a softer light with less harsh shadows. A shotgun microphone, mounted on a separate stand, or a lavalier microphone, attached to the subject's clothing, captures the audio. Backgrounds vary

Fig. 16.1   EFP setup. Source: Lindsay Gordon (2016)

from a naturalistic set to a plain black or white background, or a green or blue background screen to allow producers to key in a background later during post-production.

All this equipment creates the impression that the interview is an important investment in time and money. I refer to EFP setups as "Hollywood productions," as they mimic the style of well-funded fiction-film production. More attention is paid to the technical details of the shoot, and the documentary crew requires time to set up the crates of equipment that show up at the location. Crews usually budget for at least one hour of setup time for an EFP-style shoot. Like an actor on a Hollywood production, the documentary participant is placed on set at the last moment. The lights on set create a much brighter illumination than is normal in a room, and hair and makeup artists work with participants beforehand, applying powder to reduce the "shine" (sweat) from the heat of the lights and adding color to faces that may appear washed-out in the lighting. In these conditions, producers often have to calm participants and counsel them to ignore the camera, and they must maintain eye contact with the participant to prevent them from becoming distracted by the equipment and crew in the room.

Interviews are framed most often as a close-up or head-and-shoulders shot. When I began as a camera operator at an NBC affiliate, the director of operations instructed me that the ideal shot should frame the top of the head at the top of the image, with the philtrum (the space between the bottom of the nose and the upper lip) in the center. When I teach production, I often notice that students frequently frame shots much wider, including much of the body. Overcoming the fear of excluding the body from the shot is a difficult but necessary challenge in order to show viewers the details of a participant's face. Ramprakash Srinivasan et al. (2016) have determined the neural correlate for identifying facial expressions in the posterior superior temporal sulcus (pSTS), which is activated when someone examines action units of facial muscle groups to evaluate the emotion of another person. Eye-tracking studies (Bruce and Young 2012; Schurgin et al. 2014; Smith 2012) have repeatedly documented that viewers search out faces in shots, and saccade (small, rapid eye movements) across the eyes, upper and lower nose, upper lip and nasion (the area between the eyes, above the bridge of the noise) of the faces within a frame. The searching is driven both by stimulus factors and goal-driven strategies for recognizing the emotion expressed on the face. This behavior has evolved out of the need to identify the emotional states of others within a social group for the purpose of creating or maintaining social bonds, identifying threats and motivating others to socially beneficial actions (Keltner and Kring 1998).

These cognitive theories explain why close framing of participants is an effective (and affective) technique. Viewers seek out perceptions of facial muscle groups to ascertain the emotional cues of participants, and they involuntarily mimic their facial expressions. They develop simulations of the participant's mental state and infer a social relationship. For example, is this someone to be trusted? Are they a threat? Should I empathize with them? Though viewers largely suppress motor actions when watching an interview, the premotor regions of the brain are active as they build mental simulations of the emotions and actions they observe. Attending to facial expressions helps to build a better mental model of the participant. However, if participants become animated during an interview, waving their arms or wringing their hands, the camera operator may zoom out to capture that salient action and incorporate it into the continuous PECMA flow.

The EFP setup provides the most control over the documentary image and offers the best conditions for capturing facial expressions. The mounted camera creates a stable image, and the three-point lighting setup illuminates the face so that viewers can clearly see a participant's expressions. A key light is placed above and in front of the participant. This gives a sense of the direction of the lighting source, not unlike sunlight or an overhead room lamp, adding to the perceptual realism of the image. The fill light ensures that facial expressions are not hidden in the shadow created by the key light. Low-key lighting, using a weaker or absent fill light, may generate a more dramatic image, but it reduces perceptual realism by obscuring part of the face and activates associations with nighttime lighting conditions, lurking in the shadows or the spotlights used in police interrogations. Lighting techniques, like low-key lighting and gels that change the color of the light, foreground the image as a constructed artefact and distance it from the experience of the natural world.

ENG Interviews

The electronic news gathering (ENG) setup, otherwise known as "run-and-gun," is a much more portable and unobtrusive arrangement. Using, for example, a shoulder-mounted camera with minimal equipment (Fig. 16.2), this setup clearly differs from the more controlled static EFP

Fig. 16.2 ENG setup for the documentary *Touristic Intents* (2014, Mat Rappaport). Source: Ted Hardin (2014)

setup. Often selected for shoots on location, the ENG setup allows for smaller crews to follow participants in public spaces and crowded conditions. Cameras may be shoulder-mounted or smaller, palm-sized form factors that are lightweight and allow the camera operator to move about more freely. In some cases, crews may be indistinguishable from tourists or other people recording home videos. Illumination is limited to natural overhead lighting or a small light mounted on the camera itself, resulting in less control over the lighting conditions. Participants may wear a small lavalier microphone to capture audio, or the audio operator may suspend a small mixer over their shoulder and hold a fishpole with an attached directional microphone. Often, no audio operator is present, and the camera operator herself adjusts audio levels directly, using on-camera controls. Sometimes, the audio operator or a production assistant holds a small reflector to bounce natural light and fill in shadows, but as this would call attention to the shoot, crews often sacrifice manipulating lighting in favor of a smaller and more portable setup.

My experience has shown that participants become comfortable much more quickly during an ENG shoot than an EFP setup. A smaller crew provides less of a distraction, and the small amount of equipment and the portable setup allows producers to interview participants in settings where they feel comfortable. Overall, the setup conforms more to a natural environment than the fixed setting of an EFP shoot, and participants more easily develop a conversational speaking style during the interview. The ENG setup contributes to the natural realism of shooting in a real-world space, as well as the categorical realism of an identifiable location. However, it sacrifices technical control over the image and sound, often producing a less cinematic result. The counterintuitive effect produces an imperfect perceptual realism through the recording artefacts—imperfect lighting, handheld camera movement, background noise, and so on—that asserts that what viewers are seeing and hearing is a real event that has been recorded and then presented to them.

The technical challenges and conventions of the ENG interview contribute, I believe, to an embodied simulation in viewers. A handheld camera shot is more difficult to keep steady with a telephoto lens, so operators often shoot wide in an ENG setup. They are left with the choice of either getting unnaturally close to the participant for a close-up shot, or staying back and framing more of the participant's body within the shot. While a wider shot and reliance on natural lighting reveal less detail in facial expressions, seeing more of the body as it interacts with the environment allows viewers to perceive bodily motions like walking, reaching and grasping, and to simulate those actions on an experiential level (Gallese 2017; Gallese and Guerra 2012).

During the production of a documentary about the making of *Beloved* (Jonathan Demme 1998), producer and star of the film, Oprah Winfrey, took me by the arm, and we walked to an open field far away from the din of the production to conduct an interview. I had clipped a small microphone to her costume and balanced the camera on my shoulder. Winfrey began to talk about the long journey she had taken to make this film of Toni Morrison's book. I continued the interview by asking follow-up questions and, through my pauses, inviting revealing additions. Mostly, however, I was having a conversation. While I kept one eye on the viewfinder to confirm I had a usable shot, I focused on maintaining eye contact with her to communicate my participation in the conversation. During the interview, I held a medium shot of Winfrey from the waist up, capturing her (and her hand motions) as she walked through the field, as well as the camera shot moving through the field. Viewers see Winfrey touching the leaves on nearby trees and walking through the tall grasses, with an expression of contemplation. They hear her describe the trauma her character,

Sethe, experiences as the past possesses her. These motions situate the interview within the environment where it took place, and viewers' brains simulate them in their premotor cortices as a part of the PECMA flow. As Stefano Rozzi and Leonardo Fogassi (2017) note, simulating such observed actions in the premotor cortex, and processing them in the lateral prefrontal cortex, aids in predicting future action for the purpose of developing a behavioral goal. Viewers may connect their perceptions of Winfrey's interview to some combination of grief, sadness, serenity, interest or trust, depending on their own past experiences, including knowledge of the legacy of slavery and of the story itself (both Toni Morrison's novel and Winfrey's personal story). They may recall similar experiences of walking in natural surroundings. Knowing they are watching a recorded interview and not engaged in an interactive, interpersonal conversation, viewers use top-down processes to suppress motor action and generally do not act upon their perceptions, emotions and cognitive processes, save for potential involuntary actions like crying, a faster heartbeat or shifting their position in their seat.

Direct-Address Interviews

In both EFP and ENG setups, a participant makes eye contact slightly to one side of the camera with an off-screen interviewer. In contrast, a third type of interview setup configures the shot so that the participant looks directly at the camera lens. Tom Brown (2012) provides a comprehensive examination of the functions that breaking the "fourth wall" through direct address serve in narrative cinema. Here, I delimit the direct-address interview to a participant speaking with an interviewer in a mediated form or holding a conversation with an imagined interviewer, and do not include autobiographical documentaries, which have a range of different cognitive and embodied dynamics, the analysis of which would go beyond the scope of this chapter. When conducted alone—for example, with recorded webcam footage or using a video diary—participants control the conditions of the self-interview, including the recording apparatus. They may think of questions the interviewer would ask based on prior experiences with the interviewer, or they may infer an imagined interviewer based on their own self-examination. Sometimes, similarly to first-person documentaries, participants engage in a form of self-interrogation, introspection or confessional address when speaking directly to the camera, as if they imagine the interviewer is listening.

In cases where the participant is speaking with an actual interviewer, the direct-address setup generates the illusion of immediacy by ironically building a second layer of mediation. To record interviews in which participants look directly into the camera lens, documentary filmmaker Errol Morris invented what he calls the "Interrotron." The apparatus consists of two cameras mounted with teleprompters, devices that include a split mirror set at a 45-degree angle in front of the camera lens. The mirror allows the camera to record the participant, while the participant sees a reflection of the video from a video monitor attached above or below the mirror. The second camera points at the interviewer and feeds that footage into the teleprompter of the camera recording the participant. The result is that the participant sees an image of the interviewer in front of the lens of the camera (Fig. 16.3). Morris (2004) says the Interrotron "creates greater distance *and* greater intimacy. And it also creates the *true first person*. Now, when people make eye contact with me, it can be preserved on film" (emphasis in the original).

Cognitive models of interpersonal communication can help producers choose whether to shoot traditional EFP or Interrotron interviews. In their study of multiagent conversations, Roel Vertegaal et al. (2001) have determined that the eyes' gaze predicts with a high degree of probability

Fig. 16.3   The Interrotron. Source: Michael Grabowski (2015)

who is speaking and who is being listened to. The off-camera gaze of EFP interviews infers that a conversation is taking place between the participant and an unseen interviewer; the viewer is a third party observing the conversation. I have always rejected the notion that the viewer is a voyeur in this case, as an explicit or implicit narrator invites viewers to observe a participant's communication and action. Instead, sound bites are presented to support the narrator's assertions, in effect communicating to viewers, "This is what they told me." The Interrotron generates the illusion that the participant has become the narrator of the story and is speaking directly to the viewer in a dyadic conversation. For instance, in *The Fog of War* (2004), Morris shows Robert McNamara offering his recollections—and the lessons and regrets—of his long career; he locks his gaze onto the camera and, by extension, the viewers. When Morris interjects or asks a follow-up question from off-camera, the sound of his voice off-mic implies a third party who has overheard a conversation between the narrator and viewer and is interrupting, violating social convention.

My first experience with the Interrotron was not as a producer but as a participant. I was interviewed recently for the documentary *YouTube 2017 Upfront*, which YouTube produced at its studios in New York. When I arrived, the auditorium at the front of the office had been sectioned off with black curtains, a green screen and several lights. After a wardrobe consultation, and having my hair and makeup done, I took my mark standing in front of the green screen. In the Interrotron, I saw a color image of the producer, who began a conversation with me. During the first few minutes of the interview, I felt uncomfortable seeing what looked like a floating head speaking to me while hearing the voice of the producer from across the room. However, I quickly adjusted to the technology, and I eventually had an in-depth conversation with the producer as if she were sitting across from me, not unlike a video-chat session. The final video removed the producer's questions, segmented my interview into several sound bites, and intercut them with sound bites from other participants, resulting in the illusion that we had posed implied questions to ourselves and were sharing our experiences directly with the viewers.

Rather than acting as an alienating or foregrounding technique, direct-address interviews in documentaries, I would argue, have become more acceptable to audiences because of several environmental factors. The first is the explosion of reality television during this century, which uses the confessional as a staple technique. Producers shoot the confessional in an enclosed or otherwise separate space, in which participants comment on previously recorded events and share their feelings about them. The confessional mimics the play-by-play and color commentary of sports programming; the participant becomes a storyteller, shaping and contextualizing the narrative. New information may emerge from the confessional; however, from my own experience—and as several producers working in reality television have related to me—confessionals are often guided by producers, scripted outright or deliberately performed by the participants.

A second factor is the emergence of the aforementioned autobiographical documentaries, such as personal video-diary documentaries and direct-address videos posted on online video-sharing sites like YouTube. Although the auto-ethnographic documentary form has a long history, the widespread availability of consumer video recording equipment, webcams and mobile phone cameras has elevated its visibility. Over a hundred YouTube channels featuring direct-address videos have more than ten million subscribers (Socialblade YouTube n.d.), and young viewers (aged 13 to 24) in particular are watching more than twice as much video on the Internet than on television (Spangler 2016). YouTubers describe their fans as "friends," and YouTube encourages creators to ask their audience direct questions and incorporate viewer responses into their videos (YouTube Creator Academy 2015).

Third, video-chatting software like FaceTime, Skype and WhatsApp have become increasingly popular applications. WhatsApp reported that 55 million video calls are made each day using its software (Bell 2017). Cameras built into laptops, smartphones and tablet computers have made video-calling and chatting ubiquitous. Over the last decade, people have become more accustomed to conducting a conversation while looking at the image of the interlocutor on a screen (or, more precisely, slightly below or to one side, as the camera is next to and not behind the screen). In both EFP and ENG setups, the interviewer stands or sits next to the camera, so that the participant looks slightly off-camera, at about a 15-degree angle from center. Video chatting has much less of an angle offset, and direct-address videos and confessionals have no offset at all, implicating the viewer as a participant in the conversation.

A central premise of the PECMA flow model is that audiovisual representations tap into human brain processes that evolved within a natural environment. Multisensory perception of a human face talking, with the synchronous sound of a human voice, contributes to the natural realism of the PECMA flow. However, our experiences with mediated forms are accompanied by reality checks—top-down processes that ascertain if what we are viewing is real or fictional, natural or mediated. We respond to the on-screen face when engaged in a video chat but inhibit motor action while watching an online video or direct-address interview. These interactions become habitual and are ecological in nature: the more viewers perceive participants looking back at them, the less jarring that composition becomes.

INTERVIEW CONVENTIONS AND NEW MEDIA

The direct-address interview setup provides one example of how media environments and technologies influence conventions of production and the perception of those conventions. As more viewers become accustomed to video-chatting platforms and personal video, they will become habituated to faces looking back at them through a screen. The composition of that frame is often a close-up shot, in which only the face and shoulders are in view. This "amputation" of the body precludes embodied simulation by viewers but heightens the ability to perceive facial expressions. While the head-and-shoulders shot has long been a staple of news and documentary interviews, the prevalence of online video shot at arm's length may increase exposure to face-only shots, promoting the activation of the fusiform and occipital face areas (Kanwisher and Yovel 2006), while suppressing the simulation of embodied movements like reaching, grasping or camera movement.

Footage shot by smartphones, in particular, is shifting conventions of framing. The aspect ratios of film and video frames have maintained, from their inception, a horizontal orientation, and current smartphones are designed to shoot and display video at 16:9 aspect ratio when held sideways. However, many users never turn their phones when shooting, and the resulting video is vertically oriented, with an aspect ratio of 9:16. The mobile app, Snapchat, encourages content providers to shoot and share video vertically (Sloane 2015), and several television and online video producers have begun to incorporate vertical video. Horizontal aspect ratios conform to the natural perception of the human field of vision, but as more viewers watch video on smaller screens that are vertically oriented, they may become more accustomed to seeing interviews in this format (Thompson 2017).

In addition, webcam video is often shot from a lower angle, looking up at the face. Laptop-mounted webcams sitting on desks are typically below eye level, and the camera on a smartphone is often held below the head as the operator looks down at the phone. At its most extreme, this framing mimics a child's view of an adult's face. Fiction-film directors have used the natural realism of low-angle shots to imbue a character with power, but the convention of webcam video may assert a categorical realism, indicating a self-produced, intimate relationship with the participant. In the future, the evolved natural experience of the angle of view may conflict with the categorical realism of the webcam experience.

Handheld cameras and footage gathered from smartphones have become pervasive, and they are reducing the footprint of the recording technology, blending them into the natural environment. High-resolution 4K video footage can be gathered unobtrusively, and widespread video recording by consumers means that small documentary crews attract less attention. This development makes it easier to set up an ENG shoot and capture participants interacting in natural environments.

Perception, as Luis Antunes (2016) observes, is multisensory and multimodal. The audio and video content of documentaries stimulate other senses at the experiential level, and changes in the relationship of those senses modify perceptions. New media complicate this process, introducing more sensory stimuli and refocusing attention. The emerging medium of virtual reality (VR) engages the vestibular and proprioceptive senses, in addition to vision and hearing, by updating the point of view as viewers move their heads. Recent 360-degree documentaries, like Kathryn Bigelow's *The Protectors: Walk in the Ranger's Shoes* (2017), do away with the frame completely and rely on viewers to search out participants. Some VR devices, like the Oculus Rift, allow viewers to move through a 3D environment, activating the motor cortex as they walk through a scene. Though immersive media are in their infancy, their growing popularity suggests future changes to fiction and documentary conventions, just as video gaming and online video have already reshaped some conventions in documentary production.

COGNITIVE THEORY AND INTERVIEW STRATEGY

The PECMA flow model and embodied simulation may explain why different interview setups can generate different responses in viewers. I find that these theories can also act as a guide to conducting interviews with participants. When preparing for an interview, my goal as an interviewer is to engage the participant in a conversation and have them forget they are

being recorded. I warn students, when I teach them documentary interview techniques, that it is likely that the first ten minutes of the interview
will be unusable. Participants often begin by providing answers they think
the interviewer wants to hear, and they engage in an official, performative
style of conversation. As the interview begins, participants may attempt to
assess whether the interviewer is an ally or threat, and their answers tend
to be short, fearing they may reveal too much information.

To reduce this fear, I begin interviews by outlining the topics I want to
cover and asking the participant for permission to talk with them. I face-
tiously tell students that this is not unlike the vampire asking permission to
be invited into someone's home, but the psychological reason behind the
question is to frame the subsequent conversation as permissible. The participant has invited the questions and will understand them to be less of a
threat. I then begin a conversation that Deborah Tannen (2001) has
labelled "rapport-talk," or speech designed to build social bonds. Once I
have established a relationship with the participant and they have become
habituated to the recording technology, I begin to ask questions that serve
as prompts for them to tell their story. My follow-up questions are designed
to elicit details of those stories the participant has omitted. Throughout
this process, I act not as an inquisitor but as a guide for the participant,
enabling them to share their experiences and remember their feelings
about them.

The PECMA flow explains why these techniques work. Brain processes,
obviously, are not limited to viewers. During interviews, producers and
participants also perceive their environment, generate emotions as action
potentials, seek out and attend to significant information, make compari-
sons with memories of previous experiences, and react with motor action
that may include verbal or non-verbal communication or other body
movements. Only the most naïve participants fail to be on guard, knowing
that their words and expressions are being recorded and will be used in the
construction of a documentary. Some bring set talking points to be sure
they deliver a particular message; others take on a performative style they
have learned from watching other documentaries or reality television. My
rapport-talk serves the evolutionary social function of becoming a trusted
member of the participant's group. Not only are they more likely to provide details in the interview, but their facial expression and body language
produce social signals that are perceived as friendly and not defensive.
Researchers have found that the social function of facial perception is
tightly connected to emotion (Adolphs 2003; Carter and Pelphrey 2008).

This perception of friendly or defensive social expressions occurs automatically at the preconscious level (Freeman et al. 2014).

However, interview participants may serve different functions for the narrative. In some cases, I forgo rapport-talk, particularly when I want to capture the tension in an interview. Jerry Rothwell (2012) provides a useful taxonomy of interview narrative frames. Borrowing from a model Dorothy Heathcote advocated in theatre education, Rothwell arranges the mode of an interviewee's address based on the distance of that person's role from the story. A participant or guide has direct experience of an event, while a critic or artist provides meaning or interpretation of the event. An authority may have been a participant but uses the distance of time to more coolly reflect on a past event (pp. 242–245). Although content often determines the frame, viewers also situate the frame from emotions generated by observing participants' expressions: a participant's hostile expression, when challenged by a line of questioning, positions them differently than would a socially welcoming expression.

During the interview, I elicit some of the most revealing stories by not asking any questions at all. After a participant has shared a story as a result of my prompting, I may pause for an uncomfortable amount of time, while maintaining eye contact. This generates a response from the participant, who sees I am still engaged in the conversation but waiting for more information. They may assume I have not fully comprehended their story and will elaborate with more intimate details, attempting to make me understand the story the way they do. Because I have violated the rules of interpersonal conversation, the participant tries to preserve the conversational structure by continuing to fill the gap, often revealing information they had previously decided to hold back. Neural correlates of human conversation show that a listener is often preparing a response before the question is completed. During extended silences, participants may be compelled to contribute more information because they perceive their turn in the conversation is not yet over (Bögels and Levinson 2017).

Viewers are active listeners in the stories constructed from these interviews. Likewise, the interviewer and participant engage in a complex brain synchronicity, using both verbal and non-verbal communication (Hasson et al. 2012). fMRI scans have demonstrated that perception and action are connected when listening to a story, and synchronized brain areas include not only linguistic regions but also social-information processing centers, including those with "the capacity to discern the beliefs, desires, and goals of others" (Stephens et al. 2010, p. 14429).

In accordance with the PECMA flow model, this synchronicity works best when audiovisual material approximates unmediated experiences. Recorded audio may contribute to or detract from the perceptual realism of an interview. Although ensuring the clarity of the participant's voice is crucial, ENG setups often pick up the background ambient noise of the space where the shoot is taking place. If the background audio conforms to the visual background, the audio adds to the perception that the participant is in that space. Background noise occurring from an off-camera source may indicate a realistic source if listeners can identify the sound, but indistinguishable sounds, like humming, buzzing, crowd noise or other sounds that cannot be placed, can reduce the clarity of the participant's speech. Adding a sound bite with distracting background audio to a documentary indicates to listeners that the recorded moment is so important to the story that they should work to discern what is being said through the noise. However, it also foregrounds the means of production and reminds viewers that they are watching a constructed narrative.

Cognitive film and media theories have provided credible explanations for how viewers perceive and experience fiction and documentary films. An understanding of these processes is of use not only to scholars and critics but also to producers, who must gather the raw material to create these films. Most documentaries rely on the conventions of the genre, and the documentary interview is one of the most fundamental of these conventions. Embodied simulation and the PECMA flow model reframe interviewing as a cognitive process, one in which perceptions and emotions motivate embodied responses. The verbal and non-verbal communication during an interview, and the audiovisual presentation of that material within a documentary, generate automated naturalistic responses, categorical associations and top-down assertions. Cognitive theory can help us understand how producers can choose different interview setups and compositions to effectively engage the PECMA flow: EFP allows for steady close-ups and controlled lighting conditions that capture facial expressions with more detail; ENG situates participants within a contextualized space and permits freedom of movement, providing more opportunities for embodied simulation of participants' motor actions; and direct-address interviews conform to the increasing prevalence of on-screen faces looking back at viewers. Understanding how viewers actively engage with interviews can help producers capture that footage more effectively, and knowing how interviews are gathered can help explain what ends up on screen.

REFERENCES

Adolphs, R. (2003) "Cognitive Neuroscience: Cognitive Neuroscience of Human Social Behaviour," *Nature Reviews Neuroscience*, 4(3), pp. 165–178 [Online]. Available at: https://doi.org/10.1038/nrn1056 (Accessed: October 19, 2016).

Antunes, L. R. (2016) *The Multisensory Film Experience: A Cognitive Model of Experiental Film Aesthetics*. Bristol: Intellect.

Bell, K. (2017) "WhatsApp's Bet on Video Calling is Paying Off Big," MashebleUK, May 8 [Online]. Available at: http://mashable.com/2017/05/08/whatsapp-video-calling-stats/#SoJ3HB8k75q0 (Accessed: October 19, 2016).

Bögels, S. and Levinson, S. C. (2017) "The Brain Behind the Response: Insights Into Turn-taking in Conversation From Neuroimaging," *Research on Language and Social Interaction*, 50(1), pp. 71–89 [Online]. Available at: https://doi.org/10.1080/08351813.2017.1262118 (Accessed: December 5, 2017).

Brown, T. (2012) *Breaking the Fourth Wall: Direct Address in the Cinema*. Edinburgh: Edinburgh University Press.

Bruce, V. and Young, A. W. (2012) *Face Perception*. New York: Psychology Press.

Carter, E. J. and Pelphrey, K. A. (2008) "Friend or Foe? Brain Systems Involved in the Perception of Dynamic Signals of Menacing and Friendly Social Approaches," *Social Neuroscience*, 3(2), pp. 151–163 [Online]. Available at: https://doi.org/10.1080/17470910801903431 (Accessed: December 5, 2017).

Freeman, J. B., Stolier, R. M., Ingbretsen, Z. A. and Hehman, E. A. (2014) "Amygdala Responsivity to High-Level Social Information from Unseen Faces," *Journal of Neuroscience*, 34(32), pp. 10573–10581 [Online]. Available at: https://doi.org/10.1523/JNEUROSCI.5063-13.2014 (Accessed: October 19, 2016).

Gallese, V. (2017). "Mirroring: A Liberated Embodied Simulation and Aesthetic Experience," in Hirsch, H. and Pace, A. (eds.) *Mirror Images: Reflections in Art and Medicine*. Vienna: Verlag für modern Kunst, pp. 17–27.

Gallese, V. and Guerra, M. (2012) "Embodying Movies: Embodied Simulation and Film Studies," *Cinema: Journal of Philosophy and the Moving Image*, 3, pp. 183–210.

Grodal, T. K. (2009) *Embodied Visions: Evolution, Emotion, Culture, and Film*. Oxford: Oxford University Press.

Hasson, U., Ghazanfar, A. A., Galantucci, B., Garrod, S. and Keysers, C. (2012) "Brain-to-Brain Coupling: A Mechanism for Creating and Sharing a Social World," *Trends in Cognitive Sciences*, 16(2), pp. 114–121 [Online]. Available at: https://doi.org/10.1016/j.tics.2011.12.007 (Accessed: October 19, 2016).

Hatfield, E., Cacioppo, J. T. and Rapson, R. L. (1994) *Emotional Contagion*. Cambridge: Cambridge University Press.

Kanwisher, N. and Yovel, G. (2006) "The Fusiform Face Area: A Cortical Region Specialized for the Perception of Faces," *Philosophical Transactions of the Royal Society B: Biological Sciences*, 361(1476), pp. 2109–2128 [Online]. Available at: https://doi.org/10.1098/rstb.2006.1934 (Accessed: December 5, 2017).

Keltner, D. and Kring, A. M. (1998) "Emotion, Social Function, and Psychopathology," *Review of General Psychology*, 2(3), pp. 320–342 [Online]. Available at: https://doi.org/10.1037/1089-2680.2.3.320 (Accessed: December 5, 2017).

Morris, E. (2004) "Eye Contact: The Interrotron," *FLM Magazine* [Online]. Available at: http://www.errolmorris.com/content/eyecontact/interrotron.html (Accessed: December 5, 2017).

Plantinga, C. R. (2009) *Moving Viewers: American Film and the Spectator's Experience*. Berkeley: University of California Press.

Rothwell, J. (2012) "Interview Strategies," in de Jong, W., Kundsen, E. and Rothwell, J. (eds.) *Creative Documentary: Theory and Practice*. London: Pearson Education, pp. 239–251.

Rozzi, S. and Fogassi, L. (2017) "Neural Coding for Action Execution and Action Observation in the Prefrontal Cortex and Its Role in the Organization of Socially Driven Behavior," *Frontiers in Neuroscience* [Online]. Available at: https://doi.org/10.3389/fnins.2017.00492 (Accessed: January 10, 2017).

Schurgin, M. W., Nelson, J., Iida, S., Ohira, H., Chiao, J. Y. and Franconeri, S. L. (2014) "Eye Movements during Emotion Recognition in Faces," *Journal of Vision*, 14(13), p. 14. [Online]. Available at: https://doi.org/10.1167/14.13.14 (Accessed: January 10, 2017).

Sloane, G. (2015) "Snapchat Persuades Brands to Go Vertical With Their Video," April 26 [Online]. Available at: http://www.adweek.com/digital/snapchat-persuades-brands-go-vertical-their-video-164305/ (Accessed: January10, 2017).

Smith, M. (1995) *Engaging Characters: Fiction, Emotion, and the Cinema*. Oxford: Oxford University Press.

Smith, T. J. (2012) "The Attentional Theory of Cinematic Continuity," *Projections*, 6(1), pp. 1–27 [Online]. Available at: https://doi.org/10.3167/proj.2012.060102 (Accessed: 10 January 2017).

Socialblade YouTube (n.d.) "Top 100 YouTubers Sorted by Subscribers" [Online]. Available at: https://socialblade.com/youtube/top/100/mostsubscribed (Accessed: January 10, 2017).

Spangler, T. (2016) "Young Viewers Watch 2.5 Times More Internet Video Than TV (Study)," March 29 [Online]. Available at: http://variety.com/2016/digital/news/millennial-gen-z-youtube-netflix-video-social-tv-study-1201740829/ (Accessed: January 10, 2017).

Srinivasan, R., Golomb, J. D. and Martinez, A. M. (2016) "A Neural Basis of Facial Action Recognition in Humans', *Journal of Neuroscience*, 36(16), pp. 4434–4442 [Online]. Available at: https://doi.org/10.1523/ JNEUROSCI.1704-15.2016 (Accessed: 10 January 2017).

Stephens, G. J., Silbert, L. J. and Hasson, U. (2010) 'Speaker–Listener Neural Coupling Underlies Successful Communication," *Proceedings of the National Academy of Sciences*, 107(32), pp. 14425–14430 [Online]. Available at: https://doi.org/10.1073/pnas.1008662107 (Accessed: January 10, 2017).

Tannen, D. (2001) *You Just Don't Understand: Women and Men in Conversation*. New York: Quill.

Thompson, C. (2017) "Phones Are Changing How People Shoot and Watch Video," *Wired*, September 7 [Online]. Available at: https://www.wired.com/ story/thompson-smartphone-video/ (Accessed: January 10, 2017).

Vertegaal, R., Slagter, R., van der Veer, G. and Nijholt, A. (2001) "Eye Gaze Patterns in Conversations: There is More to Conversational Agents than Meets the Eyes," *ACM Digital Library*, pp. 301–308 [Online]. Available at: https:// doi.org/10.1145/365024.365119 (Accessed: January 10, 2017).

YouTube Creator Academy (2015) "10 YouTube Fundamentals: Interactivity (#3)" [Online]. Available at: https://www.youtube.com/watch?v=X9gxSTv8W08 (Accessed: December 5, 2017).

CHAPTER 17

Documentary Editing and Distributed Cognition

Karen Pearlman

This chapter aims to reveal, from a cognitive perspective, what documentary editing is and how it works as a creative action in filmmaking. It proposes that the editing of documentary film is a cognitive process of perceiving or imagining potential structure and rhythm in a mass of unscripted material and then shaping that material into a significant form.[1] Further, in this process, editors, directors and the raw, uncut filmed material are all contributors to the generation of ideas. Shaping raw material into a coherent documentary film, this chapter will argue, is not work done solely in the brain; rather, it is the work of an "extended mind" (Clark and Chalmers 1998; Clark 2008) and requires a comple-

---

[1] Directors often propose quite open ideas about how the material's structures and rhythms may be formed using outlines, paper edits or even drawings. Ideas for how things may come together also often originate, as will be discussed here, in the material itself. There are many analogies for the editor's work in finding the best flow of shots for the particular film they are constructing, but perhaps the most apt in this context is that "editing documentary is akin to someone handing you a bag of sentences and asking you to write a book" (Swartz, cited in Bayne 2014).

K. Pearlman (✉)
Macquarie University, Sydney, NSW, Australia
e-mail: karen.pearlman@mq.edu.au

© The Author(s) 2018   303
C. Brylla, M. Kramer (eds.), *Cognitive Theory and Documentary Film*, https://doi.org/10.1007/978-3-319-90332-3_17

mentary activation of brain, body and the "film objects" (Vertov 1984) themselves.

In support of this argument, the chapter draws on David Kirsh and Paul Maglio's (1994) theory of "epistemic actions" as extended cognitive actions done in the world (not just in the brain), and formulates a theory of five different actions in relation to editing: watching, sorting, remembering, selecting and composing. This formulation synthesizes the findings of cognitive studies with film editors' own accounts (including my own) to reveal the nexus of "perception, cognition and action" (Clark 2016, p. 186) and collaborative "improvisation" (Millard 2014) in which the thousands of editing decisions are made that shape the finished documentary film.

Outside of the confines of the edit suite, however, the actions taken to shape a film's structure and rhythm are not widely known or understood. Even inside the suite, the cognitive dimensions of editors' work are often described as "mysterious," "magical," or, at best, "intuitive"—see, for example, Gabriella Oldham's (1992) multiple interviews with editors. By juxtaposing theoretical models with empirical data drawn from direct experiences inside the "mysterious" edit suite, this chapter is itself a montage. It assembles the modes of what we might call "scientific treatise," "pedagogical discourse" and "editor's manifesto" into a hybrid form that aims to illuminate the practice of documentary editing and make some of its cognitive complexity accessible for further study.

THE EXTENDED MIND

The chapter's primary framework for understanding documentary editing from a cognitive perspective is the extended mind thesis (Clark and Chalmers 1998; Clark 2008) and its refinements, as articulated by second-wave theorists of distributed cognition (e.g. Sutton 2010). The proposition is that in order to understand editing, it is productive to understand "human cognition as essentially and multiply hybrid, involving a complex interplay between internal biological resources and external non-biological resources" (Clark 2006, p. 291).[2] The biological resources are the editors' and directors' own bodies and brains, the non-biological resources

[2] Acceptance of this premise amongst cognitive scholars varies, with one objection being that, as a thesis, it seems to be unbounded, potentially encompassing all action and interaction. This may be the case, but this chapter looks at documentary editing as an intricate and specific instance of interaction with machines, materials and collaborators that demonstrates the distributed cognition model's utility as an explanatory framework for a process that is pervasive in contemporary life, but is otherwise untheorized.

are the images and sounds that have been captured, the notes made about them and the editing gear itself, with its affordances for particular actions. Andy Clark and David Chalmers' hypothesis on the extended mind begins with an argument for "active externalism," which describes "the general tendency of human reasoners to lean heavily on environmental supports":

> Thus consider the use of pen and paper to perform long multiplication ..., the use of physical re-arrangements of letter tiles to prompt word recall in Scrabble (Kirsh 1995)... the individual brain performs some operations, while others are delegated to manipulations of external media. (Clark and Chalmers 1998, p. 61)

I propose that editing film is necessarily actively external in a way that is similar to thinking with Scrabble tiles, but more cognitively complex. Just as Scrabble tiles are manipulated—moved around to one position, then another, to form words—individual shots are manipulated to form the sequences of a film. A key difference, however, is that Scrabble tiles are manipulated to form words that can be found in a dictionary, in the precise order and construction proposed by the Scrabble player, whereas documentary film shots are manipulated into orders, rhythms, sequences and constructions that may have general narrative precedents but which, unlike Scrabble tiles, are not fixed or reliable symbolic systems with a known signification arising from known sequencing. We cannot look up proposed sequences of shots in a reference text to ensure we have the order right. Nor can we look up proposed orders of events in a script, since documentary is usually unscripted. While we may have narrative schemas that are useful guides for communication, the specific selection, order and duration of particular shots to create or realize the ideas of each new documentary are unique. Thus, whereas Scrabble tiles are helpful external aids for forming letter sequences, filmed images and sounds are more than helpful, they are essential. The cognitive activity of forming particular film sequences cannot take place without them.

Three-time Emmy Award-winner and Guggenheim Fellow, Alan Berliner, relates how this process works in his documentary practice, in which he is both director and editor:

> For me, editing is about being responsive and open to making discoveries. The key word in making discoveries is "noticing". What catches my eye?

What tickles my thought? What moves my gut? What makes me smile? The
more you notice, the more connections there are to be made. (Berliner in
Oldham 2012, pp. 162–163)

Berliner's term, "responsive," is central to the argument here concerning what editing creativity actually is, and is used to anchor the notion that
editing thinking is actively external. Without the filmed material, there can
be no response, no discoveries made by "noticing" and, most importantly,
no connections.[3]
   The making of these connections is what Kirsh and Maglio (1994,
p. 153) call "epistemic action": "actions performed to uncover information that is hidden or hard to compute mentally." As Clark and Chalmers
(1998, p. 61) explain: "Epistemic actions alter the world so as to aid and
augment cognitive processes such as recognition and search." The epistemic actions of an editor (often working closely with a director) involve
sorting, selecting and assembling shots and their durations in order to
alter their signification and associations. Altering the order and length of
shots creates structures and rhythms of ideas and experiences, first for the
editors and directors, and later, after many more alterations, for viewers.
   Kirsh and Maglio (1994) use the computer game Tetris as their example of the extension of the mind into the world. They describe "recognition and search" as two of the cognitive actions that are actively aided by
the game's external materials and mechanisms. The player first recognizes
the puzzle piece it offers and then uses its mechanics to turn the piece,
aiding the search for the piece's optimal position. Rather than just thinking about spatial organization, the player's cognition is integrated with the
game's mechanics as they turn the knobs to make the piece fit the board's
gaps. In documentary editing, the filmed material does not just aid recognition and search; it is, in fact, a partner in a process of what could be more
accurately described as "search and recognition." The search for the

---

[3] It should also be noted that in addition to the shots themselves, the use of actively external cuing systems such as file cards or screen shots pinned to a corkboard, are often important
to documentary editing. These are ways of chunking down the salient content of shots or
scenes into key words or phrases, and moving them around as chunks to determine an order
that is then tested on the shots themselves. As documentary filmmaker Catalin Brylla noted,
in private correspondence with the author in 2017, "I have used paper edits with post-it
notes on a pin board to build narrative sequences, and in some cases of very plot-driven narratives, I deliberately adhered to the narrative flow of these paper edits, trying not to be
'distracted', by affective responses to individual shots."

optimal position for each piece of filmed material is ongoing throughout the process of watching, sorting, remembering, selecting and composing. The recognition is not just the "aha!" moment of finding a functional juxtaposition of shots, but a recognition of when a combination of shots creates an idea. Thus, to extend the analogy of Tetris, finding a juxtaposition in documentary does not just fulfil the game's mechanics, it actually changes the game's landscape, generates new opportunities for other pieces and new problems to be solved or gaps to be filled in the film's evolving logic. Each new juxtaposition asks the editor to return to the search for other shots that will realize, enhance, augment or clarify the viewer's experience of the documentary's idea.

As an epistemic action, editing is iterative. It seems, from my point of view, to work similarly to Clark's (2016) description of the brain's "predictive processing." Clark puts forward the notion that: "Brains like ours... are predictive engines, constantly trying to guess at the structure and shape of the incoming sensory array" (p. 3). If we wrote "film editors" instead of "brains like ours" we would have an accurate description of editing.

In Clark's predictive processing model, just as in film editing: "Perception and action ... are intimately related and work together to reduce prediction error by sculpting and selecting sensory inputs" (p. 3). This is what editors do. We perceive and "notice" (Berliner in Oldham 2012, p. 163) salient aspects of the material. We then guess at the shape and structure of the incoming sensory array of images and sounds. What, we might ask ourselves, does this documentary want to be? We act: sculpting and selecting, structuring and shaping the material. We do not do this just in our brains, since the editor's cognition is profoundly entangled with and responsive to the propositions the images and sounds are making. Thoughts do not occur in the editor's mind and then get executed. Thoughts manifest in the process of making edits. We put sequences together to uncover the 'information that is hidden' (Kirsh and Maglio 1994, p. 513), and then we respond and revise, trying to clarify the thought by clarifying the edit. As we gain more experience as editors, we become much better predictors. But part of editing remains, importantly, being open and responsive to possibilities suggested by the material itself. No matter how experienced an editor is, every new juxtaposition gives rise to new possibilities—every cut is an epistemic action that changes the world of the film, revealing new information about what the documentary itself could become.

The editor is therefore "coupled" with the material they are cutting. The editor is:

> linked with an external entity in a two-way interaction, creating a coupled system that can be seen as a cognitive system in its own right. All the components in the system play an active causal role, and they jointly govern behavior in the same sort of way that cognition usually does. If we remove the external component the system's behavioral competence will drop, just as it would if we removed part of its brain. (Clark and Chalmers 1998, p. 69)

Removing a film editor's shots would not cause permanent brain damage, but it would—as with removing part of the brain—completely disrupt the editor's "behavioral competence," because the shots are key causal agents in editing decisions. They are not, however, the only causal agents, we must also account for editors, directors and contexts. But among these other things, the shots do govern the editor's behavior, and thus, in the extended mind thesis, they are an integral part of her own cognitive system, as well as the cognitive system consisting of all the film collaborators immediately participating in the editing process. Editing, then, is a *distributed cognitive process*—editors, their collaborators, the raw filmed material, their notes and their gear comprise an actively external, causally coupled extended mind.

Having proposed the extended mind thesis as a framework for examining documentary editing, the next section will look at some of the specific kinds of expertise of perception/ cognition/ action required to edit documentary.

THE EDITOR'S EPISTEMIC ACTIONS

What does the documentary editor do? In asking this question, we are also asking: how does a documentary editor think?

This section breaks down documentary editing into a series of expert cognitive processes. These are not comprehensive, nor are they exclusive of other approaches, though it is beyond this chapter's scope to account for specific experiences or particular cultural contexts. Instead, I propose a framework that maps cognitive processes common to all documentary editing: watching, sorting, remembering, selecting and composing.

Watching

It starts with watching the material. I watch all material—or I try to. I will say it gets more and more difficult with directors shooting three hundred and four hundred hours of film, but I do try to watch all of it. (Amend in Oldham 2012, p. 209)

Kate Amend, winner of the 2005 International Documentary Association Award for Outstanding Documentary Editing, and editor of dozens of documentaries including the Peabody Award-winning *Beah: A Black Woman Speaks* (LisaGay Hamilton 2003), says of her editing process that it "starts with watching." But what is this "watching," and is it different in an editor than in a lay person?

If we accept the enactive approach to perception that "perceiving is a kind of skillful bodily activity" (Noë 2004, p. 2), it is possible to argue that the editor's watching, as a form of perception, is more or differently skilled due to their particular training and experience. As Jonathan Oppenheim (in Oldham 2012, p. 88), editor of *Paris is Burning* (Jennie Livingston 1990) and many other highly acclaimed documentaries, says, his watching is a form of "responding in a way that's both receptive and active."

As noted earlier, Berliner (in Oldham 2012, p. 168) distinguishes what he does from ordinary watching by calling it "noticing." In the same collection of interviews with editors, Amend describes her watching in a similar way:

I do sit and watch the footage and check my first reaction to what I see. If I laugh, I make a note of it. If I cry—and I do cry watching dailies—then I know that if it resonates with me, it's going to resonate with an audience. That's what I do to begin, and then I start to build the story or scene and make those connections. (Amend in Oldham 2012, p. 209)

Oppenheim, Berliner and Amend each distinguish between watching as done by an audience for a film and expert watching as done by an editor as part of the filmmaking process. The quotes from these editors about their processes suggest that an editor is a trained watcher who can simultaneously *have* felt responses and *notice* these embodied responses to filmed material. They further suggest that as the editors notice their responses, they begin a process of imagining a composition.

During watching, felt responses and key images or sounds of shots are mentally linked and embedded in the editor's consciousness (and often noted or sorted, as will be discussed later, inside the editing software itself or on paper as combined reminders of a shot's name, position and the feeling the editor experiences on watching). These coupled images and sensations become triggers for imagining the as-yet uninvented sequences into which they may be eventually composed. Watching, for the expert editor, is perceiving and responding affectively, noticing the perception and the feelings, and filing—mentally, physically, or both—the combination of image and response to be accessed when building a film.

Sorting

Watching will often be accompanied by note-taking and sorting or logging the material by giving it a name and placing it in a digital folder (or bin, when using real film) with other potentially related material. As Berliner says:

> Naming something… profoundly impacts how your associative memory will be able to link to it, connect with it, and generate new (or old) contexts for it. Not only that, but calling a shot, a sound or a sequence with an appropriate name will also help you remember it. And that's important, because amid the throes of intense editing, important elements and details can often get lost in the crowd if they're not given names that facilitate an active—and memorable—engagement with them. (Berliner in Oldham 2012, p. 159)

As Berliner describes it, during the sorting process editors shift some of their cognitive load into the external, non-biological resources that they work with—their named bins full of hanging strips of celluloid or named digital folders linking to named digital forms of the images and sounds. Sorting, as an epistemic action, alters the world in which the creative process unfolds. It is, in a sense, the creation of a map.[4] There are, as yet, no guidelines for navigating a route through the terrain but, by naming material and placing it in the neighborhood of other material related either

---

[4] In fiction filmmaking, the script is often referred to as a map or blueprint for production and editing. In documentary, detailed scripts are usually not written prior to filming, but even if they are, these scripts are generally abandoned as real life takes control of unfolding events.

through given names or the feelings associated with it, the potential for navigation is created.

The editor names the bins and clips, generally in discussion with the director, but in such a way that she will be able to find them again, by association. For example, a clip shows a woman running, stumbling and falling. She quickly recovers and runs off screen. What name do we give this clip and where do we put it? If the woman is a named person in the film, we might name it "Anna run-trip-recover" and place it in a bin called "Training Day 1." But if the film is about the dangers of the coastal region, and the woman is a random example, we might instead name it "stumble by sea" and file it in a bin named "Risk Taking." From there, the material might be sought if building a sequence on Training Day 1 or on Risk Taking, but it might also, due to the associations formed when watching and naming, be accessed in a context related to neither of these at some future point when, for example, a shot is needed of the sea or of Anna alone.

Sorting thus enhances the actively external agency of the filmed material itself, giving it a signaling system through which it can suggest possibilities. Once sorted, the editor can make her way through the material by following signposts that aid her search for certain moments, remind her of feelings, help retrieve particular information embedded in the material and suggest associations.

Sorting, in many instances, also shifts the management of cognitive processes of collaboration more into the editor's realm of responsibility. It shifts the decision-making processes more firmly into editors' bodies and minds because they are in direct contact, from this point forward, with the physical resources, whereas the director will begin experiencing these resources through the filter of the editor's access to them. This assertion is not made in order to diminish the importance of the director's thoughts in the composition of the whole, but merely to augment an understanding of the editor's cognition. As creative problems arise in the composing of a film, editors will draw on their sorting systems in an expert way to solve problems. Because they have created the sorting systems and are physically manipulating them (like tiles on a Scrabble tray)[5] to solve problems, theirs

---

[5] Sorting systems, and the software in which they reside in contemporary editing practice, have varying degrees of opacity for directors. For some, once the material has been digitized into the editing software, it is as though the editor has a tray of Scrabble letters that is hidden from the director. For other directors, the "letters" are visible but cannot be moved around

will be the minds and memories through which at least some of the lateral connections between things are made or the solutions to problems found. It is crucial, when talking about shifting material physically into the editor's hands, not to fall prey to the notion that there is some reliable distinction that can be made between thinking and doing. As Doris McIlwain and John Sutton (2014, p. 656), drawing on a number of studies in physical expertise and embodied cognition, note: "Expert thinking is not an inner realm behind practical skill, but an intrinsic and entirely worldly aspect of certain forms of real time, on-the-fly engagement in complex, culturally embedded physical activities." Thus, from a cognitive standpoint, it would be incorrect to suggest that the editor functions as a pair of hands *rather* than as a thinker in the editing process. Documentary editing is an instance of integrated cognition and action.

When we understand that sorting and organizing material shifts some of the decision-making process from the director's to the editor's body, we can see that the collaboration itself is a process of distributing cognition between director and editor. The director's mind is now extended through and with the editor, as hers is extended through and with the material that she has sorted to optimize her cognitive interaction with its possibilities. Thus, in the process of composing a documentary that has no a priori form, we can begin to see that editor's sorting and organizational skills are not merely the administration of intelligence, they are part of the imaginative intelligence that creates documentary story, structure and flow.

Remembering

When I was cutting film, I would be given maybe forty or fifty hours of material and I thought that was a lot. But I could pretty much memorize the footage and readily access something I was looking for. (Amend in Oldham 2012, p. 210)

Memorizing forty or fifty hours or material is certainly an expert feat of memory. This expert remembering is part of the documentary editor's skillset.

---

on the tray—only the editor can move them. Thus, the process of shifting the knowledge from the director's realm of expertise to the editor's can vary from being a source of great relief to directors to a source of great frustration, depending on the dynamic between the two and the individual proclivities of each.

This feat of memory is complex: it includes at least three key kinds of memory. One is the *contextual memory* of the principles of film storytelling and the context of the production. This knowledge could be considered a kind of scaffold, the part of memory where associations of image and feeling are, in a sense, "filed" when watching. For example, on first seeing shots of the triumphant ascent of a peak in a documentary about mountain climbers, editors might mentally file and/or physically make a note of the images and their associated elation as potential material for the film's climax. This is a simplistic example, and documentary structures are rarely as direct as a journey to a peak, but the underlying scaffold of "beginning, middle and end," where the editor may have mentally filed shots when watching and physically filed them when sorting, is doubtless part of the process that aids the retrieval of memories.

Another type of memory is *memory of shot content and valence*. These memories are called upon to imagine juxtapositions and possible positive or negative emotional dynamics. In this imagining, the scaffold of a possible structure offers, in a sense, problems to be solved or gaps to be filled. The editor's memories of shots and feelings, in tandem with their hunt through their sorting system, respond with notions or rather glimmers of ideas of combinations that might work. These ideas are not fully formed at a conscious level and are almost never spoken out loud by editors. Rather, memories of moments or movements in the material, gestures, expressions or statements come to mind and suggest, through some inherent quality they hold, possible pairings with material visible in the physical sorting system. Any number of pairings of shots or patterns of movement may suggest themselves in this process of memory collaborating with the material.

The third part of this complex cocktail of memory is *memory of how to use the editing gear*, which is the visible aspect of editing. Its visibility might lead to the mistaken impression, when observing an editor at work, that the physical skill of using the gear is the substance of the job. Without undermining the operational expertise required, it is important to note that using gear is not the most cognitively complex part of editing, and it does not solely constitute the editor's actual expertise. It is the seamless integration of the procedural memory of operating the workstation and the software with the other two kinds of memory that makes an editor an expert.

For editors, the process of remembering is not just in the brain but is corporeal. They scroll through their digital folders, click on shots and glance through them to trigger memories and affects. These "external, non-biological resources" (Clark 2006, p. 291) are part of the functional distributed cognition that makes the film. When the editor's memory collaborates with the gear's mechanical memory (for example, the logged rushes and the stored edited sequences) to find a combination of shots, this combination might, as we shall see when looking at "selecting and composing," throw all of the director's and editor's initial plans and ideas into disarray. Each new combination becomes a new memory partnering the hundreds and thousands of other possibilities as the iterative process continues.

The importance of an editor's expert memory is, in part, self-evident: someone has to hold, at some level, a mental catalogue of the available material in order to be able to think of its possible inclusion in a film, and to find it or even to use the trigger of accidentally stumbling upon it (when looking for something else) productively.

Beyond this search for and recognition of material, however, this cocktail of memory systems is essential to creative filmmaking because it is, I propose, part of what Dee Reynolds (2007) might call "kinaesthetic imagination." Reynolds coins this term to describe the ways that choreographers imagine original movements into being and into patterns that make up their dances. I have argued elsewhere that editing is a form of choreography (Pearlman 2016), but in the editor's case, the movement is not originally generated by their bodies, it is inherent in the moving images. However, as in choreography, its composition as a shot-to-shot flow of movement and as a narrative, emotional and physical dynamic, does not yet exist. This composition must be imagined through the processes of watching, sorting, and the multi-modal remembering described above, in order to ultimately scaffold the processes of selecting and composing.

Selecting and Composing

I make connections that I didn't expect and everything evolves. (Oppenheim in Oldham 2012, p. 88)

Perception and action are thus locked in a kind of endless circular embrace. (Clark 2016, p. 7)

The "connections" that editor Jonathan Oppenheim refers to in the quote above are both physical and conceptual. A shot is selected. It is juxtaposed in a composition with another shot. The juxtaposition gives rise to a new thought, in answer to which another shot is selected to extend the composition, or the new thought may suggest an alternative composition that may require a different selection.

Selecting and composing as an iterative process of film editing has remarkable resonance with Clark's model of "predictive processing" that he puts forward in his book, *Surfing Uncertainty: Prediction, Action and the Embodied Mind* (2016). Selecting and composing could be described as a visible, macro instance of this perception model, which he describes as "a dynamic, self-organizing system in which the inner (and outer) flow of information is constantly reconfigured according to the demands of the task and the changing details of the internal (interoceptively sensed) and external context" (p. 3).

In the predictive processing model, Clark (2016, p. 3) describes "perception, understanding, action and imagination" as being "co-constructed courtesy of our ongoing attempts at guessing the sensory signal." Similarly, documentaries are co-constructed, in a "kind of endless circular embrace" (p. 7) between the documentary editors' actions and perceptions and the filmed material itself. The documentary editor selects and composes by "guessing the sensory signal" (p. 3) that will work in the context of the moment of the film she is constructing. Being informed by watching, sorting and remembering, as well as years of training and experience (including implicit and explicit knowledge of principles of structure, rhythm and juxtaposition), does not make the selection any less of a guess. Selecting a piece of material is implicitly a question that could be verbalized as: "Is this the shot the film needs?" Placing a selected shot into an evolving composition is a hypothesis, a guess that "yes, this is the needed shot" or "this is the place it is needed," or possibly, "it is only needed for this particular duration."

However, as Berliner (in Oldham 2012, p. 158) notes in his description of his selecting and composing process, there is "much trial and error— and a lot of bad ideas!" In the composing process done by documentary editors, as in predictive processing done by brains: "Failed guesses generate 'prediction errors' that are then used to recruit new and better guesses" (Clark 2016, p. 1). The only difference between the expert and the novice editor's guessing is the number of prediction errors that the expert has already accumulated and can implicitly draw upon in order to reach "better guesses" more directly.

Thus, the shaping of a mass of material into a composed form is a cognitively extended "improvisation" with the material. As Kathryn Millard (2014, pp. 98–99) says, "improvisation requires skill and expertise... Far from requiring no preparation, improvisation most often occurs within a loosely prepared structure." The structure within which the expert documentary editor improvises is created by the production's intentions and context, and most importantly, by the material itself, which structures what an editor can think.

In the creation of documentary, the captured materials are "cognition-amplifiers" (Sutton 2006, p. 239). They are the source of thought, which manifests in their physically evolving forms. Little if any of the editor's "thought" lives solely in the editor's head. Although the fruits of their labors are manifestly ideas, *the ideas are the film*—they are neither conceived nor articulated in any other form than in the film. The film in its composed form is not a record of the editor's thoughts, it *is* their thoughts.

It is beyond the scope of this article to describe the particular kinds of things that may influence the specific selections and compositions of the movement of story, movement of emotion and movement of image and sound (Pearlman 2016), which vary from project to project. Thus, the cognitive actions may feel different, and it is not unusual to hear editors say that they feel as though they are learning to edit anew at the beginning of each project. However, I would argue that they are not learning the expertise of watching, sorting, remembering, selecting and composing anew. Rather, they are learning what a given project has to teach them about editing that particular project, as opposed to editing a project in general.

CONCLUSION

By revealing the editor's epistemic actions and identifying how they function in the creative process of documentary-making, one of my aims has been to reveal the creative contributions of editors. I have, at the same time, revealed the creative contributions of the film itself. Should the editor and the film be credited differently in the evaluation of a film? Possibly. As Clark and Chalmers (1998, p. 62) put it: "Epistemic action, we suggest, demands spread of epistemic credit."

Nevertheless, I would like to suggest that maybe asking who, or what, should get credit for one or another part of this integrated creative activity is asking the wrong question. What we need to be asking is: how are ideas generated in a distributed cognitive system? Can we move away from the idea of a lone genius to understand, at least on some level, that editing is filmmaking and is the shared thinking of filmmakers' extended mind? The distinct but interrelated cognitive operations during editing described in this chapter take place in the process of perceiving, imagining and shaping a mass of material into a coherent and compelling whole. These mental, corporeal and technical operations are not just helping the creative thinker, they are the creative thinking of an extended mind.

Having positioned documentary editing as an instance of the functioning of an extended mind, and broken down the editor's epistemic actions into watching, sorting, remembering, selecting and composing, it is not difficult to see why editors are 'invisible' (Vaughan 1983), or at least under-credited, in the evaluation of film. These seemingly mundane cognitive mechanisms are not the sorts of processes usually associated with the generation of creative work. They could certainly appear to be "just" responsive to material rather than generative of material.

Still, a question arises for further research as to whether responsiveness and editing are actually under-theorized aspects of the generation of ideas. This question has significant ramifications for the evaluation of artists, the understanding of collaboration, and even the historical positioning of women's contributions to partnerships, where men are highly visible and women seemingly occupy invisible and responsive positions, not dissimilar to the perceived position of editors themselves. However, having dissected and articulated some of the cognitive complexities of working responsively as a documentary editor, it is certainly possible to say that the long-held, clichéd conception of artists as being generative rather than responsive requires further scrutiny—a scrutiny that could indeed challenge understandings of the term "creativity." In terms of editing, this scrutiny could begin with excising the word "just" from the valuation of the complex cognitive actions involved in editing. Editing is not "just" responsive; editors' responsiveness is a highly developed form of cognitive expertise. Watching, sorting, remembering, selecting and composing are the cognitively distributed, responsive epistemic actions that ultimately create the form, flow and audience impact of a documentary film.

Acknowledgements The author gratefully acknowledges the input and advice of John Sutton, Kathryn Millard, Alan Berliner and the editors of this volume in responding to drafts and ideas proposed in this chapter.

REFERENCES

Bayne, G (2014) *If You Want to Learn How to Tell a Story, Edit a Documentary.* No Film School [Online]. Available at: http://nofilmschool.com/2014/10/ if-you-want-learn-how-tell-story-edit-documentary (Accessed: September 25, 2017).

Clark, A. (2006) "Material Symbols," *Philosophical Psychology,* 19(3), pp. 291–307 [Online]. Available at: https://doi.org/10.1080/09515080600689872 (Accessed: May 3, 2017).

Clark, A. (2008) *Supersizing the Mind.* New York: Oxford University Press [Online]. Available at: https://doi.org/10.1093/acprof:oso/9780195333213.001.0001 (Accessed: May 3, 2017).

Clark, A. (2016) *Surfing Uncertainty: Prediction, Action and the Embodied Mind.* New York: Oxford University Press [Online]. Available at: https:// doi.org/10.1093/acprof:oso/9780190217013.003.0004 (Accessed: May 3, 2016).

Clark, A. and Chalmers, D. (1998) "The Extended Mind," *The Philosopher's Annual,* XXI, pp. 59–74 [Online]. Available at: http://www.jstor.org/ stable/3328150 (Accessed: December 3, 2016).

Kirsh, D. (1995) "The Intelligent Use of Space," *Artificial Intelligence,* 73, pp. 31–68.

Kirsh, D. and Maglio, P. (1994) "On Distinguishing Epistemic from Pragmatic Action," *Cognitive Science,* 18(4), pp. 513–549. Available at: https://doi. org/10.1207/s15516709cog1804_1 (Accessed: May 3, 2016).

McIlwain, D. and Sutton, J. (2014) "Yoga from the Mat Up: How Words Alight on Bodies," *Educational Philosophy and Theory,* 46, pp. 655–673. Available at: https://doi.org/10.1080/00131857.2013.779216 (Accessed: May 3, 2017).

Millard, K. (2014) *Screenwriting in a Digital Era.* Basingstoke: Palgrave Macmillan.

Noë, A. (2004) "The Enactive Approach to Perception: An Introduction," *Action in Perception,* pp. 1–34 [Online]. Available at: http://mitpress.mit.edu/ books/chapters/0262140888chap1.pdf (Accessed: May 3, 2017).

Oldham, G. (1992) *First Cut: Conversations with Film Editors.* Berkeley: University of California Press.

Oldham, G. (2012) *First Cut 2: More Conversations with Film Editors.* Berkeley: University of California Press.

Pearlman, K. (2016) *Cutting Rhythms: Intuitive Film Editing.* 2nd edn. New York: Focal Press.

Reynolds, D. (2007) *Rhythmic Subjects: Uses of Energy in the Dances of Mary Wigman, Martha Graham, and Merce Cunningham.* Binstead, Hampshire: Dance Books.

Sutton, J. (2006) "Distributed Cogntion, Domains and Dimensions," *Pragmatics & Cognition*, 14(2) [Online]. Available at: https://doi.org/10.1075/is.9.1.10aro (Accessed: May 3, 2017).

Sutton, J. (2010) "Exograms and Interdisciplinarity: History, the Extended Mind, and the Civilizing Process," in Menary, R. (ed.) *The Extended Mind*. Cambridge, MA: MIT Press, pp. 189–225.

Vaughan, D. (1983) *Portrait of an Invisible Man: The Working Life of Stewart McAllister, Film Editor*. London: BFI Books. Available at: http://www.jstor.org/stable/20687638 (Accessed: May 3, 2017).

Vertov, D., Michelson, A. (ed.) and O"Brien, K. (trs.) (1984) *Kino-Eye: The Writings of Dziga Vertov*. Berkeley: University of California Press.

Index[1]

[1] Note: Page numbers followed by 'n' refer to notes.

© The Author(s) 2018   321
C. Brylla, M. Kramer (eds.), *Cognitive Theory and Documentary
Film*, https://doi.org/10.1007/978-3-319-90332-3

Mind and body, 25, 26, 33
Miners Shot Down (2014), 12, 135,
 137–143, 146
Minsky, Marvin, 230
Mirren, Helen, 84
Mirroring, 211, 283
Mirtahmasb, Mojtaba, 71
The Missing Picture (2013), 232
Mitchell, David, 270
Mitman, Gregg, 173
Mixed genres, 43n3
Mobile phone cameras, 293
Modernism, 60
Montage, 29, 31, 33–35, 67, 237,
 239
Moore, Michael
 Bowling for Columbine, 106, 127
 characterization, 123, 124, 126–128
 Fahrenheit 9/11, 127
 post-truth society, 100–101, 103,
  106–107, 109
 Roger & Me, 100–101, 103, 123,
  124, 127
 spectatorship and "difficulty," 65
Moral allegiance, 168, 170, 174
Moral emotions, 89, 159, 192
Morality, 98, 105, 192, 196, 197
Moral judgement, 127, 128,
 132, 159
Morally ambiguous characters, 149,
 151, 156, 160
Morin, Edgar, 125
Morris, Errol
 A Brief History of Time, 130
 characterization, 118, 122–124,
  126, 130
 The Fog of War, 118, 124, 130, 292
 Gates of Heaven, 130
 Interrotron, 291, 292
 limits of difficulty, 70, 71
 Standard Operating Procedure, 122
 Tabloid, 130

The Thin Blue Line, 70–72, 123,
 130
The Unknown Known, 124, 130
Vernon Florida, 130
Morrison, Toni, 289, 290
Mosaic narratives, 272
Moss, Jesse, 125
Motor system, 81
Movement, 218, 219, 314
Multidimensional network theories of
 emotions, 191
Multisensoriality, 206, 209, 213–215,
 217, 219
The Multisensory Film Experience
 (Antunes), 206
Murder on a Sunday Morning (2002),
 127–128
Murdoch, Rupert, 94
Music, 25, 28–29, 51, 66–67, 69, 217
Myrick, Daniel, 231

N
Nagel, Thomas, 166
Nanook of the North (1922), 75, 93,
 126
Narration, 118
Narration in the Fiction Film
 (Bordwell), vi
Narrative
 characterization, 115, 118
 fiction and nonfiction film, 24
 fragmentation, 273
 limits of difficulty, 72
 nonhuman character engagement,
  166
 Østergaard, self and imagination,
  22, 26, 29, 32–3, 36
 slow TV, 205–209
 social stereotyping, 264, 268, 269,
  272–273, 275
Narrative schemas, 267, 305